Women, Politics, and American Society

Fourth Edition

Nancy E. McGlen
Niagara University

Karen O'Connor
American University

Laura van Assendelft
Mary Baldwin College

Wendy Gunther-Canada
University of Alabama–Birmingham

PEARSON
Longman

New York San Francisco Boston
London Toronto Sydney Tokyo Singapore Madrid
Mexico City Munich Paris Cape Town Hong Kong Montreal

Vice President and Publisher: Priscilla McGeehon
Executive Editor: Eric Stano
Senior Marketing Manager: Elizabeth Fogarty
Production Manager: Denise Phillip
Project Coordination, Text Design, and Electronic Page Makeup: Electronic
    Publishing Services Inc., NYC
Cover Design Manager: Wendy Ann Fredericks
Cover Designer: Kay Petronio
Cover Photos: Background political campaign buttons: © Comstock Royalty Free/
    Fotosearch Stock Photography, Inc.; Hillary Clinton: Ramin Talaie/CORBIS;
    Margaret Chase Smith: Bettmann/CORBIS; Sojouner Truth: Bettmann/CORBIS;
    "Women Work/Women Vote" poster: Walter P. Reuther Library, Wayne State
    University; and Equal Rights Amendment Rally: Bettmann/CORBIS. All other
    images: © PhotoDisc.
Manufacturing Buyer: Roy Pickering
Printer and Binder: Phoenix Color Corporation
Cover Printer: Phoenix Color Corporation

Library of Congress Cataloging-in-Publication Data

Women, politics, and American society / Nancy E. McGlen ... [et al.].-- 4th ed.
    p. cm.
    Rev. ed. of: Women, politics, and American society / Nancy E. McGlen, Karen
O'Connor. 3rd ed. 2001.
    Includes bibliographical references and index.
    ISBN 0-321-20231-7 (pbk.)
    1. Women's rights--United States. 2. Women in politics--United States. I. McGlen,
Nancy E., 1952- II. McGlen, Nancy E., 1952- Women, politics, and
American society.

HQ1236.5.U6M394 2005
305.42'0973--dc22

                                                                        2004001126

Please visit our website at http://www.ablongman.com

ISBN 0-321-20231-7

1 2 3 4 5 6 7 8 9 10—PHH—07 06 05 04

Contents

PART III **FAMILIAL AND REPRODUCTIVE
RIGHTS AND REALITIES 235**

5 **THE STRUGGLE FOR FAMILIAL AND
REPRODUCTIVE RIGHTS 238**

Preface

Historically, many of the first steps of women in the public sphere to assert their rights as citizens in a democracy were motivated by the energy of friendships nurtured in the private sphere. Karen and Nancy have worked together for nearly thirty years and have lived through many of the changes chronicled in this book. The third and fourth editions add the perspective of a new generation of scholars in women and politics, Laura and Wendy, best friends and working mothers who have dealt firsthand with many of the policies discussed in the chapters that follow. Just as Nancy was Karen's professor, Karen was Laura's, showing how multigenerational the study of women and politics has become. The four of us are united in our passion for the subject of women and politics and inspired by our students, who throughout the years have challenged us with difficult questions and sparked lively debates in our classrooms.

In this text we share our enthusiasm for the study of women and politics. It is our experience that many people are woefully unaware of the battles that many heroic women and women's organizations have fought since the 1800s to garner basic, fundamental rights. This book addresses women and politics in American society by combining historical and topical approaches with a focus on political rights, education and employment, and familial and reproductive rights.

THE FOURTH EDITION

In the fourth edition we suggest that the women's movement entered a new phase in 1995 that can be characterized by both a "feminist malaise" and a realignment of issues and support. In light of the dramatic gains for women during the 1992 Year of the Woman, the 2002 elections were a disappointment, increasing women's representation in Congress by only one seat. At the same time that the feminist label continues to come under attack, new groups of women are mobilizing around an expanded agenda. How these changes unfold will define the next period of the women's movement.

Updates to the Fourth Edition

- Three thematic boxes appearing throughout: (1) Profiles in Leadership boxes focusing on the backgrounds and contributions of individual women leaders; (2) Women and Politics boxes highlighting critical political issues and events relevant to women; and (3) Global Awareness boxes providing cross-national statistics on current issues.

- New tables, charts, and graphs highlighting current public opinion regarding women and politics with cross-national comparisons of women's issues.

- Cartoons and websites are included in each section to stimulate discussion and interactive learning.

- Additional coverage of the gender gap, women and media, women in the military, Title IX, and the mothers movement.

Our goal is to spark debate over historical as well as contemporary issues, events, and leaders in women in politics. This text offers our readers a more comprehensive understanding of where women stand today in America and the battles they have fought. It also provides strategies for changes that still need to be made before full equality can be reached. We hope that this book produces as many questions as it answers and motivates readers to pursue subjects of particular interest in greater detail.

ACKNOWLEDGMENTS

Over the years, many women's organizations and research institutes—including the Center for American Women and Politics, Women and Politics Institute, the Institute of Social Research at the University of Michigan, the National Women's Political Caucus, the National Organization for Women, Concerned Women for America, EMILY's List, the Ms. Foundation, the Congressional Caucus for Women's Issues, the Reproductive Freedom Project of the American Civil Liberties Union, and the White House Project—provided us with valuable information. We would also like to acknowledge the Inter-University Consortium for Political and Social Research, the Louis Harris Association, the Roper Organization, and Philip Morris for survey data and summaries used throughout the book. We would also like to thank our colleagues in the Women's Caucus for Political Science and the Organized Women and Politics Section for always being there to support research of this nature. Finally, we extend our thanks to those reviewers who commented on the third edition to help us prepare for this fourth: Lisa S. McLeod Simmons, Virginia Wesleyan College; Susan Johnson, University of Wisconsin–Whitewater; and Gary Aguiar, University of Hawaii at Hilo.

We would especially like to thank Nancy and Karen for giving us the opportunity to update a text that we have used so often in our classrooms and to add our insights about women and politics to the third and fourth editions. We have been invigorated by the task and humbled by their generous support. We hope that our service to the profession and our accomplishments as scholars are a credit to the women who have been our mentors and friends.

Nancy E. McGlen
Karen O'Connor
Laura van Assendelft
Wendy Gunther-Canada

Introduction:
Women's Movements in America

Women's efforts to gain political, economic, and social equality in America are as old as the United States itself. As early as March 31, 1776, Abigail Adams wrote to her husband, John, who was in attendance at the Continental Congress:

> In the new Code of Laws . . . I desire you would Remember the Ladies, and be more generous and favorable to them than your ancestors. Do not put such unlimited power into the hands of the Husbands. Remember all Men would be tyrants if they could. If particular care and attention is not paid to the Laidies [sic] we are determined to foment a Rebelion [sic], and will not hold ourselves bound by any Laws in which we have no voice, or Representation.[1]

The rebellion predicted by Abigail Adams, however, did not begin for more than half a century.

In 1848, a woman's rights convention was held in Seneca Falls, a small town in central New York. Present at that meeting were many women who soon were to become leaders of what we call the first woman's movement, including Elizabeth Cady Stanton and Lucretia Mott. Today these women are most remembered for their efforts to secure female suffrage; in 1848, however, their goals were much broader in scope.

At the Seneca Falls Convention, a Declaration of Sentiments modeled after the U.S. Declaration of Independence was drawn up by attendees.[2] Later, at the same meeting, a series of resolutions calling for the abolition of legal, economic, and social discrimination against women was passed. Twelve days later, a larger meeting was held in Rochester, New York. At that meeting, which was presided over by a woman (a controversial move at the time), an even more revolutionary set of resolutions was drafted. Both documents reflected these women's dissatisfaction with contemporary moral codes, divorce and criminal laws, and the limited opportunities for women to obtain an education, participate in the church, and enter careers in medicine, law, and politics. While the agenda of rights for women set forth at these conventions has been expanded over the years, women today continue to work toward many of the goals first publicly enunciated at Seneca Falls.

VINDICATING THE RIGHTS OF WOMAN

Abigail Adams's appeal to her husband and his fellow lawmakers to "Remember the Ladies" in their new legal code was not a solitary cry at the end of the eighteenth century. For at least a hundred years, women authors had addressed the issue of the education of their sex and how their role as wives limited the possibilities of their lives. In seventeenth century England, Mary Astell wrote a tract aimed at expanding female education. In *A Serious Proposal to the Ladies* first published in 1695, Astell argued for the creation of female seminaries so that women who chose to live a contemplative life rather than marry could pursue advanced studies while educating younger women for their duties in the family. She asserted, "The Ladies I'm sure, have no reason to dislike this Proposal, but I know not how the Men will resent it to have their enclosure broken down, and Women invited to taste of the Tree of Knowledge they have so long unjustly monopoliz'd. But they must excuse me, if I be as partial to my own sex as they are to theirs, and think Women are capable of learning as men are, and that it becomes them well."[a] A century later, the discussion of women's education became a debate about women's rights. In 1792, Mary Wollstonecraft published *A Vindication of the Rights of Woman*, a political tract that argued for coeducation of the nation's children and the extension of civil rights to English women. Wollstonecraft commented, "The conclusion which I wish to draw, is obvious; make women rational creatures, and free citizens, and they will quickly become good wives and mothers; that is—if men do not neglect the duties of husbands and fathers."[b] Like Adams, Wollstonecraft believed that it might take another revolution for women to achieve their birthright as citizens. In nineteenth-century America, Elizabeth Cady Stanton and Susan B. Anthony wrote articles on woman suffrage for their newspaper, *The Revolution*, under a portrait of Mary Wollstonecraft.

---

[a]Mary Astell, *A Serious Proposal to the Ladies* (London: J. Wilken, 1695), 70.

[b]Mary Wollstonecraft, *A Vindication of the Rights of Woman*, ed. Carol Poston (New York: Norton, 1988), 178. For a larger discussion of Wollstonecraft's gender politics, see *A Vindication of Political Virtue: The Political Theory of Mary Wollstonecraft* (Chicago, University of Chicago Press, 1992) by Virginia Sapiro and *Rebel Writer: Mary Wollstonecraft and Enlightenment Politics* (DeKalb: Northern Illinois University Press, 2001) by Wendy Gunther-Canada. An excellent historical overview of women's political writing that includes selections from Astell and Wollstonecraft is *Women's Political and Social Thought: An Anthology*, ed. Hilda Smith and Bernice Carroll (Bloomington: Indiana University Press, 2001).

Since 1848, however, the pursuit of women's rights has been intermittent. There have been periods of high activity, when pressure for reforms has been keen. Most often these phases have been followed by years of little visible or public organized effort. Historically there have been three high points of activity when definable women's rights movements existed: (1) the early woman's movement (1848–1875), (2) the suffrage movement (1890–1925), and (3) the women's rights movement (1966–1995). We examine these three periods of women's rights activity by detailing the rise and development of each movement, its philosophy, and its accomplishments in three issue areas: (1) politics; (2) education and employment; and (3) personal rights, including those within the family and those dealing with reproductive freedom.

Where appropriate, we trace the development and activities of organizations or social movements that arose to oppose these women's movements' efforts for expanded rights. We also examine the nature of the movements themselves and why they developed when they did. Thus, we pay particular attention to factors that social movement theorists consider important to the rise or development of social movements: (1) an organizational base and organizational support that includes government support and the presence of pre-existing groups upon which to build, (2) the availability of leaders or organizers (who often have experience in other groups), (3) the existence of communications networks to facilitate expansion of a movement, and (4) the role of crises (or what we term *critical mobilizing events*) to foster or even to reinvigorate a movement. Also key to our discussion is an examination of the kinds of rights sought by women in the various women's rights movements. It is our contention that those movements that sought rights that could be termed by some as *public goods*, which by definition are available to all and therefore often threatening to many, are less likely to succeed. An example of a public good would be the proposed equal rights amendment that was defeated in 1982. Had it been ratified, equal rights would have been guaranteed to *all* women, whether or not they personally favored the amendment. Movements seeking public goods, which often are viewed by some as public bads, are more likely to encounter strong opposition than movements whose goals are more limited.

This analysis facilitates a better understanding of the current status of women's rights activism. To trace the development of women's rights—and the role that organized women's groups have played in the achievement of those rights—this book is divided into three parts: Part I, Political Rights and Realities; Part II, Employment and Educational Rights and Realities; and Part III, Familial and Reproductive Rights and Realities. The first chapter of each section describes the political efforts undertaken to obtain various rights. Because these endeavors were strongly influenced by the particular characteristics of each women's rights movement, as well as by a number of other political and social factors, we attempt to show how these several factors interacted to affect the successes of each movement. The second chapter of each section then focuses on the social changes still needed to obtain the conditions necessary for the full exercise of rights. The transformation of public opinion, especially that of women, toward women's participation in each area is of special interest. This is followed by a discussion of how hard-fought-for rights have been translated into realities, and what legal and social barriers remain to the achievement of full equality for women.

Although we have divided "rights" into three general areas, they often overlap. Efforts to achieve success in one area have often affected progress in others. Changes in social institutions that allow for the fuller exercise of political rights, for example, have often influenced participation in the economic or social spheres. This has been particularly true of women's role within the family. Changes in marital age, number of children, and other aspects of family life have important ramifications on political and economic participation.

Perhaps most importantly, we cannot ignore the fact that only women give birth, which has permeated their efforts to seek expanded rights. Assumptions about women's child-rearing capabilities as well as their "motherhood" duties are a common theme that has linked debates concerning political, employment, and educational rights.

Women in the United States clearly have made major legal, political, and social advances since 1848 and especially in the past forty years. Yet much remains to be accomplished for women to secure parity in political representation and equity in the household and workplace with men. The so-called Nannygate debacle that occurred in the first Clinton administration, when charges were made that only female and not male nominees for cabinet positions were asked about their child-care arrangements, is but one example of the problems that continue to plague women in their effort to reach the full equality first demanded at Seneca Falls. Many political observers had a sense of déjà vu when a female designated for a cabinet slot in the Bush administration had her nomination withdrawn over allegations concerning her household help. The sexual division of labor in the home and the sexual segregation of women in the workforce limit opportunities for women seeking election or appointment to political office. Today in the United States, women represent 52 percent of the population, yet only 13.7 percent of the membership of the House of Representatives and the Senate. We hope that as you read the pages to follow, you will gain a fuller appreciation of the activities of those who have gone before you, learn what changes still need to occur, and be inspired to carry on the mission.

AN OVERVIEW OF WOMEN'S RIGHTS MOVEMENT ACTIVITY

The Early Woman's Movement (1848–1875)

During much of the early nineteenth century, a prime topic of discussion and of women's writings was women's proper role in society. Nevertheless, no organized activity for women's rights occurred. In the 1840s, as an outgrowth of religious revivalism, however, both men and women were encouraged to work for those less fortunate than themselves. The temperance and abolition movements, both developed by followers of revivalism, attracted large numbers of supporters. Women were initially assigned minor roles in these efforts, and the battle over their right to take action in "political causes" was often heated. Nevertheless, women eventually took an active and vocal role, especially within the more liberal branch of the antislavery movement headed by William Lloyd Garrison. Garrison, the editor of *The Liberator*, a leading abolitionist newspaper, theorized that the rights of blacks and women to vote and otherwise participate in government followed from the proposition that all men and women were created equal. Thus, both groups possessed the same inalienable rights to life, liberty, and the pursuit of happiness.

This view fostered the formation of numerous local and national female antislavery societies in the mid-1800s. These organizations brought women together for the first time and gave them the opportunity to develop leadership and political skills.

One of the first women to speak out publicly was Maria W. Stewart, a writer for Garrison's *Liberator*, who gave a series of four public addresses in Boston. At a time when public speaking for women was a rarity—except at Quaker meetings—Stewart's speeches were even more notable because she was African American.[3] Actions of women including Stewart and the Grimké sisters of South Carolina, Sarah and Angelina, who first gained fame as abolitionists, earned for other women the right to speak out on political issues. The social code that made it unladylike for women to speak in public was bent to accommodate the perceived need for action against a horrible evil—slavery.

Participation in the antislavery movement helped to spark women's recognition that they, as a *class*, were subjected to discrimination. More specifically, in 1840, Lucretia Mott and Elizabeth Cady Stanton accompanied their husbands to a meeting of the World Anti-Slavery Society in London, England. After their long and arduous trip, the women were denied the right to participate in the meeting. A lengthy and vehement debate by the assembled delegates ensued. In the end, Mott and Stanton were told to take seats in the balcony because, as *women*, they could not participate in the meeting. This stinging rejection led them to realize that their position in society was not much better than that of the slaves they were working to set free. Mott and Stanton immediately resolved to call a convention of women to petition for their rights. Both women had families to raise, so it was not until eight years later that they convened a meeting in Stanton's hometown of Seneca Falls, New York, believing that the time was opportune to press for additional rights.

Friendships among other women active in the abolitionist cause produced a set of linkages, which with the aid of abolitionist newspapers and annual conventions served as a communications network of sorts for the fledgling woman's movement until after the Civil War. No independent national women's rights organizations, however, were formed until the late 1860s. In 1869, after a disagreement over endorsement of the Fifteenth Amendment occurred, two rival organizations, the National Woman Suffrage Association (NWSA) and the American Woman Suffrage Association (AWSA), were founded. From that time through the mid-1870s, women's groups lobbied for a variety of reforms advocated at Seneca Falls. Generally, they focused on "woman suffrage," but their efforts were to no avail, as no state added women to its list of eligible voters during that period. Women's work for expanded rights, including suffrage, was grounded in their belief that "the gender hierarchy of male dominance and female submission was not natural but arbitrary."[4] Their anger at the unfairness of this system often came through loud and clear. Not surprisingly, as women continued to press for women's rights during the next few decades, they met with little success. Their views were simply seen by many as too radical.

The Suffrage Movement (1890–1925)

In 1890, after years of limited activity, NWSA and AWSA were merged to create the National American Woman Suffrage Association (NAWSA) with Susan B. Anthony, a longtime close friend of Elizabeth Cady Stanton, at its helm. Anthony, in fact, had founded NWSA along with Stanton.[5]

We date the beginning of the suffrage movement as 1890, but other social trends also helped to foster the second push for equality. Both the temperance and progressive movements were instrumental to the development of the suffrage movement in the late nineteenth and early twentieth centuries. The Woman's Christian Temperance Union (WCTU), whose primary focus was the abolition of liquor, was founded in 1874 and promoted woman suffrage as early as 1879. Its phenomenal growth to more than 200,000 members by the early 1900s helped a large number of women to perceive the need for suffrage.[6] In the North and West, the Progressive Era gave birth to the settlement house movement, the National Consumers' League (NCL), and the Women's Trade Union League (WTUL). Both organizations were made up largely of white, middle-class women who sought to improve the working conditions of less fortunate children and women. Eventually, many women active in these organizations came to see the ballot as a prerequisite for their success. They claimed the vote would allow women to reform society, a task that they, as women, were particularly well suited to do.

This ideology clearly buttressed these women's limited demand for the vote. Most supporters of suffrage were avowedly content with their roles as mothers and wives. In fact, their position and the logic used to support it were the ideology of the earlier movement in reverse. While Stanton, the intellectual leader of the woman's movement, had claimed that motherhood and marriage were only *incidental roles* for women with respect to any claim for rights, leaders of the suffrage movement viewed motherhood and marriage as an *important basis* for the right to vote.

The existence of strong women's organizations, especially the WCTU, helped to spread this idea to women who had been untouched or unconvinced by women's rights advocates of the earlier era. In particular, the WCTU was especially effective in the South, where it was able to cloak the "radical" vote idea under the rubric of temperance. Thus, the WCTU was responsible for organizing women in a region that had previously seen few women's organizations.

The temperance and progressive movements also provided training for suffrage leaders. For example, two later presidents of NAWSA came to the suffrage movement via their activities in the temperance movement. Indeed, an interlocking directorate of sorts developed between the various reform groups and the NAWSA, as depicted in Table I.1.

The progressive and temperance movements alone, however, probably would have been insufficient to produce an effective women's movement were it not for the development of a large organizational base of women that came from the tremendous growth of women's clubs in the 1880s and 1890s. White middle-class women, freed from many domestic tasks by the development of labor-saving devices, devoted some of their extra time to participation in self-improvement groups such as reading societies or book clubs, as they are called in some communities today.[7] An important club movement also began among well-educated and affluent African American women, who often joined these clubs for companionship and self-improvement. But, unlike most white women, African American women also saw these groups as a way of alleviating racial injustice and underscoring their own religiosity and character.

When women in these clubs became involved in social causes, they quickly realized their own inferior political position. Thus, in 1914, the immense General Federation of Women's Clubs (GFWC) decided to support the suffrage movement, which added the organizational strength necessary for a successful social movement. Other organizations of professional, university, and even working women also began to support woman suffrage and

TABLE I.1 Social Movement Connections

Women's Rights/Suffrage Advocate (year of birth)	Religious Revivalism	Temperance	Moral Reform	Abolition	Peace	Settlement House/ National Consumers' League
Sarah Grimké (1792)	X	X	X	X	X	
Lucretia Mott (1793)	X	X	X	X	X	
Angelina Grimké (1805)	X	X	X	X	X	
Elizabeth Cady Stanton (1815)		X		X	X	
Lucy Stone (1818)		X		X		
Susan B. Anthony (1820)		X	X			
Anna Howard Shaw (1847)		X				
Alice Stone Blackwell (1857)		X		X	X	X
Florence Kelley (1859)					X	X
Carrie Chapman Catt (1859)					X	
Jane Addams (1860)				X	X	X

Note: All women listed, except for Lucretia Mott and the Grimké sisters, were officers of the National American Woman Suffrage Association.

Source: Adapted from Alice S. Rossi, ed., *The Feminist Papers: From Adams to de Beauvoir* (New York: Columbia University Press, 1973).

became affiliated with NAWSA. The result was a powerful movement that was able to mount what Carrie Chapman Catt called a "Winning Plan" to coordinate the efforts of thousands of women to lobby for the vote.

By 1920, this alliance was able to secure passage of the Nineteenth Amendment, which gave women the right to vote. The fragile coalition that made up the suffrage movement soon disintegrated, however, when its diverse constituent groups could no longer agree on a new postsuffrage agenda.[8]

The Women's Rights Movement (1966–1995)

After the demise of the suffrage movement, there was little organized protest activity by women for women until the 1960s. What we call the women's rights movement, which began in the 1960s, had two distinct personas reflecting the origins, leadership, and goals of each branch. What we term here the *younger* branch of the women's rights movement was far more radical in its orientation than what we term the *older* branch of the movement as originally personified by the National Organization for Women (NOW) and its more traditional, rights-oriented strategies and demands.* Today many of the goals of the younger branch have been incorporated into those of the older branch or have become smaller special interest movements, such as the battered women's, domestic violence, rape, or feminist health clinic movements, or have become subsumed in the broader women's rights movement.[9]

The Younger Branch.   Initially, most women active in the younger branch of the women's rights movement were involved with other protest movements. In the early 1960s, many women working in the civil rights movement, a significant number of whom were college students or recent graduates, began to sense that men in these organizations failed to value women's con-

---

*Various authors use different terms to describe not only the overarching movement that we call the women's rights movement but also the initial strains of this movement. Zillah R. Eisenstein, *The Radical Future of Liberal Feminism* (Boston: Northeastern University Press, 1993), for example, labels this movement *liberal feminism*. Jo Freeman, *The Politics of Women's Liberation* (New York: Longman, 1975), was the first to delineate the younger and older branches of the movement. Sarah M. Evans, *Born for Liberty: A History of Women in America* (New York: Free Press, 1989), 270–91, calls what we term the younger branch the *women's liberation movement*, and our women's rights movement, the *new feminist movement*. See also Cynthia Harrison, *On Account of Sex: The Politics of Women's Issues 1945–1968* (Berkeley: University of California Press, 1988), and Nancy F. Cott, *The Grounding of Modern Feminism* (New Haven: Yale University Press, 1987). Flora Davis, *Moving the Mountain: The Women's Movement in America Since 1960* (New York: Simon and Schuster, 1991), delineates several names and strains within what we term the *younger branch*. See also Alice Echols, *Daring to Be Bad: Radical Feminism in America, 1967–1975* (Minneapolis: University of Minnesota Press, 1989); Judith Evans, *Feminist Theory Today: An Introduction to the Political Theories of Second Wave Feminism* (Beverly Hills: Sage Publications, 1996); Rosemary Tong, *Feminist Thought: A More Comprehensive Introduction* (Boulder, CO: Westview Press, 1998); Stacey Young, *Changing the Wor(l)d: Discourse, Politics and the Feminist Movement* (Boston: Routledge, 1997); and Imelda Whelehan, *Modern Feminist Thought: From the Second Wave to Post-Feminism* (New York: New York University Press, 1995).

tributions. Like Stanton and Mott more than a century before, they came to see their position as analogous to the blacks for whom they were seeking expanded rights. Around the same time this recognition began to occur, civil rights groups such as the Southern Christian Leadership Council (SCLC), the Congress of Racial Equality (CORE), and the Student Non-Violent Coordinating Committee (SNCC) were organized. As some of these organizations entered a "Black Power" phase, they drove most white activists into other movements, especially the growing leftist student antiwar movement. There, too, women experienced sexism. At a 1965 meeting of Students for a Democratic Society (SDS), for example, "catcalls, storms of ridicule and verbal abuse"[10] were hurled at women who broached the women's issue. When a women's rights plank was introduced at the next annual SDS meeting, its sponsors "were pelted with tomatoes and thrown out of the convention."[11] A similar situation occurred the next year at the National Conference for a New Politics. When two women, Jo Freeman and Shulamith Firestone, both former civil rights activists, demanded that the convention address issues of sexism, they were patted on the head and told to "calm down, little girl."[12] The conference then decided not to deal with these women's "trivial complaints."[13] Freeman left to found a radical women's group in Chicago; Firestone did the same in New York City.

Subsequently, often without knowledge of what was happening in other areas of the country, women began to hold meetings in cities across the United States. This new idea of women's liberation was spread mainly through the existing infrastructure and communications network of the student movement and counterculture. SDS women and those from other New Left groups, in particular, were well suited to the task of organizing the women's groups that sprung up in many parts of the country. The development of a new form of organization, the consciousness-raising group, allowed these women to spread ideas, especially the notion that the problems they experienced were not the result of individual failures or situations, but instead had roots in the dominant culture and thus were common to all women.

Since the early to mid-1970s, these local groups and their progeny have played an important role in establishing feminist women's health care centers, rape crisis centers, shelters for battered women, and even feminist women's bookstores.[14] They have also sought to work with more traditional groups within the system, and after a period of relative quiet, many reemerged to play key roles in the pro-choice arena. In fact, the specter of major limitations on abortion rights that emerged in the 1980s may have brought about the same kind of merger in diverse women's groups that occurred in 1890, when NWSA and AWSA merged to become the National American Woman Suffrage Association.[15]

The Older Branch.   The United States has long been a nation of joiners. At least since the 1890s, many national organizations were composed largely of women. After 1920, however, few of those organizations were politically active for women's rights. Nevertheless, some groups, most notably the National

League of Women Voters (LWV), the National Federation of Business and Professional Women's Clubs (BPW), and the National Council of Negro Women (NCNW), had long been pursuing improvement in women's status in the legislative arena. These groups provided a potential leadership base for a social movement, but they needed to be galvanized to act.

Several events occurred to motivate these women's groups to action. The civil rights movement and the resultant awareness of rights, along with the publication of Betty Friedan's *The Feminine Mystique* in 1963, helped to disseminate the idea of group oppression to women across the United States.[16] Also occurring in 1963 was the issuance of a report by John F. Kennedy's newly created President's Commission on the Status of Women. This report, *American Woman*, documented in great detail the extent of discrimination against women in all areas of life. Following JFK's lead, the governors of all fifty states established state commissions on the status of women. These commissions soon began to issue their own state reports on women's status.

What finally mobilized some women on the president's commission to take action was the failure of the Equal Employment Opportunity Commission (EEOC) to enforce provisions of the 1964 Civil Rights Act, which prohibits sex discrimination in employment. In 1966, at the Third National Conference of Commissions on the Status of Women, attendees learned that conference bylaws prohibited them from passing a resolution demanding that the EEOC treat sex discrimination complaints seriously. Thus, several of the women present decided to form an independent pressure group—the National Organization for Women (NOW). Most of NOW's original members had served on the president's commission, and its leadership was drawn almost exclusively from the commission's ranks.

Unlike founders of the younger branch, these women were well trained as leaders, but there were few organizers among them. Not surprisingly then, NOW's initial growth was slow. Additionally, other women's rights organizations were formed after NOW, often because of some disagreement with NOW over tactics. The formation of many of these new organizations, as well as the increasing political activity of existing women's groups, often was fostered by women connected with NOW or the various state commissions on the status of women. Little new ground was broken in terms of reaching beyond these organizational bases until 1970. Indeed, the movement might have failed when the limits of this base were reached had it not been for widespread free publicity.

This came early in 1970 when the national media finally began to focus on the women's rights movement. The *New York Times, Newsweek, New York* magazine, and the national television networks all devoted time or space to women's issues.[17] According to Jo Freeman, "The cumulative impact of the series of stories was tremendous. Within the short space of a few months the movement went from a struggling new idea to a national phenomenon."[18] When NOW organized a strike to commemorate the fiftieth anniversary of the

THE FEMINIST LABEL

Historian Nancy F. Cott tells us the term *feminist* entered the English language sometime around 1910. Then, as now, it meant a "complete social revolution" in the roles of women. Cott explains that early feminism had "two dominating ideas: the emancipation of woman both as a human-being and as a sex-being."[a] Its goals were the elimination of all barriers that prevented women from achieving complete development as individuals. More radical in its demands than the suffrage movement, it attracted only a few of the youngest and most educated women of its day. It persisted organizationally as the National Woman's Party, with its demand for complete constitutional equality of women and men (see Chapter 1).

The premises of modern-day feminism are traceable to its roots in early feminism. Three main tenets of this philosophy continue today.

1. Women should be the equal of men. No gender is superior.
2. Women's roles and status are a product of the social structure and thus changeable.
3. Women are self-identified as a social group; thus they are positioned to act "as a group" to change their status.[b]

Cott claims that both early and modern feminism contain paradoxes, emphasizing sexual equality but sexual differences, individual freedoms but collective action, unity but diversity among women, and gender consciousness but elimination of gender roles.

Increasingly, the term *feminist* evokes a negative connotation. In 1998, only 32 percent of women and 37 percent of men had a favorable impression of feminists. In a 1999 Gallup poll, only 26 percent of Americans identified themselves as feminists. Despite this unwillingness to identify with the feminist label, two-thirds of both men and women are favorable toward the women's movement and support efforts to change the status of women.[c] Education and income, two closely related factors, are strongly associated with a woman's willingness to label herself a "strong feminist."

---

[a]Nancy F. Cott, *The Grounding of Modern Feminism* (New Haven, Conn.: Yale University Press, 1987).

[b]Ibid.

[c]Leonie Huddy, Francis K. Neely, and Marilyn R. Lafay, "Poll/Trends: Support for the Women's Movement," *Public Opinion Quarterly* 64, no. 3 (2000), http://www.journals.uchicago.edu/PDQ/journal/contents/v64n3.html.

ratification of the Nineteenth Amendment, extensive reporting of the event further helped to familiarize millions of American women with the existence of the women's movement. Practically overnight, NOW's membership burgeoned as its ideas were carried to a nationwide audience. The publication of *Ms.* magazine in 1972 and the fanfare surrounding it spread the word of the new movement even further as it provided a communications network for isolated women around the country.

NOW's push for the equal rights amendment (ERA) and the quick support it garnered from most other women's groups provided the necessary cohesion to cement and focus the new movement. NOW pushed for the ERA believing that passage of an amendment to the U.S. Constitution was the easiest way to bring about a guarantee of equality. Prior to 1971, the U.S. Supreme Court had declined to find that women were protected from state discrimination by the equal protection clause of the Fourteenth Amendment. Even if the Court interpreted the Fourteenth Amendment to protect women from some forms of discrimination, without a specific constitutional guarantee of equality, women might always be less than full citizens under the law. Thus, final passage of the ERA in both houses of Congress in 1972 provided an emotional high to movement activists, who turned their energies to ratification by the states.[19]

The media attention that aided development of the older branch, however, also contributed to the development of a countermovement. By the mid-1970s, some women came to perceive additional rights for women as a threat to their way of life. The proposed ERA and the legalization of abortion that occurred in 1973 with the Supreme Court's decision in *Roe v. Wade* were viewed as particularly ominous changes (see Chapter 5). Using the organizational base of fundamentalist religious groups and other conservative political organizations, prominent conservative Republican Phyllis Schlafly and others created a countermovement that effectively blocked passage of the ERA. Schlafly's Eagle Forum was initially devoted to stopping passage of the ERA. More recently, the Eagle Forum as well as Concerned Women for America (CWA), founded by Beverly LaHaye, have effectively mobilized to stop passage of many bills supported by the liberal women's rights movement, including, until 1993, passage of the Family and Medical Leave Act.

The women's rights movement and the conservative countermovement continue to go head to head most notably in the area of reproductive freedom rights. Prior to 1989, lacking the single unifying factor of an equal rights amendment, the current women's rights movement appeared to be in disarray. On July 3, 1989, however, the U.S. Supreme Court issued its opinion in *Webster v. Reproductive Health Services*, legalizing increased restrictions on abortions (see Chapter 5). A few weeks before the decision, pro-choice supporters, galvanized by the threat of the Court's overruling *Roe v. Wade*, organized a march of more than half a million people—the largest ever to occur up to that time in Washington, D.C. The Court's decision clearly spurred women's rights supporters to action.[20]

The Clarence Thomas hearings also galvanized liberal women's rights supporters. In 1991, many women around the nation sat aghast, watching their televisions, as the all-male and all-white Senate Judiciary Committee questioned African American Anita Hill for hours during the hearing on the appointment of Clarence Thomas to the U.S. Supreme Court.[21] Initially, his appointment to the bench had been fought by women's rights groups that believed he would provide the fifth and deciding vote to overrule *Roe v. Wade.* It was then learned that while Thomas headed the EEOC—the federal agency charged with investigating claims of sex discrimination *including* sexual harassment—one of his young assistants believed she had been the object of Thomas's improper sexual behavior. As white male senator after white male senator questioned law professor Anita Hill's veracity, mental stability, and morals, many white women around the country were outraged while black women struggled to cope with this public battle.[22] It was clear to many women, regardless of race, that most of the members of the all-male Judiciary Committee "just didn't get it." Many women decided on the spot to run for public office; others decided to get involved in politics. These revitalized women, and the reenergized women's rights movement, contributed to the election in 1992 of the largest number of women ever to the U.S. House and Senate. In 1994, however, women stayed home from the polls (see Chapter 2) and Republicans took control of both houses of Congress.

The Feminist Malaise or a Realignment? (1995 to present)

> The pioneer feminists were hard-hitting individuals, and modern young woman admires them for their courage, even while she judges them for their zealotry and their inartistic methods. . . . They fought her battle, but *she* does not want to wear their mantle [original emphasis].[23]
> *"Feminist—New Style" in Harpers 1927*

The absence of an organized general movement for women's rights today suggests a period of transition, similar to those following previous eras of highly focused activity. Women today lack a unifying symbol, crisis, or mobilizing event needed to reinvigorate the movement, although individual groups have worked hard to prevent a rollback of women's rights under the Bush administration. In January 2001, for example, some of the nation's largest pro-choice women's groups and civil rights organizations held a joint press conference to oppose President Bush's nomination of John Ashcroft for Attorney General of the United States. Ashcroft's record of challenging a woman's right to choose brought together a diverse coalition of feminist organizations committed to protecting reproductive rights, including the National Organization for Women, the Coalition of Labor Union Women, the Feminist Majority, the Rainbow/PUSH Coalition, and the National Council of La Raza. More recently, women's organizations joined forces in a battle to save Title IX (see Chapter 3). Despite continued attacks on the gains of women in these areas, a 2003 survey revealed that reproductive rights and Title IX are not ranked highly as priorities among a majority of women. Instead, women rank domestic violence and equal pay at the top of their agenda. Women support a broad array of issue priorities, with no single issue dominating the agenda (see Table I.2.). As the new women's rights agenda has emerged, support for an organized movement has declined.

In 1970, as the women's rights movement was just gaining visibility, polls revealed that less than a majority (40 percent) of women favored efforts to "strengthen or change women's status in society." By 1985, a majority of women worked outside the home, either part time or full time, and women overwhelmingly favored an improved status for women (77 percent). By the end of the 1980s, most women (58 percent) reported that change would occur "as a matter of course without any organized effort on the part of women."[24] Only 37 percent indicated that an organized women's movement was needed to work for further improvements for women. A 2001 survey revealed that African American and Hispanic women are more likely to believe that a movement is needed to improve the status of women in the United States. Sixty-eight percent of Hispanics and 63 percent of African Americans but only 41 percent of white women agreed strongly that the United States continues to need a strong women's movement to push for changes that benefit women. Overall, 47 percent of women agreed strongly with the statement. Support declined to only 43 percent by 2003.

Changes in issue priorities and the growing diversity of women supporting equal rights perhaps signals a feminist realignment. At the same time,

TABLE I.2 **Women's Views About Top Priority Issues for the Women's Movement**

Issue	% labeling as a "top priority"
Domestic violence and sexual assault	92
Equal pay for equal work	90
Child care	85
Women's health care	83
Time off from work to care for family	74
Drug and alcohol addiction	72
Sexual harassment	71
More women in math, science, and technology	66
Women in other parts of the world	64
Electing more women to political office	61
Keeping abortion legal	41
More girls in sports	38

Source: "Progress and Perils: New Agenda for Women," Center for the Advancement of Women (April 2003) http://www.advancewomen.org.

"GENERATION X FEMINISM— THE THIRD WAVE"

In the late 1980s, it became popular to identify feminists who had joined the women's rights movement in the 1970s as the "second wave." By the mid-1990s, a new generation of feminists had joined the ranks of activists working toward gender equity and sexual equality in America. The Third Wave Foundation is a national organization that seeks to promote a feminist social and political agenda among young people age fifteen to thirty. Currently there are more than 4,000 members of the Third Wave of both sexes who are working to create a diverse feminist community. The organization sponsors the "Why Vote?" lecture series to encourage younger Americans to get involved in politics and funds the "Why Give?" campaign to raise grant money for feminist programs across the country. Third Wave members pay a dollar a year for each year of their lives.[a] The emerging leaders of the next generation of the women's rights movement continue to advocate reproductive freedom and political reform, but the Third Wave agenda also includes efforts to eradicate homophobia, racial inequality, and economic injustice. In 2002, the Third Wave Foundation began the ROAM (Reaching Out Across Movements) project to bring together young women activists involved in the social justice movement throughout America. The ROAM program has reached the Southeast, Pacific Northwest, and Southwestern states to create a nationwide network of young leaders involved in progressive politics.

[a]For more information about the Third Wave and the ROAM program, go to their website, http://www.thirdwavefoundation.org.

young women coming of age today are increasingly disengaged from the goals of the women's rights movement. A generation removed from the mobilizing events of the Roe decision and the struggle to ratify the equal rights amendment, most "Generation Xers" find it difficult to identify with the feminist label and embrace a feminist agenda. To move beyond this "feminist malaise" to protect and extend the hard-fought gains for greater choice in women's lives will require a generation of new leaders. Some young women, such as those active in the "Third Wave Foundation," have started their own organizations to voice their concerns and advocate for women's rights issues. Although many advances toward the goals first enunciated in Seneca Falls more than 150 years ago have occurred, many remain unmet. These unmet goals and the strategies and changes needed to meet them are the focus of the remainder of this book.

NOTES

1. H. L. Butterfield, Mark Friedlaender, and Mary-Jo Kline, eds., *The Book of Abigail and John: Selected Letters of the Adams Family, 1762–1784* (Cambridge, Mass.: Harvard University Press, 1975), 121, quoted from a letter dated March 31, 1776.
2. A complete text of the Declaration of Sentiments can be found at "created equal," http://www.rochester.edu/SBA/declare.html.
3. See "Maria W. Miller Stewart," in *Notable American Women*, vol. 3, ed. Edward T. James (Cambridge, Mass.: Belknap Press of Harvard University, 1971), 377–78.
4. Nancy F. Cott, *The Grounding of Modern Feminism* (New Haven, Conn.: Yale University Press, 1987), 18.
5. See generally Lois W. Banner, *Women in Modern America: A Brief History*, 3rd ed. (New York: Harcourt Brace, 1994). See also Suzanne M. Marilley, *Woman Suffrage and the Origins of Liberal Feminism in the United States, 1820–1920* (Cambridge, Mass.: Harvard University Press, 1997).
6. Janet Zollinger Giele, *Two Paths to Women's Equality: Temperance, Suffrage, and the Origins of Modern Feminism* (Old Tappan, N.J.: Twayne, 1995).
7. Karen J. Blair, *The Clubwoman as Feminist: The Womanhood Redefined, 1868–1914* (New York: Holmes and Meier, 1980).
8. Sara Hunter Graham, *Woman Suffrage and the New Democracy* (Baton Rouge: Louisiana State University, 1996).
9. See, for example, Flora Davis, *Moving the Mountain: The Women's Movement in America since 1960* (New York: Simon and Schuster, 1991), who argues that the distinction disappeared in the mid-1970s.
10. Quoted in Judith Hole and Ellen Levine, *Rebirth of Feminism* (New York: Quadrangle Books, 1971), 112.
11. Ibid.
12. Ibid., 113–14.
13. Quoted in ibid., 113–14.
14. Maria Bevacqua, "Rape on the Public Agenda: Feminist Consciousness and the Politics of Sexual Assault" (Ph.D. diss., Emory University, 1997).
15. Myra Marx Ferree and Patricia Yancey Martin, eds., *Feminist Organizations: Harvest of the New Women's Movement* (Philadelphia: Temple University Press, 1995). But see Nancy Whittier, *Feminist Generations: The Persistence of the Radical Women's Movement* (Philadelphia: Temple University Press, 1995).
16. Betty Friedan, *The Feminine Mystique* (New York: Norton, 1963).
17. See a history of NOW at http://www.now.org/history/history.html, and Toni Carabillo's *The Feminist Chronicles 1953–1993* at http://www.feminist.org/research/chronicles/chronicl.html.
18. Jo Freeman, *The Politics of Women's Liberation* (New York: Longman, 1975), 150.
19. Jane Mansbridge, *Why We Lost the ERA* (Chicago: University of Chicago Press, 1986).
20. Karen O'Connor, *No Neutral Ground: Abortion Politics in an Age of Absolutes* (Boulder, Colo.: Westview Press, 1996).
21. For accounts of the Clarence Thomas hearings, see Jill Meyer and Jill Abramson, *Strange Justice: The Selling of Clarence Thomas* (New York: Houghton Mifflin, 1994), and Timothy M. Phelps and Helen Winter-Mintz, *Capitol Games: Clarence Thomas, Anita Hill, and the Story of a Supreme Court Nomination* (New York: Hyperion, 1995).
22. See Toni Morrison, *Race-Ing Justice, En-Gendering Power: Essays on Anita Hill, Clarence Thomas, and the Construction of Reality* (New York: Pantheon, 1992), and

Anita Hill and Emma Coleman Jordan, eds., *Race, Gender and Power in America: The Legacy of the Hill-Thomas Hearings* (New York: Oxford University Press, 1995).

23. Quoted in Sarah Jane Deutsch, "From Ballots to Breadlines 1920–1940," in *No Small Courage: A History of Women in the United States*, ed. Nancy Cott (New York: Oxford University Press, 2000), 424.

24. Specific wording used in Virginia Slims poll. All statistics derived from Virginia Slims poll conducted by the Roper Center.

Political Rights and Realities

As early as 1875, the U.S. Supreme Court confirmed that American women were citizens of the United States, but the Court also held that citizenship did not include a basic political right—suffrage. It took Congress and the states an additional forty-five years to ratify a constitutional amendment guaranteeing women the right to vote.

Today, few laws bar women's participation in the political arena, but vestiges of past barriers remain. Cultural and social attitudes continue to impede women's exercise of political rights. These extralegal barriers affect the composition of state and national legislative bodies. Only 13.7 percent of the lawmakers in the 108th Congress are women, and the sexual composition of other legislative and judicial bodies is only slightly more representative.

The ability of a women's movement to gain supporters and ultimately to achieve its goals often has hinged on the public's perception of the rights sought. During the suffrage movement, for example, opponents often characterized the franchise as something that would affect both men and women negatively. Thus, a critical element in achieving the vote was the suffrage leaders' ability to counter these arguments by stressing the limited nature of voting rights for women and by emphasizing potential benefits to society.

Some efforts for expanded political rights have been successful without producing strong countermovements, especially when the goals sought have not appeared to pose any significant threat to the political or social order. In the mid-1800s, for example, when few gave the suffrage cause much chance of victory, no significant antisuffrage movement developed. Likewise, in the 1970s, women in the younger branch of the women's rights movement received only token opposition to one of their goals—replacement of the present political system—largely because of the remote possibility of their success. During the same period, however, the proposed equal rights amendment drew fierce opposition, and its supporters were not able to counter its opponents in enough states to gain ratification. Clearly, the nature and implications of the political rights sought and the probability of victory have often been critical parts of the battle.

The battle for rights and the ensuing problems of implementing those rights are the topics of the next two chapters. Chapter 1 discusses women's attempts to gain access to the political arena and to gain equal rights in general. Chapter 2 then examines the impact of altering those political rights and examines how, why, and to what extent women have participated in the political process since the early 1900s. Finally, remaining barriers to the attainment of a full and equal civic role for women are discussed.

WEB EMPOWERMENT TOOLS

Women and Politics Institute at American University
http://www.american.edu/oconnor/wandp

National Women's History Project
http://www.nwhp.org

Roper Center for Public Opinion Research (Public Perspective Magazine)
http://www.ropercenter.uconn.edu

Gallup Organization
http://www.gallup.com

Center for American Women and Politics (CAWP)
http://www.rci.rutgers.edu/~cawp

EMILY's List
http://www.emilyslist.org

The WISH List
http://www.thewishlist.org

The White House Project
http://www.thewhitehouseproject.org

Federal Election Commission
http://www.fec.gov

League of Women Voters
http://www.lwv.org

Women Leaders Online
http://www.wlo.org

American Association of University Women
http://www.aauw.org

Ms. Foundation
http://www.ms.foundation.org

Institute for Women's Policy Research
http://www.iwpr.org

National Organization for Women (NOW)
http://now.org

Inter-Parliamentary Union
http://ipu.org

Center for the Advancement of Women
http://www.advancewomen.org

Women's Campaign School at Yale University
http://www.wcsyale.org

Feminist Majority Foundation
http://www.feminist.org

The Struggle for Political Rights

At the time of the Seneca Falls Convention in 1848, "woman suffrage" was a radical idea. In fact, a resolution supporting expanding the "elective franchise" to women received only a bare majority of votes. Given that convention attendees were more liberal than most, it becomes easier to understand why many long, hard years of organizing, petitioning, and educating both the public and government officials were necessary before women finally attained suffrage by constitutional amendment in 1920. In 1923, after that victory, some women sought fuller rights for women through the addition of another amendment to the U.S. Constitution—the equal rights amendment (ERA). As we shall see, that effort was not nearly as successful as the more simple demand for the vote. During the battle for ERA ratification, some women's groups continued to pursue expanded political opportunities for women. After the ERA's defeat in 1982, even more women turned their energies in that direction. High on their list of priorities was the election and appointment of women to public office. To understand the underrepresentation of women in politics, the history of efforts to obtain the right to vote and equal rights under the Constitution must first be understood. In 1998, a diverse group of women met in upstate New York to celebrate the 150th anniversary of the Seneca Falls Convention. To mark the event, the National Women's History Project produced an Anniversary Proclamation with resolutions noting the positive impact the struggle for women's rights has had upon the life choices of American women. Yet the authors of this Proclamation remind us of the fact that the history of "this century-and-a-half of efforts now spanning seven generations of unceasing work to achieve equality for fully half the American population still, regrettably, remains unknown and unrecognized by our nation's citizens."[1]

THE WOMAN'S RIGHTS MOVEMENT AND THE BALLOT

The women who attended the Seneca Falls Convention were primarily concerned with securing greater economic and social rights. In fact, at least initially, the right to vote was only a secondary concern. Lucretia Mott, in

21

particular, feared that a demand for the franchise would make women look "ridiculous" and urged her sisters to "go slowly."[2] In spite of her caution, however, the ballot was demanded on the basis of the belief that women were first and foremost individuals and citizens and deserved not only the same economic and social rights but also the same political rights as men. Paraphrasing the Declaration of Independence, women at the Seneca Falls Convention proclaimed: "We hold these truths to be self-evident: that all men *and women* are created equal; that they are endowed by their Creator with certain inalienable rights; that among these are life, liberty, and the pursuit of happiness"[3] (emphasis added).

Involvement in the abolition effort led many leaders of the woman's movement to see the issues of slavery and women's rights as intimately linked. Most believed that once society accepted the concept of individual rights as embodied in the Declaration of Independence as the rationale for freeing and enfranchising slaves, suffrage logically would be extended to women, regardless of color. Although Elizabeth Cady Stanton and Lucretia Mott's logic may have been correct, their estimation of the public's reaction to woman suffrage was not. Woman's movement leaders failed to realize that their demands for female suffrage directly challenged socially determined role divisions between men and women. And because demands for female suffrage often were coupled with calls for more controversial changes in women's status, many came to link suffrage with the reform of other issues, including divorce, education for women, or child custody. This was in spite of the fact that the New Jersey Constitution of 1775 granted all inhabitants worth "50 pounds a year" the right to vote. Election officials allowed propertied women to vote, and New Jersey and its women citizens apparently suffered no long-lasting dire consequences.

Prior to the Civil War, woman's rights activists chose not to form a national association to press for greater rights. Rather, they continued to rely largely on abolitionist associations to spread their ideas. Northern and midwestern organizational activity was limited to little more than yearly conventions to address women's common problems and to discuss strategy to obtain the vote. Often announcements of these meetings were carried in abolitionist newspapers as well as in women's magazines. In addition to these conventions, petition campaigns—a tactic regularly employed by abolitionist-based female antislavery societies—were used to demand suffrage in some states. These petition campaigns presented the signatures of men and women supporting a particular issue to legislators. While they sometimes resulted in positive legislative change involving property or material rights, petition campaigns failed to produce any state constitutional suffrage amendments.

With the advent of the Civil War, even these minimally independent efforts for women's rights were abandoned as many women focused their energies on the war effort and the campaign for an antislavery amendment. Fully expecting women's rights to be granted simultaneously with Negro rights, Susan B. Anthony and Elizabeth Cady Stanton, among others, helped to form the National Women's Loyal League (NWLL) to work for an amendment to end slavery.

Hopes for granting simultaneous rights to blacks and women were soon dashed. Republican politicians, the major proponents of abolition, feared that support for woman suffrage would doom the chances for ratification of an amendment enfranchising Negroes. To ensure that their party would be "rewarded" with the votes of 2 million southern Negro males, the Republican-controlled Congress opted not to mix the two issues.

Many abolitionist men also turned a deaf ear to the call for woman suffrage. In 1866, for example, the American Anti-Slavery Society rejected appeals to unite the two causes, prompting women to form a new abolitionist organization with men who supported female suffrage. The stated purpose of the new American Equal Rights Association (AERA) was universal suffrage for blacks and women.

The Civil War Amendments

Even AERA, however, soon abandoned woman suffrage when it supported the proposed Fourteenth Amendment to the U.S. Constitution. When a majority of its members agreed that "Now is the Negro's hour," Stanton, Anthony, and their followers were furious. They were particularly incensed by AERA's support of text contained in the Fourteenth Amendment, which introduced the word *male* into the U.S. Constitution for the first time.[4] Not only did Stanton and Anthony argue that women should be included in any attempt to secure fuller rights for Negroes, who had been freed from slavery with passage of the Thirteenth Amendment in 1865, but they also voiced fears that this clause would necessitate yet another constitutional amendment before women could vote in national elections. Even though they felt betrayed by AERA's support of the Fourteenth Amendment, Stanton, Anthony, and other supporters of woman suffrage were not yet ready to sever their ties with the organization they had helped to found.

The event that finally caused Stanton and Anthony to leave AERA was its support of the proposed Fifteenth Amendment, which called for giving Negro males the right to vote. The then-controversial amendment read, "The right of citizens of the United States to vote shall not be denied or abridged by the United States or by any State on account of race, color, or previous condition of servitude." Feverish attempts to have the word *sex* included proved futile, as women once again were told that the rights of Negro men must come first.

Interestingly, until passage of the Fifteenth Amendment, woman's movement leaders believed that the question of voter qualifications was a matter for the individual states. With enactment of the Fifteenth Amendment, however, it became clear that an amendment to the U.S. Constitution would in all likelihood be necessary before women could vote in national elections.[5]

New Groups Founded

Faced with the apparent need to alter their strategy, which had sought suffrage legislation on a state-by-state basis, and abandoned by AERA, which had failed to support a proposal to call for a woman suffrage amendment, Stanton and

Anthony founded the National Woman Suffrage Association (NWSA) in 1869. NWSA dedicated itself to the joint causes of securing greater rights for women in *all* spheres of life—especially in education, work, marriage, and the family— and securing a national constitutional amendment to enfranchise women.

Later that year, Lucy Stone, who had remained a member of AERA, founded the more conservative American Woman Suffrage Association (AWSA), which stressed the feasibility of a state-by-state route to woman suffrage. In AWSA's pursuit of that lone goal, it tried to avoid association with controversial issues that could cloud the suffrage issue.

Unlike NWSA, whose leaders had few dealings with abolitionists, AWSA leaders continued to expect that abolitionists and Republicans would adopt their cause as soon as the issue of Negro rights was resolved. This hope and the strategies adopted to support it (the state-by-state route, for example, was proposed to leave the federal arena open for debate on Negro suffrage) were counter to everything Stanton and Anthony believed. AWSA's organizational structure was also fragmented. Composed of official state delegations and strong local affiliates, AWSA required that new members be sponsored by at least two existing members.

NWSA's far more informal structure reflected Stanton's and Anthony's more liberal beliefs. Because they believed that a federal amendment was preferable to AWSA's state-by-state approach, NWSA initially made little effort to establish a state or local associational structure. This failure often resulted in the loss of potential members. State woman's rights associations often affiliated with AWSA because their participation appeared more appreciated there and their efforts, seemingly, could have greater impact.

Only gradually did Anthony and Stanton realize that, unlike abolitionists who faced few problems in convincing slaves of their oppressed status, many women were completely satisfied without the vote. Thus, shortly after ratification of the Fifteenth Amendment, Stanton, Anthony, and NWSA began a concerted effort to organize more women. Reaching out beyond the abolitionist movement, they attempted to attract the support of women they had met during the Civil War. Those who belonged to the National Women's Loyal League (NWLL) or those who volunteered in hospitals or collected money to buy much-needed medical supplies for the war effort were early targets of their organizing efforts. These largely middle-class women had not previously been active in politics or in the abolitionist movement. Stanton and Anthony also sought to gain sympathizers from those women who were members of the short-lived postwar Working Woman's Association (WWA). WWA members, as wage earners, also had not been involved in any women's rights activity previously. Women from both groups, however, were considerably more conservative about the position of women in society than either Anthony or Stanton. Consequently, efforts to attract these women eventually led to a considerable toning down of NWSA's radical demands for divorce reform and equal rights and to an increasingly narrow focus on suffrage. However, before it toned down its rhetoric, NWSA's image as an organization dedicated to altering society was fairly well established.

Profiles in Leadership

ELIZABETH CADY STANTON
AND SUSAN B. ANTHONY

"The prolonged slavery of woman is the darkest page in human history. A survey of the condition of the race through those barbarous periods, when physical force governed the world, when the motto, 'might makes right,' was the law, enables one to account for the origin of woman's subjection to man without referring the fact to the general inferiority of the sex, or Nature's law."[a]

Elizabeth Cady Stanton was born in 1815 in West Point, New York, the same year that her father was elected to the U.S. House of Representatives. Her first memory was the birth of a baby sister when she was four years old and overhearing family friends exclaim that it was a pity the baby was a girl. In a family of five sisters and one brother, Stanton recalls that she felt warmly for the child but that, at her young age, "I did not understand at the time that girls were considered an inferior order of beings."[b] Her fate as a female limited her educational opportunities, as she received formal instruction only after the death of her elder brother. Elizabeth Cady Stanton never understood the subordinate status accorded to females and spent her life advocating equality between the sexes. In this battle she acquired a friend of fifty years, Susan B. Anthony. Anthony was born in Adams, Massachusetts, in 1820, the second of seven children. Raised in a Quaker household, she was given a solid education first at home and later in a female seminary in Philadelphia. The two women did not meet until 1851 following an antislavery meeting in Syracuse, New York. Stanton had been married many years and was the mother of four sons. Anthony was an unmarried teacher eager to be introduced to the woman who, with Lucretia Mott, had organized the first women's rights conference in Seneca Falls in 1848. Their brief encounter developed into a partnership that would change American politics forever. Stanton famously described their relationship in her autobiography as a meeting of the minds. "It is often said, by those who know Miss Anthony best, that she has been my good angel, always pushing and goading me to work, and that but for her pertinacity I should never have accomplished the little I have. On the other hand it has been said that I forged the thunderbolts and she fired them. Perhaps all this is, in a measure, true. With the cares of a large family I might, in time, have become wholly absorbed in a narrow family selfishness, had not my friend been continually exploring new fields for missionary labors."[c]

(continued)

Together the women worked on campaigns for temperance, abolition, educational reform, and woman suffrage. Anthony energetically pursued worthy causes, leading an exhausted Stanton (eventually the mother of seven children) to remark, "Say not one word to me about another convention, any paper, or any individual for I swear to you that while I am nursing this baby I will not be tormented with suffering humanity."[d] When their concerted efforts failed to effect policy change, Stanton and Anthony recognized that, without the vote, women lacked the most important political tool. As political scientist Anna Harvey argues, they concluded that "vote-minded legislators were not particularly concerned about the policy preferences of a nonvoting group."[e] Thus, in 1869, Stanton and Anthony organized the National Woman Suffrage Association to secure the vote for women. In 1890, the National Woman Suffrage Association merged with Lucy Stone's American Woman Suffrage Association to form the National American Woman Suffrage Association. At NAWSA's first convention, Stanton, as president of the new organization, delivered the keynote speech. "Wherever and whatever any class of women suffer whether in the home, the church, the courts, in the world of work, in the statute books, a voice in their behalf should be heard in our conventions."[f] Yet six years later, after the publication of Stanton's controversial *Women's Bible*, Anthony pleaded with NAWSA delegates not to censure her old friend. She cautioned delegates: "you would better not begin resolving against individual action or you will find no limit. This year it is Mrs. Stanton; next year it may be I or one of yourselves who will be the victim. If we do not inspire in women a broad and catholic spirit, they will fail, when enfranchised, to constitute that power for better government which we have always claimed for them."[g] Delegates voted to disavow the *Women's Bible*. Historian Sara Hunter Graham suggests that "Stanton's radicalism can best be seen in her belief that all movements for freedom were linked inextricably, and that suffrage was part and parcel of that radical tradition."[h] Her emphasis on sexual equality and a secular society distanced Stanton from more traditional women who had joined the suffrage movement. She retreated to her home, where she worked on the *History of Woman Suffrage* with Anthony and Matilda Joslyn Gage, which was published in two volumes in 1898.

Elizabeth Cady Stanton died in 1902, marginalized by the movement she had begun over a half-century earlier. To Anthony, the loss of her dear friend was almost more than she could comprehend. She wrote: "It was an awful hush—it seems impossible—that the voice is hushed—that I have longed to hear for 50 years."[i] Anthony lived to advocate women's rights at the International Council in Berlin and lobby President Theodore Roosevelt to support woman suffrage. At her death in 1906, Susan B. Anthony was eulogized by Anna Shaw as a woman of good works whose name would not be forgotten. "The ages to come will revere her name. . . . Her work will not be finished, nor will her last word be spoken, while there remains a wrong to be righted or a fettered life to be freed in all the earth."[j]

Women achieved suffrage with the ratification of the Nineteenth Amendment to the Constitution of the United States of America in 1920. Today, the amendment is popularly referred to as the Susan B. Anthony amendment.

---

[a] Elizabeth Cady Stanton, Susan B. Anthony, and Matilda Joslyn Gage, eds., *History of Woman Suffrage*, vol. 1 (New York: Arno and the New York Times, 1881/1969), 13.

[b] Elizabeth Cady Stanton, *Eighty Years & More* (New York: Schocken, 1898/1971), 4.

[c] Ibid., 165.

[d] Kathleen Barry, *Susan B. Anthony: A Biography of a Singular Feminist* (New York: New York University Press, 1988), 74.

[e] Anna Harvey, *Votes Without Leverage: Women in American Electoral Politics, 1920–1970* (Cambridge: Cambridge University Press, 1998), 73. Harvey argues: "In the estimation of the founders of the suffrage organizations, it was simply wasted effort for women's elites to continue to lobby legislators on behalf of a group that could neither reward nor punish legislators for their actions" (ibid., 84).

[f] Elizabeth Cady Stanton and Susan B. Anthony, *Correspondence, Writings, and Speeches*, ed. Ellen Carol DuBois (New York: Schocken, 1981), 226.

[g] Sara Hunter Graham, *Woman Suffrage and the New Democracy* (New Haven: Yale University Press, 1996), 44.

[h] Ibid.

[i] Barry, *Susan B. Anthony*, 341.

[j] Ibid., 358.

Woman Suffrage and the Fourteenth Amendment

Aware of its image problems, NWSA attempted to "conservatize" and to narrow its goals. For example, Francis Minor was a prominent attorney whose wife, Virginia, was the president of the Missouri Woman Suffrage Association (MWSA) and a close friend of Anthony. In 1869, he wrote persuasively about his belief that women, as citizens, were entitled to vote under the existing provisions of the Fourteenth Amendment. Minor believed that if his theory was used as the basis for litigation challenging the disenfranchisement of women, demands for suffrage would be perceived as much less frivolous.

Minor's ideas were widely publicized by NWSA leaders. Along with an explanatory letter from Minor, they were published in two consecutive issues of *The Revolution*, a newspaper founded by Anthony and Stanton to publicize the movement. The impetus for a concerted effort to test the logic of Minor's argument, however, did not arise until January 1871 when Victoria Woodhull, a controversial figure herself, made a presentation to Congress. Using arguments very similar to those posited by Minor, she urged legislators to pass enabling legislation to give women the right to vote under the newly enacted Fourteenth Amendment.[6]

When Woodhull chose to address Congress on the opening day of NWSA's 1871 annual convention, her actions attracted considerable public attention. As editor of a controversial newspaper, she was an open advocate of "free love" and was reported to be living with a man who was not her husband. In spite of her reputation, NWSA leaders invited Woodhull to repeat her remarks later that day when their meeting opened.

Woodhull's appearance had mixed benefits for NWSA. On the negative side, NWSA's alliance with Woodhull caused some members of the press to ridicule the organization openly and to link NWSA and suffrage with declining moral standards. Numerous articles and cartoons were printed depicting Woodhull and those in favor of votes for women as "free lovers." In response, the more conservative AWSA, trying hard to preserve its own public image, quickly passed the following resolution in an effort to disassociate itself from NWSA and free love:

> Resolved . . . That the claim of woman to participate in making the laws she is required to obey, and to equality of rights in all directions, has nothing to do with special social theories, and the recent attempts in this city and elsewhere to associate the woman suffrage cause with the doctrines of free love, and to hold it responsible for the crimes and follies of individuals, is an outrage upon common sense and decency, and a slander upon the virtue and intelligence of the women of America.[7]

Sometimes more astute than NWSA leaders, AWSA leaders recognized that linkages between suffrage and more radical issues, particularly those as controversial as free love, would damn their cause.

On the positive side, the "Woodhull Convention" infused NWSA members with a new sense of purpose and generated some favorable publicity along with the bad. The *Washington Republic*, for example, described the annual meeting as follows:

> It was thus a convention with a new idea . . . indicating healthy life in the movement. The consequence was that the cause of woman's enfranchisement made a new, sudden, and profound impression in Washington.[8]

Litigating for the Franchise. Francis Minor quickly moved to seize upon the enthusiasm that Woodhull's remarks inspired and to counter any adverse publicity that Woodhull brought to NWSA. He urged that test cases quickly be brought to determine if the courts would obviate the need for additional legislative action. A number of legal scholars and judges had publicly agreed with Minor's arguments. More importantly, the chief justice of the United States, Salmon Portland Chase, offered his belief that it would be wise for women to test the parameters of the Constitution to determine if they were enfranchised by its provisions.

While this change in strategy was met with great excitement, it appears that NWSA leaders did not actually expect a favorable decision from the courts. The leaders clearly anticipated a strong written dissent from the chief justice and believed that his opinion could be used as a means to educate and to inform the public on the issue of woman suffrage.[9] In essence, litigation was attempted to convince the public that female suffrage was not a passing fad or something evil. Indeed, the need for enlightened and favorable discussion of woman suffrage was particularly acute. The Woodhull affair had tarnished both suffrage and NWSA's image.

Litigation was viewed by NWSA leaders as a conventional tactic to focus serious national attention on suffrage. Only one of the three major test cases brought by NWSA members, however, was given a full hearing by the U.S. Supreme Court. Fittingly, it involved Virginia Minor. In *Minor v. Happersett* (1875),[10] Minor, with her husband, Francis as coplaintiff (as a married woman, she had no right to sue in her own name), sued a St. Louis voter registrar after he refused to allow her to register to vote. Francis Minor claimed that his wife's rights under the Fourteenth Amendment were violated because she was denied "the privileges and immunities of citizenship, chief among which is the elective franchise." This argument was rejected by the Missouri courts, and the Minors appealed their case to the U.S. Supreme Court. In 1875, a unanimous Court upheld the Missouri court's determination. Writing for the Court, the new chief justice, Morrison R. Waite (Chase died in 1873), maintained that suffrage was *not* a right of citizenship.

After the *Minor* decision, NWSA turned to more commonly used modes of political activity. The unanimous decision in *Minor* made it clear that a real victory in the courts would not be forthcoming any time in the near future. To litigate further would only destroy any credibility NWSA had established. Its leaders, therefore, refocused their efforts on obtaining a constitutional amendment.

Toward a Constitutional Amendment

While NWSA viewed litigation as important, it never really abandoned its drive for a constitutional amendment. From 1868 to 1875, its leaders made many attempts to have a female suffrage amendment added to the Constitution. In the 1870s, for example, NWSA members testified before Congress in support of a bill that would have given women in the District of Columbia the right to vote. Their efforts were of no avail, even on that limited level.

NWSA also continued to use other avenues to advocate its goals. By necessity, many of its efforts were aimed at education. NWSA leaders realized that the public as well as elected officials needed to be better informed on the question of suffrage and its actual potential consequences before suffrage could be attained.

This strategy of education and agitation can be traced to the exposure of several woman's rights leaders to Garrisonian abolitionism. William Lloyd Garrison had previously argued that to bring about social and legal change one must first change ideas. So, in addition to testifying before congressional committees on the necessity of a woman suffrage amendment, NWSA leaders staged a number of what today would be called "media events." For example, as late as July 4, 1876, at the U.S. Centennial celebration in Philadelphia,

Anthony led a delegation of women onto the platform where assorted dignitaries were assembled. She handed a woman's rights declaration to the chair of the event and then turned and marched out of the hall with other women who handed out copies of the document to the startled audience. Once outside, the women mounted another platform and read the Declaration on the Rights of Women to the large crowd assembled in Independence Square. They demanded, among other things, the inclusion of women on juries and the end of taxation without representation.[11]

In these as well as other efforts, AWSA members never joined NWSA. Indeed, AWSA continued to take every precaution to distance itself from its more radical sister and even chose a different strategy to obtain the vote. While NWSA pursued its quest for a national suffrage amendment, AWSA persisted in its attempts to change state constitutions. Neither organization, however, made many inroads after 1875. Suffrage had been sufficiently complicated by NWSA's advocacy of other goals to produce considerable antisuffrage reaction in the public, even though no strong opposition group arose.

The Antisuffrage Movement

Woman suffrage had many detractors. Arguments against it were numerous. Some critics argued that the Bible counseled the exclusion of women from politics. Antisuffrage forces relied heavily on the book of Genesis and the writings of St. Paul to maintain that God created separate spheres for men and women—men's place was out in the world, which included politics, whereas women's proper place was in the home, away from politics. Suffrage opponents further argued that women's "natural roles" were those of wife and mother. Thus, any change in this natural order would destroy society. Others claimed that the founding fathers had framed the Constitution according to the principle espoused by John Locke that the male head of the household represented the interests of the family in government. Detractors argued that there was no need for suffrage because a woman's husband would fully protect her rights. Some worried that if women got the vote, the only result would be to set wife against husband, which would result in the destruction of the family. In the first U.S. Senate debate on the question of woman suffrage, Senator George H. Williams summarized many of these arguments:

> It has been said that "the hand that rocked the cradle ruled the world," . . . by their elevated social position, [women] can exercise more influence upon public affairs than they could coerce by the use of the ballot. When God married our first parents in the garden . . . they were made bone of one bone and flesh of one flesh; and the whole theory of government and society proceeds upon the assumption that their interests are one. . . . The woman . . . who undertakes by the use of some independent political power to contend and fight against man, displays a spirit which would, if able, convert all the now harmonious elements of society into a state of war, and make every home a hell on earth.[12]

These and similar sentiments probably were shared by most men and women in the 1860s. Catherine Beecher, the sister of Harriet Beecher Stowe, authored a tract in which she argued against woman suffrage because she believed that the right to vote would be an additional burden on women already busy with the duties of wives and mothers. Beecher proposed that the status of women could be improved by educating them for their role as manager of the private household.[13] Public opinion, including that of most women, was generally negative, and more often than not, hostile, toward expanded political rights for women. These negative attitudes were exacerbated by the advocacy of controversial ideas by some woman's movement members. Most people viewed notions of divorce reform and free love with horror. The reluctance of the Republican Party to support woman suffrage foreclosed the possibility of a quick, national solution. NWSA's weak organizational structure, which was limited to a loose national leadership group with few actual members, made any mass uprising to demand the vote impossible. These factors, along with the creation of rival groups in 1869, and the movement's limited source of potential supporters, help explain the minimal headway made toward suffrage. It was not until reconciliation occurred between NWSA and AWSA in 1890 that a new source of supporters was made available, and significant progress toward attaining the ballot was made.

THE SUFFRAGE MOVEMENT: THE QUEST FOR THE VOTE CONTINUES

In 1890, largely on account of the efforts of Alice Stone Blackwell, Lucy Stone's only daughter, NWSA and AWSA joined forces to become the National American Woman Suffrage Association (NAWSA).[14] To that time, efforts to secure the ballot had borne little fruit, although the territory of Wyoming enacted a suffrage law in 1869. Numerous suffrage campaigns in the states, however, met with failure. The state campaigns suffered from poor organization, a limited number of women who supported suffrage efforts, and a lack of more general popular support. In addition, state suffrage campaigns often faced stiff opposition from liquor interests, which feared that temperance-minded suffrage workers would vote for Prohibition—the banning of the sale of alcoholic beverages. Clearly, additional respectability and organization were necessary before women would receive the vote. Even though these changes ultimately occurred, the result was a radically altered women's movement. In fact, the transformation was so great that by 1890 a new movement, called the suffrage movement, emerged.

Constituent Groups

In ideology, NAWSA more closely resembled the more conservative AWSA, whose philosophy slowly became dominant. Although some of the broader goals earlier espoused by NWSA had been achieved—greater educational opportunities for women, for example—many others, including significant divorce reform, trade unionism, and the legalization of prostitution, were dropped by NAWSA in favor of a single cause—woman suffrage.

The chances for success of a new movement spearheaded by NAWSA were aided by a variety of factors. First, thousands of previously unorganized, more conservative women were mobilized.[15] This process began in the 1870s with the founding and subsequent marked growth of the Woman's Christian Temperance Union (WCTU).[16] The campaign to eliminate the sale and consumption of alcohol in the nineteenth and early twentieth centuries was one of the first major political efforts undertaken by women acting independently of men. The WCTU spearheaded the campaign to abolish the liquor trade. At a peak membership of 176,000, it was the largest women's organization ever to exist up to that time. (To put this in perspective, in 1997 NOW claimed 250,000 members; Concerned Women for America, 600,000.) The WCTU was able to restrict the sale of liquor in many communities, and for a limited time, the whole nation, after it lobbied successfully for passage of the Eighteenth (Prohibition) Amendment. Women linked temperance to family issues. Some men wasted money on liquor, while their wives and children went hungry. Some women also associated domestic violence and sexual assaults with drinking liquor.

Attempts to link the WCTU and woman suffrage were at first resisted by temperance leaders, but under the leadership of Frances Willard, the former dean of the Women's College of Northwestern University, the two movements were entwined. Elected president of the WCTU in 1879 on a prosuffrage platform, Willard argued that prohibition would come only if women could vote for it. She convinced WCTU members that suffrage was a necessary antecedent to attaining prohibition. In the Midwest, the association between the two causes was strongest, and campaigns for the vote relied heavily on local chapters of the WCTU. Eventually Willard was able to bring many of WCTU's members, most of whom were traditional, religious women, into the suffrage cause. The WCTU's endorsement of suffrage was particularly important in the South, where it found support with religious fundamentalists. Of course, many southern women held strong biases against the specter of African American voters— male or female. The influx of WCTU members into the suffrage movement further exacerbated the rightward, conservative drift of NAWSA, as WCTU leaders began to become powerful forces in the new suffrage movement. From the perspective of the liquor industry, the tie between the WCTU and woman suffrage meant that both causes were legitimate targets. Fearful that Willard was right and that giving women the vote would bring about the end to the liquor traffic, the industry pumped thousands of dollars (a lot of money at the time) into the antisuffrage effort. Thus, the ties between the WCTU and the woman suffrage movement were a mixed blessing, drawing supporters who might not have originally favored suffrage but also mobilizing a well-financed foe.

The growth of what is termed the club movement—so dubbed because many middle-class women joined a variety of self-improvement clubs in the

1880s and 1890s—was a second factor assisting the development of the suffrage movement. In 1888, for example, Susan B. Anthony, recognizing the possible political usefulness of these clubs for the suffrage cause, helped to create an alliance called the National Council for Women. An even larger and more powerful umbrella association, the General Federation of Women's Clubs (GFWC), claimed a membership of more than 2 million by 1910.

In general, two types of clubs were affiliated with the GFWC. The first type consisted of self-improvement groups, such as book clubs. These groups tended to attract white, educated, married, middle-class women. Confined to the home for most of the day, these women sought female companionship and intellectual stimulation to fill their leisure time. The second and more important type, however, consisted of the civic and department clubs that sprang from and were a part of the progressive movement. Most of the civic clubs were organized to improve municipal services and to bring about government reform, whereas the department clubs promoted specific issues such as abolition of child labor or improved conditions for working women.[17]

African American women, too, had their own groups. By 1916, the National Association of Colored Women, founded in 1896, had twenty-eight state federations and a membership of more than 50,000. Its first president, Mary Church Terrell, was appointed to the District of Columbia school board in 1895, becoming the first African American woman in the country to hold such a position. The association sponsored Mother's Congresses and Mother's Clubs to foster teaching of home skills to poorer women. It also lobbied for improvements in public education and was at the forefront of the battle against lynching.[18]

Within these progressive organizations, many women came to recognize their inferior political status and the need for the ballot. Without the ballot, they saw little chance to enact government reform or legislation to improve the status of working women or children. Thus, like WCTU members, many club women and those allied with the progressive movement became active in the suffrage cause, even though the GFWC did not formally endorse woman suffrage until 1914.

Like temperance workers, these new supporters of woman suffrage were fairly conservative. Many believed that a woman's proper place was in the home. Indeed, many chose to do club work rather than to seek employment outside of the home because club activities allowed them to pursue what they viewed as their more important domestic duties. They viewed progressivism and efforts to secure unadulterated foods, child labor laws, and better government as merely extensions of their traditional roles of wife and mother. Even those who joined the National Consumers' League (NCL), a progressive association formed to improve working conditions for women and children, were in basic agreement with the idea that a woman's "sphere" was the home. Although the NCL and other groups fought for improved factory conditions, they did so to make certain that poor women would be able to be better mothers and homemakers.

Educated Suffrage.   These women were undeniably considerably more conservative than those in the first movement, but their conservatism was in many ways merely a reflection of the ideological changes that most members of their social class had undergone since the Civil War. The postbellum era spawned several trends and changes that altered the native-born, white, middle-class view of democracy and politics. In the South, newly freed slaves and northern carpetbaggers helped to produce the turmoil and corruption of Reconstruction. In the North, waves of immigrants crowded into urban areas where their votes often formed the backbone of powerful and corrupt political machines. The West also had its fair share of political machines. In view of this seemingly nationwide political corruption, many came to believe that certain elements in society (blacks and immigrants) should be kept out of politics or, at least, that only the "better" elements of society should be in positions of political control. The notion that all humankind was endowed with inalienable, natural political rights quickly gave way to the idea of "political capacity" or "educated suffrage." These phrases were used to describe the philosophy that only those who had the ability to participate should have the right to do so. Antisuffrage forces, in fact, began to voice the opinion that adding women to the list of voters would only increase the number of "poor, ignorant, and immoral" elements, thus outnumbering the "patrician, intelligent, and impeccably proper" voters.[19]

Profiles in Leadership
IDA B. WELLS AND THE CLUB MOVEMENT

Ida B. Wells was born in 1862 in Mississippi of slave parents. She was educated at a freedman's high school during Reconstruction. At the age of fourteen, after the death of both parents, she lied about her age to secure a teaching position in a rural school. Later she moved to Memphis, where she taught in the city's Negro school system while she pursued her education at Fisk University. While a student there, she refused to give up her seat on a train to take a seat in the coach reserved for colored passengers and was forcibly removed. Undaunted, she sued the Chesapeake & Ohio Railroad and won her case in the state circuit court. Although the decision was overturned by the Tennessee Supreme Court in 1887, she actually challenged the segregated train system nine years before the U.S. Supreme Court decided *Plessey v. Ferguson* (1896).[a]

Wells's courage brought her to the attention of the leader of the Negro Press Association, who urged her to use her talents to write for small Negro-owned papers. Her court case and her numerous articles criticizing the inadequate education given to Negro children led the school board to fire her, so she then turned all of her energies to writing.

After three of her friends were lynched in 1892, she became a one-woman crusade against lynching. She founded antilynching societies and conducted in-depth analyses of lynchings in the South. She also was a member of a delegation that visited President William McKinley in 1898 to demand that federal action be taken to stop lynchings.

Wells married a Chicago lawyer in 1895. Her interest in the welfare of Negroes led her to found Negro women's clubs and the first Negro woman suffrage association. As president of the Ida B. Wells Club of Chicago, she worked to provide kindergartens and music instruction for the community. She also founded the Negro Fellowship League, which included a social center and a reading room that could be used to help assimilate the thousands of African Americans who were leaving the South and settling in Chicago. She also worked with national suffrage leaders, including Jane Addams of Hull House, and participated in the 1913 suffrage march on Washington, D.C., and the 1916 women's demonstration at the Republican National Convention to demand the inclusion of a suffrage plank in the platform.

Wells died in Chicago at age sixty-nine. In 1940, the city dedicated the Ida B. Wells Housing Project to honor her many achievements on behalf of African Americans and all Chicagoans.[b]

---

[a] 163 U.S. 537 (1896).

[b] For more information on Wells, see Alfreda M. Duster, ed., *Crusade for Justice: The Autobiography of Ida B. Wells* (Chicago: University of Chicago Press, 1970/1991), and Linda O. McMurry, *To Keep the Waters Troubled: The Life of Ida B. Wells* (New York: Oxford University Press, 1999).

NAWSA members and leaders also were often unwilling to associate suffrage with what some termed *the colored problem*. In 1898, Mary Church Terrell spoke at NAWSA's annual meeting and urged the convention to pass a resolution demanding that "suitable accommodation" be created on trains. As one African American delegate put it, "educated colored women should not be hindered from working for the improvement and moral elevation of their less fortunate sisters."[20] Traveling for suffrage and self-improvement was intolerable for African American activists who were barred from sitting in all but the worst cars of passenger trains.

Southern women in attendance strongly objected to the resolution. To assuage this important source of support, Susan B. Anthony told the convention that it was beyond the scope of NAWSA's charge to pass "resolutions against railroad corporations or anybody else."[21] These examples of political expediency and political strategy exacerbated the breach between black women and the predominately white suffrage movement. Suffragists proclaimed that they had the necessary "capacity" to exercise the franchise and defended their ability on two grounds. First, they reasoned that *as women* they had special contributions to make to the more efficient and honest running of government. Second, they argued that their capacity rested in their membership in that segment of society best suited to participate—the native-born, white, middle class. NAWSA's arguments and actions were often racist in nature as it tried to build support in the South.

One version of NAWSA's first line of reasoning was that women were inherently less corruptible and less influenced by partisan loyalties. Its leaders argued that women would become an important bloc of voters in passing progressive legislation and in defeating political machines. Suffragists even asserted that the moral nature of women would mean a reduced likelihood that the nation would go to war if women were allowed to vote.

A closely related position was that women had a duty to bring their expertise into the legislative process. Their status as homemakers and mothers became the prime reason for giving women the ballot. While motherhood was an important argument for suffrage, the belief of many of its proponents that middle-class, native-born women would be better voters by virtue of their social status was often carried to extremes. Taking on racist overtones, some maintained, for example, that the votes of native-born, white women could be used to outweigh those of African Americans in the South or immigrants in the North. Others, including Stanton, called for the imposition of literacy or educational qualifications to reduce the number of immigrant and black voters. Excluded from the NAWSA by the color of their skin, black women formed the Colored Woman's Progressive Franchise Association to promote political equality and economic security for their race.[22] But as late as 1919, in denying the membership application of another African American women's organization, NAWSA justified its action, noting that if it welcomed black women, supportive votes of southern Democrats in Congress would be jeopardized.

There is, however, ample evidence that more than simple political expediency was also present. Racism and nativism were also evident. In 1893, for example, the following resolution was passed by NAWSA:

> *Resolved*, that without expressing any opinion on the proper qualifications for voting, we call attention to the significant facts that in every state there are more women who can read and write than all Negro voters; more white women who can read and write than all foreign voters; so that the enfranchisement of such women would settle the vexed question of rule by illiteracy, whether of homegrown or foreign-born production.[23]

Given these kinds of statements, it is surprising that women like Ida B. Wells or groups like the National Association of Colored Women had anything to do with NAWSA. NAWSA was not only racist but also politically conservative in nature. For example, NAWSA initially attempted to secure the vote on a state-by-state strategy and did not work for a national constitutional amendment. This tactic was adopted, at least in part, so as not to offend southern women or politicians who were wedded to the notion of states' rights. NAWSA's organizational structure was consistent with its pursuit of the state strategy. Like AWSA, it was composed of state organizations with a loose national leadership, at least until 1915. In fact, to gain greater southern support, in 1903 it even adopted its own states' rights plank allowing each state to set its own membership standards, thereby allowing southern affiliates to exclude black women.[24]

Suffrage Flounders.   These policies virtually guaranteed state organizational autonomy but did little to help women actually win the vote on the state level. While there were some early suffrage victories in Colorado (1893) and Idaho (1896), after Wyoming (1890) and Utah (1896) entered the Union as suffrage states, no other states joined the suffrage column until 1910.[25] Although tremendous efforts were expended on state suffrage campaigns (noted historian Eleanor Flexner cites 480 efforts in thirty-three states, seventeen actual referendum votes, but only two victories from 1870 to 1910), these efforts went largely unrewarded.[26] It became increasingly clear to NAWSA that it could never win adoption of woman suffrage provisions in every state constitution.

Reasons for suffragists' failure to win victories along the East Coast in particular were numerous. First, NAWSA leaders were often ineffective, providing little direction for suffrage supporters. NAWSA had no national headquarters; the hometown of each NAWSA president became the organization's temporary base of operations. It also had a series of weak presidents, and without national direction, state associations floundered. Moreover, states where suffrage campaigns were launched were chosen in a haphazard fashion that often led to needless expenditures of time and energy on lost causes.

NAWSA also faced an increasingly sophisticated, well-organized, and well-financed opposition. Suffrage victories in Washington (1910) and California (1911), and in Arizona, Kansas, and Oregon in 1912, convinced opponents that the issue was alive and well. Liquor interests and political machines, sometimes financed by big business, began impressive antisuffrage campaigns that often were combined with voting fraud. Opposition to suffrage was so widespread in the South that chances for success there seemed particularly slim. In 1915, organized opposition contributed to the defeat of a suffrage referendum in four states in a period of but a few weeks. These defeats and recognition of the growing organization of antisuffrage forces finally led NAWSA leaders to recognize the need for a new strategy. Although the election of Carrie Chapman Catt as NAWSA president in late 1915 facilitated change, a new strategy was being tried even before she reorganized NAWSA.

Toward a National Amendment

In late 1912, the NAWSA board appointed Alice Paul, who had worked with the more militant British suffragettes, to its Congressional Committee. She quickly infused new life into the committee and immediately began to tap and build existing support for a *national* constitutional suffrage amendment. Within a few months, Paul was able to organize more than five thousand women to parade through the streets of Washington, D.C., for suffrage the day before Woodrow Wilson's presidential inauguration. Marchers dressed in white, some even on horseback, slowly made their way down Pennsylvania Avenue, where they encountered antagonism from some spectators. Although NAWSA had obtained a parade permit, when a riot ensued as mobs of spectators turned on the women, police offered the marchers no assistance. Many other citizens who watched the parade were outraged about the absence of protection for females. This sense of outrage at the violence directed at women, plus the very size of the parade that was staged at a time when all eyes were on the U.S. capital, resulted in a spectacular media event that brought incalculable press attention to the suffrage movement. Capitalizing on this free, favorable publicity, the committee launched a national woman suffrage petition drive and began to send regular delegations to see President Wilson to press for a national solution.

Paul, sensing momentum and believing in a national strategy, formed a new organization, the Congressional Union, in April 1913, to work exclusively for a national amendment. Although she remained chair of the NAWSA Congressional Committee, a break with the larger organization was inevitable. At the NAWSA convention in 1913, Paul's insistence that a federal amendment be the sole target of suffrage forces was at odds with the beliefs of most NAWSA leaders, who continued to cling to the state-by-state approach. Not surprisingly, Paul was removed as chair of the Congressional Committee.

After her fall from grace with NAWSA, Paul devoted her full energies to the Congressional Union. Following the lead of British suffragettes, the Congressional Union began to hold the party in power responsible for failure to pass a suffrage bill, a tactic also strongly opposed by NAWSA. In 1914, union members actively campaigned against congressional candidates of the Democratic Party, which had failed to endorse woman suffrage. All the while, the union, later called the National Woman's Party (NWP), pressed Congress for an amendment to the U.S. Constitution. Its effort resulted, at least, in a renewed interest in a suffrage amendment, a proposal that had been nearly dormant for more than twenty years. Like NAWSA, it also used racist appeals, particularly in the South, where it tried to appease fears that a constitutional amendment would complicate what it called "the race problem."[27]

A Winning Plan.   Many of NAWSA's own members, excited by the Congressional Union's enthusiasm and focus, pressed its leaders to work more actively for a constitutional amendment. Carrie Chapman Catt needed little convincing. After decisive state referenda defeats in 1916, she devised what was called a Winning Plan; its object was to direct all NAWSA's resources and cooperating organizations toward the goal of achieving a woman suffrage amendment to the U.S. Constitution by 1922. A key component of the plan was national coordination whereby *all* state associational activity was to be geared toward the single goal of an amendment to the U.S. Constitution.[28]

Catt's Winning Plan was quite detailed. Associations in suffrage states were to pressure their legislators to request that Congress pass a constitutional amendment. Additionally, national officers handpicked states for new campaigns where passage of state amendments was seen as feasible. Other state associations were to direct their efforts toward presidential suffrage or voting rights for women in party primaries in states that allowed state legislatures to make those changes. Catt believed that it was critical "to keep so much 'suffrage noise' going all over the country that neither the enemy nor friends will discover where the real battle is."[29] To keep the battle national in scope, Catt targeted southern and northern states for intense activity to break the spirit of suffrage opponents. To speed up the process even more, Catt planned to have support for the suffrage amendment included in both party platforms by 1920 to facilitate state ratification by 1922.

While World War I, like the Civil War before it, diverted much of the suffrage leaders' energies, Catt wisely insisted, unlike Stanton and Anthony earlier, that suffrage work continue to come first and that NAWSA continue to follow her plan. Yet her support for the war effort was criticized by many. Speaking to the members of the New York Woman Suffrage Party, Catt argued: "We ask woman suffrage as a war measure as the emancipation of the slaves was a war measure."[30] Slowly the Winning Plan began to produce results. The antisuffrage "solid South" was cracked in March 1917 when women in Arkansas won the right to vote in state primary elections. In addition, several legislatures enacted presidential suffrage laws. In the same year, New York voters approved the addition of a suffrage amendment to their state constitution.

These events resulted in the enfranchisement of more women, but strong opposition in the U.S. Senate prevented proponents from securing the two-thirds majority required for a constitutional amendment. Southern senators stood firmly against the amendment and were joined by others from New England and some eastern states. Opposition was justified on the rationale of states' rights, but many women, particularly those in southern suffrage associations, rejected this claim. Southern senators, for example, supported a Prohibition amendment and were not upset by the national government's intrusion into that area. In fact, southern proponents believed that the true motive of Senate opponents was a combination of resistance to any change in women's roles and fear of what female suffrage might do to the lucrative cotton industry in the South and Northeast. Manufacturers there relied heavily on female workers, child workers, and oppressed black workers. Senate suffrage opponents believed that manufacturers' cheap labor resources would be threatened if the amendment passed and women voters used their ballot strength to secure enactment of equal pay or factory inspection laws.

Recognizing that changes had to be made in the composition of the U.S. Senate before passage of the suffrage amendment could become a reality, NAWSA leaders launched a campaign to defeat their opponents who stood for reelection in 1918. The political clout of the suffragists produced the defeat of two powerful opponents of the amendment. When this show of force was

coupled with the addition of several more states into the suffrage column—
South Dakota, Michigan, Oklahoma, Iowa, Minnesota, Missouri, Ohio, Wisconsin, and Maine—quick passage of the Nineteenth Amendment was
virtually assured.

Meeting in a special session in the spring of 1919, first the House of Representatives and then the Senate passed the suffrage amendment. Ratification
by the necessary thirty-six states was completed in 1920, and the first national
election with full woman suffrage occurred in November of that year. In spite
of the Nineteenth Amendment, black women in the South were still effectively
disenfranchised by a variety of practices that kept most African Americans—
male or female—from voting.

Suffrage Not Enough—The Beginning of the End

Women in NAWSA, its constituent groups, and the NWP celebrated the ratification of the Nineteenth Amendment, or the Susan B. Anthony amendment,
as it was sometimes called. The Anthony amendment, however, did not
appease the desire of the NWP for full equality. Its leaders, in fact, quickly
turned their energies toward the passage of an amendment to ban *all* discrimination based on sex. Their view of women's roles, however, differed from
that held by most women. Even a majority of suffragists wanted no further
changes made in women's status. Their single agreed-upon goal had been suffrage. Once suffrage was secured, the base of the suffrage movement quickly
began to disintegrate.

Without another common issue or set of issues to unite them, the many
and varied women's groups that had made possible the passage of the Nineteenth Amendment began to go their separate ways. Some suffrage leaders
tried to counter this phenomenon by starting new organizations. Some members of NAWSA founded the National League of Women Voters (LWV) in 1919
to work to educate female voters concerning the elective and legislative
processes. Other, more radical women, such as Catt, became involved in the
growing movements for peace, birth control, or equal rights. These efforts
aside, many felt powerless to stop fractionalization of the movement. Even
while state ratification of the Anthony amendment was pending, Anna
Howard Shaw, a past NAWSA president, lamented, "I am sorry for you young
women who have to carry on the work in the next ten years, for suffrage was
a symbol, and now you have lost your symbol. There is nothing for women to
rally round."[31]

The Women's Joint Congressional Committee.   Some suffrage leaders, particularly those active in the newly formed LWV, believed that there was a chance
to save the movement. They sensed that most participants in the suffrage movement were issue oriented and that their continued involvement in the political
process could be had if the right kind of association could be formed. Therefore,
the LWV moved to create an umbrella-type organization composed of a variety
of women's groups previously active in the suffrage cause. The Women's Joint

Congressional Committee (WJCC) was established in late 1920 to identify and to lobby for the enactment of national legislation of concern to women. With fourteen sponsoring organizations and a total membership of 10 million, WJCC quickly moved to become a clearinghouse for women's issues and to avoid duplication of effort among its constituent groups.

WJCC, however, soon fell into disarray. Initially it was able to mobilize its constituent groups to pressure Congress effectively for enactment of citizenship and prenatal care legislation for women. But controversy over goals and the growing recognition of legislators that women *did not* vote as a bloc led to an immediate decline in its power over Congress. Also contributing to its decreasing prestige was the widely publicized disagreement that occurred among women's groups over the prospect of an equal rights amendment.[32]

The NWP and the Equal Rights Amendment.   Writing about the early 1920s, noted historian William H. Chafe commented, "No issue divided women's organizations more than the Equal Rights Amendment to the Constitution."[33] As first submitted to the Congress in December 1923 by Daniel Anthony (R-Kans.), Susan B. Anthony's nephew, the proposed amendment read, "Men and women shall have equal rights throughout the United States and every place subject to its jurisdiction."

The NWP's support of the amendment immediately split the already faltering suffrage movement into two distinct coalitions: (1) militant feminists and (2) social feminists. NWP leaders, as spokespersons for militant feminists, rejected pleas from WJCC social feminists to work for causes such as peace, birth control, and social reform. Instead, they saw these efforts as diverting their energies from the ultimate goal—equality—and thus a waste of time. The powerful National Consumers' League, in particular, found itself forced to take a public stand against the amendment because of the clear indications that the ERA, as written, would negate all protective labor legislation for women—legislation that the NCL believed imperative to the health and well-being of female workers.

The division among women over the ERA continued into the 1930s, although no real women's rights movement was evident. Nevertheless, in 1940, the Republican Party added support of the amendment to its platform.[34]

Largely because of the NWP's continued pressure, some form of an ERA was introduced in at least one house of Congress every session between 1923 and 1971. The House of Representatives held hearings on the proposed amendment in 1948 but failed to do so again until 1971. In contrast, the Senate held hearings in several sessions, and in 1950 and 1953 it passed the proposed amendment. Reflecting the militant/social feminist split, however, on both of those occasions the Senate version included a rider guaranteeing that protective legislation for women would not be affected.

Unlike many social feminists, the NWP continued to insist that women, like blacks, had to be guaranteed equality in all spheres and that such change could not come about easily without a specific constitutional amendment. But the NWP was clearly more radical than most other women's groups. Thus, it was not until the development of the current women's rights movement that passage of an equal rights amendment came close to reality.

THE DRIVE FOR WOMEN'S POLITICAL RIGHTS

Initially, women's rights groups gave little thought to expanded political rights per se, although they clearly shared the goal of greater representation of women in government. For example, in one of the National Organization for Women's (NOW's) first letters to prospective members, its purpose was explained:

> to initiate or support action, nationally or in any part of this nation, by individuals or organizations, to break through the silken curtain of prejudice and discrimination against women *in government* . . . the *political parties*, the *judiciary* . . . and in every field of importance in American society[35] (emphasis added).

These women saw that the civil rights movement had been able to make impressive changes in the status of African Americans—now they wanted similar progress for women.

Nowhere among NOW's specific goals enunciated at its first national meeting was a specific call for additional political rights. This absence is largely attributable to the fact that by 1967 the political inequalities experienced by women were quite different from those encountered by leaders of the early woman's and suffrage movements. While a variety of laws and practices kept women out of jobs or hampered their abilities for advancement in the 1960s, women enjoyed most basic political rights. Consequently, NOW and other older-branch groups devoted most of their early efforts to alleviating discrimination in the economic, educational, and social spheres, where problems were more immediate, and to the passage of the equal rights amendment. Many NOW members, as well as other supporters of women's rights, believed that once equality came in those spheres, especially through passage of an ERA, fewer of their efforts would have to be directed at blatant types of discrimination (because such practices would be unconstitutional), freeing them to work toward their goal of greater representation of women in government.

Women in the younger branch were even less interested in expanded political rights per se. Two factors largely account for their lack of participation. Most in the younger branch either rejected the political system as corrupt or believed that the end of women's oppression would not come about through participation in or alteration of the political system. Some, for example, believed that women's oppression was traceable to racism, capitalism, imperialism, the patriarchal system, or some combination of those factors. Hence, women's inferior status could be remedied only when these systems were overthrown and replaced by a new political order.

Some in the younger branch argued that an end to oppression and discrimination against women in the political arena would come only after sex-role stereotypes and their supporting structures (traditional courtship and

Women and Politics

WOMEN SEEK RIGHTS THROUGH LITIGATION

While most women's rights activists lobbied for an equal rights amendment, some groups, realizing the successes that the National Association for the Advancement of Colored People (NAACP) had in securing additional rights for blacks through the courts, began to explore the feasibility of a litigation strategy designed to seek a more expansive judicial interpretation of the scope of the Fourteenth Amendment. Although prior forays into the courts such as the *Minor* case in 1875 and others as recently as 1948 had ended unfavorably,[a] some believed that the times had changed enough for the justices (or some of the justices) to recognize that sex-based differential treatment of women was unconstitutional.

The Fourteenth Amendment protects all U.S. citizens from state action that violates equal protection of the laws. Early on, the Supreme Court decided that certain rights were entitled to a heightened standard of review. When fundamental rights such as First Amendment freedoms or suspect classifications such as race are involved, the Court uses a heightened standard of review called *strict scrutiny* to determine the constitutional validity of the challenged laws. In legal terms, this means that if a statute or governmental practice makes a classification based on race, for example, the statute is presumed to be unconstitutional unless the state can provide "compelling affirmative justifications"—that is, unless the state can prove the law is necessary to accomplish a permissible goal. During the 1960s and into the 1970s, the Court routinely struck down as unconstitutional statutes that discriminated on the basis of race.

Many believed that the status of women and the climate for change were sufficiently positive to convince even a conservative Court that some change in its interpretation of the Fourteenth Amendment was necessary. The first group to seek the elevation of statutory classification based on gender to a suspect classification status (thus entitling it to strict scrutiny) was the American Civil Liberties Union (ACLU). Its first women's rights case was *Reed v. Reed* (1971).[b] Ruth Bader Ginsburg, a member of the ACLU board who in 1993 would become the second woman to serve on the U.S. Supreme Court, argued the case before the Court. Her enthusiasm and interest in the expansion of women's rights via constitutional interpretation led the ACLU to found the Women's Rights Project (WRP).

(continued)

At issue in *Reed v. Reed* was the constitutionality of an Idaho statute that required that males be preferred to females as administrators of estates for those who die intestate (without a will). The National Federation of Business and Professional Women, the National Organization for Women, and the Women's Equity Action League all filed amicus curiae briefs urging the Court to interpret the Fourteenth Amendment to prohibit discrimination against women as well as African Americans.

Reed v. Reed turned the tide in terms of constitutional litigation. While the Court did not rule that sex was a suspect classification, it concluded that the equal protection clause of the Fourteenth Amendment prohibited unreasonable classifications based on sex. Two years later, in another WRP case, *Frontiero v. Richardson* (1973),[c] the Court fell one justice short of elevating gender to a suspect classification. Finally, in 1976, after a series of cases had been brought to it by Ginsburg and other women's rights lawyers, the Court ruled that sex-discrimination complaints would be judged by a new, judicially created intermediate standard of review a step below strict scrutiny. In *Craig v. Boren* (1976),[d] the owner of the Honk 'n' Holler Restaurant in Stillwater, Oklahoma, and Craig, a male under age twenty-one, challenged the constitutionality of the state law that prohibited the sale of 3.2 percent beer to males under the age of twenty-one and to females under the age of eighteen. The state introduced a considerable amount of evidence in support of the statute, including the following:

> Eighteen- to twenty-year-old males were more likely to be arrested for driving under the influence than were females of the same age.
>
> Youths aged seventeen to twenty-one are more likely to be injured or to die in alcohol-related traffic accidents, with males exceeding females.
>
> Young men were more inclined than females to drink and drive.

The Supreme Court found that this information was "too tenuous" to support the legislation. In coming to this conclusion, the justices carved out a new, two-tiered test to be used in examining claims of sex discrimination. According to the Court, "to withstand constitutional challenge, . . . classifications by gender must serve important governmental objectives and must be substantially related to achievement to those objectives." As *Craig* demonstrates, men, too, can use the Fourteenth Amendment to fight gender-based discrimination. Since 1976, the Court has applied that intermediate standard to most claims involving gender that it has heard. Thus, the following kinds of practices have been found to violate the Fourteenth Amendment:

Single-sex public nursing schools.[e]

Laws that consider males adults at age twenty-one but females at age eighteen.[f]

Laws that allow women but not men to receive alimony.[g]

State supported all-male military academies.[h]

In contrast, the Court has upheld the following governmental practices and laws:

Draft registration provisions for males only.[i]

Statutory rape laws that apply only to female victims.[j]

State failure to allow employees to take full twelve weeks of unpaid leave as required by the federal Family and Medical Leave.

The level of review used by the Court is crucial. Clearly, a statute that excluded blacks from a draft registration would be unconstitutional. But, because gender is not subject to the same higher standard of review that is used in racial discrimination cases, the exclusion of women from the requirements of the Military Selective Service Act was ruled permissible because the government policy was considered to serve "important governmental objectives."

One can perhaps better understand, then, why women's rights activists continue to argue that, until the passage of an equal rights amendment, women will never come close to enjoying the same rights as men. An amendment would automatically raise the level of scrutiny that the Court applies, although there is concern about how *equal* would be applied to situations of gender difference such as maternity.[k]

---

[a] *Goessaert v. Cleary*, 335 U.S. 464 (1948).

[b] 404 U.S. 71 (1971).

[c] 411 U.S. 677 (1973).

[d] 429 U.S. 190 (1976).

[e] *Mississippi University for Women v. Hogan*, 458 U.S. 718 (1982).

[f] *Stanton v. Stanton*, 421 U.S. 7 (1975).

[g] *Orr v. Orr*, 440 U.S. 268 (1979).

[h] *U.S. v. Virginia*, 116 S.Ct. 2264 (1996).

[i] *Rostker v. Goldberg*, 453 U.S. 57 (1981).

[j] *Michael M. v. Superior Court of Sonoma County*, 450 U.S. 464 (1981).

[k] See Laura Woliver, "The Equal Rights Amendment and the Limits of Legal Reform," *Polity* 21 (Fall 1988): 183–200.

Source: Adapted from Karen O'Connor and Larry J. Sabato, *American Government: Continuity and Change* (Boston: Allyn and Bacon, 1997), 209–10.

sexual double standards, the traditional family, etc.) were abolished. Other women maintained (and continue to do so) that the patriarchal, social, and political systems as well as the capitalist economic system must be overthrown before women will be free. While some in the younger branch called for the "full participation [of women] in the decision-making processes and positions of our political, economic, and social institutions,"[36] the focus of most of these small groups was largely on raising individual women's consciousness as a prelude to social and hence political revolution or providing limited help to local women in specific issue areas. Moreover, when these groups mobilized to act, they usually did so at the local level. Their activist work in rape crisis centers, battered women's shelters, and health clinics, for example, empowered these women at the *local* level.[37]

Just as different strategies for political change emerged among women activists involved in NOW, a split also emerged among women authors of various ideological perspectives. Feminist theorists sought unity between theory and practice, and their attempts to present a unified political agenda revealed important differences among women. Women such as Betty Friedan, who sought to reform the political system by challenging sexual inequality in the courts, were labeled liberal feminists because they worked within the existing legal structure. Younger feminists challenged these tactics by older, liberal feminists, because they argued these reforms only served to prop up an oppressive system. For example, women who identified themselves as radical feminists chose to break with patriarchal society and form separatist communities among themselves. These women, such as Andrea Dworkin, Ti Grace Atkinson, and Mary Daly, viewed society as misogynistic, and they encouraged other women to create safe spaces for themselves outside of the dominant culture. Dworkin's *Women Hating: A Radical Look at Sexuality* (1974), Atkinson's *Amazon Odyssey* (1974), and Daly's *Gyn/Ecology: The Metaethics of Radical Feminism* (1978) examined how heterosexuality and patriarchy oppress women. Other feminists claimed that women's subordinate status in society was determined by our capitalist economic system. These women, active in the socialist party, the communist party, and the New Politics movement, argued that only a revolution in the means and relationships of production would substantively change the sexual division of labor that supported capitalism and patriarchy. Socialist feminists like Sheila Rowbotham and Zillah Eisenstein focused on the connection between reproductive and productive labor. Rowbotham's *Women's Consciousness, Man's World* (1973), and Eisenstein's edited volume, *Capitalist Patriarchy and the Case for Socialist Feminism* (1979), treated the history of women as a sex-class working toward political liberation through collective action.[38]

While often disagreeing on the focus, both branches of the movement agreed that changes had to be made in the political or legal system. It was the more conventional route to change—the addition of a constitutional amendment guaranteeing equality of rights to all women—however, that became the first major rallying point for change.[39]

The President's Commission on the Status of Women and NOW

In 1961, President John F. Kennedy created the President's Commission on the Status of Women. The commission was created in large part as a payback for a political debt to the women who had worked so hard for his election. Those supporters were outraged when President Kennedy appointed few women to major governmental positions. To appease these women, and some say to avoid the question of the ERA, which he opposed, Kennedy established the commission with activist and former First Lady Eleanor Roosevelt as its chair.[40]

In June 1963, the commission's report, *American Woman*, recommended increased appointment of women to important political positions. The sole advocate of the ERA on the commission, Marguerite Rawalt, persuaded other commission members to temper their rejection of the need for an ERA. Thus, the commission report "concluded that a constitutional amendment need not *now* be sought," paving the way for a possible future recommendation to the contrary.[41]

Five years after the President's Commission on the Status of Women Report, however, many women's groups still did not greet the concepts embodied in the ERA with enthusiasm. In fact, when NOW endorsed the ERA in 1967, some of its members resigned in protest, voicing fears similar to those noted earlier by social feminists and many existing women's groups: the proposed amendment would negate protective labor legislation.

Later in 1967, Martha Griffiths (D-Mich.), one of the few women in the House of Representatives, used a discharge petition to force the amendment out of the House Judiciary Committee. It had been blocked there since 1948 by its powerful committee chair, Emanuel Celler (D-N.Y.). After extensive hearings, on August 10, 1970, the full House had its first occasion ever to vote for the ERA. After eloquent presentations by female representatives, it passed on a vote of 350 to 15.

A somewhat different pattern emerged in the Senate. In May 1970, prior to the House vote, the Senate Subcommittee on Constitutional Amendments held hearings. Several representatives from the AFL-CIO testified in opposition to the amendment. No women's groups spoke out against it. A similar pattern emerged when new hearings were held by the full Senate Judiciary Committee, after the House vote. Most of those who testified, including the John Birch Society, the AFL-CIO, and the National Council of Catholic Women, spoke against the amendment. Senator Sam Ervin (D-N.C.) proposed a rider that prohibited the drafting of women into the armed forces. It also contained language limiting the ERA's effect on protective legislation such as maximum-hour laws; initially his amendment had substantial support.

In 1970, the Citizens Advisory Council on the Status of Women (which replaced the President's Commission on the Status of Women) reported to President Richard M. Nixon its belief that an amendment was necessary, thus rejecting the earlier recommendation of the original commission. Included in its report was a legal analysis of the ERA's impact on protective legislation that concluded that when benefits were given to women, they would be extended

---

THE PROPOSED EQUAL RIGHTS AMENDMENT

Section 1: Equality of rights under the law shall not be denied or abridged by the United States or by any State on account of sex.

Section 2: The Congress shall have the power to enforce, by appropriate legislation, the provisions of this article.

Section 3: This amendment shall take effect two years after the date of ratification.

---

to men. That report gave impetus to the tremendous effort that was launched by myriad women's organizations, culminating in a Senate vote of 84 to 8 for the ERA on March 22, 1972.

The Ratification Effort

General agreement existed about how the ERA would affect political, educational, and employment opportunities. Controversy over its impact on family relations, especially divorce, alimony, and child support laws, and the specter of military service for women should there be another draft, were present from the beginning.

In fact, once the ERA was sent to the states for their approval, the real battle over its ratification began in earnest. Initially, ratification seemed a virtual certainty. Supreme Court rulings striking down most protective legislation as unlawful under the Civil Rights Act of 1964 (see Chapter 3) helped to bring into the ERA camp most of the social feminist and labor groups that had initially opposed it. Even some women in the younger branch who saw little to be gained from a constitutional change supported the amendment, perceiving it to be a symbol and a possible tool to facilitate the acquisition of additional rights. Additionally, public opinion polls revealed growing national support for the ERA.

Between March 1972 and January 1973, twenty-eight states quickly moved to ratify the amendment, prompting Martha Griffiths to predict confidently in March 1973, "ERA will be a part of the Constitution before the year's out."[42] These early victories, however, were not an indication of an easy road ahead. States that failed to ratify the amendment, especially in the South, often had political cultures resistant to innovative legislation or expanded women's rights. Additionally, many ERA supporters failed to recognize growing grassroots opposition.

During the drive for the Nineteenth Amendment, NAWSA acted as an umbrella organization and as *the* single major representative of prosuffrage forces. NAWSA also had strong state and local affiliates upon which to rely once the ratification effort turned from the national to the state level. In contrast, the women's rights movement had no spokesperson, no Winning Plan, and few state affiliates. These deficiencies became increasingly grave in the wake of growing and well-organized state and local opposition. Weak or nonexistent state organization was particularly critical, given that Congress attached a seven-year time limit for ratification of the amendment.

ERA—The First Stage (1972–1977). During this stage, NOW, the LWV, and the National Federation of Business and Professional Women's Clubs (BPW) sponsored letter and telegram campaigns, provided expert testimony, and supported pro-ERA candidates. State groups were reactive and were created or mobilized only in response to anti-ERA activity. While pro-ERA groups defeated some state legislators who opposed ratification, only five states ratified the ERA after 1973.[43]

During this period, BPW funded a study that recommended that women's rights groups band together to form a more organized and well-financed national headquarters to coordinate state campaigns and solicit money. In addition to being among its earliest supporters, BPW played a key role in funding the movement for the ERA, billing its members $1.50 per year for support of the ratification effort. Its financial and political resources allowed BPW to be an instrumental force in seeing the ERA through Congress. It also was a leading force in bringing together key organizations in ERAmerica in January 1976, in an attempt to orchestrate states' efforts to get the needed legislative support at that level. But ERAmerica, which relied on member organizations for help, soon turned out to be relatively poor and powerless. Thus, without a strong national coordinating organization, actions to ratify the ERA relied almost exclusively on the efforts of individual groups, particularly NOW, BPW, and LWV, as well as ad hoc coalitions. Not only did each of these groups pursue different strategies, but all sought to become the leader in the ratification effort.

ERA—The Second Stage (1977–1979). In 1977, NOW adopted different tactics "which marked the ascendancy of NOW as the leading proponent of the ERA."[44] Its rise to the forefront was triggered by the adoption of two campaigns. First, NOW called for an economic boycott of states where ratification had not yet occurred. Generally, this boycott took the form of having large national associations cancel or threaten to cancel conventions scheduled in cities located in unratified states. Even the American Political Science Association voted not to hold its annual meeting in Chicago, Illinois, a state where ratification had not occurred, after extensive lobbying by women in the Women's Caucus for Political Science. Second, given the impending deadline for ratification—March 1979— a resolution to extend that deadline an additional seven years was introduced in Congress at the urging of numerous women's groups. In addition, these groups, as suffragists had done before, sponsored a march on Washington, D.C., that attracted more than 100,000 participants. Many dressed in white as suffragists had done long before in their quest for the Nineteenth Amendment. These well-planned efforts ultimately led Congress to approve a thirty-nine-month extension period for ratification, over the strong objections of amendment opponents.

Both of these strategies were national in nature and quite unlike the Winning Plan devised earlier by Carrie Chapman Catt. In fact, the then-president of NOW, Eleanor Smeal (later head of the Fund for a Feminist Majority), justified the necessity of a national campaign, saying that "this is an unratified country. We communicate as a nation . . . our states are economically interdependent [and] [o]ur opposition is national."[45] This kind of determination to pursue a national strategy in the wake of growing anti-ERA and New Right strength in nonratified states' legislatures is noteworthy, given that the amendment could not be ratified without the approval of those states.

Anti-ERA forces were best mobilized at the state level. Drawing women from the organizational bases of the conservative wing of the Republican Party, fundamentalist churches in the South, and a reenergized antiabortion movement (see Chapter 5), Phyllis Schlafly effectively organized STOP ERA, which led the fight against ratification of the amendment. Schlafly, the editor of the conservative monthly *Phyllis Schlafly Report* and a former speech writer for Senator Barry Goldwater (R-Ariz.), laid the groundwork for an anti-ERA movement as early as 1967.[46]

Schlafly was a master at grassroots mobilization, which was a key factor in defeating the ERA at the state level. Schlafly and the Eagle Forum, a group she founded in 1975 to fight ratification, lobbied state legislators in key states, while pro-amendment forces continued to work largely on the national level.

Building on her conservative base, Schlafly became the symbol of the anti-ERA movement as she effectively argued that the amendment would mean:

1. Private schools would have to be coed.
2. All sports, including contact sports, would be coed.
3. All persons would pay the same income tax regardless of their income.
4. Abortions would be government funded.
5. Homosexuals could be schoolteachers.
6. Women would be forced into combat.
7. Men could refuse to support their wives.
8. A woman's right to her home and support of her children could be denied.
9. Homosexual marriages would be legal.
10. Homosexuals would be allowed to adopt children.[47]

Other ERA opponents argued that it would legalize unisex toilets and pornography.[48] The ambiguity surrounding the ERA encouraged many to view it as a threat to the status quo. As the ERA was portrayed by its opponents, the traditional family, the institution of marriage, and the right of a wife to be supported by her husband would be jeopardized by ratification. Phyllis Schlafly, in answer to the question of who would profit from the ERA, wrote in an often reprinted quotation, "Women will lose, families will lose, society will lose."[49]

ERA—The Third Stage (1979–1982). In spite of the apparent success of STOP ERA's *state* efforts and public perception problems, in late 1979 NOW fully devoted itself to implementation of a new *national* plan of action. By 1982, NOW was receiving more than $1 million a month for ERA ratification and had formed several political action committees (PACs) to elect pro-ERA candidates. It also used a variety of other traditional and nontraditional strategies. For example, "ERA missionaries" went door to door seeking support in unratified states, and pro-ERA entertainers went on television to gain support and publicity. A variety of forms of protest also occurred. For example, some women chained themselves to Republican headquarters, while others conducted hunger strikes or performed acts of vandalism.

These tactics came too late and generally occurred at the wrong level of government. Even in states such as Illinois, which were the targets of massive pro-ERA efforts, few votes were changed. The amendment was finally defeated on June 30, 1982, when the time period for ratification expired. The lack of a coordinated effective effort, however, was probably just one of several factors that contributed to the ERA's defeat. In fact, had it not been for the activities of anti-ERA groups with their close ties to state legislators and corporate interests, the amendment's chances of passage would have been far greater.[50] By the early 1980s, however, the political tide in the nation had turned. Conservative Ronald Reagan was elected president in 1980, and a backlash against many gains by women was soon to begin.[51]

The Aftermath of the ERA Ratification Effort: Women's Groups Mobilize for Expanded Political Opportunities

When the ERA was not ratified, NOW chose to continue to press for the amendment at least in part because ERA direct-mail solicitations stimulated donations. But, many other groups sought to focus their efforts elsewhere. Many turned their energies toward preservation of abortion rights that were under attack from conservatives and the Reagan administration (see Chapter 5). Others concentrated on litigation to press the courts for expanded constitutional rights for women. Without an ERA guaranteeing women's equality under the U.S. Constitution, women were forced to look for statutory remedies to prevent discrimination. We explore many of these efforts in Chapter 3.

Former vice-presidential candidate Geraldine Ferraro is fond of telling female audiences, "If you don't run, you can't win."[52] Sentiments like these led to the creation of several groups to encourage women to do just that, as well as to provide support for those who chose to run. Some women opted to work within the existing two-party structure. And both parties, but especially the Democratic Party, took measures to encourage women to participate and even run for office. For example, the Women's Council of the Democratic Senatorial Campaign Committee gave $1.5 million to the ten Democratic women who ran for the Senate in 1992. Some groups, most notably the National Women's Political Caucus (NWPC), the Coalition for Women's Appointments, the Fund for a Feminist Majority, and Black Women Organized for Action, were founded with

Women and Politics

MADAM PRESIDENT? A WOMAN IN THE WHITE HOUSE

In 1984, Geraldine Ferraro (D-N.Y.), a three-term member of the U.S. House of Representatives, became the first woman nominated by a major party for the position of vice president of the United States. The selection of Ferraro by Walter Mondale was the result of a campaign by the women's rights movement to place a woman on the Democratic Party ticket. The leaders of this effort believed a woman would make the Democratic Party victorious, but the election of Ronald Reagan to a second term indicated Ferraro had little impact on the choice of voters.[a]

Almost twenty years later, in their book *Madam President: Women Blazing the Leadership Trail*, journalists Eleanor Clift and Tom Brazaitis examined Geraldine Ferraro's historic role in the rise of women to prominence across the political spectrum. "Whether Ferraro's candidacy had advanced or set back the cause of a woman on the ticket is a question still being debated. Women answered themselves by increasing their presence as voters and candidates, validating women at every level of politics, as if to say one losing election is no big deal. Still, so powerful was the Ferraro hangover that it would not be until 2000 that the two major political parties would again contemplate a woman on the ticket as a vice presidential contender."[b] Even though a number of women were considered for the vice presidential nomination in 2000, both George W. Bush and Al Gore chose men as their running mates.

Since Ferraro's pioneering bid for second place on the national ticket, several women have considered running for the highest office in the land. In 1988, Representative Patricia Schroeder (D-Colo.) explored the possibilities of a run for president but tearfully bowed out of the race a few months later. In 1999, Elizabeth Dole announced her decision to seek the Republican nomination for president in 2000. Dole had held cabinet positions in two previous Republican administrations and spent eight years as president of the American Red Cross, where she was a successful fundraiser. Yet Dole's inability to raise enough money to effectively challenge front-runner George W. Bush doomed her campaign. Now retired from Congress, Patricia Schroeder speculated about why no woman has ever been elected president of the United States: "Women don't feel entitled, and until we do, we're not going to do much about it. If women spent half what they spent on make-up last year on a candidate, we could have a woman in the White House."[c]

Clift and Brazaitis argue that the first woman to be electe
dent of the United States will most likely be a moderate Re
from a Western state. The number of women elected to sta
tures has vastly increased in recent years, filling the pipeline ic.
higher office. Today, women are lieutenant governors in seventeen
states, the governors in eight states, fifty-nine members of the House
of Representatives, and fourteen Senators. They note that four of the
last five presidents were former governors, suggesting that voters
look for executive experience in a candidate for the nation's highest
public office. "Electing women senators and governors may be the
best way to nurture ambition and hurry history."[d] In February 2003,
former Senator Carol Moseley-Braun (D-Ill.), who served as ambas-
sador to New Zealand in the Clinton administration, announced her
intention to run for the Democratic Party nomination for president.
Speaking to the Democratic National Committee, she declared: "In
these difficult times for America, I believe women have a contribution
to make to move our country toward peace, prosperity, and progress.
I am Carol Moseley-Braun, and I want to be your nominee for president of the United States because now is the time for inclusion, equality, and real democracy."[e] Entering a race already filled with male
presidential hopefuls, Braun won praise from women's groups for her
decision to run in the presidential primary. "Moseley-Braun is a longtime women's rights supporter with a record to back up her rhetoric,
said Kim Gandy, president of the National Organization for Women.
"With Carol at the table, women's issues will be central in shaping the
debate."[f] Marie Wilson, president of the White House Project, underscored the importance of having Carol Moseley-Braun in the race for
the presidency. "She'll bring a different voice to the race and she'll
make sure, just because she's there, that men around her really have
to think, more than they ordinarily do, about women."[g] On January
15, 2004 Caroll Moseley-Braun ended her presidential bid.

---

[a] Kathleen A. Frankovic, "The 1984 Election: The Irrelevance of the Campaign," *PS* (Winter 1985): 39–47.

[b] Eleanor Clift and Tom Brazaitis, *Madam President: Women Blazing the Leadership Trail* (New York: Routledge, 2003).

[c] Ibid., 300.

[d] Ibid., 78.

[e] Allison Stevens, "Moseley-Braun Runs for President and More," National Women's Political Caucus, http://www.nwpc.org/topstories.html.

[f] "Feminist Explores Presidential Race, NOW Applauds Moseley-Braun Announce-ment," National Organization for Women Press Release, February 19, 2003, http://www.now.org/press/02-03/02-19.html.

[g] Ibid.

Global Awareness

WOMEN ELECTED TO EXECUTIVE OFFICE

Around the world women have been elected to executive office. Women leaders have served their nations as president or prime minister in Europe, Asia, Africa, and the Americas. When will a woman be elected president in the United States?

Source: Adapted from data compiled by the Women's Environment and Development Organization and The Center for Asia-Pacific Women in Politics.

the electoral process as their primary target. Other women's organizations, including the League of Women Voters, the American Association of University Women, and NOW, also began to focus their energies on the enhanced political participation of women in electoral politics. And, in response to campaign law reform that occurred in the early 1970s, a variety of women's PACs, including the Women's Campaign Fund, EMILY's List, and the WISH List, became important sources of financial support for women candidates.

The National Women's Political Caucus (NWPC)

Founded in 1971, the NWPC is a national, grassroots organization dedicated to increasing the number of feminist women elected at all levels of government.[53] Its founders included leaders of many major women's organizations, among them Gloria Steinem, Bella Abzug, and Betty Friedan. Rep. Shirley Chisholm (D-N.Y.), another founder, was elected to Congress in 1968 and actually ran in the New York State Democratic presidential primary in 1972. (Although she lost, Chisholm received 151.5 votes on the first ballot at the 1972 Democratic Party's national convention, becoming the first African American woman to run for president.) LaDonna Harris, a Comanche Indian, was also a founder of the NWPC. (The first congressional wife ever to testify before

Congress, Harris later ran for vice president of the United States on the Citizens Party ticket.)

NWPC goals include increasing support for women candidates and appointed officials, and reforming party structures to assure equitable representation for women. The organization also publicizes women's issues when they are at stake in elections, monitors the selection of women delegates to party conventions, and holds regional training sessions for women candidates and campaign workers throughout the United States. NWPC is unique in its multipartisan base. To accommodate the needs of its members and to fulfill its commitment to increased representation in the political parties, however, it maintains special Democratic and Republican task forces.

Since its creation, NWPC has had a noticeable impact on Democratic Party rules, in particular. At the 1976 Democratic National Convention, it led the move for a written guarantee that women would constitute 50 percent of the delegates at the 1980 convention. To prevent an embarrassing floor fight, soon-to-be-nominated candidate Jimmy Carter met with women's rights leaders to reach a compromise. The resultant agreement involved Carter's promise to appoint women to high-ranking positions in his administration should he be elected. Other parts of the compromise included provisions in the party rules that mandated that "future conventions shall promote equal division between delegate men and delegate women"[54] and required the Democratic National Committee (DNC) to encourage the state parties to adopt rules to effectuate this goal. In 1978, the DNC actually passed a resolution that required that 50 percent of the future convention delegates be women.

Since 1976, the NWPC has been at the forefront of efforts to increase the number of women appointed to high-ranking, policy-making federal jobs. It convened the Coalition for Women's Appointments, composed of representatives from more than seventy women's and public interest groups, to identify qualified female candidates, collect and forward their résumés to the White House, and then lobby for their appointment. The appointments coalition forwarded the names of many eventual nominees to the Carter, Bush, and Clinton administrations. Now called the Women's Appointment Project, the project supported the four women who were appointed to George W. Bush's cabinet. The NWPC also works with the Federation of Women Judicial Lawyers Screening Panel and NOW to identify qualified women for the federal bench. The NWPC has provided leadership programs for candidates and campaign staff across the country. More recently, NWPC has begun to offer leadership training programs aimed at teenage girls, young women, and women of color in order to prepare the next generation of pro-choice political leaders.

The bipartisan orientation of the National Women's Political Caucus was highlighted by the election of Rosalyn O'Connell, a Republican pro-choice activist, in 1999. In 2002, the NWPC endorsed fifty-two women candidates running for Congress, four women seeking the office of governor, and two women in bids to be elected secretary of state. Under O'Connell's leadership, the NWPC sponsored a 2003 convention in Washington, D.C., entitled "Strong

Women for Tough Times," which brought together scholars, candidates, and activists to strategize how to increase the number of women in all levels of government in the 2004 election cycle.

The Feminist Majority Foundation

The Fund for a Feminist Majority (now the Feminist Majority) was created in 1987 by Peg Yorkin, a prominent feminist producer and philanthropist, and Eleanor Smeal, a former president of NOW, who had guided that organization through much of the ERA ratification effort. One of the Feminist Majority's major activities is its nationwide campaign to recruit more women to run for political office. It also provides a much-needed source of feminist news from around the world and offers Web links to many less well financed women's organizations.[55] The Feminist Majority Foundation sponsors a variety of campaigns directed at young women on college and university campuses. A campus program called the Feminist Majority Leadership Alliance fosters leadership training and organizing skills, and the "Get out HER Vote" and "Rock for Choice" campaigns aim at registering and mobilizing young people to vote.

The League of Women Voters

The League of Women Voters was one of the original members of the Women's Joint Congressional Committee. It soon, however, abandoned its support of women's issues, preferring to call itself "a citizen's group rather than a women's organization."[56] It did not endorse the ERA until the early 1970s and only truly came to feminist activism in the 1990s. The League specifically targeted racial and ethnic minorities and eighteen- to twenty-four-year-olds in its Get Out the Vote effort, partnering itself with MTV's Rock the Vote, begun by MTV before the 1992 elections to educate and motivate young voters. The organization took the lead in efforts to lobby for the passage of the National Voter Registration Act (the Motor Voter Law). After women stayed home in droves in 1994, the League, in combination with its efforts to implement the Motor Voter Law, also launched comprehensive campaigns in 1996 and 1998 to get out the vote, with the goal of achieving 85 percent registration and turnout rates. It worked in conjunction with the *Ladies Home Journal* magazine to highlight issues of women's political participation and its consequences. The League termed its strategy "up close and personal" by delivering a message that brought politics home. "It's about your children's education, your taxes, your Social Security, your Medicare, and your safe streets. It's about you and your family. Vote."[57] While voter turnout declined somewhat in 1996, areas that had been targeted by the League actually had higher numbers of citizens going to the polls.

The controversy surrounding election results in Florida following the 2000 presidential campaign led the League of Women Voters to champion election reform with an online petition drive that encouraged members of the 107th Congress to implement "best practices" voting systems. The League also called for the abolition of the electoral college as an "archaic and unnecessary" institution at odds with the principles of one person, one vote.[58] In 2001, the League conducted the "Good Enough is not Good Enough" election reform survey, which exposed inadequacies in voter access, vote counting, the election workforce, and voter education across the country and proposed policy recommendations to remedy these problems to "ensure that *every* vote *always* counts."[59] To encourage greater civic engagement, the League of Women Voters developed DemocracyNet, which is an online voter education service, and campaigned for the Political Campaign Broadcast Activity Improvements Act to provide free air time for political candidates.

The American Association of University Women

The American Association of University Women (AAUW) was formed in 1881 to help women find jobs and network in business. The organization became more extensively involved in politics after the 1994 elections resulted in a conservative Republican-controlled Congress. It saw this Congress as "threaten[ing] to devastate every initiative that AAUW had worked for [for] decades."[60] Thus, it launched the AAUW Voter Education Campaign in July 1995. This campaign was divided into two parts. The first consisted of an organized nationwide fax campaign and e-mail network to inform women on how issues before Congress affected their lives: "Biweekly Get the Facts alerts were produced in partnership with 43 organizations in a nonpartisan, issue-based coalition, the Women's Network for Change."[61] The second part of its campaign was a get-out-the-vote effort designed to organize AAUW members to encourage *drop off voters*—those who voted in 1992 but stayed home in 1994—to go to the polls in 1996. Members used phone banks to call nearly one million women in fifty key congressional districts. In subsequent election cycles, AAUW continued to encourage women's participation in the voting booth and the public policy-making process through Get the Facts alerts and the distribution of fact sheets and position papers on their website.

The American Association of University Women continues to lobby Congress on numerous educational and equity issues of concern to girls and women. The organization's Congressional Outlook in recent years has highlighted reproductive choice, civil rights, economic security, and expanded educational opportunity. Members of AAUW lobbied the 107th Congress for increased access to mifepristone/RU486, reforming Social Security, and passage of the Educating America's Girls Act. During the 108th Congress, the organization put the strength of its membership behind efforts to achieve pay equity, protect affirmative action and Title IX, expand family and medical leave, and increase education and training programs as part of welfare reauthorization. Recognizing that balancing work and family can leave little time for civic activism, AAUW launched the "Two-Minute Activist" feature on its website, allowing members to quickly contact lawmakers about legislation affecting their busy lives.

The National Organization for Women

After the defeat of the ERA, NOW "began to focus less on trying to influence men in power and more on electing feminists to replace them."[62] In 1992, it joined the chorus of women's organizations seeking more women in elective office with its Elect Women for a Change campaign. NOW is the nation's largest feminist organization, with more than 500,000 members who are active in more than 550 chapters in all fifty states. The organization has used the strength of its membership to help women candidates succeed in being elected to office through the formation of two political action committees, NOW/PAC and NOW Equality PAC.

NOW also supports gender equity in political appointments and is a member of the Coalition for Women's Appointments. On the state level, NOW has also targeted the appointment of more women. "Gender balance" on boards and commissions continues to be a goal of state NOW chapters especially in states that require governors' appointments to be divided equally between the sexes.[63]

The National Organization for Women President Kim Gandy remarked following the 2002 midterm elections, "Now it's up to us to organize, organize, organize to protect our rights."[64] The organization remains committed to the passage of an equal rights amendment as the key to protecting and expanding women's rights to political representation, educational opportunity, and economic equity. NOW provides valuable information about public policy debates ranging from campaign finance reform to family friendly initiatives in the workplace. NOW posts "Action Alerts" on its website to educate and activate members about feminist issues.

Women's PACs

As a result of changes in the national campaign finance laws, in 1974, it became possible for organizations to create political action committees (PACs) to raise money for candidates running for public office. In response, several women's organizations, including NOW, BPW, and NWPC, created PACs in the 1970s, although they generally supported both women and men candidates. The exception was the now defunct Women's Campaign Fund, organized in 1974, with the express purpose of contributing solely to the campaigns of women candidates.

During the 1980s, new PACs for women candidates or candidates supporting women's issues were established almost every year, but these groups were generally small and underfunded. By 1989, thirty-three PACs gave money primarily to women candidates. According to the Center for the American Woman and Politics (CAWP), in 1988, seventeen of those PACs gave more than $1.1 million to 464 candidates. The big breakthrough year for PACs supporting women candidates came in 1992. Not only were twelve new PACs founded, raising the total number of PACs supporting only or mainly women candidates to more than forty, but the contributions to those PACs skyrocketed. Collectively, PACs contributed nearly $12 million to women candidates running for public office in the fall elections. This represented almost a qua-

SIPRESS

"Today I'm announcing I've decided to get out of my family so I can devote more time to politics."

drupling of these groups' donations from 1990. One reason for the rise in women's campaign contributions was that the conservative groups like Phyllis Schafly's Eagle Forum and Beverly LaHaye's Concerned Women for America also funded successful PACs. Throughout the decade, PACs increased their contributions to candidates running for public office, and these funds often made the difference in crucial races. Recent data from CAWP, however, indicate that the actual number of women's PACs declined from a high of fifty-eight in 1997 to forty-nine in 2002.[65] The top women's PACs were EMILY's List and those of the National Organization for Women.

NOW/PAC and NOW Equality PAC.   In 1977, NOW created two PACs to put individual contributions together to fund the candidacies of feminists. NOW/PAC supports candidates for national election. NOW Equality PAC fills up the political pipeline by supporting women candidates at the state and local levels. The Equality PAC is not regulated by federal law. NOW/PAC claims to be the only "women's rights PAC that bases its endorsements on a broad feminist agenda" including pay equity, welfare reform, and a vast range of economic issues.[66] Like the Women's Campaign Fund, NOW's two PACs allow it to endorse Republican, Democratic, and independent women at all levels of government, believing that "lower level offices serve as a pipeline to the highest levels of office."[67] NOW prides itself on endorsing strong feminists "in ways that defy conventional political wisdom."[68] NOW/PAC, for example, was an early supporter of Cynthia McKinney, who was deemed "too young, too liberal and, with her cornrow hairstyle, too black to win."[69] With NOW/PAC support, McKinney won election to the U.S. House of Representatives in 1992, 1994, and even in 1996, when her district was dramatically redrawn in a way that excluded a large proportion of black voters. Said Carol Moseley-Braun (D-Ill.) of her own campaign, "Without [NOW] there would be no Carol, candidate for the Senate."[70] From 1996 to 2000, NOW/PAC contributed over $500,000 to the campaigns of feminists running for federal office.

In 1997, NOW/PAC and NOW Equality PAC launched a campaign to greatly increase the number of women officeholders at all levels of government, from city hall to Congress. The campaign dubbed "Victory 2000—The Feminization of Politics" had the goal of electing two thousand feminist candidates by the year 2000. The Republican sweep in 2000 led NOW to revitalize efforts to identify, support, and elect feminist leaders at all levels of government. In 2002, NOW's PAC funds helped to elect one Senator, seven new members of the House of Representatives, and nine governors. New campaign finance laws that limit soft money contributions have made NOW's PACs all the more important to feminist candidates preparing to run for office. NOW President Kim Gandy noted the significance of NOW PACs to future campaign finance reform. "We believe that the system is flawed, but we cannot opt out until it's fixed. We will never elect the kind of candidates who will push for real change if we don't use the NOW PACs to their full potential."[71]

EMILY's List.   The largest of the women's PACs is EMILY's List ("Early Money Is Like Yeast—It Makes the Dough Rise"), which was founded in 1985 to support viable, pro-choice Democratic women running in congressional and gubernatorial races. Its goal is to raise money early in the election cycle to put more women in elective office. It tries to do this by putting them on its list and encouraging its members to support endorsed women. Each election cycle, members of EMILY's List agree to contribute no less than $100 to at least two of the recommended candidates on the list. (It costs $100 to become a member of EMILY's List.) Unlike other PACs, whose boards decide how members' contributions are to be spent, EMILY's List members write their checks to the candidates of their choice. They are then bundled together and sent directly to the candidate by EMILY's List. Since 1988, EMILY's List has been the largest financial resource for women candidates. (See Figure 1.1.) It also supported House candidates for the first time that year.

Aware that money was not enough, EMILY's List's leaders recognized the tremendous opportunity presented by the reapportionment of the House of Representatives that was to take place in 1990. To prepare to seize that opportunity, in 1989 EMILY's List held a debriefing conference for the candidates it supported in 1988 and published "Campaigning in a Different Voice," a study of gender-related issues faced by female candidates for the House. Soon after, in 1990, it commissioned a national poll on the choice issue and how it affects female Democratic candidates. It also worked with the National Committee for an Effective Congress, using the committee's huge computer capacity to identify likely new congressional seats for 1992. Representatives from EMILY's List met with pro-choice Democratic women to brief them on ways to keep abreast of the potential district boundary changes and to suggest ways to keep their districts winnable. It also made an extensive search for viable candidates. Its efforts were key to women's successes in 1992. EMILY's List raised more than $6.2 million that year, which it donated to the campaigns of fifty-five women candidates, making it the largest PAC supporting congressional candidates—male or female.[72] Most of the women elected in the "Year of the Woman" were supported by EMILY's List.

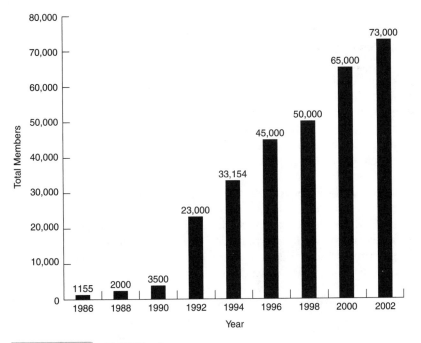

FIGURE 1.1   **EMILY's Army**

EMILY's List also provides professional training for candidates and their staffs, conducts surveys and issue research, and helps with campaign message development.[73] In 1996, like many other women's organizations, EMILY's List tried to mobilize women voters to vote for pro-choice female candidates. Its WOMEN VOTE project raised more than $3 million to use to turn out additional pro-choice women voters. It also contributed an additional $12 million directly to candidates in 1996.[74]

In the 2000 elections, EMILY's List members contributed $9.2 million directly to pro-choice Democratic women candidates, and raised $10.8 million for efforts to educate women voters and get them to the polls. Said Ellen Malcolm, founder and president of EMILY's List, "EMILY's List helped bring as many new pro-choice Democratic women to the U.S. Senate in the 2000 elections as in 1992, the 'Year of the Woman.' We worked hard to reach that high-water mark and add more women's voices to the World's Most Exclusive Club."[75] The impact of EMILY's List financial assistance and other forms of campaign support can be seen in the 2000 election of Senator Debbie Stabenow (D-Mich.). Armed with poll data that suggested the first-term GOP Senator Spencer Abraham could be defeated, EMILY's List's leaders approached Stabenow, who was serving in the House of Representatives, and encouraged her to challenge Abraham for his seat in the Senate. Throughout a tough campaign, in which Abraham raised over $15 million from conservative groups, Stabenow was backed by the significant resources of EMILY's List. The PAC contributed nearly $1.4 million directly to her campaign, plus donated over $600,000 to the Michigan Democratic Party to call and canvass women voters, and spent another $1.3 million on television advertisements encouraging women to vote. Following her victory, Stabenow said, "Long before I was a candidate for the United States Senate, I was a proud member of EMILY's List."[76]

In November 2002, EMILY's List support once again made the difference in the election of Jennifer Granholm, Michigan's first woman governor. Kathleen Sebelius in Kansas and Janet Napolitano in Arizona were also victorious in gubernatorial races in their states with the endorsement of EMILY's List. Ellen Malcolm believes that these newly elected women governors are ready for the challenges ahead. "These incoming governors have their work cut out for them. All are inheriting budgetary nightmares during a national economic downturn. But they demonstrated to voters during their campaigns that they are tough enough and smart enough to lead their states through these and any crises."[77] These Democratic victories at the state level were particularly sweet in an election cycle that gave the Republicans control of Congress. Malcolm and members had hoped that redistricting following the 2000 U.S. Census would give women candidates an edge in the 2002 midterm Congressional elections, but when the lines were redrawn, there were few open seats to contest. While only two new women who received EMILY's List endorsement won election to the House of Representatives, Diane Watson (D-Calif.) and Linda Sanchez (D-Calif.), all of the sponsored incumbents were reelected to Congress. EMILY's List has helped to elect seven women governors, eleven women Senators, and fifty-five women members of the House of Representatives since its founding. These women leaders are changing the face of American politics.

The WISH List.   The success of these liberal women's PACs led to the creation of the WISH List (Women in the Senate and House) in 1992. Like EMILY's List, viable candidates for the Senate, House, and governorships are recommended to members, who send their checks directly to the group, where they are bundled. It supports Republican pro-choice women, including Senators Olympia Snow (R-Maine), Kay Bailey Hutchison (R-Texas), and Susan Collins (R-Maine), and Hawaii Governor Linda Lingle. Since its inception, contributors to the WISH List provided almost $3 million to pro-choice Republican candidates. In the 2000 elections, all the WISH List incumbents were reelected, and the 107th Congress included the largest group of Republican women ever to serve. Many of their campaigns were funded in part by the organization. "WISH has helped secure a 50 percent increase in the number of pro-choice Republican Congresswomen and a three-fold jump in pro-choice GOP members of the U.S. Senate." Said Representative Nancy Johnson (R-Conn.) of these gains, "The WISH List is a tremendously important resource for Republican women. . . . Its leadership and success in candidate recruitment and development is vital to the continued strength of the Republican Party."[78] In 2002, only a decade after its founding, WISH List members contributed $765,000 to more than two hundred Republican women candidates, and a majority of them won on election night. The organization has broadened its scope to meet the challenges of a new century, with campaign schools for candidates, "living room groups" to meet and greet political hopefuls and elected officials, and campus outreach programs to recruit young Republican leaders.

CONCLUSION

Women have made tremendous strides since they first gathered in 1848 in Seneca Falls, hesitant to demand the vote. It took two eras of women's movement activity to win the franchise, and much longer to move toward parity in the political process.

Once the Nineteenth Amendment was ratified, women's groups were divided over what goals to pursue. Social feminists wanted to continue their work for protective legislation, a goal that was in direct odds with the NWP's major goal—the addition of an equal rights amendment to the Constitution. Although the NWP worked hard for passage, it was not until the rise of the current women's rights movement that an ERA seemed likely to become a reality. But amendment supporters failed to learn from the lessons of history: their failure to mobilize at the state level in the face of well-organized opposition stymied their efforts.

The period 1970–1982—years critical to the development of the current women's rights movement—was one of intense mobilization and growth, but most efforts were concentrated on the ratification of the ERA. Some groups such as the NWPC, however, remained focused on women's access to the political process. Women's organizations' continued efforts allowed women's PACs, especially EMILY's List, to take advantage of the unique circumstances present in the 1992 election cycle—open seats caused by reapportionment, congressional scandals, a revitalized women's rights movement motivated by a fear of losing access to abortion rights, and women's anger at the Senate Judiciary Committee's treatment of Anita Hill during the Clarence Thomas hearings. All of these unique factors combined to make 1992 the "Year of the Woman." The 1994 midterm elections were not kind to progressive women. Women's groups then stepped up their efforts, and again record numbers of women joined legislative bodies all over the United States, often encouraged and aided every step of the way by women and women's groups.

President Bill Clinton's reelection in 1996 was welcome news to supporters of women's rights. But presidential leadership on issues such as pay equity, welfare reform, and access to reproductive health care would not be enough to secure legislative gains in Clinton's second term in office.

The women who met again at Seneca Falls in 1998 to discuss the struggle for women's rights in America looked to the past to make sense of women's current status in society. The Anniversary Proclamation recognized that the Declaration of Resolutions and Sentiments created an agenda for change. As a result, the "Women's Rights Movement has had a profound and undeniable impact on all aspects of American life, and has opened new and well-deserved opportunities for women in all fields of endeavor, including among others commerce, athletics, business, education, religion, the arts and scientific exploration."[79] The Anniversary Proclamation focused on the future of the women's movement, stating that "the twenty-first century will find an ever-increasing need for both women and men to share in the fundamental responsibilities of our national life and the blessings that must result from full and equal participation in society."[80]

Yet, more than a century and a half after Seneca Falls, the authors of the Anniversary Proclamation noted that "there still remain substantial barriers to the full equality of America's women before our freedom as a nation can be called complete."[81] It is to those barriers that we now turn our attention.

NOTES

1. National Women's History Project, Women's Rights Movement Anniversary Proclamation, http://www.legacy98.org/proclamation.html.
2. Quoted in Eleanor Flexner, *Century of Struggle* (New York: Atheneum, 1974), 76.
3. Elizabeth Cady Stanton, Susan B. Anthony, and Matilda Joslyn Gage, eds., *History of Woman Suffrage*, vol. 1, 1848–1861 (Rochester, N.Y.: Charles Mann, 1881), 70–71.
4. The critical section of the amendment reads: "Section 2 . . . or in any way abridged, except for participation in rebellion, or other crime, the basis of representation therein shall be reduced in the proportion which the number of such *male* citizens

shall bear to the whole number of *male* citizens twenty-one years of age in such State" (emphasis added).

5. Ellen Carol DuBois, *Feminism and Suffrage: The Emergence of an Independent Women's Movement in America, 1848–1869* (Ithaca, N.Y.: Cornell University Press, 1978).

6. This legislation would have been easier for proponents to secure. A constitutional amendment requires a two-thirds majority vote; enabling legislation requires but a simple majority.

7. Elizabeth Cady Stanton, Susan B. Anthony, and Matilda Joslyn Gage, eds., *History of Woman Suffrage*, vol. 2 (New York: Fowler and Wells, 1882), 810–11.

8. Reprinted in ibid., 441–42.

9. Much of this discussion comes from Karen O'Connor, *Women's Organizations' Use of the Courts* (Lexington, Mass.: Lexington Books, 1980), chap. 3.

10. 88 U.S. 162 (1875).

11. For the full text of the Declaration of Rights, see Mari Jo Buhle and Paul Buhle, *The Concise History of Woman Suffrage* (Urbana: University of Illinois Press, 1978), 297–303.

12. *Congressional Globe*, 39th Cong., 2d sess., 1867, pt. 1: 56.

13. Catherine Beecher, *A Treatise on Domestic Education* (New York: Schocken, 1977).

14. Sara Hunter Graham, *Woman Suffrage and the New Democracy* (New Haven, Conn.: Yale University Press, 1996).

15. See Nancy F. Cott, *The Grounding of Modern Feminism* (New Haven, Conn.: Yale University Press, 1987), for an excellent account of the constituent groups and their diverse philosophies.

16. For more on the WCTU, see Janet Zollinger Giele, *Two Paths to Women's Equality: Temperance, Suffrage, and the Origins of Modern Feminism* (Old Tappan, N.J.: Twayne, 1995).

17. See generally Karen J. Blair, *The Club Woman as Feminist* (New York: Holmes and Meier, 1980).

18. See Pat McKissack and Frederick McKissack, *Mary Church Terrell: Leader for Equality* (Springfield, N.J.: Enslow, 1991).

19. See Aileen Kraditor, *The Ideas of the Woman Suffrage Movement, 1890–1920* (New York: Columbia University Press, 1965; Anchor Books, 1971), 20.

20. Quoted in Judith Papachristou, *Women Together* (New York: Knopf, 1976), 142–43.

21. Ibid., 143.

22. "Like the WCTU, black women regarded the right to vote not as an abstract, universal right to which they were entitled as members of the human race, but as a powerful tool to improve their own lives and those of their people." Harriet Sigerman, "Laborers for Liberty," in *No Small Courage: A History of Women in the United States*, ed. Nancy Cott (New York: Oxford University Press, 2000), 344.

23. Quoted in Papacristou, *Women Together*, 100.

24. Graham, *Woman Suffrage*.

25. Flexner, *Century of Struggle*, 222.

26. Ibid.

27. For more about the NWP, see Doris Stevens, *Jailed for Freedom: The Story of the Militant American Suffragist Movement* (New York: Schocken, 1976), and Christine A. Lunardini, *From Equal Suffrage to Equal Rights: Alice Paul and the National Woman's Party, 1910–1928* (New York: New York University Press, 1986).

28. William H. Chafe, *The Paradox of Change: American Women in the 20th Century* (New York: Oxford University Press, 1991), 18–21.

29. Flexner, *Century of Struggle*, 281.

30. Jacqueline Van Voris, *Carrie Chapman Catt: A Public Life* (New York: Feminist Press, 1987), 143.
31. See Mary Carroll, "Wanted—A New Feminism: An Interview with Emily Newell Blair," *Independent Woman*, December 9, 1930, 499, for a discussion of Shaw's concerns.
32. Chafe, *The Paradox of Change.*
33. William H. Chafe, *The American Woman: Her Changing Social, Economic, and Political Role, 1920–1970* (New York: Oxford University Press, 1972), 112. See also Susan Ware, *Beyond Suffrage: Women in the New Deal* (Cambridge: Harvard University Press, 1987), and Kristi Anderson, *After Suffrage: Women in Partisan and Electoral Politics Before the New Deal* (Chicago: University of Chicago Press, 1996).
34. Janet K. Boles, *The Politics of the Equal Rights Amendment: Conflict and the Decision Process* (New York: Longman, 1991).
35. Quoted in Papachristou, *Women Together*, 220.
36. "Chicago Women Form Liberation Group," pamphlet reproduced in ibid., 229.
37. For more about women at the local level, see Laura Woliver, *From Outrage to Action: The Politics of Grassroots Dissent* (Urbana: University of Illinois Press, 1993).
38. For a systematic overview of the historical development of different branches of feminist theory, see Rosemarie Putnam Tong, *Feminist Thought: A Comprehensive, Introduction*, 2nd ed. (New York: Westview Press, 1998).
39. Anne N. Costain, *Inviting Women's Rebellion: A Political Process Interpretation of the Women's Movement* (Baltimore: Johns Hopkins University Press, 1992).
40. For an excellent discussion of the founding of NOW and the creation of the commission, see Toni Carabillo, *The Feminist Chronicles—Part 1a*, http://www.feminist.org./research/chronicles/part1a.html.
41. Groups supporting the proposed amendment during this period included the National Federation of Business and Professional Women's Clubs and the National Association of Women Lawyers. See Catherine East, "The First Stage: ERA in Washington, 1961–1972," *Women's Political Times*, September 1982, 7.
42. Quoted in Carol Felsenthal, *The Sweetheart of the Silent Majority* (Garden City, N.Y.: Doubleday, 1981), 235.
43. Much of this discussion comes from Janet Boles, "Building Support for the ERA: A Case of 'Too Much Too Late,'" *PS* 15 (Fall 1982): 572–77. See also Jane Mansbridge, *Why We Lost the ERA* (Chicago: University of Chicago Press, 1986).
44. Boles, "Building Support," 574.
45. Quoted in "Organizations Supporting Equal Rights Amendment," *National NOW Times*, May 13, 1980, 14–15.
46. Felsenthal, *The Sweetheart.*
47. List derived from Felsenthal, *The Sweetheart.* See also, Pamela Johnston Conover and Virginia Gray, *Feminism and the New Right: Conflict Over the American Family* (New York: Praeger, 1983); Boles, *The Politics of the Equal Rights Amendment*; Suzanne Crowell, "Four Days in Houston—Watershed for Women's Rights," *Civil Rights Digest* 10 (Winter 1978): 3–13; and Mansbridge, *Why We Lost the ERA.*
48. John Hebers, "Equal Rights Amendment Is Mired in Confused and Emotional Debate," *New York Times*, May 28, 1978, 1, 44. See also Rex E. Lee, *A Lawyer Looks at the ERA* (Provo, Utah: Brigham Young University Press, 1980).
49. *Phyllis Schlafly Report*, July 1975, 4.
50. See Mansbridge, *Why We Lost the ERA*, 295–96, for a discussion of the role that numerous insurance companies played in the defeat of the ERA, which would have brought with it unisex insurance rates. See also Mary Frances Berry, *Why ERA*

Failed: Politics, Women's Rights and the Amending Process of the Constitution (Bloomington: Indiana University Press, 1988).

51. Susan Faludi, *Backlash: The Undeclared War Against Women* (New York: Crown, 1991).

52. Geraldine Ferraro, speech delivered at Women and the Constitution: A Bicentennial Perspective, Colony Square Hotel, Atlanta, Georgia, February 11, 1988.

53. National Women's Political Caucus, http://feminist.com/nwpc.htm.

54. See http://feminist.com/nwpc.htm.

55. See http://www.feminist.org/home.html.

56. Leila J. Rupp and Verta Taylor, *Survival in the Doldrums: The American Women's Rights Movement, 1945 to the 1960s* (New York: Oxford University Press, 1987), 49.

57. "Promoting Democracy in America: Read About Voting Rights," League of Women Voters, http://www.lwv.org/where/promoting/votingrights_read-pg6.html.

58. League of Women Voters, http://www.lwv.org/where/promoting/election_reformstatement.html.

59. League of Women Voters, "Good Enough is not Good Enough: League Survey Findings," http://www.lwv.org/where/promoting/election.html.

60. Get the Facts, http://www.aauw.org/5000/votedini.html#j4.

61. Ibid.

62. http://www.now.org/nnt/05-96/nowpac.html.

63. Jane Gross, "At NOW Convention, Goal Is Putting More Women in Office," *New York Times*, July 1, 1990, A1.

64. Linda Berg, "NOW Fired Up by Election, Vows to Fight," http://www.now.org/nnt/fall-2002/election.html.

65. "Women's PACs and Donor Networks: A Contact List," Fact Sheet, Center for American Women and Politics (October 1999).

66. NOW PAC's Election Report, http://www.now.org/pac/facts.html.

67. Ibid.

68. Ibid.

69. Ibid.

70. Ibid.

71. Linda Berg, "Campaign Finance Reform Makes NOW's Political Action Committees More Important than Ever," http://www.now.org/nnt/summer-2002/finance.html.

72. See the Federal Election Commission report, http://www.fec.gov/finance/pacdisye.htm.

73. "EMILY's List: The Facts," http://www.irsociety.com/ertukel3.html.

74. Ibid.

75. Quoted in "Women Celebrate Historic Senate Victories," in "Notes from Emily," December 2000, 1.

76. Quoted on EMILY's List Homepage, http://www.emilyslist.org.

77. "Historic Gubernatorial Wins, Pelosi Victory Offset Congressional Losses," http://www.emilyslist.ort/newsroom/newsletter//2002-12-10.238.html.

78. Quoted from "What is WISH?" Wish List Homepage, http://www.thewishlist.org/whatis.htm.

79. National Women's History Project, Women's Rights Movement Anniversary Proclamation, http://www.legacy98.org/proclamation.html.

80. Ibid.

81. Ibid.

Women's Political Participation

To the dismay of suffrage leaders, the removal of legal barriers to political participation failed to result in equality between the sexes in the political arena. African American women, poor white women, and recently immigrated women often were denied the right to vote and participate in politics because of practices such as poll taxes and unfairly administered literacy tests. It appears, however, that one of the most significant factors that kept many women from exercising their political rights was the existence of negative cultural attitudes about women engaging in political activity. Historically, these attitudes have led to voter resistance toward women candidates and an unwillingness on the part of women to get involved in the political process. Cultural attitudes toward and restrictions on women's political activity have also resulted in other barriers to women's full political equality: the lack of preparation of women for political activity and outright sex discrimination by party leaders and government officials. While these barriers and the attitudes that underlie them have diminished over time, other system-specific problems continue to prevent women from achieving parity with men in the political arena.

CULTURAL ATTITUDES ABOUT THE POLITICAL PARTICIPATION OF WOMEN

Our knowledge of societal attitudes toward women's political participation both before and shortly after 1920 is scant. In the 1930s, the first nationwide opinion polls revealed that public attitudes toward the participation of women in politics were decidedly negative. At a time when only a handful of women held public office, 60 percent of all citizens polled rejected the idea that "we need more women in politics."[1] This aversion to the involvement of women in politics was particularly strong with respect to elective office. More than half of those surveyed were opposed to women serving as

"Have you and Tim picked out a name for the
career obstacle yet?"
Source: © The New Yorker Collection 2001 Michael Crawford from
cartoonbank.com. All rights reserved.

governors or senators. When asked in 1937 about their willingness to vote
for a qualified woman for president, only 27 percent of all men and 40 percent of all women polled answered affirmatively.

Biases against political activity by women continued. In 1946, for example, an astounding 88 percent of all men and 87 percent of all women polled
responded that the office of mayor "should nearly always be held by a man."
In 1949, almost half of those polled reported that they would not vote for a
woman for president even if she was qualified for the office and nominated
by the party for which they regularly voted. These negative attitudes did not
extend to all areas of political activity. Nearly half of all respondents to a 1946
survey favored a woman over a man as head of a Red Cross chapter or president of a Parent-Teacher Association. Community activity was and still is often
considered to be an extension of a woman's primary roles of mother and
homemaker. These kinds of activities were not even considered politics in the
late nineteenth century because women did them; politics was understood to
be party politics and was restricted to men.[2]

Polls conducted in the 1950s and 1960s found only small changes in attitudes toward women in politics. Most respondents continued to agree that
women could or should take part in school affairs, but more than 40 percent
of those interviewed in 1955, 1963, and 1969 responded that they would not
vote for a woman for president.

Impact of the Women's Rights Movement on Political Rights and Political Participation

Public support for women's participation in politics increased considerably by the late 1960s. E. M. Schreiber attributes this change to the women's rights movement and the publicity it received. He reports that it was among the educated public—those most exposed to the women's movement by the media—that the greatest changes in attitudes occurred. For example, among women college graduates, support for a female president rose from 51 percent in 1967 to 88 percent in 1975; the figures for college men were actually higher—58 and 91 percent.[3]

Willingness to elect women to other political offices, such as mayor or governor, also increased. As early as 1975, more than 80 percent of the public reported that they would support a qualified woman for those positions.[4] Similarly, in sharp contrast to the public's attitudes toward women judges in the 1930s (when three-quarters of those polled objected to a woman Supreme Court justice), Sandra Day O'Connor's appointment to the Supreme Court in 1981 was approved by 87 percent of all women and 84 percent of all men.[5] By the 1990s, in the wake of government scandals such as the savings and loan crisis, the House check-bouncing fiasco, and the U.S. Senate Judiciary Committee's treatment of Anita Hill, voters began to turn to women candidates at the same time more women sought elective office. According to Patricia Ireland, former president of NOW, "certainly voters perceive women candidates as more honest . . . and as advocating issues that make our world a better place to live."[6] Whereas in 1984 only 28 percent of Americans believed that increasing the number of women in elected office would be beneficial, by 2000 support for women increased to 57 percent. A 2000 Gallup Poll also indicated that 93 percent of women and 91 percent of men would vote for a qualified woman for president if she was nominated by their party. When Gallup first asked this question in 1937, only 33 percent of Americans said they would support a woman presidential candidate.[7]

Continuing Cultural Barriers

Even with changes in cultural beliefs, stereotypes continue to impede women's political participation. When asked to list reasons why there were not more women in public office, the respondents to a 1999 poll said one of the most important factors is "Many Americans aren't ready to elect a woman to higher office."[8] In 2000, 40.7 percent of Americans polled agreed that it is much better for everyone involved if the man is the achiever outside the home and the woman takes care of the home and family. Moreover, 25 percent of men and 22 percent of women agreed with the statement "Most men are better suited emotionally for politics."[9]

Furthermore, some people continue to question the effectiveness of women elected officials. For instance, as shown in Table 2.1, a 1999 survey revealed that on the top issues of importance to Americans, including foreign policy, law and order, and the economy, a sizable number of respondents

TABLE 2.1 **Expectations of Presidential Job Performance of Women vs. Men**

Question: When it comes to _____, which type of American president would you expect to do a better job, a man or a woman?

Issue	Woman	Man	No Difference
Foreign policy	15	45	36
Law and order	14	42	41
Economy	22	31	44
Governmental problems	21	31	44
Social issues	46	13	38
Moral questions	48	13	36

Source: "Women in Elected Office," report prepared for Deloitte and Touche by Roper Starch Worldwide, Inc. (2000). Data provided by Deloitte and Touche.

believe that a male president would perform better than a female president. Respondents in the survey were more likely to believe that men would possess the most important characteristics of a good president. Males were rated higher than females in terms of preparedness to go to war (64 percent vs. 6 percent), ability to lead the nation (51 percent vs. 12 percent), and ability to make difficult decisions (38 percent vs. 18 percent). The sexes were rated equally on intelligence and ability to compromise. Females were expected to be more honest (37 percent vs. 14 percent), trustworthy (36 percent vs. 16 percent), and better able to understand ordinary people (45 percent vs. 15 percent).[10]

Polls reveal that in the last thirty years, women have gained confidence in their ability to direct the military, strengthen the economy, and conduct diplomatic relations with other countries. Still, men are more likely than women to say that women do not have the mental or emotional toughness to succeed in politics. Twenty-three percent of men agreed that men make better leaders than women, but only 13 percent of women. Likewise, 18 percent of men but only 13 percent of women agreed that women are not tough enough for politics.[11] Given these views, it is easy to see how some women are disadvantaged when they run for office, especially for higher office. Women candidates start out with a certain percentage of the electorate predisposed *not* to vote for them, depending on the office. Moreover, questions still linger about women's abilities to perform well in certain positions. Relatedly, societal views may encourage many women to reject a role in politics, deeming it an activity more appropriate for the other sex.

POLITICAL SOCIALIZATION

One byproduct of negative cultural attitudes toward political involvement by women is that girls traditionally have not been socialized to take an active role in politics. Studies of young children show that boys and girls differ in significant ways in their orientation to politics. Most research finds young girls to be less attentive to, less informed about, and less interested in politics than are boys.[12] According to the 2000 Virginia Slims Poll, more than 42 percent of the respondents believed that one of the main reasons there are so few women in politics is that young girls are not inclined to aspire to careers in politics.[13] In an effort to change these gender stereotypes, the White House Project teamed up with Mattel, Inc., to introduce President Barbie in 2000. As Marie C. Wilson, president of the White House Project explained, "Girls nationwide own an average of eight Barbies. Since Barbie is such a large part of girls' lives, we want to be there with a message that encourages them to become tomorrow's leaders."[14] The White House Project also created a "Ms. President" patch for Girl Scouts to earn through civic and educational activities.

Surveys and focus groups among eighteen- to twenty-four-year-old Americans have underscored the importance of early political socialization in developing interest in political participation among young women. Those women who are most interested in running for office have parents who vote in every election, have been told that they should run for office, and believe that they can make a difference in solving problems. Demographically they are more likely to be white, full-time college students, daily Internet users, and registered voters. They are also more likely to volunteer in their communities, to have held leadership positions, to pay attention to politics, and have high levels of political efficacy.[15] (See Table 2.2.)

The process of political socialization does not end with a college education. Some political scientists think that the birth of a woman's first child is a critical point at which gender stereotypes come into play.[16] Other scholars have found that over the course of their adult lifetimes, many women, at least those living through the 1970s, became more politically active and aware, in part as a correlate to their increasingly gender-egalitarian beliefs.[17]

TABLE 2.2 **Differences in Attitudes and Experiences Among Young Women by Interest in Running for Office**

	Very or Somewhat Interested	*Solidly Not Interested*
Have leadership experience	82%	39%
Are involved in community	80	36
Believe they can make a difference	66	35
Have been encouraged to run	63	14
Think politics is too complicated	52	68

Source: Lake Snell Perry and Associates, "Pipeline to the Future: Young Women and Political Leadership," The White House Project 2000, http://www.womensleadershipfund.org/programs/youth_research.pdf.

POLITICAL RESOURCES

The socialization of women into the dominant cultural beliefs about the appropriateness of politics for them has echoes in the relative levels of psychological involvement or preparedness of women to participate in politics. Relatedly, stereotypes about women's roles as breadwinners mean women are less likely to have the money or professional involvement necessary for some forms of political activity. Research on political participation of average men and women has found that the absence of both types of political resources—money and professional involvement—is part of the explanation for women's lower involvement in our country's affairs.[18]

Citizen Duty

The belief that a citizen has an obligation to vote is perhaps the most elementary civic attitude. It constitutes the single best predictor of whether a person casts a ballot in an election. In 1923, interviews with women nonvoters in Chicago indicated that more than 10 percent believed it was wrong for women to vote.[19] In fact, one female nonvoter's response was: "Women should not 'stick their noses in politics.' . . . Only men and widows should vote. Women do not understand politics and so should not 'butt in men's work.'"[20] As voting became a more acceptable activity for women, there was a corresponding increase in women's feelings of civic obligation. By 1980, women recorded slightly higher levels of citizen duty than men.[21]

Psychological Involvement in Politics

For participation other than voting, political scientists have emphasized the critical importance of political interest and attention to public affairs in determining who participates. These orientations have been labeled by Sidney Verba and Norman Nie as "psychological involvement" in politics.[22] When women and men are compared on these dimensions, we begin to see the legacy of the societal views examined earlier.

In one early survey, for instance, nearly 33 percent of all women nonvoters interviewed in Chicago in 1923 reported "no interest in politics" as their reason for not voting, as compared to only 15 percent of nonvoting men.[23] Even in the 1960s, the interest of women at all educational levels in politics and national affairs was lower than that of similarly educated men.[24]

The dawning of the women's movement and changes that began in the 1970s have not completely eliminated this disparity between the sexes. In 2000, 36 percent of men but only 25 percent of women said they were very interested in politics and national affairs.[25] In at least one area of politics—presidential campaigns—women are almost as involved as men. Whereas studies in the 1940s and 1950s found that women were less interested than men in presidential campaigns, in the 1964 election no such difference was found. Additionally, there is some indication that even in those elections since 1952 when women as a group indicated less campaign interest than men, the interest gap was much smaller or even nonexistent among citizens with at least some college education.[26]

Women's lower psychological involvement in politics appears to be closely associated with levels of political information. A recent study by Nancy Burns, Kay Lehman Schlozman, and Sidney Verba confirmed earlier findings that men know more about politics than women. In their Citizen Participation Study, women and men were asked the names of public officials and a series of knowledge questions about government and politics. Men were more likely than women to provide the correct answer for nine out of the ten questions. Women outscored men on one item—the ability to name the head of the local public school system.[27]

Comparisons with information gaps in decades past, moreover, show no signs that things are improving. The only area where women appear to be as informed as men is local politics—the policy arena where their participation has been seen as acceptable for many decades.[28] This disparity in political information is likely to continue. A national survey of first-year college students conducted in the fall of 2002 reported that young women are less likely than young men (29 vs. 38 percent) to identify keeping up with political affairs as essential or very important.[29] Jeffrey Mondak and Mary Anderson, however, suggest that at least part of the knowledge gap may be an illusion, arguing, "There are systematic differences in how men and women go about answering knowledge questions, and these differences artificially inflate knowledge scores for men."[30] Still, even a small knowledge gap is not surprising, given the greater levels of interest in politics among men.

Political Efficacy

Political efficacy is an individual's belief that he or she can influence governmental decision making. Confidence in one's ability to affect governmental actions is closely related to a willingness to undertake political activity. Early interviews with women revealed their lack of self-confidence about political matters. Although nearly equal numbers of nonvoting men and women doubted the effectiveness of their vote, women were more likely to report "timidity" when it came to casting their ballots. One female nonvoter explained why she had never voted: "I ain't got the nerve."[31]

Since the 1950s, women have routinely reported lower levels of efficacy in several areas. One involves awareness of and confidence in the use of political participation other than voting. In every presidential election between 1956 and 1972, women were more likely than men to believe that "voting is the only way to influence government."[32] By 1980, there was no significant difference between male and female respondents across educational categories.

In one respect, however, the political efficacy of women continues to lag behind men. Perhaps tied to their lower levels of attention to and information about politics, women still report much lower confidence in their understanding of politics. Our analysis of the 2000 NES found, for example, that 64 percent of women but only 50 percent of men indicated that politics was too complicated for them to understand.[33]

In contrast, the more nearly equal levels of local political interest and local political information between men and women result in more similar overall confidence in understanding local issues and politics by the two sexes. A 2000 survey found that women were slightly more likely than men to disagree strongly with the statement "The people running my community do not really care what happens to me." Women were also no more likely than men to list "lack of information or not knowing how to begin" or "feeling that you cannot make a difference" as obstacles to community involvement.[34]

Other Resources

Although attitudes go a long way toward explaining women's lower involvement in politics, recent research also finds that women may not be as active as men in some forms of political activity because they earn less than men or contribute a smaller share than their husbands to the family income. A 2000 survey found women more likely than men to identify work schedules or inadequate child care as obstacles to political involvement.[35] Relatedly, women's jobs are generally not as likely as men's to prepare them for political life. Women seem only to be advantaged by their involvement in nonpolitical organizations such as church groups, which boosts women's political activity more than men's.[36]

SEX DISCRIMINATION: THE HIDDEN BARRIER

Historically, sex discrimination has been a powerful deterrent to political activity. Unfortunately, discrimination is difficult to study or document. Few men are willing to admit that they discriminate. Additionally, what many women see as discrimination against them may be viewed otherwise by men who believe they are simply complying with traditional cultural mores or widely accepted patterns of political behavior.

Two factors seem to motivate most sex discrimination: (1) cultural stereotypes about the abilities and appropriate position of women in politics and (2) self-interest on the part of male voters and politicians who are reluctant to share their power with women or any other "out group." It is difficult, however, to determine where cultural attitudes end and self-interest begins. Politicians in the 1920s and 1930s, for example, could be openly hostile to the active participation of women in politics. For instance, a 1924 gubernatorial candidate proclaimed, "women's place in politics is about four feet from the kitchen sink."[37] Although today few would be so blunt, some have questioned the efficacy of women holding public office. When Senator Pam Murray first ran for office, she was told, "You can't make a difference, you're just a mom in tennis shoes."[38]

Women of color often face discrimination from men of color who believe that, after years of race discrimination, women should let men go first. Shirley

Chisholm, who faced opposition from male political leaders in her first race for Congress, noted that "Black males feel that the political seats are owed to them because of historical circumstances; therefore, opportunities should redound to them first of all."[39]

POLITICAL PARTICIPATION

Given the legacy of public attitudes about the appropriateness of political activity for women and the evidence of women's lower psychological involvement, we would expect women to be less involved as citizens than men. It is possible, however, that women overcome these factors and are equal to men in their participation in politics. An examination of various types of activities supports both of these predictions.

Voter Turnout

The first major study of women's electoral turnout in the 1923 Chicago mayoral election found nearly two-thirds of all men but only one-third of all eligible women voted. Other research on this era finds similar, if somewhat smaller, disparities.[40]

Many women chose not to vote in the early decades after ratification of the Nineteenth Amendment. Reluctance to vote was especially pronounced among classes of women—immigrant and uneducated women—where there were strong cultural stereotypes concerning appropriate male and female roles. In the South, where attitudes toward women's roles were more conservative, and where the poll tax and racial discrimination eliminated the possibility of voting for poor white women and African American men and women, only a few women went to the polls. In contrast, in the West, where support for women's suffrage had a long heritage, women were apparently voting in the early 1920s at rates nearly equal to those of men.[41]

Suffrage movement leaders saw women's lack of information and training as the main barriers to the full and equal participation of women in politics. To correct this problem, they established the National League of Women Voters (LWV) to help educate women about politics and political activity. Just how many women benefited from the League's efforts is difficult to measure, although only a small minority of the original suffrage movement members joined the new organization. Moreover, the League's policy of remaining aloof from partisan politics may have diminished the chances that those who became involved would become active in partisan politics, although many women elected officials claimed membership in it.[42] Although the League may have played a role in mobilizing middle-class women, Kristi Andersen's research indicates political parties probably were more important for women generally. Examination of the data on registration rates of women and men in the 1920s (where available) finds that in those areas where it was advantageous to political parties to register women, registration rates for women were higher.[43]

The Great Depression of the 1930s also played a key role in the mobilization of women, especially those with fewer resources, both political and economic. This crisis politicized large numbers of immigrants, lower-class women, and young people who had previously remained outside the political arena.[44] Work by Courtney Brown indicates that although women voters in the 1920 presidential election overwhelmingly favored the Republican Party, voters who were drawn to the polls for the first time in their adult life by the economic crisis surrounding the 1932 election adopted strong ties to the Democratic Party and to the electoral process.[45]

As revealed in Table 2.3, from 1964 to 1978, women continued to vote at rates slightly lower than men. Since the 1980 presidential election, however, women have voted at rates higher than men. As Table 2.4 indicates, among African Americans, Hispanics, and whites, the proportion of eligible women who voted exceeded the proportion of eligible men who voted during the last five elections. The number of women voting also exceeded the number of men voting in each subgroup in each election since 1980. Although whites have the

TABLE 2.3 Gender Differences in Voter Turnout Rates, 1964–2000 (percentage of eligible adults who voted)

Year	Women	Men	Difference (% Women–% Men)
2000	56.2	53.1	+3.1
1998	42.4	41.4	+1.0
1996[a]	55.5	52.8	+2.7
1994	44.9	44.4	+0.5
1992[a]	62.3	60.2	+2.1
1990	45.4	44.6	+0.8
1988[a]	58.3	56.4	+1.9
1986	46.1	45.8	+0.3
1984[a]	60.8	59.0	+1.8
1982	48.4	48.7	−0.3
1980[a]	59.4	59.1	+0.3
1978	45.3	46.6	−1.3
1976[a]	58.8	59.6	−0.8
1974	43.4	46.2	−2.8
1972[a]	62.0	64.1	−2.1
1970	52.7	56.8	−4.1
1968[a]	66.0	69.8	−3.8
1966	53.0	58.2	−5.2
1964[a]	67.0	71.9	−4.9

[a] Presidential election years.

Source: "Sex Differences in Voter Turnout," *CAWP Fact Sheet*, March 2002. Data from the U.S. Bureau of the Census.

TABLE 2.4   **Gender Differences in Community Involvement (percentage who participated in last 12 months)**

	Men	Women
Signed a petition	35%	36%
Attended a political meeting or rally	18	15
Worked on a community project	37	38
Participated in demonstrations, boycotts, or marches	9	6
Participated in church activities other than attending services	35	44
Participated in sports club, league, or outdoor activity club	26	16
Participated in youth organization	22	22
Participated in parent association or other school support group	19	25
Participated in veterans groups	14	5
Participated in neighborhood association	23	19
Participated in seniors groups	13	15
Participated in charity or social welfare organization	28	35
Participated in service or fraternal organization	14	14
Participated in ethnic, nationality, or civil rights organization	7	6
Participated in political group	11	7
Participated in literary, art, or musical group	15	20
Participated in hobby, investment, or garden club	30	20

Source: Social Capital Benchmark Survey, 2000 (Saguaro Seminar on Civic Engagement in America, John F. Kennedy School of Government, Harvard University), http://www.ropercenter.uconn.edu.

highest participation rates, the largest gender gaps are among African Americans and Hispanics.[46]

Sandra Baxter and Marjorie Lansing trace the higher participation rates of African American women to their greater feminist beliefs, products of being doubly oppressed by both sex and race discrimination.[47] It is also possible that the higher levels of voting by African American and Hispanic women are traceable to their greater ties to the community, especially to the church. Susan A. MacManus, Charles S. Bullock III, and Barbara P. Grothe speculated that the Mexican American women in their study might also participate more than the men in their community as a function of the role of women as agents of change and upward mobility for their families.[48]

Although the barriers to women's voting have diminished significantly since 1920, the one factor that may still negatively affect the voting participation of some women is the presence of small children, who make it difficult for some women to get to the polls. This seems to be particularly true for single mothers.[49]

When the disparity in voter turnout is combined with the greater number of women in the electorate (52 percent of all voters were women in 2000), we can see what a powerful voting bloc women could form if they wanted to do so.[50] But do women cast their ballots differently from men? The leaders of the suffrage movement (and even suffrage opponents) clearly expected women would be distinct in their attitudes and political behavior. Until recently, however, these differences were not evident. A prerequisite to establishing the voting bloc envisioned by the suffrage leaders would be for women and men to take different stands on questions of public policy.

Issue Positions

Survey data reveal few significant gender differences across views about most issues, with a few notable exceptions. Since the 1930s, women have typically led men in their opposition to war and the use of force more generally. Tom Smith's extensive research on the use of military force from the 1930s through the 1980s found gender differences on 87 percent of the questions, with an average 9 percent gap.[51] In 1952, for example, 45 percent of the women compared to only 37 percent of the men interviewed believed the United States should have stayed out of the Korean War. Similar differences of opinion surfaced during the Vietnam War. During the 1991 Persian Gulf War, women were on average 14.3 percent more likely than men to think the United States had made a mistake in sending troops to the area. At one point, only 37 percent of women but 61 percent of men supported that war.[52]

The September 11, 2001, terrorist attacks on the World Trade Center and the Pentagon seemed to erase these earlier gender differences. Whereas a 2001 poll conducted prior to the attacks reported that only 24 percent of women favored increased military spending compared to 41 percent of men, a month after the attacks 47 percent of women and 53 percent of men favored increased spending. Women also increased their support for a national missile defense system from 52 percent before the attacks to 64 percent a month later. Support among men remained the same at 65 percent.[53] The salience of military affairs for women also increased after September 11. A December 2001 Gallup Poll reported that women were much more likely than men to say that September 11 was a "life-altering experience" (42 percent vs. 24 percent respectively).[54] The Center for Gender Equality reported that 87 percent of women in a national survey were still following the news about terrorism very or somewhat closely two months after the attacks.[55] In early 2003, the prospects of a war with Iraq revealed no significant gender gap.[56] Once the war began, a slight gender gap reemerged, although not as large as observed in previous wars. A Gallup Poll the day after the war began reported that 78 percent of men and 74 percent of women approved the decision to go to war with Iraq.[57]

Although the gender gap on most issues is not very large, there are some persistent patterns. The gap cannot be explained simply by differences on "women's issues." Lydia Saad, a senior Gallup Poll editor, explains, "By virtue of being older, less financially secure, more religious, and less likely to be in the workforce, women may, on average, have slightly different worldviews than men, and the net effect may be more favorable for the Democratic Party than the Republican."[58]

In general terms, the Center for the American Woman and Politics (CAWP) has found, when compared to men, women are:

- Less militaristic on issues of war and peace.
- More often opposed to the use of force in nonmilitary situations.
- More likely to favor measures to protect the environment and to check the growth of nuclear power.
- More often supportive of programs to help the economically disadvantaged.
- More often supportive of efforts to achieve racial equality.
- More likely to favor laws to regulate and control various social vices (e.g., drugs, gambling, pornography).
- Less likely to be optimistic about the country's future.[59]

Although some research suggests these gender differences in attitudes may be limited to only feminists or conditioned by the careers women and men choose,[60] a national survey of first-year college students in 2002 found large differences of opinion between men and women on the legalization of marijuana, prohibition of homosexuality, control of handguns, affirmative action, racial discrimination, treatment of immigrants, and increased federal government spending on the military. On all issues, the gap was over 10 percent, with women always more likely to choose the more liberal position.[61]

The gender gap does not always appear where it might be expected. Analysis of attitudes toward reproductive rights including abortion, for example, reveal more differences among women and among men than between the sexes. However, even on issues where men and women agree, there are gender differences in the salience of these issues. Recent research by Kathleen Dolan suggests that women's issues such as abortion, family leave, and sexual harassment affect vote choices only when the "electoral environment" emphasizes gender. If women candidates and women's issues receive large amounts of attention during the campaign, the influence of gender on the vote increases.[62]

Party Identification

Party identity—whether or not an individual views himself or herself as a Republican, Democrat, or something else—generally is believed to be an exceptionally important determinant of the vote. Prior to 1968, however, men and women showed little difference in their tendency to affiliate with either party, when age and region of the respondents were controlled. In that year, however, significant differences began to occur in male-female patterns of party identification, with women significantly more likely than men to identify with the Democratic Party. Figure 2.1 illustrates this gender difference in party identification since 1972.

Since 1982, the difference between men and women does not disappear when age, race, and education controls are introduced. Indeed, some of the greatest disparities are found among the youngest voters and the well educated. Women tend to view the Democratic Party as more concerned about women's issues and closer to them on a wide range of domestic policy questions. This gap in party identification has parallels in the voting choices of women and men.

Voting Patterns

In recent years, gender-based differences in issue positions and party identification have tended to manifest themselves in differences in male-female support for political candidates—producing an electoral gender gap. As revealed in Figure 2.2, women have given greater support than men to the Democratic candidate since 1980. In the aftermath of the 1980 presidential election when Eleanor Smeal, then director of NOW, first coined the term "gender gap" to draw attention from the media to the differences in voting behavior among women and men, it was believed that a feminist agenda was driving the women's vote. Many assumed the Republican Party's failure to endorse the equal rights amendment contributed to Reagan's "woman problem." Awareness of the gap prompted both political parties to respond to women as a voting constituency in the 1984 presidential election. Democrats falsely assumed that nominating a woman, Geraldine Ferraro, as the vice presidential candidate was enough to mobilize the

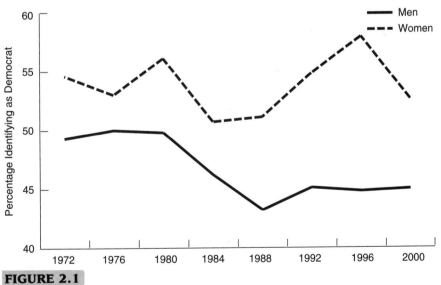

FIGURE 2.1
Gender Differences in Democratic Party Identification
Source: American National Election Studies, Center for Political Studies, University of Michigan; data made available through the Inter-University Consortium for Political and Social Research.

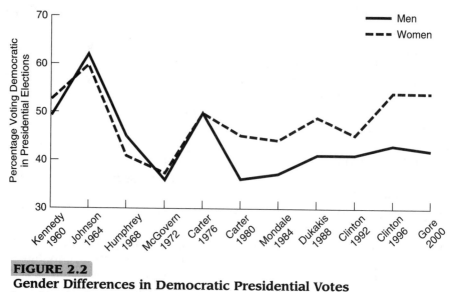

FIGURE 2.2

Gender Differences in Democratic Presidential Votes

Source: "American Opinion," *Wall Street Journal,* June 22, 2000, A10. Updated by author with 2000 Voter News Service Data, *CAWP Fact Sheet,* "Gender Gap in the 2000 Election" November 2000.

women's vote. The Democratic Party chose not to use Ferraro as a vehicle to champion women's issues, in fear of alienating male voters. In contrast, Ronald Reagan's pollster Richard Wirthlin conducted a detailed analysis of the issues important to women. The data collected allowed Republicans to target specific subgroups of women on the basis of economic interests. Elizabeth Dole convinced Reagan that he simply needed to communicate his record on women's issues. The strategy worked, and Reagan won by a landslide with majorities of both women and men.[63]

Since the gap was recognized in 1982, both political parties have targeted women voters, yet political scientists have not agreed on theories about the underlying causes of the gap. Jane Mansbridge's analysis of the 1980 election pointed out that even if all pro-ERA voters had voted against Reagan, it would only explain about a third of the gender gap, due to the similarities between men and women in their support of the ERA.[64] Kathleen Frankovic argues that attitudes toward the use of military force help to explain the gender gap, demonstrating that the gender gap in 1980 disappears after controlling for aggressiveness in foreign policy.[65] Others suggest that the lower socioeconomic status of women explains women's preference for the Democratic Party. The feminization of poverty contributes to greater empathy among women for the disadvantaged and increased support for an activist governmental role in addressing social welfare issues.[66] In contrast, Karen Kaufman and John Petrocik suggest that the gap reflects changes in the behavior of men, who left the Democratic Party during the late 1970s and early 1980s in greater numbers than women.[67]

The research clearly indicates differences between the policy preferences of woman and men, and several complex models have emerged to explain the implications for voting behavior.[68] However, Anna Greenburg argues that "excessive attention to these gender differences obscures important political differences between women." Greenburg focuses on the interaction between class, race, and values—political ideology as well as religious involvement and affiliation—in explaining how subgroups of women drive the gender gap, rather than women as a group. Greenburg finds that economically disadvantaged women favor the Democratic Party, but that social or religious conservatism mutes economic interests in driving women toward the Republican Party. Minority women, however, are the most loyal to the Democratic Party despite their high levels of religious commitment.[69]

Additional research is needed to completely understand the relationship between gender and voting behavior. The continued presence of the gender gap signals the increased importance of women as voters, forcing candidates to acknowledge and target women as a constituency. As former NOW President Patricia Ireland notes, "Because of the gender gap, women's votes put us in the driver's seat."[70]

POLITICAL ACTIVISM

Political activity is another area where gender differences exist. Here, we divide our discussion into three sections: (1) lobbying and community involvement, (2) campaign and party work, and (3) office holding.

Lobbying and Community Involvement

Since the latter half of the nineteenth century, women have played a vital role in their communities, organizing charitable and civic projects and dominating the activities of groups such as the PTA and local library boards. Women have also taken the lead in pressing local officials to include family, children's, and women's issues on the agendas of local legislative bodies. This practice of lobbying, petitioning, and protesting for social needs originated with women's groups because they were unable to pressure politicians with their votes. Kristi Andersen argues that as a result of women's domination of this activity at the turn of the century, it was not even seen as politics. Politics was connected with activities on behalf of political parties and elections and was the exclusive sphere of men.[71]

Recent research by scholars reveals the continued pervasive lobbying activity of women at the local level. Janet Boles and others have documented how women in feminist groups have altered the policies of local libraries to include more material of interest to women, worked to expand child-care services, broadened support for abused women and their children, and provided centers for victims of rape.[72] Similarly, conservative women's groups often lobby for the removal of certain books from libraries or for a return to traditional school curricula. Many of these issues have traditionally been seen as outside of politics, but women activists and elected officials are transforming the policy agenda to make personal matters political in nearly every community in the United States.

Some of the most unrecognized work has been done by African American women and other women from ethnic and racial minorities. African American women, for instance, played a vital role in antilynching campaigns and, later, the civil rights movement, organizing the bus boycott in Montgomery, managing the poor people's cooperatives in Mississippi, running freedom schools, and directing voter registration drives.[73] More recently, Nydia M. Veláquez, for example, organized a Hispanic voter registration drive in New York City. Unlike countless other women who have worked to expand opportunities for women in their communities, Veláquez's work resulted in her eventual election to the House of Representatives, where she became the first Puerto Rican woman to hold that office.[74]

Although women's contributions at the local level have been notable, research has found men slightly more likely than women to report that they had worked informally to deal with a community problem and to have contacted a public official with a problem. For women and men who engaged in some form of political activity other than voting, there was only a slightly greater tendency for women over men to restrict such activity to local affairs. Only with respect to religious institutions were women more active than men.[75] (See Table 2.4.) Interestingly, when women become active, they often focus on different issues than men. Compared with men, women generally are more concerned with education, and African American and Hispanic women more with basic human needs such as drug and crime prevention.[76] In 2000, Robert Putnam's book *Bowling Alone* drew attention to the more general trend of disengagement in community involvement among both women and men. Declining rates of political and civic involvement—measured on a variety of indicators from campaign work, philanthropy, and religious activity, to picnics and dinner parties—have reduced the connections Americans have with their communities.[77] Amy Caiazza and Robert Putnam suggest that the level of social capital is linked to the status of women in a community, arguing:

> Women fare better where civic engagement is greater, and they fare worse where people are isolated and disconnected from their communities. Engaging more women in civic and political participation may be a crucial tool for advancing their status more generally—and improving women's status may be important to improving the overall civic health of the country.[78]

Campaign and Party Work

There are several reasons to expect that women will not participate as extensively as men in partisan activities. First, such involvement has often run counter to cultural expectations about a woman's role in public life. Whereas community involvement has been seen as a natural extension of women's homekeeping role, partisan politics was viewed as exclusively male. Party politics and campaigning in the nineteenth and early twentieth centuries in many ways took on the appearance of a "males only" sporting event with two groups of players: the candidates and their respective groups of partisan "fans." There were marching groups, parades, and smoke-filled rooms. Polling places often were located in pool halls and bars. While progressive movement reforms, including the secret ballot, weakened political party machines, the Nineteenth Amendment and the addition of women to the electorate also altered the game of politics.[79] Even today, however, many citizens still see politics as "dirty" or corrupt and reject the idea of an active political role for women in party affairs and campaigns.

Second, while levels of interest in local affairs, especially among better-educated women, prepare them for community activities, the generally lower levels of political interest, involvement, information, and efficacy of women concerning politics or national affairs might be a serious obstacle to their participation in extralocal political campaigns and party work. Last, the relative absence of women in certain "power" positions, including those of union leaders and corporate executives, may result in women not being asked to become involved in campaigns.

In the years immediately following passage of the Nineteenth Amendment, women received a mixed message concerning party work. While some women leaders, including Carrie Chapman Catt, urged women to take an active role in the parties, the League of Women Voters adopted a nonpartisan posture.[80] Although a few followed Catt's advice, most women tended to avoid all partisan work, including campaign activity. The decline of political machines eventually forced party leaders to rely on volunteers, including women, to run campaigns. Even so, the first national survey of citizen-level campaign activity in 1952 found that women were considerably less involved in campaigns than men.[81]

Since 1952, there has been a gradual decline in the overall disparity in campaign activity between the sexes. In 1980, only slightly fewer women than men reported engaging in at least one of the following campaign acts: contributing money, attending a political meeting, influencing another's vote, or displaying a button or poster. Our analysis of the 2000 NES data found that women continued to lag slightly behind men on these measures. For instance, in the most common form of campaign activity, trying to influence another person's vote, more men than women reported engaging in this activity. Women also were less likely to wear a campaign button, attend a political rally, or contribute money to a candidate or political party. Studies suggest the small differences that do exist can be traced largely to women's lower levels of political and economic resources. For instance, because women earn less than men, they generally are less frequent campaign contributors. In 2000, 17 percent of men contributed money but only 9 percent of women.[82] The more developed civic skills of men also help to explain their slightly higher campaign participation.[83]

In spite of these continued differences, there is considerable evidence that women are essential to the maintenance of both major political parties. Informal reports and research on party activists indicate it is women who do the daily work of keeping the parties functioning.[84] One recent study, moreover, found few gender differences in the amount of time devoted to local party politics.[85] Indeed, because of the aggressive affirmative action efforts of the Democratic Party, about 50 to 60 percent of its state party officials are African Americans or women.[86]

At the national level, since 1972, both major parties have included more women in their presidential nominating conventions than ever before. From 1980 to 2000, half of the delegates to the Democratic conventions, and more than one-third of those at the Republican conventions, have been women.[87]

There is some evidence that the women who take the most active roles in national campaigns, as participants in the party caucuses, are ideologically distinct from the men activists in their parties, with women more liberal on social and foreign policy questions and more supportive of women's issues in both of the major parties.[88] A study of local party activists also found women in both parties to be more liberal on these issues.[89]

Office Holding

Women have long been severely underrepresented in elective office. During any single year between 1917 and 1970, women never constituted more than 5 percent (and generally far less) of the members of the U.S. Congress or of the state legislatures. In 1971, slightly more than 2 percent of the members of Congress and less than 5 percent of state legislators were women. By 1991, these numbers had climbed marginally, as women made up less than 6 percent of the Congress and 18.3 percent of the state houses.[90] (See Figures 2.3 and 2.4.)

Heralded as the Year of the Woman, 1992 was a breakthrough year for women candidates as they vied for all levels of political office in unprecedented numbers. In all, 108 women won their parties' nomination for seats in the House and eleven for positions in the U.S. Senate. Moreover, 2,375 women ran for state legislative posts, up from 2,063 in 1988. Even more importantly, more women than ever before were elected to the House and Senate, increasing their representation to 10 percent. The gains in 1992 were particularly dramatic for women of color. The first African American woman ever to take a seat in the Senate, Carol Moseley Braun, was elected from the state of Illinois. In the House of Representatives, five new African American women were elected, raising the total to nine.[91]

The "Decade of the Woman," however, never materialized. Although women have increased significantly their representation at all levels of elective office, the dramatic successes of 1992 have not been repeated. Even redistricting in 2002 failed to create comparable opportunities for women. Women gained only one new Senate seat in the 2002 elections, and the overall number of women in the House remained unchanged from 2001. Women represent 13.7 percent of the 108th Congress, including fourteen women in the Senate (nine Democrats, five Republicans), fifty-nine in the House of Representatives (thirty-eight Democrats, twenty-one Republicans), and three additional Democratic women serving as nonvoting delegates.[92] (See Figure 2.3.)

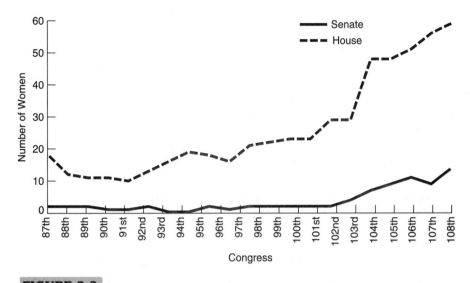

FIGURE 2.3
Number of Women in the U.S. Congress, 87th to 108th Congresses
Source: "Women in Elective Office 2003," *CAWP Fact Sheet*, February 2003.

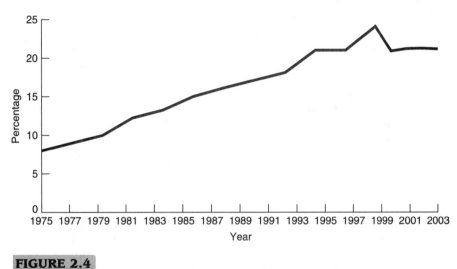

FIGURE 2.4
Percentage of Women in U.S. State Houses, 1975–2003
Source: "Women in State Legislatures 2003," *CAWP Fact Sheet*, February, 2003.

Of the seventy-three women serving in the 108th Congress, eighteen (25 percent) are minorities, a decrease from twenty-two (29 percent) in the 107th Congress. Women of color comprise 3.4 percent of Congress and all of them serve in the U.S. House. There are eleven African Americans and seven Latinas, including the first sisters in Congress, Linda and Loretta Sanchez (D-Calif.).[93]

Women and Politics

THE YEAR OF THE WOMAN GOVERNOR

If 1992 was The Year of the Woman in Congress, I think this year, 2002, is going to be The Year of Women Governors. We're going to elect a record number of women in November. Three is actually the biggest number of women we've elected governor in one election; we could triple that this year.[a]

> Ellen Malcolm, President, EMILY's List

In 2002, women entered more than half of the thirty-six gubernatorial races, twice as many as ever before. Ten women advanced to the general election—including for the first time two women from the same state—and four won, increasing the number of women governors to a record six (four Democrats, two Republicans). Joining their ranks in 2003 were Lieutenant Governor Olene Walker (R), who replaced Mike Leavitt as governor of Utah following his appointment as head of the EPA, and Lieutenant Governor Kathleen Blanco (D), who defeated Bobby Jindal (R) in a run-off election to become the first woman governor of Louisiana. A total of twenty-five women (seventeen Democrats, eight Republicans) have served as governor. Three replaced their husbands, five became governor by constitutional succession (one of whom subsequently won a full term), and seventeen were elected in their own right. Six of the eight women governors serving in 2003 were first elected in races for open gubernatorial seats.[b] As Ellen Malcolm reported of the 2002 elections, "These new women governors won extraordinarily hard-fought, difficult races. They were able to do that because they had impressive records in office, built strong coalitions, and attracted Independents and a large outpouring of support from women voters."[c]

Despite breaking records, women gubernatorial candidates were expected to do better. Similarly, expectations ran high for women running for Congress in 2002, as many anticipated that redistricting would create new opportunities for women to increase their representation in the House of Representatives. In the end, the total number of women governors increased from five to six and women increased their representation in Congress by one Senate seat. What happened? Unlike the Year of the Woman in 1992, when domestic issues favoring women were emphasized, the 2002 elections focused on the economy, terrorism, and the impending war with Iraq. Budget shortfalls at the state level placed particular pressure on women lieutenant governors and state treasurers—all four who ran lost their gubernatorial races. In Congress, incumbents prevailed, with Republicans even picking up a handful of seats, defying historical trends of presidential party losses at midterm. President George W. Bush contributed to their success by raising funds and campaigning relentlessly for fellow Republicans despite criticism that he was risking his political capital. Democrats, and Democratic women in particular, were not advantaged in the political climate of the 2002 elections.

Still, the increase in the number of women governors to eight in 2003 is significant. Eleanor Clift and Tom Brazaitis argue in *Madam President* that the first woman president is more likely to be a governor than a member of the House or Senate because, as governor, women have the opportunity to demonstrate their executive leadership skills.[d] The future first woman president could be among the eight women currently serving in office.

Women Governors in 2003

Governor	Political Party	State	Year First Term Began
Kathleen Blanco	D	Louisiana	2003
Jennifer M. Granholm	D	Michigan	2002
Linda Lingle	R	Hawaii	2002
Judy Martz	R	Montana	2000
Ruth Ann Minner	D	Delaware	2000
Janet Napolitano	D	Arizona	2002
Kathleen Sebelius	D	Kansas	2002
Olene Walker	R	Utah	2003

[a] "2002: Year of the Woman Governor," *EMILY's List Quote Sheet*.

[b] "Statewide Elective Executive Women 2003," *CAWP Fact Sheet*, November 2003.

[c] Janet Harris, "Women Gain Record Number of Governorships," *EMILY's List Press Release*, November 6, 2002.

[d] Eleanor Clift and Tom Brazaitis, *Madam President: Women Blazing the Leadership Trail* (New York: Routledge, 2003).

At the state level, gains have come more gradually. Women held 18.3 percent of state legislative seats in 1991. In 2003, 22.3 percent of all legislators are women, a slight decrease from 22.7 percent in 2002. Currently a record 12.4 percent of all women state legislators are African American, 3.7 percent are Latinas, 1 percent (twenty-three) are Asian/Pacific American, and nine Native American women were state legislators.[94] (See Figure 2.4.)

In statewide elected offices, women now hold 25.3 percent of executive positions, a slight decrease from 27.6 percent in 2001. The total number of women governors increased to a record six (four Democrats, two Republicans) after the 2002 elections. An additional seventeen women served as lieutenant governor,

ey general, ten as secretary of state, and nine as state treasurer.[95] In
ant Governor Olene Walker (R-Utah) replaced Governor Mike Leav-
g his confirmation as head of the EPA. Democrat Kathleen Blanco
publican Bobby Jindal in a run-off election to become the first female
f Louisiana, increasing the number of female governors to eight.

At the local level in 2003, women are mayors in fifteen of the largest one
hundred cities, 20.8 percent of the mayors in cities with populations over
30,000, and 15.9 percent in cities with populations of 100,000 or more.[96] The
ability of women to get elected to office below the national level is a good indicator of their future ability to achieve higher political office, as state and local
offices often are a jumping-off point for political positions at the national level.
The increase in female governors is promising, given that four of the last five
presidents were former governors. However, the 2002 elections were a setback
for women in terms of state legislative and statewide elective offices. As Debbie Walsh, director of the Center for American Women and Politics, explains:
"With fewer women in state legislatures and statewide offices, we're draining
the pool of potential candidates for governorships, the women who could rise
to national office."[97] These recent setbacks are a reminder of how far women
have yet to go before they achieve parity with men.

BARRIERS TO WOMEN IN ELECTED AND APPOINTED POSITIONS

Historically, the barriers that have kept women out of political office seem to fall
into five general categories: (1) stereotypes, (2) career choice and preparation, (3)
family demands, (4) sex discrimination, and (5) the political system itself.
Although most of these barriers have been eliminated or weakened in the other
areas of political activity, they continue to be much more powerful vis-à-vis political office. Moreover, other system-specific problems limit the likelihood that
every election year will afford record gains like those made by women in 1992.

These barriers act in two ways to keep the numbers of women in public
office low: first, they deter many women from running for office, and second,
they keep those who run from succeeding. Studies of women who actually
seek elective office indicate that this first set of hurdles, such as the initial decision to seek public office, can be the most formidable.[98] When women run for
office as challengers, incumbents, or open seat candidates, they are just as
likely to win as male candidates. Gender differences in fundraising have also
been erased. As a result of these findings, many have looked toward the
pipeline of women entering male-dominated careers that often are stepping
stones to elective office. Recent research by Richard Fox and Jennifer Lawless,
however, suggests that women who have reached elite status and are "eligible" to run for political office are less likely than elite males to emerge as candidates for political office.[99] Thus, it is the failure of women to toss their hats
in the ring that contributes most to the absence of women in the political arena.

Stereotypes

When public opposition to women running for political office was at its peak, the most likely explanation for women not running for office was that most women and men thought such activity was inappropriate. Evidence of the continued influence of these stereotypes can also be seen in places where women are still underrepresented in state legislatures, notably the South— a region where traditional views about women continue to hold sway. Half of the ten state legislatures with the lowest percentages of women in 2003 were from this region.[100]

The legacy of cultural stereotypes is also apparent in the ambition levels of women participants in party politics. Research focusing on party activists in California from 1964 to 1986 found women less likely at every time interval to be as interested as men in seeking elective and appointive office.[101] A 2001 survey of citizen political ambition likewise revealed gender differences in candidate emergence. When asked if they had considered running for office, 59 percent of men but only 43 percent of women responded that it had at least "crossed their mind." Women were 50 percent less likely to take additional steps toward candidacy, including finding out how to get their name on the ballot, or discussing running with potential donors, party leaders, community leaders, family members, or friends. Fox and Lawless note: "what started out as a gender-balanced eligibility pool winnows to one that is dominated by men."[102]

A recent survey by the White House Project found that both young women and men perceive barriers that may ultimately deter interested women from actually running. The vast majority (80 percent) agree that it is very or somewhat hard for a woman to run for political office, while only 7 percent say it is hard for a man to run for political office. Eighty-two percent of women and 78 percent of men agree that women have a hard time breaking into politics. Although women are more likely to believe that government can help solve problems with the right people involved (71 percent vs. 62 percent of men), women were more likely than men to say that they would not know how to get involved in politics even if they were interested.[103]

Media Bias

For women who actually decide to run for office, stereotypes about their abilities continue to present problems. Kim Fridkin Kahn finds evidence of this in the press coverage of women and men candidates in Senate and gubernatorial races. She reports that women senatorial candidates are routinely portrayed as less viable than male candidates. Women also receive less issue coverage. No such bias was evident in the articles about women candidates for governor.[104] Using an experimental design, Kahn finds this difference contributes to voters rating men candidates as more competent to deal with military issues, and women candidates as less viable, more honest, and better able to deal with health issues. Kahn argues that this combination of stereotyping articles and reader reaction might help to explain women's lower success rates in races for the Senate, a legislative body that traditionally has focused more on defense than health issues. She reasons that because the press does not diminish the viability of women gubernatorial candidates, the same stereotypes about women's issue expertise help to explain their greater success in gubernatorial races, where key issues are those for which women are seen as better prepared.[105] James Devitt argues that media bias is possibly "diminishing the pipeline of women's leadership."[106] His analysis of six 1988 female gubernatorial races found that although male and female candidates received the same quantity of coverage, the content of the news articles differed significantly. Reporters were more likely to focus on personal characteristics of female candidates, including age, marital status, family, personality, and appearance, in contrast to highlighting the issue positions, voting records, or leadership abilities of male candidates. Male candidates were also more frequently quoted backing their claims with reason or evidence.[107]

Martha Kropf and John Boiney support these findings in their analysis of Senate races from 1988 to 1992. They argue that gender plays a role in establishing the viability of a candidate and that news media coverage can disadvantage women candidates. While increased exposure to television news about male candidates increased the likelihood of mentioning something positive about the candidate, female candidates did not appear to reap the same benefits.[108]

Recent research suggests that media bias played a role in Elizabeth Dole's inability to establish her credibility as a viable candidate in the 2000 presidential election. Analysis of Dole's campaign by Caroline Heldman, Susan J. Carroll, and Stephanie Olson suggests that Dole did not receive the quantity or quality of coverage that she deserved as the number two candidate in the race. Dole received less coverage than Bush or McCain, and the coverage she did receive had greater emphasis on personality and appearance. Although Dole received issue coverage comparable to her male competitors, there was noticeable bias in the coverage of "horserace" and fundraising, with Dole receiving more negative coverage. The media also focused on the novelty of the first serious female contender, labeling Dole in a way that probably decreased her viability.[109] Marie Wilson, president of the White House Project, argues: "There's a subtle undermining of women's authority when the emphasis in the press is all about hair, husbands, and hemlines."[110]

Women candidates who run for office also have to be mindful of public perceptions when they produce their campaign commercials. An analysis of the ads of men and women senatorial candidates in 1992 found that women dressed more formally and used male announcers, perhaps in a subtle effort to overcome stereotypes about competence and strength. Correspondingly, they stressed their compassionate side and their empathy for voters' needs more than men.[111] The emphasis on domestic issues as the Cold War ended also helped women candidates.

A recent study by the White House Project identified continued barriers to women's executive leadership and offered some strategic recommendations based on analysis of over 400 television spots as well as testing of sample ads on dial groups. The findings suggest that women must present themselves differently from men in order to achieve the same level of effectiveness. Voters have more negative predispositions about the effectiveness, toughness, and proven records of female candidates than male candidates. To compensate, the White House Project emphasizes the need for women to provide a proven record with tangible examples, preferably using nontraditional issues such as crime, taxes, or the economy, and a more formal setting to convey a seriousness of purpose.[112]

Career Choice and Preparation

The socialization of women to pursue occupations that are either incompatible with political careers or are perceived as such by officials who supervise candidate selection processes (or by voters) also constitutes a barrier to and limit on the potential number of female office seekers. Many traditionally female occupations such as teaching or nursing are less compatible with politics than are more male-dominated professions. Historically, women were barred from, or had difficulty entering, the legal profession, a common springboard to public office. R. Darcy, Susan Welch, and Janet Clark present convincing evidence that the relative paucity of women from the "eligible pool" of potential political candidates until recently is an important reason, although not the only one, for their relative absence from state legislatures, especially in the "upper" or more prestigious houses.[113] Christine B. Williams's research on the relationship between the number of women lawyers in a state and the number of women in the state legislature indicates that the lack of "eligible" women continues to help explain the disparity between the number of men and women in state legislatures.[114]

Research suggests the careers of women and men running for Congress are increasingly converging. In the 108th Congress, 75 percent (forty-four) of the women serving in the House of Representatives have held previous elective office, and more than half (twenty-four) of these women held more than one post.[115] Although women are still less likely to be lawyers, the gap with men is declining. An examination of the careers of women officeholders, moreover, finds that many successful women candidates have pursued "women's careers."[116] It may be that as the public assesses the issues facing the nation in the twenty-first century, women's careers and experiences in education, health, and social services will make them more and more attractive candidates. As former State Senator Nita Rinehart of Washington notes, the benefit from having more women in office may come from their difference from men in educational and career backgrounds: "There's a wider array of perspectives now when you have more women."[117]

Family Demands

Another major barrier that has affected women candidates is a public perception that women with children (especially young children) are less suited for public office. According to one woman state legislator serving in the

1970s who had postponed running until her children were older: "To be very frank, I couldn't have done it. I really couldn't have been an effective legislator if my children were little. . . . I would have carried too much of a load of guilt."[118] Half of the women in Jeane Kirkpatrick's 1974 study of female state legislators ran for office only after their children were grown. Only one had attempted it when she had a child under age six.[119] Interviews with a broader group of women political officials a decade later by CAWP also found that women officeholders were less likely than men officeholders to have young children. Moreover, these women officeholders were more likely to agree that "my children being old enough for me to feel comfortable not being home as much" was very important to their decision to run.[120] Men, however, did not appear to hold reservations about running for or serving in public office while they had children.[121]

Until recently, the conflict between parenthood and politics channeled many women away from not only elected office but also partisan or campaign activity, at least while their children were young. This gave women a late start in partisan politics, which had important ramifications on the eventual success of women in getting into office. Even if a woman could reject or overcome the alleged incompatibility of the two roles of mother and politician, she might not run for office for fear of the public's or her own family's negative reaction. Mothers of young children who have run for office tell many stories about the hostile and snide questions asked by some voters and reporters about who was taking care of their children. Jane Swift, who was pregnant with her first child when she was elected lieutenant governor of Massachusetts in 1998 and pregnant with twins when she replaced Paul Cellucci as active governor in 2001, was widely criticized by both the press and the public as she attempted to balance a political career and family. Referred to as "supermom on a power trip," Swift, a Republican, made headlines in 2000 for asking staff members to babysit and for using a state police helicopter to fly home over Thanksgiving to tend to her sick toddler.[122] In 2001, when she was hospitalized with premature labor with her twins, she conducted meetings using a speaker phone from her hospital bed while Democratic opponents threatened to challenge the constitutionality of her actions.[123] Ironically, Swift was challenged for reelection by a Democratic mother of a two-year-old. Ultimately her own party convinced her to step down and endorse Mitt Romney, a millionaire businessman who gained prominence as the president and CEO of the Salt Lake Organizing Committee for the 2002 Winter Olympics. Swift commented to reporters, "I guess I should be accustomed to powerful men trying to tell me that they know better than I do what it is I should be doing."[124]

Stereotypical attitudes about a "woman's place" can be particularly problematic for women who run for national office. Nancy Pelosi (D-Calif.) explains, "I came to Congress in my 40s, after my five children were grown. Most of my male colleagues had a 10-year advantage in terms of seniority. The single biggest difference in women rising to the highest levels of power would be to have young women coming in and building the seniority and experience and judgment needed to be governor, Senator, President. We have to make politics more family-friendly."[125] A 1999 survey revealed that 17 percent of respondents would be less likely to vote for a female presidential candidate if she had a child under age five, compared to just 6 percent who would vote against a male candidate with a young child. Almost a third of Americans said they would be less likely to vote for a female presidential candidate if she was pregnant, in contrast to only 5 percent who would not vote for a male presidential candidate if his wife was pregnant.[126]

Research suggests that negative attitudes toward balancing motherhood and a political career may be less prevalent at lower levels of office.[127] However, young children may produce another kind of problem or barrier for some women seeking elective or appointive office. Two women President Clinton considered nominating for attorney general in his first term withdrew from consideration after it was revealed that they had employed undocumented aliens to care for their children. On the heels of what many pundits dubbed Nannygate, Clinton then nominated Janet Reno, an unmarried, childless, Dade County, Florida, prosecutor, to the nation's top law enforcement position. In 2001, President George W. Bush's Department of Labor nominee, Linda Chavez, withdrew her nomination, admitting that she had not been forthcoming about hiring an illegal immigrant.[128]

Historically, another closely related aspect of role conflict that has kept many married women out of politics was spousal preference. Surveys of political officeholders of both sexes in the 1970s found evidence that acceptance and encouragement of political activity by one's spouse and family were more critical for a woman than for a man.[129] Again, this may be especially true for offices that require relocation or spending considerable amounts of time away from home. It may be that one of the reasons so few women ran for office before the 1970s was that husbands willing to provide the necessary support for a wife who wanted to be active in politics were rare. One of the benefits of the women's rights movement and a factor in the rise in the number of women in office may well be the growth of the idea of shared marriages where both partners have careers. Recent research, moreover, suggests women candidates today may be less concerned with spousal support than are men candidates. Although more women than men officeholders claim their spouses are supportive, fewer women than men said that spousal support was important to their decision to run. The main reason for the difference seems to be that many more women than men elected officials are not married.[130]

Thus, women are apparently confronted with a conflict between their roles as mothers and wives and their political roles. When faced with this role conflict, following the pattern of women in other high-powered careers, women politicians appear to solve the problem either by remaining childless, having fewer children, delaying their political career until their children are older, remaining single, or marrying a supportive spouse.

Discrimination

Historically, there was considerable reason to believe that the male gatekeepers of political office, the party leaders, were not very supportive of women candidates. Susan Carroll's survey of women who ran for state or national office in 1976 found that women were seldom recruited by their party and often discouraged from running. When women were recruited to run, they were often meant to serve as "sacrificial lambs" in races they could not be expected to win.[131] Former Representative Patricia Schroeder (D-Colo.), however, presents a realistic view of the process: "A lot of women think they're going to be asked to run. But this is not a dance. There are a lot of sharp elbows trying to get to the front of the line."[132]

More recent research finds little continued discrimination by party leaders. Women and men are equally as likely to be recruited by party leaders, although there is evidence that women are still disproportionately encouraged to run in unwinnable races or where the seat is a "woman's seat," that is, one previously held by a woman.[133]

African American women and other women of color often face a special or double burden in running for political office because both their race and their gender limit their chances for success. R. Darcy, Charles D. Hadley, and Jason F. Kirksey point out that based on state legislative seats, African American women are more severely underrepresented than African American men.[134] They argue that African American men hold nearly 90 percent of the seats they could expect to hold at the state level based on population; African American women hold only 30 percent of the seats they "deserve." Irene Natividad of the National Women's Political Caucus argues that minority women are especially hampered by their perceived lack of credibility as serious candidates.[135] Other research by R. Darcy and Charles D. Hadley, however, suggests African American women have been able to do better than white women in securing elected office. In their study, African American women held 18.8 percent of all state legislative seats occupied by African Americans, while the percentage of white seats held by white women was 14.5.[136] Part of the problem facing women of both races is an electoral system that magnifies the disadvantages faced by women running for office.

The Political System

Several key components of the political system—money, campaign finance laws, party organization, winner-take-all electoral systems, and incumbency—all affect the ability of women to run and wage successful campaigns for public office.

Money. Adequate funding is the lodestone of a successful campaign. Elizabeth Dole abandoned her candidacy for the presidency only six months after forming her exploratory committee. Unable to match the resources and fundraising abilities of George W. Bush, Dole told reporters in a press conference on October 20, 1999, "it would be futile to continue."[137] Most women candidates believe that it is more difficult for women than men to obtain the funds needed to run.[138] This may be a function of the fact that women are generally challengers who have a more difficult time raising money than incumbents. Gary Jacobson's research on congressional campaigns documents the fundraising advantages of incumbents, who win over 90 percent of their reelection bids. As Jacobson explains, "The better a candidate's prospects, the more contributors of all kinds are willing to invest in the campaign."[139]

Indeed, if women want to achieve political equality, they have to raise more money than the male incumbents they need to unseat. As discussed in Chapter 1, the rise in women's PACs has fueled dramatic increases in women's fundraising. Whereas traditional PACs follow "access strategies," funding incumbents to secure influence, women's PACs use "electoral strategies," giving money to the maximum number of candidates that support the group's agenda. The seed money provided by women's PACs helps women candidates establish the credibility they need to attract traditional sources of campaign funding.[140] Women's PACs mobilize *women* to contribute campaign funds, tapping into an underutilized political resource.[141]

Burrell's research on women candidates for the House finds that the campaign fund deficit of women in the 1970s (except for 1972) declined in the 1980s. In 1988 and 1992, women actually outraised men once the status of the candidate (incumbency) and party were controlled.[142] Follow-up studies indicate that political experience and incumbency status have greater influence on fundraising than gender; controlling for these two factors, women continue to raise as much as men.[143] The founder of EMILY's List, Ellen Malcolm, commented on the change in women's behavior: "Women have learned that if they want to see themselves represented, they have to get behind women candidates with their contributions as well as their volunteer hours and their votes."[144]

Although women overall may be facing an improved ability to raise funds, African American and other women of color may still have a particularly difficult time because of fewer contacts with monied individuals and the low economic status of the people living in their districts.[145] In 2002, over eighty women met at the National Council of Negro Women Headquarters in Washington, D.C., and formed the first national African American women's political action committee. Women Building for the Future, or the Future PAC, supports progressive black women candidates committed to improving the quality of life for African Americans. Donna Brazile, the foremost African American campaign consultant, who led the Gore presidential campaign, argues: "It's time for Black women to become bigger players in the political process. . . . We're not underrepresented in political office. Underrepresentation would signal we were in the pipeline. We're invisible."[146]

Campaign Finance Laws.   Former Representative Geraldine Ferraro (D-N.Y.) had to sell property and take out personal loans to raise money for her campaign. She lamented, "Unfortunately, that's the way women have to do it. Women have got to learn to write checks for other women."[147]

Since 1984, many women have heeded Ferraro's words, and the growth of political action committees (PACs) made legal by the 1974 campaign finance reforms has helped. The Center for American Women and Politics currently reports a total of forty-nine PACs, including twelve national donor networks and thirty-seven state or local PACs, representing a decrease from 1997, when there was a total of fifty-eight donor networks.[148] Recent efforts by women's PACs including EMILY's List, NOW PAC, the Women's Campaign Fund, and Women in the Senate and House (WISH), have been critical in alleviating the financial obstacles faced by women candidates. EMILY's List ranked second in the 1999–2000 election cycle for both receipts and disbursements. Moreover, reports submitted to the FEC do not include "bundled" funds, or checks written directly to candidates, collected and distributed by EMILY's List. Although this highly successful fundraising tactic has been challenged by Republican reform proposals, it was not included in the 2002 Bipartisan Campaign Reform Act. The new law bans soft money contributions, increases the amounts that individuals can contribute to candidates and political parties, and places new restrictions on political ads close to the election.

Party Organization.   Historically, women candidates also faced another problem—limited organizational help in the form of campaign workers, in part because of marginal party support.[149] This, however, appears to have changed. Both major parties now support the notion of electing more women. According to Burrell's analysis, they have backed their statements with money and other forms of support.[150] An analysis of party contributions to candidates finds women may actually get more money than men from the party. The Republican Party, however, appears to have more difficulty recruiting women to run for Congress. This may be related to the party's strength in the South, a region less hospitable to women candidates. In 2002, 113 women Democrats entered U.S. House races, but only seventy-three women Republicans. A majority of both Democratic and Republican women won their primaries (69 percent vs. 63 percent) and nearly half proceeded to win in the general election (49 percent vs. 46 percent). Of the eleven women (eight Democrats, three Republicans) who ran for the Senate in 2002, one Democrat and two Republicans won.[151] The success of women's PACs that give early money disproportionately to female Democrats may provide the Democratic Party a recruitment advantage.[152] The concentration of women in the Democratic Party may also be a function of the party's support of issues benefiting women.[153] However, research suggests that when Republican women emerge as candidates they may now have an advantage over Democratic women. Since 1994, Republican women running in open seat contests have a 50 percent success rate versus a 38 percent success rate among Democratic women.[154]

Interviews with elected officials indicate that groups other than parties, especially women's groups, now play a key role not only in funding women's races but in encouraging and championing them more generally. Political consultant

Cathy Allen calls it "the triple play of women in politics—more women deciding to run, more women contributing money, more women working in campaigns."[155]

Electoral Systems.   The traditional barriers facing women running for office may be diminishing. Yet some problems unique to the U.S. political system make it very hard for women to be elected in as large numbers as in other democracies. Currently women hold an average of 14 percent of parliamentary seats worldwide. With 13.7 percent of the seats held by women in Congress, the United States continues to fall below the international average. The International Institute for Democracy and Electoral Assistance reports that the ten highest-ranking countries all use proportional representation systems. Party-established quotas, or systemwide quotas for candidates or actual seats are additional means used by other

---

Global Awareness

WOMEN IN ELECTIVE OFFICE

National Rankings of Women Representatives

Country	% Seats in Lower or Single House	% Seats in Upper House	Rank
Sweden	45.3		1
Denmark	38.0		2
Netherlands	36.7	26.7	3
Finland	36.5		4
Norway	36.4		5
Germany	32.2	24.6	9
New Zealand	29.2		14
Spain	28.3	24.3	15
Australia	25.3	28.9	23
Belgium	23.3	28.2	25
Switzerland	23.0	19.6	26
China	21.8		32
Canada	20.6	32.4	36
United Kingdom	17.9	16.4	49
Mexico	16.0	15.6	55
United States	13.6	14	58

Source: The Inter-Parliamentary Union, http://www.ipu.org/wmn-e/classif.htm.

A woman has served as either president or prime minister in more than thirty-two countries. Women preside over twenty-five legislative bodies, constituting 10.4 percent of the total number of presiding officers. Women also hold 14.7 percent of parliamentary seats. In contrast, the

(continued)

United States ranks fifty-eighth in the world in terms of female representation in national government.[a] Other countries have increased the representation of women in elective office by experimenting with affirmative action strategies, which Pippa Norris divides into three categories: (1) rhetorical strategies that, "articulated in leadership speeches, party guidelines, or official party platforms, aim to change the party ethos by affirming the need for social balance in the slate of candidates"; (2) recruitment and training programs that "aim to encourage applicants by providing training sessions, advisory group targets, financial assistance, as well as systemic monitoring of the outcome"; and (3) positive discrimination strategies that "set mandatory group quotas for the selection of candidates from certain social or political groups."[b] Sweden, for example, uses "sandwich nomination lists" requiring a woman to be listed every other name on the party's nomination list. Argentina requires by law that 30 percent of the legislature is female. Political parties in Spain and Mexico have adopted quotas to increase female representation. In the United States, however, structural and cultural barriers continue to impede the progress of women in elective office.

[a] "Why Women Matter: Lessons About Women's Political Leadership From Home and Abroad," The White House Project 2003.

[b] Pippa Norris, "Breaking the Barriers: Positive Discrimination Policies for Women," in *Has Liberalism Failed Women? Parity, Quotas, and Political Representation*, ed. Jyette Klausen and Charles S. Maier (New York: St. Martin's Press, 2001), quoted in "Why Women Matter: Lessons About Women's Political Leadership From Home and Abroad."

countries to bolster female representation.[156] Work by Rebecca Davis documents the advantages women have in obtaining political appointments in multiparty, multiple-member districts.[157]

In contrast, the U.S. electoral system of single-member, "winner-take-all" districts—meaning only one candidate wins in each district—continues to hinder women. Studies show that when a system has multiple winners (multimember districts) who are selected from lists of candidates prepared by the party, women are more likely to be included on these lists. More women candidates generally means more women win a seat in the legislature.[158] This is true not only in other countries, but also in the United States. In the few states and localities where multimember districts exist, women have a much better chance of election. Indeed, a number of states with higher than average representation of women in their legislatures elect their officials this way.[159] In recent decades, however, the number of states using multimember districts has declined.[160] African American women seem particularly disadvantaged by this trend.

Incumbency.   The political system favors incumbents, making it hard for newcomers, which most women are, to break into politics. It is common for 90 percent or more of all members of Congress to seek reelection and to win. Barbara Palmer and Dennis Simon describe this lack of competition as a "political glass ceiling" for women congressional candidates, who strategically will choose not to run against a safe incumbent.[161] The number of women candidates thus reflects the number of competitive opportunities available to women in the form of open seats or districts in which the incumbent is vulnerable. As of 2003, only three out of fifty women challengers have ever won in the Senate. In the House, twenty-two of the 543 challengers (4 percent) have won.[162] Many women first win office in special elections, races where the incumbent has left office between elections. A study of the women elected to the House between 1979 and 1992, for example, found that a third obtained their seats in special elections.[163] Eight women in the 108th Congress won their seats in special elections.

Kim Fridkin Kahn and Edie Goldenberg's analysis of U.S. Senate races suggests that when women run in races where there is an incumbent, they get less media coverage than men in similar races. This hurts women's electoral chances in races already difficult.[164] Some commentators argue that a "woman's nature" makes it more difficult for a woman to run against an incumbent. Jane Danowitz, former director of the Women's Campaign Fund, notes, "To get anyone out of office, you have to explain to voters why [that person] shouldn't be in office, and that means negative campaigning."[165] She says this is harder for women to do because it goes against their image of what women should do.

Indeed, 1992 was the Year of the Woman in large part because there were an unprecedented number of open seats. A record number of House incumbents (fifty-four) did not seek reelection or were defeated in primaries (nineteen). This allowed more women candidates than ever—one-third of all candidates—to run in races where there were no incumbents, which greatly increased their chances of winning. The media's coverage of the Year of the Woman also may have made women look more viable as candidates. Kathleen Dolan argues that the gendered context of the 1992 election stimulated a voting pattern that has not been repeated in later years, when candidate sex and gender-related issues did not receive the same media attention. When the "electoral environment" focuses on gender issues including abortion, family leave, and sexual harassment, the voters approach female candidates differently.[166] In this context, Paul Herrnson, J. Celeste Lay, and Atiya Stokes suggest that women gain a strategic advantage when they run "as women" emphasizing issues that have a positive association with women candidates.[167]

One political innovation that may weaken the incumbency advantage is term limits. If incumbents, mostly men, were forced to retire after a few terms, women would be able to run for those open seats. The problem remains, however, in recruiting women to run. A 1999 study of the effects of term limits at the state level found that while the number of women increased in state houses, the number of women in state senates decreased as term-limited women incumbents forced to vacate their seats were not replaced by women.[168]

Congressional incumbents so far have avoided term limits. In 1995, the U.S. Supreme Court struck down state-imposed term limits on members of Congress, and thus far proposals to amend the Constitution have been unsuccessful.[169] When women reach incumbent status, they enjoy the same advantages as men. The average incumbency rate for women from 1978 to 2000 is 85 percent in the Senate and 96 percent in the House.[170]

PROBLEMS FACED BY WOMEN IN ELECTED POSITIONS

Election to public office often does not end a woman's problems. Interviews with women public officials indicate that many of the barriers to election also may act to keep women in secondary positions once in office.[171]

Positions of power in legislatures are gained generally according to length of time served. Women often come to politics later in life due to child-rearing demands. This places them at a disadvantage in terms of seniority. Women who break into leadership positions, moreover, usually have to fight male resistance to get there. A 1991 CAWP report, for example, found almost half of the women in state legislatures believe men try to keep women out of leadership positions.[172] This problem is not restricted to the state level. In 1996, Representative Louise Slaughter (D-N.Y.) was defeated in her effort to become the ranking member of the Budget Committee (the person who would become chair if Democrats controlled the House), even though she had the most seniority on the committee. Democratic women were especially angered by Slaughter's defeat because of the key role women had played in electing Clinton and House Democrats. As Slaughter rightly noted, "Half of our governing body of the United States doesn't have any representation."[173]

By some measures, however, women appear to be moving up in the power structure. Nancy Pelosi (D-Calif.) made history in 2003 as the first woman to serve as Minority Leader of the House of Representatives. Women hold eleven leadership positions in the 108th Congress, representing a significant increase from just one position in the 102nd Congress a decade ago. (See Table 2.5.)

TABLE 2.5 **Women in Congressional Leadership Roles**

	Senate		House		Total
108th Congress 2003–2005	4 D	1 R	4 D	2 R	11
107th Congress 2001–2003	3 D	2 R	3 D	2 R	10
106th Congress 1999–2001	2 D	2 R	6 D	4 R	14
105th Congress 1997–1999	1 D	2 R	4 D	5 R	12
104th Congress 1995–1997	1 D	1 R	4 D	4 R	10
103rd Congress 1993–1995	2 D	0 R	1 D	1 R	4
102nd Congress 1991–1993	0 D	0 R	1 D	0 R	1

Source: "Women in Congress: Leadership Roles and Committee Chairs," *CAWP Fact Sheet,* April 2003.

Profiles in Leadership
NANCY PELOSI

> She grew up as the only daughter of an old-fashioned urban ward
> boss and never forgot what her father taught her: that politics is a
> matter of winning votes, not spinning philosophies.
> *David Von Drehle and Hanna Rosin, Washington Post*[a]

U.S. Representative Nancy Pelosi (D-Calif.) broke a political glass ceiling in the 107th Congress when she became the first woman to serve as Minority Whip in the House of Representatives. Just thirteen months later, when Dick Gephardt stepped down to focus on his 2004 presidential campaign, Pelosi was elected to replace him as Minority Leader of the House of Representatives in the 108th Congress, making her the highest-ranking woman ever in Congress. "I didn't run as a woman," Pelosi said, "I ran as a seasoned politician and an experienced legislator. It just so happens that I am a woman and we have been waiting a long time for this moment."[b]

Pelosi's childhood was immersed in politics. Pelosi's father, Thomas "Big Tommy" D'Alesandro Jr., represented Baltimore in the U.S. House from 1939 to 1947 and then served as mayor for twelve years, running the city under a tight political machine. Her brother, Thomas D'Alesandro III, followed in his footsteps as mayor. Despite growing up in a politically active family, Pelosi did not follow a traditional career path into politics. She married Paul Pelosi a year after graduating from Trinity College, a women's Catholic school in Washington, D.C., in 1962. After moving to San Francisco, where her spouse started his career in investment banking and real estate, Pelosi gave birth to five children in six years and "made a sacrament out of ironing."[c] Balancing family with her interest in politics, Pelosi served as Chair of the Northern California Democratic Party from 1977 to 1981 and State Chair of the California Democratic Party from 1981 to 1983. Her daughter Alexandra remembers the family weekend projects of assembly-line envelope stuffing for Democratic candidates. Pelosi also served as a Democratic National Committeewoman from California for two decades, from 1976 to 1996. Her first bid for Congress came in 1987 when Democratic Representative Sala Burton, dying of cancer, made Pelosi promise to run for the vacant seat.[d]

In Congress, Pelosi quickly established her reputation as an astute and assertive leader, serving as a senior member of the Appropriations Committee and as the ranking Democrat on the Select Intelligence Committee. She has been an active supporter of the environment, AIDS prevention and treatment, and human rights, particularly in China. Although labeled a "San Francisco liberal," she quickly ascended to a leadership

(continued)

position though her political skills, her collegiality, and perhaps most importantly, her ability to raise funds. As Steve Rosenthal, outgoing political director of the AFL-CIO characterizes her, "She's a technician, a nuts-and-bolts person, smart enough to see that how she represents her district is one thing, and how she leads the Democratic Party in the House is another."[e] Pelosi describes politics as a tennis match, "You can move to the right or to the left, but you always have to come back to the middle."[f] Like her father, Pelosi pays close attention to personal relations. "She acknowledges reporters by name in the hallways with a bright smile, lavishes colleagues with personal attention and is the queen of thank-you notes, even to the most minor volunteer helper."[g]

For years, Pelosi cultivated support behind the scenes by raising money for fellow Democrats, often without being asked. Loretta Sanchez (D-Calif.) recounts how her first campaign for Congress in 1996 was being ignored by others when Pelosi called to say, "'Here are a couple of dates. If you can come up here, I can raise you $40,000.' I said, 'OK. What's your name again?'"[h] Pelosi ultimately raised twice as much at the event.[i] During the 2000 election, Pelosi raised a record $3.9 million for Democratic candidates, contributing to her defeat of Steny Hoyer for the coveted position as minority leader.[j] In an interview the day after her swearing-in ceremony, Pelosi commented, "Over 200 years of our history, no woman has ever risen to these heights in the Congress of the United States. No woman has gone to the White House in the capacity of senior, in a senior position in the Congress to sit at the table with the President, to discuss the issues facing our country and the President's agenda. And so it's pretty exciting."[k]

---

[a] David Von Drehle and Hanna Rosin, "The Two Nancy Pelosis," *Washington Post*, November 14, 2002, A1.

[b] Edward Walsh, "House Democrats Take Pelosi to Be Their Leader," *Washington Post*, November 15, 2002, A11.

[c] Von Drehle, A1.

[d] Ibid.

[e] Ibid.

[f] Ibid.

[g] Juliet Eilperin, "The Making of 'Madam Whip,'" *Washington Post National Weekly Edition*, January 14–20, 2002, 7.

[h] Susan Ferrechio, "Rep. Nancy Pelosi," *Congressional Quarterly Weekly Report*, December 28, 2002, 55.

[i] Ibid.

[j] Eilperin, 7.

[k] "Rep. Nancy Pelosi," a News Hour with Jim Lehrer Transcript, February 7, 2002, http://www.pbs.org/newshour/bb/congress/jan-june02/pelosi_2-7.html.

However, women have yet to hold the coveted positions as Speaker of the House or Majority Leader. At the state level, three women serve as presidents of state senates and five women are speakers of state houses.[174]

Another indicator of the difficulties women face can be seen in their committee assignments. Most of the work of legislatures is done in committees. The appointment of women to committees that control important legislation is critical to their ability to influence legislation. Interviews at the state level in the late 1980s, however, found women more likely than men *not* to be appointed to at least two prestige committees—finance and revenue. Instead, they were appointed disproportionately to committees concerned with traditional women's issues such as health or education. Women also were more unhappy with their committee appointments than were men. Their discontent stemmed largely from being placed disproportionately on unpopular committees or as tokens on committees with few or no women.[175] More recently, women have made advancements as committee chairs as a result of their longer tenure.[176] In 2001, women held 18.8 percent of committee chair positions in state legislatures nationwide.[177]

Although more women are getting prestigious committee assignments in Congress, their prospects for these slots are often worse than those for men in their same class. Most prestigious committees have but token positions for women.[178] The real power on a committee, moreover, goes to its chair, and few women have held such a position in either the House or the Senate. A record two women serve as chair of Senate standing committees in the 108th Congress, both from Maine: Olympia Snowe on Small Business and Susan Collins on Governmental Affairs.[179]

Media bias also continues to play a role once a woman is elected to office. In an analysis of Sunday morning talk shows, the White House Project found that women account for one in seventeen appearances by an elected official despite a one in seven ratio in Congress. During an eighteen-month period, male Senators made 245 repeat guest appearances in contrast to eight by female Senators.[180] Through interviews with press secretaries, David Niven and Jeremy Zilber reveal gender bias in reporters' treatment of House members. Press secretaries of women members were more likely to believe their members were treated unfairly by the press, including insufficient coverage of their member's priorities and accomplishments. They argue that the media focus on women members primarily as representatives of women, highlighting their support of women's issues. This narrow definition of their role as gender representatives marginalizes their influence within the House. Niven and Zilber quote one press secretary as saying, "The day the media spend as much time pointing out that [Senate Majority Leader] Trent Lott was a cheerleader in college, spend as much time worrying about how the men in this body take care of their young kids while they're in office, and start asking why these men don't care about family issues instead of why we [women Representatives] do, then you can ask me if the media are fair and I won't have to laugh out loud."[181]

IMPACT OF WOMEN IN ELECTED POSITIONS

Political theorist Hannah Pitkin asserts that political representation "means acting in the interest of the represented, in a manner responsive to them."[182]

Political Scientist Jane Mansbridge goes farther to note that descriptive representation enhances substantive representation.[183] Some male legislators may seek to advance women's interests, and others may argue that all issues are women's issues, but a large and important body of research by political scientists indicates that the presence of women in legislative bodies makes a difference not only in what gets discussed, but also in what kinds of legislation are advanced.

Much of the early research on the impact of women legislators was confined to analysis of state and local legislatures simply because there were insufficient numbers of women in the U.S. House or Senate to allow for any kind of exacting quantitative analysis. Research conducted at the state and local level, however, ultimately provided testable hypotheses to examine the impact of women in the House of Representatives.

Women Legislators at the State and Local Level

The impact of women legislators at the state and local level is evident in their different conceptualization of problems and solutions.[184] Women legislators of both parties are more likely to advance "women's issues," define women's issues more broadly than men, put them at the top of their legislative agendas, and take a leadership role in those issue areas.[185] As a result, bills dealing with children, education, and health care are becoming legislative priorities.[186] Women legislators are also more likely to support new programs to help women.[187] Even nonfeminist women are more likely than nonfeminist men colleagues to work on legislation affecting women.[188]

Gender differences also emerge in how legislators perform constituency service. Women legislators receive more constituent casework requests than their men colleagues and are three times more likely to agree that they would do more if they had more staff.[189] Women not only are more responsive to constituent requests but are more likely to be persistent in their follow through to get a favorable resolution for their constituents.[190] Women legislators believe that they need to help other women transcend barriers to success.[191]

The perceptions of women legislators about their roles suggest a different style of leadership. Women view themselves as more prepared, more diligent, and more organized than male colleagues.[192] Women describe using a "hands on" approach emphasizing collegiality and collaboration instead of a hierarchical "command" approach.[193] Women tend to rely on a wider range of individuals in formulating policy, creating more sensitive and thoughtful policy making.[194] Female committee chairs, for example, use their positions to facilitate interaction among committee members rather than to control and direct the debate. This affects the behavior of witnesses and other committee members.[195] Male legislators report that women in the legislative body help sensitize them to women's issues.[196]

Although first-term women sponsor less legislation than their male counterparts, senior women offer more than their male counterparts.[197] Women who meet as a caucus are more likely to work on bills dealing with women's rights.[198] In general, women-sponsored legislation has a slightly higher rate of passage.[199]

In particular, women's priority bills on women's issues become law at a higher rate than men's.[200] When women are less than 15 percent of the legislative body, their status constrains their behavior.[201] States with the lowest percentage of women in their legislatures pass the lowest number of women's bills.[202]

Women in Congress

The findings of the research noted above provide conclusive proof of the impact that women have as state and local legislators. Of course, given the smaller number of women in Congress until lately, many of their local and state-based studies cannot yet be replicated, particularly in the U.S. Senate. Still, all of the quantitative studies of women in the House of Representatives have reached the same conclusions about women in that body. As the late Congresswoman Patsy Mink (D-Hawaii) noted: "I always felt that we [women] were serving a dual role in Congress, representing our own districts and, at the same time, having a voice to the concerns of the total population of women in the country."[203] It is clear that the vast majority of women in Congress feel this way. This sentiment is underscored by quantitative studies of women in Congress, finding that women get women's issues on the agenda, widening the range of policy solutions proposed and framing the policy debate in different terms.[204] Congresswomen give more attention and support to women's issues than men, regardless of their party affiliation or ideology.[205] Overwhelmingly, women members introduce most women's legislation.[206] Women are also more likely than men to cosponsor legislation dealing with women's issues.[207]

Women use the Congressional Caucus for Women's Issues to champion women's issues.[208] Without Caucus initiatives, many women's policies would not have been enacted.[209] Strategic positions by women legislators make the difference in drafting legislation and on the floor.[210] Women use their positions on committees to advance legislation benefiting women. Women also use conference committee assignments to advance and protect women's policy issues.[211] However, women continue to be overlooked for committee chairmanships.

Thirty decades of methodologically sophisticated social science research proves women make a difference. The question now should be how to get more women elected to public office.

PROBLEMS FACED BY WOMEN IN APPOINTED POSITIONS

Many of the problems faced by women in elective office also apply to women in appointed governmental positions. Until recently, women have made few inroads in this area.

The Executive Branch

Franklin D. Roosevelt was the first president to select a woman for a cabinet-level position—Frances Perkins as Secretary of Labor in 1933. FDR also appointed an African American woman, Mary McLeod Bethune, to the board of the National Youth Administration. She and three African American men constituted the "black cabinet" in the Roosevelt administration, advising the president on issues affecting their race.[212] Since Jimmy Carter's presidency, every president has appointed one or two women to his cabinet. (See Table 2.6.)

TABLE 2.6 **Cabinet Positions Held by Women**

Year Appointed	Department	Person	President
1933	Labor	Frances Perkins	Roosevelt/ Truman
1953	Health, Education, and Welfare	Oveta Culp Hobby	Eisenhower
1975–77	Housing and Urban Development	Carla Anderson Hills	Ford
1977	Commerce	Juanita M. Kreps	Carter
1979	Housing and Urban Development	Patricia Roberts Harris	Carter
1979	Health and Human Services	Patricia Roberts Harris	Carter
1979	Education	Shirley Mount Hufstedler	Carter
1981	United Nations Ambassador[a]	Jeane Kirkpatrick	Reagan
1983	Health and Human Services	Margaret M. Heckler	Reagan
1983	Transportation	Elizabeth H. Dole	Reagan
1987	Labor	Ann Dore McLaughlin	Reagan
1989	Special Trade Representative[a]	Carla Anderson Hills	Bush
1989	Labor	Elizabeth H. Dole	Bush
1991	Labor	Lynn Martin	Bush
1992	Commerce	Barbara H. Franklin	Bush
1993	Energy	Hazel O'Leary	Clinton
1993/1997	Health and Human Services	Donna Shalala	Clinton
1993/1997	Attorney General	Janet Reno	Clinton
1993	United Nations Ambassador[a]	Madeleine K. Albright	Clinton
1997	State	Madeleine K. Albright	Clinton
1997	Labor	Alexis Herman	Clinton
2000	Labor	Elaine Chao	G. W. Bush
2000	Interior	Gale Norton	G. W. Bush
2000	Agriculture	Anne Veneman	G. W. Bush

[a] Presidents Reagan and Clinton included this as a cabinet position.

Clinton's desire to appoint a first-term cabinet that looked "like America," along with pressure from the Coalition for Women's Appointments, which decided it was time to go after one of the "big four" power positions—Defense, State, Justice, and Treasury—resulted in his selection of four women to that cabinet, including the first woman to serve as attorney general, heading the Justice Department.

In his second term, Clinton again nominated four women to cabinet posts, including the first woman, Madeleine Albright, to the second of the "big four" slots: the State Department. "She's a strong lady. She is a courageous lady," said Senator Jesse Helms (R-N.C.), not one known for bestowing accolades on Democratic nominees.[213] A protégé of former National Security Advisor Zbigniew Brzezinski during the Carter years, Albright was serving as chief delegate to the United Nations when Clinton tapped her to lead his foreign policy team.

In 2001, President George W. Bush appointed three women to his cabinet, although none held "big four" slots. Additional elite women initially serving in the Bush administration included Condoleezza Rice, the first woman to serve as National Security Advisor; Karen Hughes, White House Counselor; Mary Matalin, Assistant to the President; and Christine Todd Whitman, Administrator of the Environmental Protection Agency.

Recent research by MaryAnne Borrelli finds evidence of gender bias in both the nomination and confirmation process for cabinet secretaries. Borrelli argues that although presidents clearly recognize women as a constituency, the media and the Senate perceive only men as fully qualified to lead. Borrelli describes women cabinet secretaries as "routinized tokens," concluding that, "Too often, the women nominees have contributed more to the image than to the practice of gender inclusivity, the mechanisms for decision-making reinforcing the harsh dictates of masculinism."[214]

The Federal Judiciary

Former President Clinton appointed record-breaking numbers of women to the federal bench, including 28.5 percent of District Court seats and 32.8 percent of Appeals Court seats.[215] In addition, Clinton appointed Ruth Bader Ginsburg to the U.S. Supreme Court. As indicated in Table 2.7, this record was an improvement over that of his predecessors. In 1981, Ronald Reagan had appointed Sandra Day O'Connor the first woman to the Supreme Court, but he nominated only twenty-eight women to fill the 368 judicial vacancies that arose in his eight years in office. Most observers believe Reagan had a hard time finding women who could meet his strict test of ideological conservatism. George H. W. Bush appointed fewer women, but they comprised a larger percentage of his overall appointments than Reagan's.[216] George H. W. Bush is likely to be remembered, however, for his nomination of Clarence Thomas to the Supreme Court, an act that mobilized many women to run against Senators who voted to confirm the man accused of sexually harassing Anita Hill.

TABLE 2.7 **Diversity on the Bench: New Seats and Minority Seats**

Proportion of nontraditional lifetime judges in active service on courts of general jurisdiction November 3, 1992, through January 1, 2001

	1992 % (N)	2001 % (N)	% increase
U.S. District Courts			
Women	10.5%[a] (68)	18.9%[b] (130)	91.2%
African American	5.3% (34)	10.7% (71)	108.8%
Hispanic	4.5% (29)	4.7% (31)	8.9%
Asian	0.6% (4)	0.8% (5)	25.0%
Native American	0.0% (0)	0.2% (1)	NA
Total nontraditional	19.1% (123)	32.2% (214)	74.0%
U.S. Courts of Appeals			
Women	13.2%[c] (22)	21.0%[c] (35)	59.1%
African American	5.4% (9)	7.1%[d] (12)	33.3%
Hispanic	2.4% (4)	6.0% (10)	150.0%
Asian	0.6% (1)	0.6% (1)	0.0%
Total nontraditional	21.0% (35)	31.1% (52)	48.8%
U.S. Supreme Court			
Women	11.1%[e] (1)	22.2%[e] (2)	100.0%
African American	11.1% (1)	11.1% (1)	—
Total nontraditional	22.2% (2)	33.3% (3)	50.0%
All three court levels			
Women	11.1% (91)	19.9% (167)	83.5%
African American	5.4% (44)	10.1%[d] (84)	90.9%
Hispanic	4.0% (33)	4.9% (41)	24.2%
Asian	0.6% (5)	0.6% (6)	20.0%
Native American	0.0% (0)	0.1% (1)	NA
Total nontraditional	19.5% (160)	32.0% (269)	68.1%

The total does not double count those who were classified in more than one category.

[a] Out of 645 authorized lifetime positions on the U.S. district courts in 1992.

[b] Out of 664 authorized lifetime positions on the U.S. district courts in 2001.

[c] Out of 167 authorized lifetime positions on the numbered circuits and the U.S. Court of Appeals for the District of Columbia Circuit, all courts of general jurisdiction.

[d] Includes Roger Gregory, given a recess appointment on December 27, 2000.

[e] Out of nine authorized positions on the U.S. Supreme Court.

In sharp contrast, Clinton's first appointment to the U.S. Supreme Court, Ruth Bader Ginsburg, was not only a coauthor of the first important text on sex discrimination,[217] but also the architect of the legal strategy to convince the Supreme Court to apply the equal protection clause of the Fourteenth Amendment to invalidate gender-based laws.[218] A moderate with impeccable credentials, Ginsburg fits the pattern that defines Clinton's judicial legacy. As seen in Table 2.7, Clinton had a dramatic impact on the diversification of the federal judiciary.

George W. Bush, as governor, appointed four Texas Supreme Court judges; one was a woman and all four were considered moderate on controversial issues such as abortion.[219] Two years into his presidency, twenty-one (19 percent) of Bush's 110 confirmed nominees were women.

IMPACT OF WOMEN IN APPOINTED POSITIONS

With more women selected to serve in the executive and judicial branches, an interesting question is whether they, like their sisters in the legislative branches, act in ways distinct from men. Research on this question generally finds they do. Among President Carter's executive-branch appointees, the women were found to be more feminist than the men; so, too, were women appointed to high state government positions.[220] Women appointees in the Clinton administration, moreover, appeared to select more women to serve under them than did men, thus bringing more women into the opportunity structure. As Secretary of State during the Clinton administration, Madeleine Albright launched the Vital Voices Democracy Initiative to promote the advancement of women as a U.S. foreign policy objective. An outgrowth of the U.N. Fourth World Conference on Women in Beijing, Vital Voices coordinates conferences throughout the world to help establish a global network of women and to provide women with the resources to empower themselves.[221]

The impact of women judges is beginning to be evaluated. There is evidence that women judges generally are more supportive of women in court.[222] Their very presence on the bench, particularly at the appellate level, seems to make other jurists more sensitive to problems of sex discrimination. It appears that during her first term on the Supreme Court, Sandra Day O'Connor, although generally voting with the conservative bloc of the Court, adopted positions advocated by women's rights activists in gender-based discrimination cases 66 percent of the time. Just as important was the fact that all eight other justices became more supportive of women's rights claims after she joined the Court.[223] Clearly her vote in *Planned Parenthood of Southeastern Pennsylvania v. Casey* (1992)[224] was crucial in convincing two other justices not to overrule *Roe v. Wade* (1973).[225] The appointment of Ruth Bader Ginsburg in 1993 added an even more vocal advocate of gender equality.

The fact that large numbers of women have been appointed to the federal bench has prompted more women to run for state court judgeships and has led to wider public acceptance of women in these positions. Ultimately, however, the number of women in appointed positions (both judicial and executive) will depend on the chief executive.

CONCLUSION

Five interrelated barriers exist that continue to prevent women from fully exercising their political rights: (1) stereotypes, (2) career choice and preparation, (3) family demands, (4) sex discrimination, and (5) the political system. As the discussion of various political activities has shown, these obstacles have gradually diminished. Indeed, with respect to certain citizen-level activities, women today face few difficulties in participating on an equal footing with men. Barriers to political activity, while diminished since 1920, can still be formidable. System-level barriers, especially those that favor incumbents, make it difficult for women to reach parity even if the public and male party officials are increasingly enlightened as to the need to elect and appoint more women to public office.

The women's rights movement has had an impact on all aspects of women's involvement in politics. Women's groups support women who run for office and pressure governors and presidents to appoint more women. And there is evidence that once they are in office, women, especially feminist women, are more likely to return the favor by supporting legislation and policies benefiting women.

Yet the nation is far from achieving the goal of political equality voiced by the women at Seneca Falls and supposedly achieved by the leaders of the suffrage movement. As former U.S. Representative Patricia Schroeder observes, "We've passed laws, but we haven't changed attitudes; we must now engage in some serious culture-cracking." She urged, "Young women, take government back. . . . Don't wring your hands about government—roll up your sleeves and do something about it!"[226]

NOTES

1. This figure and those that follow are reported in Hazel Erskine, "The Polls: Women's Role," *Public Opinion Quarterly* 35 (1971): 275–90.
2. Kristi Andersen, *After Suffrage: Women in Partisan and Electoral Politics Before the New Deal* (Chicago: University of Chicago Press, 1996), 13–14.
3. E. M. Schreiber, "Education and Change in Opinions on a Woman for President," *Public Opinion Quarterly* 42 (1978): 171–82. See also Myra Marx Ferree, "A Woman for President? Changing Responses: 1958–1972," *Public Opinion Quarterly* 38 (1974): 390–99.
4. Sandra Baxter and Marjorie Lansing, *Women and Politics: The Invisible Majority* (Ann Arbor: University of Michigan Press, 1980), 140.
5. *The Gallup Report*, no. 191, August 1981, 4.
6. "Election 1992," *Chicago Tribune*, June 28, 1992: 4C.
7. "Majority of Americans Say More Women in Political Office Would Be Positive for the Country," *Gallup Poll Release*, January 4, 2001, http://www.gallup.com/poll/releases/pr010104.asp.
8. Data from the 2000 Virginia Slims Opinion Poll conducted by Roper Starch Worldwide Inc. Data provided by Philip Morris, USA.
9. General Social Science 1972–2000 Cumulative Datafile, http://csa.Berkeley.edu:7502/cgi-bin12/hsda3.

10. "Women in Elected Office," report prepared for Deloitte and Touche by Roper Starch Worldwide, Inc. (2000). Data provided by Deloitte and Touche.

11. 2000 Virginia Slims Opinion Poll.

12. Dianne Owen and Jack Dennis, "Gender Differences in the Politicization of American Children," *Women & Politics* 8 (1988): 30–33.

13. 2000 Virginia Slims Opinion Poll.

14. The White House Project, "Barbie Is Running for President! President Barbie Plays a Key Role in The White House Project's 'Pipeline to the Presidency Strategy.'" Press Release, April 19, 2000, http://www.thewhitehouseproject.org/news.html.

15. Lake Snell Perry and Associates, "Pipeline to the Future: Young Women and Political Leadership," The White House Project 2000, http://www.womensleadershipfund.org/programs/youth_research.pdf.

16. Virginia Sapiro, *The Political Integration of Women* (Urbana: University of Illinois Press, 1983).

17. Sue Tolleson Rinehart, "The Life Course and Intergenerational Change: A Brief Note on the Transmission of Political Roles from Mother to Daughter" (paper delivered at the annual meeting of the American Political Science Association, Washington, D.C., 1988), 23.

18. Kay Lehman Schlozman, Nancy Burns, and Sidney Verba, "Gender and the Pathways to Participation: The Role of Resources," *Journal of Politics* 56 (1994): 984.

19. Charles Merriam and Harold Gosnell, *Non-Voting: Causes and Methods of Control* (Chicago: University of Chicago Press, 1924), 37.

20. Ibid., 113.

21. Nancy E. McGlen and Karen O'Connor, *Women's Rights: The Struggle for Equality in the 19th and 20th Centuries* (New York: Praeger, 1983), 89.

22. Sidney Verba and Norman H. Nie, *Participation in America: Political Democracy and Social Equality* (New York: Harper and Row, 1972), 83.

23. Merriam and Gosnell, *Non-Voting*, 161.

24. Judy Bertelsen, "Political Interest, Influence, and Efficacy: Differences between the Sexes and among Marital Status Groups," *American Politics Quarterly* 2 (1974): 415.

25. Social Capital Benchmark Survey, Saguaro Seminar on Civic Engagement in America, John F. Kennedy School of Government, Harvard University (2000), http://www.ropercenter.uconn.edu.

26. In 1940, only 23 percent of all women but 33 percent of all men in Erie County, Ohio, expressed an interest in that year's presidential campaign. Paul Lazarsfeld, Bernard Berelson, and Hazel Gaudet, *The People's Choice*, 3rd ed. (New York: Columbia University Press, 1968), 45. See also Angus Campbell et al., *The American Voter* (New York: Wiley, 1960), 489; Susan Welch, "Women as Political Animals? A Test of Some Explanations for Male-Female Differences in Political Participation Differences," *American Journal of Political Science* 21 (1977): 723; McGlen and O'Connor, *Women's Rights*, 90.

27. Nancy Burns, Kay Lehman Schlozman, and Sidney Verba, *The Private Roots of Public Action: Gender, Equality, and Political Participation* (Cambridge: Harvard University Press, 2001), 102–3.

28. Laura van Assendelft and Karen O'Connor, "Backgrounds, Motivations and Interests: A Comparison of Male and Female Local Party Activists," *Women & Politics* 14 (1994): 77–92.

29. Linda Sax, Jennifer Lindholm, Alexander Astin, William Kern, and Kathryn Mahoney, *The American Freshman: National Norms for Fall 2002* (Los Angeles: Higher Education Research Institute, UCLA, 2002).

30. Jeffrey J. Mondak and Mary R. Anderson, "A Knowledge Gap or a Guessing Game?" *Public Perspective* (March/April 2003), 6–9.
31. Merriam and Gosnell, *Non-Voting*, 37.
32. John W. Soule and Wilma E. McGrath, "A Comparative Study of Male-Female Political Attitudes at Citizen and Elite Levels," in *A Portrait of Marginality*, ed. Marianne Githens and Jewel L. Prestage (New York: McKay, 1977), 183.
33. 2000 NES data analyzed by authors.
34. 2000 Social Capital Benchmark Survey.
35. 2000 Social Community Benchmark Survey.
36. Schlozman, Burns, and Verba, "Gender and the Pathways," 972–85.
37. Quoted in Andersen, *After Suffrage*, 101.
38. Barbara Mikulski et al., *Nine and Counting: The Women of the Senate* (New York: HarperCollins, 2001), 40.
39. Quoted in Irene Natividad, "Women of Color and the Campaign Trail," in *The American Woman: 1992–1993*, ed. Paula Ries and Anne J. Stone (New York: Norton, 1992), 136.
40. Andersen, *After Suffrage*, chap. 3.
41. Ibid, 56.
42. Susan J. Carroll and Wendy S. Strimling, *Women's Routes to Elective Office: A Comparison with Men's* (New Brunswick, N.J.: Center for the American Woman and Politics, 1983), 88.
43. Andersen, *After Suffrage*, 66.
44. Kristi Andersen, "Generation, Partisan Shift, and Realignment," in *The Changing American Voter*, ed. Norman H. Nie, Sidney Verba, and John R. Petrocick (Cambridge: Harvard University Press, 1976), 74–95. Other research suggests that the 1928 presidential campaign, with a Catholic presidential candidate, mobilized many immigrant women.
45. Courtney Brown, *Ballots of Tumult* (Ann Arbor: University of Michigan Press, 1992); Andersen, "Generation, Partisan Shift, and Realignment," 90.
46. "Sex Differences in Voter Turnout," *CAWP Fact Sheet*, March 2002. Data from the U.S. Bureau of the Census.
47. Baxter and Lansing, *Women and Politics*, 101–2, 107–10.
48. Susan A. MacManus, Charles S. Bullock III, and Barbara P. Grothe, "A Longitudinal Examination of Political Participation Rates of Mexican American Females," *Social Science Quarterly* 67 (1986): 605, 610.
49. C. Richard Hofstetter and William A. Schultze, "Some Observations about Participation and Attitudes among Single Parent Women: Inferences Concerning Political Translation," *Women & Politics* 9 (1989): 93.
50. U.S. Census Bureau, "Voting and Registration in the Election of November 2000," Current Population Reports P20-542, February, 2002.
51. Tom W. Smith, "The Polls: Gender and Attitudes toward Violence," *Public Opinion Quarterly* 48 (1984): 384–96.
52. "Women and the Use of Force," *Public Perspective* 2, no. 3 (1991): 85–86.
53. David W. Moore, "War Support and the Education Gap," *Gallup News Service*, February 11, 2003.
54. David W. Moore, "For One-Third of Americans, 9/11 Was a 'Life-Altering' Experience," *Gallup News Service*, January 2, 2002.
55. Center for Gender Equality, "National Survey of Women Post-September 11 Reveals Women Are Slightly More Concerned About Financial Security Than Being the Victim of a Terrorist Attack," *PR Newswire*, December 6, 2001.

56. David W. Moore, "War Support and the Education Gap."
57. Frank Newport, David W. Moore, Jeffrey M. Jones, and Lydia Saad, "Special Release: American Opinion on the War," *Gallup News Release*, March 21, 2003, http://www.gallup.com/poll/tb/goverpubli/20030325.asp.
58. Lydia Saad, "Pondering Women's Issues, Part II" *Gallup Poll Report*, February 18, 2003.
59. Center for the American Woman and Politics, *CAWP Fact Sheet*, September 1992.
60. Pamela Johnston Conover, "Feminists and the Gender Gap," *Journal of Politics* 50 (1988): 985–1010. Others disagree with Conover's results; see Elizabeth Adell Cook and Clyde Wilcox, "Feminists and the Gender Gap—A Second Look," *Journal of Politics* 53 (1991): 1111–22. Research on women's foreign policy views finds occupation can make a difference. See Nancy E. McGlen and Meredith Reid Sarkees, *Women and Foreign Policy: The Insiders* (New York: Routledge, 1993).
61. Sax et al., *The American Freshman: National Norms for Fall 2002*.
62. Kathleen Dolan, "Electoral Context, Issues, and Voting for Women in the 1990s," *Women and Politics* 23 (2001): 21–36.
63. Linda Witt, Karen M. Paget, and Glenna Matthews. *Running as a Woman: Gender and Power in American Politics*. (New York: Free Press), 153–80.
64. Jane Mansbridge, "Myth and Reality: The ERA and the Gender Gap in the 1980 Election," *Public Opinion Quarterly* 49 (1985): 164–78.
65. Kathleen Frankovic, "Sex and Politics—New Alignments, Old Issues," *PS: Political Science and Politics* 15 (1982): 439–48.
66. Frances F. Piven, "Women and the State: Ideology, Power and the Welfare State," in *Gender and the Life Course*, ed. Alice S. Rossie (New York: Aldine, 1985); Martin Gillens, "Gender and Support for Reagan: A Comprehensive Model of Presidential Approval," *American Journal of Political Science* 32: 19–49; and Mary E. Bendyna and Celinda C. Lake, "Gender and Voting in the 1992 Presidential Election," in *Year of the Woman: Myths and Realities*, ed. Elizabeth Adell Cook, Sue Thomas, and Clyde Wilcox (Boulder, Colo.: Westview Press, 1994).
67. Karen M. Kaufman and John R. Petrocik, "The Changing Politics of American Men: Understanding the Sources of the Gender Gap," *American Journal of Political Science* 43 (1999): 864–87.
68. Janet A. Flamming. *Women's Political Voice: How Women Are Transforming the Practice and the Study of Politics* (Philadelphia: Temple University Press, 1997); Carole Kennedy Chaney, R. Michael Alvarez, and Jonathan Nagler, "Explaining the Gender Gap in U.S. Presidential Elections, 1980–1992," *Political Research Quarterly* 51, no. 2 (June 1998): 311–39.
69. Anna Greenburg, "Deconstructing the Gender Gap," a working paper accessed April 25, 2003 at http://www.ksg.Harvard.edu/prg/greenb/gengap.htm.
70. Quoted in Diane Minor, "New Year, New Congress," *National NOW Times*, January 1997, 1.
71. Andersen, *After Suffrage*, 13–14.
72. Janet K. Boles, "Local Based Social Welfare Policies: The Impact of Local Feminist Networks" (paper delivered at the annual meeting of the Midwest Political Science Association, Chicago, 1988); Woliver, *From Outrage to Action*; Irene Diamond, ed., *Families, Politics, and Public Policy* (New York: Longman, 1983).
73. Vicki L. Crawford, Jacqueline Anne Rouse, and Barbara Woods, eds., *Women in the Civil Rights Movement: Trailblazers and Torchbearers, 1941–1965* (Brooklyn, N.Y.: Carlson, 1990); Jo Anne Gibson, *The Montgomery Bus Boycott and the Women Who Started It* (Knoxville: University of Tennessee Press, 1987).

74. Profile of Nydia M. Veláquez, "The New Congress," *Congressional Quarterly Report* 51, supplement to no. 3 (1993): 113.
75. Kay Lehman Schlozman, Nancy Burns, Sidney Verba, and Jesse Donahue, "Gender and Citizen Participation: Is There a Different Voice?" *American Journal of Political Science* 39 (1995): 274.
76. Ibid., 281–83.
77. Robert Putnam, *Bowling Alone: The Collapse and Revival of American Community* (New York: Simon and Schuster, 2000), and *The Status of Women in the States* (New York: Simon and Schuster, 2000).
78. Amy Caiazza and Robert D. Putnam, "Women's Status and Social Capital Across the States," Briefing Paper, Institute of Women's Policy Research, 2002.
79. Andersen, *After Suffrage*, chap. 6.
80. Ibid., 40–45.
81. Kristi Andersen, "Working Women and Political Participation, 1952–1972," *American Journal of Political Science* 19 (1975): 442.
82. 2000 NES data analyzed by authors.
83. Schlozman, Burns, and Verba, "Gender and Pathways," 980–85.
84. Edmond Costantini, "Political Women and Political Ambition," *American Journal of Politics* 34 (1990): 763–65.
85. van Assendelft and O'Connor, "Backgrounds, Motivations and Interests."
86. Natividad, "Women of Color," 129.
87. Burrell, *A Woman's Place*, 90.
88. Ronald B. Rapoport, Walter J. Stone, and Alan I. Abramowitz, "Sex and the Caucus Participant: The Gender Gap and Presidential Nominating Conventions," *American Journal of Political Science* 34 (1990): 725–40.
89. van Assendelft and O'Connor, "Backgrounds, Motivations and Interests."
90. "Women in the U.S. Congress 1993," *CAWP Fact Sheet*, January 1993, 2; "Women in State Legislatures 1993," *CAWP Fact Sheet*, January 1993, 1.
91. "Women of Color in Elective Office 2001," *CAWP Fact Sheet*, February, 2001.
92. "Women in Elective Office 2003," *CAWP Fact Sheet*, February 2003.
93. "Women of Color in Elective Office 2003" *CAWP Fact Sheet*, February 2003.
94. Ibid.
95. "Election 2000: Summary of Results for Women," *CAWP Fact Sheet*, November 2000; "Election 2000: Firsts and Records for Women in Congressional and Statewide Races," *CAWP Fact Sheet*, November 2000.
96. "Women in Elective Office 2003," *CAWP Fact Sheet*, March 2003.
97. "First Election Results Show Women Losing Ground," *CAWP Press Release*, January 2, 2003.
98. Burrell, *A Woman's Place*, 90.
99. Richard L. Fox and Jennifer L. Lawless, "The Gender Gap in Candidate Emergence: Sex Differences in Political Ambition" (paper presented at the annual meeting of the Midwest Political Science Association, Chicago, Illinois, April 3–6, 2003).
100. The states with the lowest percentages were South Carolina (9.4), Alabama (10.0), Kentucky (10.9), Oklahoma (11.4), Mississippi (12.6), Pennsylvania (13.8), North Dakota (14.9), Louisiana (15.3), Virginia (15.7), and South Dakota (16.2), "Women in State Legislatures 2003," *CAWP Fact Sheet*, February 2003.
101. Costantini, "Political Women and Political Ambition," 749–51. See also van Assendelft and O'Connor, "Backgrounds, Motivations and Interests." Susan Carroll also finds some evidence of low career ambitions among women elected offi-

cials. Susan J. Carroll, *Women as Candidates in American Politics* (Bloomington: Indiana University Press, 1985), chap. 7.

102. Fox and Lawless. "The Gender Gap in Candidate Emergence," 7–8.

103. Lake Snell Perry and Associates, "Pipeline to the Future: Young Women and Political Leadership," The White House Project 2000, http://www.womensleadershipfund.org/programs/youth_research.pdf.

104. Kim Fridkin Kahn, "Does Gender Make a Difference? An Experimental Examination of Sex Stereotypes and Press Patterns in Statewide Campaigns," *American Journal of Political Science* 38 (1994): 168–70.

105. Ibid., 185–91.

106. James Devitt, "Framing Gender on the Campaign Trail: Women's Executive Leadership and the Press." *Report to the Women's Leadership Fund* (1999): 12.

107. Ibid.

108. Martha E. Kropf and John A. Boiney, "The Electoral Glass Ceiling? Gender, Viability, and the News in U.S. Senate Campaigns" *Women & Politics* 23 (2001): 79–101.

109. Caroline Heldman, Susan J. Carroll, and Stephanie Olson, "Gender Differences in Print Media Coverage of Presidential Candidates: Elizabeth Dole's Bid for the Republican Nomination" (prepared for delivery at the annual meeting of the American Political Science Association, Washington, D.C., August 31–September 3, 2000).

110. Robin Gerber, "Female Candidates Still Battle for Serious Attention," *USA Today*, January 3, 2002: A11.

111. Leonard Williams, "Political Advertising in the Year of the Woman," in *The Year of the Woman: Myths and Realities*, ed. Elizabeth Adell Cook, Sue Thomas, and Clyde Wilcox (Boulder, Colo.: Westview Press, 1994), 202.

112. "Barriers and Opportunities to Women's Executive Leadership: Results and Strategic Recommendations from Dial Groups," The White House Project 2002, http://www.thewhitehouseproject.org.

113. R. Darcy, Susan Welch, and Janet Clark, *Women, Elections, and Representation* (New York: Longman, 1987), 93–108.

114. Christine B. Williams, "Women, Law and Politics: Recruitment Patterns in the Fifty States," *Women & Politics* 10 (1990): 103–23.

115. "Women in the U.S. House of Representatives 2003," *CAWP Fact Sheet*, January 2003.

116. Carroll and Strimling, *Women's Routes to Elective Office*, 17–23.

117. Andrea Stone and Dee Ann Glasmer, "Lawmakers and Laws Change," *USA Today*, February 12, 1993: 6.

118. Quoted in Jeane J. Kirkpatrick, *Political Woman* (New York: Basic Books, 1974), 235.

119. Ibid., 234–35.

120. Carroll and Strimling, *Women's Routes to Elective Office*, 28–9.

121. Virginia Sapiro, "Private Costs of Public Commitments or Public Costs of Private Commitments? Family Roles versus Political Ambition," *American Journal of Political Science* 26 (1982): 265–79.

122. Jennifer Frey, "Supermom's Power Trip," *Washington Post*, January 22, 2000, C1.

123. Pamela Ferdinand, "Childbirth Only One of Governor's Challenges," *Washington Post*, May 11, 2001, A3.

124. Associated Press, "Massachusetts Governor Drops Election Bid," *New York Times*, March 19, 2002.

125. Jane Ciabattari, "Who Would You Vote For?" *Parade Magazine*, June 2, 2002, 6.

126. Deloitte and Touche (2000).

127. Joanne Bay Brzynski and Bernadette Nye, "Recruitment of Women Candidates in the 1992 Congressional Election" (paper delivered at the annual meeting of the American Political Science Association, Washington, D.C., 1993), 6.

128. Dana Milbank and Thomas B. Edsall, "Chavez Pulls Out as Labor Nominee, Bush Pick Acknowledges She 'Wasn't Forthcoming' on Illegal Immigrant Issue," *Washington Post*, January 10, 2001, A1.

129. Marilyn Johnson and Susan Carroll with Kathy Stanwyck and Lynn Korenblit, *Profile of Women Holding Office*, 2 (Metuchen, N.J.: Scarecrow Press, 1978), 17A; and Carroll, *Women as Candidates*, 30.

130. Carroll and Strimling, *Women's Routes to Elective Office*, 24–26.

131. Carroll, *Women as Candidates*, 30–56.

132. Elizabeth A. Brown, "Why Most Public Officials Are Still Men," *Christian Science Monitor*, February 15, 1991, 11.

133. Carroll and Strimling, *Women's Routes to Elective Office*, 61–82; Darcy, Welch, and Clark, *Women, Elections, and Representation*, 35–36.

134. R. Darcy, Charles D. Hadley, and Jason F. Kirksey, "Electoral Systems and the Representation of Black Women in American State Legislatures," *Women & Politics* 13 (1993): 73–6.

135. Natividad, "Women of Color," 134–8.

136. R. Darcy and Charles D. Hadley, "Black Women in Politics: The Puzzle of Success," *Social Science Quarterly* 69 (1988): 633.

137. Dan Balz, "Dole Drops Bid for GOP Nomination," *Washington Post*, October 21, 1999, A1.

138. Both the Carroll study of women candidates in 1976 and the Carroll and Strimling research on women elected officials in the 1980s found women complaining about a lack of funds. Carroll, *Women as Candidates*, 49–55; Carroll and Strimling, *Women's Routes to Elective Office*, 111–3.

139. Gary C. Jacobson, *The Politics of Congressional Elections*, 5th ed. (New York: Longman, 2000), 40.

140. Peter L. Francia, "Early Fundraising by Nonincumbent Female Congressional Candidates: The Importance of Women's PACs," *Women & Politics*, 23 nos.1–2 (2001): 7–20.

141. Christine L. Day and Charles D. Hadley, "Who Contributes? Similarities and Differences Between Contributors to EMILY's List and WISH List," *Women & Politics* 24 (2002): 53–67.

142. Burrell, *A Woman's Place*, 105.

143. Francia, "Early Fundraising by Nonincumbent Female Congressional Candidates."

144. Quoted in Beth Donovan, "Women's Campaigns Fueled Mostly by Women's Checks," *Congressional Quarterly Weekly Report* 50, no. 41 (1992): 3270.

145. Natividad, "Women of Color," 133–4.

146. Lonnae O'Neal Parker, "Essence," http://www.essence.com/workandwealth/atwork/0,16109,411669,00.html.

147. Quoted in Anita Shreve and John Clemans, "The New Wave of Women Politicians," *New York Times Magazine*, October 19, 1980, 31.

148. "Women's PAC and Donor Networks: A Contact List," *CAWP Fact Sheet*, October 1999.

149. Carroll, *Women as Candidates*, 51–6.

150. Burrell, *A Woman's Place*, 94–8.

151. "Election 2002: Summary of Women Candidates," *CAWP Fact Sheet*, February 2003; "Women in Elective Office 2003," *CAWP Fact Sheet*, February, 2003.

152. Francia, "Early Fundraising by Nonincumbent Female Congressional Candidates."

153. "Women in State Legislatures 2001" *CAWP Fact Sheet*, February 2001.

154. Kim U. Hoffman, Carrie Palmer, and Ronald Keith Gaddie, "Candidate Sex and Congressional Elections: Open Seats Before, During, and After the Year of the Woman," *Women & Politics* 23 (2001): 37–58.

155. Quoted in Stone and Glasmer, "Lawmakers and Laws Change," 6.

156. "Why Women Matter: Lessons About Women's Political Leadership From Home and Abroad," The White House Project 2003, 12.

157. Rebecca Howard Davis, *Women and Power in Parliamentary Democracies: Cabinet Appointments in Western Europe, 1968–1992* (Lincoln: University of Nebraska Press, 1997).

158. Wilma Rule, "Electoral Systems, Contextual Factors and Women's Opportunity for Election to Parliament in Twenty-three Democracies," *Western Political Quarterly* 40 (1987): 477–98. The same problem affects women running for local office. In localities with multicandidate races, women are more likely to get nominated and elected. Carroll, *Women as Candidates*, 40–41, 107–8.

159. Darcy, Hadley, and Kirksey, "Electoral Systems," 74, 85; Wilma Rule, "Why More Women Are State Legislators: A Research Note," *Western Political Quarterly* 43 (1990): 437–48.

160. Sue Thomas, "Women in State Legislatures: One Step at a Time," in *The Year of the Woman*, ed. Cook, Thomas, and Wilcox, 146.

161. Barbara Palmer and Dennis Simon, "The Political Glass Ceiling: Gender, Strategy, and Incumbency in U.S. House Elections, 1978–1998," *Women & Politics* 23 (2001): 59–78.

162. "Women Candidates for Congress 1974–2000," *CAWP Fact Sheet*, November 2000; "Women Candidates for Congress and Statewide Office," *CAWP Fact Sheet*, December, 2002.

163. David L. Nixon and R. Darcy, "Special Elections and the Growth of Women's Representation in the House of Representatives," *Women & Politics*, 16 (1996): 102.

164. Kim Fridkin Kahn and Edie N. Goldenberg, "Evaluations of Male and Female U.S. Senate Candidates: An Investigation of Media Influence" (paper delivered at the annual meeting of the Midwest Political Science Association, Chicago, 1988). See also Pippa Norris, ed., *Women, Media and Politics* (New York: Oxford University Press, 1996), and Kim Fridkin Kahn, *The Politics of Being a Woman: How Stereotypes Influence the Conduct and Consequences of Political Campaigns* (New York: Columbia University Press, 1996).

165. Quoted in Brown, "Why Most Public Officials Are Still Men."

166. Kathleen Dolan, "Electoral Context, Issues, and Voting for Women in the 1990s" *Women and Politics* 23 (2001): 21–36.

167. Paul S. Herrnson, J. Celeste Lay, and Atiya Kai Stokes, "Women Running 'as Women': Candidate Gender, Campaign Issues, and Voter-Targeting Strategies," *Journal of Politics* 65 (2003): 244–55.

168. Sue Carroll and Krista Jenkins, "Term Limits and the Representation of Women, Minorities, and Minority Women: Evidence from the State Legislative Elections of 1998" (paper delivered at the annual meeting of the Southern Political Science Association, Savannah, Georgia, November 3–6, 1999).

169. *U.S. Term Limits, Inc. v. Thornton*, 115 U.S. 1842 (1995).

170. "Women Candidates for Congress 1974–2000," *CAWP Fact Sheet*, November 2000. 2000 statistics updated by author.

171. See generally Karen Foerstel and Herbert N. Foerstel, *Climbing the Hill: Gender Conflict in Congress* (New York: Praeger, 1996); Clara Bingham, *Women on the Hill: Challenging the Culture of Congress* (New York: Times Books, 1997).

172. Debra L. Dodson and Susan J. Carroll, *Reshaping the Agenda: Women in the State Legislatures* (New Brunswick, N.J.: Center for the American Woman and Politics, 1991), 87.

173. Donna Cassata, "Leadership Lineup Stays Intact, but Centrists Gain Influence," *Congressional Quarterly Weekly Report* 54, no. 47 (1996): 3304.

174. "Women in State Legislatures, 2003," *CAWP Fact Sheet*, February, 2003.

175. Susan J. Carroll and Ella Taylor, "Gender Differences in the Committee Assignments of State Legislators: Preferences or Discrimination?" (paper delivered at the annual meeting of the Midwest Political Science Association, Chicago, 1989).

176. Kathleen Dolan and Lynne E. Ford, "Women in the State Legislatures: Feminist Identity and Legislative Behaviors," *American Politics Quarterly*, 23 (1995): 96–108.

177. "Women State Legislators," *CAWP Fact Sheet*, December 2001.

178. Sally Friedman, "Committee Assignments of Women and Blacks in Congress: 1964–1990" (paper delivered at the annual meeting of the Midwest Political Science Association, Chicago, 1990).

179. "Women in Congress: Leadership Roles and Committee Chairs," *CAWP Fact Sheet*, April 2003.

180. The White House Project, http://www.thewhitehouseproject.org.

181. David Niven and Jeremy Zilber, "How Does She Have Time for Kids and Congress? Views on Gender and Media Coverage from House Offices," *Women & Politics* 23 (2001): 160.

182. *The Concept of Representation* (Berkely: University of California Press, 1967).

183. Jane Mansbridge, "Should Blacks Represent Blacks and Women Represent Women? A Contingent Yes," *Journal of Politics* 61 (1999): 628–57.

184 Lyn Kathlene, "In a Different Voice: Women and the Policy Process," in *Women and Elective Office: Past, Present, and Future*, ed. Sue Thomas and Clyde Wilcox (Boulder, Colo.: Westview Press, 1999); Lyn Kathlene, "Words That Matter: Women's Voice and Institutional Bias in Public Policy Formation," in *The Impact of Women in Public Office*, ed. Susan J. Carroll (Bloomington: Indiana University Press, 2001); Marcia Whicker and Malcolm E. Jewell, "the Feminization of Leadership in State Legislatures," in Thomas and Wilcox, *Women in Elective Office*; and Cindy Simon Rosenthal, "Gender Styles in State Legislative Committees: Raising Their Voices in Resolving Conflict," *Women & Politics* 21 (2001): 21–46.

185. Janet Boles, "Local Elected Women and Policymaking: Movement Delegates or Feminist Trustees," in Carroll, *The Impact of Women in Public Office*; Susan J. Carroll, "Representing Women: Women State Legislators as Agents of Policy-Related Change," in Carroll, *The Impact of Women in Public Office*; Sue Thomas and Susan Welch, "The Impact of Gender on Activities and Priorities of State Legislators," *Western Political Quarterly* 44 (June 1991): 445–56; Sue Thomas, "Why Gender Matters: The Perceptions of Women Officeholders," *Women & Politics* 17 (1997): 27–54; Debra Dodson and Susan J. Carroll, "Reshaping the Agenda: Women in State Legislatures" (New Brunswick, N.J.: Rutgers University, Center for American Women and Politics, 1991); Edith J. Barrett, "Gender and Race in the State House: The Legislative Experience," *Social Science Journal* 34 (1999): 134–44; Shelah Gilbert Leader,

"The Policy Impact of Elected Women Officials," in *The Impact of the Electoral Process*, ed. L. Sandy Maisel and Joseph Cooper (Beverly Hills, Calif.: Sage, 1977); Thomas H. Little, Dana Dunn, and Rebecca Dean, "A View from the Top: Gender Differences in Legislative Priorities Among State Legislative Leaders," *Women & Politics* 22 (2001): 29–50; Beth Ringold, *Representing Women: Sex, Gender, and Legislative Behavior in Arizona and California* (Chapel Hill, University of North Carolina Press, 2000); Michelle A. Saint Germain, "Does Their Difference Make a Difference? The Impact of Women on Public Policy in the Arizona Legislatures," *Social Science Quarterly* 70 (1989): 956–68; and Sue Thomas, *How Women Legislate* (New York: Oxford University Press, 1994).

186. Carroll, *The Impact of Women in Public Office*; Joanne V. Hawks and Carolyn Ellis Staton, "On the Eve of Transition: Women in Southern Legislatures, 1946–1968," in *Women in Politics: Outsiders or Insiders*, ed. Lois Lovelace Duke (Englewood Cliffs, N.J.: Prentice Hall, 1993): Jeanne J. Kirkpatrick, *Political Women* (New York: Basic Books, 1974); and Lynne E. Ford and Kathleen Dolan, "Contemporary Women State Legislators: A Diverse Group With Diverse Agendas," in *Women in Politics: Outsiders or Insiders*, 2nd ed., ed. Lois Lovelace Duke (Englewood Cliffs, N.J.: Prentice Hall, 1996).

187. Boles, "Local Elected Women."

188. Debra L. Dodson, "Acting for Women: Is What State Legislators Say What They Do?" in Carroll, *The Impact of Women in Public Office.*

189. Lilliard E. Richardson Jr. and Patricia Freeman, "Gender Differences in Constituency Service Among State Legislators," *Political Research Quarterly* 48 (1995): 169–79.

190. Susan Abrams Beck, "Acting as Women: The Effects and Limitations of Gender in Local Governance," in Carroll, *The Imact of Women in Public Office.*

191. Thomas, "Why Gender Matters."

192. Beck, "Acting as Women," and Thomas, "Why Gender Matters."

193. Cindy Simon Rosenthal, "Determinants of Collaborative Leadership: Civil Engagement, Gender or Organizational Norms?" *Political Research Quarterly* 51 (1998): 847–68.

194. Kathlene, "Power and Influence"; Janet Flammang, "Female Officials in the Feminist Capital: The Case of Santa Clara County," *Western Political Quarterly* 38 (1985): 94–118.

195. Kathlene, "Power and Influence"; Sue Tolleson Rinehart, "Do Women Leaders Make a Difference? Substance, Style and Percpetions," in *Gender and Policy Making: Studies of Women in Office*, ed. Debra Dodson (New Brunswick, N.J.: Center for American Women and Politics, 1991); Whicker and Jewell, "The Feminization of Leadership in State Legislatures"; and Cindy Simon Rosenthal, "Getting Things Done: Women Committee Chairpersons in State Legislatures," in Thomas and Wilcox, *Women and Elective Office.*

196. Boles, "Local Elected Women."

197. Kathlene, "Words That Matter."

198. Thomas, *How Women Legislate*, and Thomas and Welch, "The Impact of Women."

199. Mark Ellickson and Donald Whistler, "A Path Analysis of Legislative Success in Professional and Citizens Legislatures: A Gender Comparison," *Women & Politics* 21 (2000): 77–103.

200. Sue Thomas and Susan Welch, "The Impact of Women in State Legislatures: Numerical and Organizational Strength," in Carroll, *The Impact of Women in Public Office.*

201. Rosabeth Moss Kantor, *Men and Women of the Corporation* (New York, Basic Books, 1977).

202. Thomas and Welch, "The Impact of Women."

203. Fern S. Ingersoll. "Former Congresswomen Look Back," in *Women in Washington: Advocates for Policy Change*, ed. Irene Tinker (Beverly Hills, Calif.: Sage, 1983).

204. Christina Welch, *The Politics of Women's Rights* (Princeton, N.J.: Princeton University Press, 2000); Debra Dodson et al., *Voices, Views, Votes: The Impact of Women in the 103rd Congress* (New Brunswick, N.J.: Center for American Women and Politics, 1995); Kathleen Frankovic, "Sex and Voting in the U.S. House of Representatives," *American Politics Quarterly* 5 (1977): 315–30; Barbara Burrell, *A Woman's Place Is in the House: Campaigning for Congress in the Feminist Era* (Ann Arbor: University of Michigan Press, 1994); Dena Levy, Charles Tien, and Rachelle Aved, "Do Differences Matter? Women Members of Congress and the Hyde Amendment," in *Women and Congress: Running, Winning, and Ruling*, ed. Karen O'Connor (New York: Haworth Press, 2002).

205. Julie Dolan, "Support for Women's Interests in the 103rd Congress: The Distinct Impact of Congressional Women," *Women & Politics* 18 (1997): 81–93; Raymond Tatlovich and David Sheier, "The Persistence of Ideological Cleavage in Voting on Abortion Legislation in the House of Representatives, 1973–1988," *American Politics Quarterly* 21 (1993): 125–39; Christina Wolbrecht, *The Politics of Women's Rights* (Princeton, N.J.: Princeton University Press, 2000); Frieda L. Gehlen, "Women Members of Congress: A Distinctive Role," in *A Portrait of Marginality: The Political Behavior of American Women*, ed. Marianne Githens and Jewell Prestage (New York: David McKay, 1977); Leader, "The Policy Impact"; Janet Clark, "Women at the National Level," in Thomas and Wilcox, *Women and Elective Office*; and Michele Swers, "Are Congresswomen More Likely to Vote for Women's Issue Bills Than Their Male Colleagues?" *Legislative Studies Quarterly* 23 (1998): 435–48.

206. Wolbrecht, *The Politics of Women's Rights*, and Michele Swers, *The Difference Women Make: The Policy Impact of Women in Congress* (Chicago: University of Chicago Press, 2002).

207. Karen O'Connor, "Thirteen and Counting (and Making a Difference): Women in the U.S. Senate," *Journal of Women's Imaging* (November 2001): 119–22; Wolbrecht, *The Politics of Women's Rights*; Karin Tamerius, "Sex Gender, and Leadership in the Representation of Women," in *Gender, Power, Leadership, and Governance*, ed. Georgia Duerst-Lahti and Rita Mae Kelly (Ann Arbor: University of Michigan Press, 1995); Katherine Cramer Walsh, "Enlarging Representation: Women Bringing Marginalized Perspectives to Floor Debate in the House of Representatives," in Rosenthal, *Women Transforming Congress*; and Swers, *The Difference Women Make*.

208. Irwin Gertzog, *Congressional Women: Their Recruitment, Integration, and Behavior*, 2nd ed. (Westport, Conn.: Praeger, 1995); and Dodson et al., *Voices, Views, Votes*.

209. Debra Dobson, "Representing Women's Interests in the U.S. House of Representatives," in Thomas and Wilcox, *Women and Elective Office*.

210. Swers, *The Difference Women Make*; Noelle H. Norton, "Transforming Policy from the Inside: Participation in Committee," in Rosenthal, *Women Transforming Congress*.

211. Norton, "Transforming Policy from the Inside," and Richard L. Hall, *Participation in Congress* (New Haven, Conn.: Yale University Press, 1996).

212. B. Joyce Ross, "Mary McLeod Bethune and the National Youth Administration: A Case Study of Power Relationships in the Black Cabinet of Franklin D. Roosevelt,"

in *Black Women in American History: The Twentieth Century*, ed. Darlene Clark Hine (Brooklyn, N.Y.: Carlson, 1990), 1021–49.

213. Carroll J. Doherty, "Senate Confirms Albright," *Congressional Quarterly Weekly Report* 55, no. 4 (1997): 248.

214. MaryAnne Borrelli, *The President's Cabinet: Gender, Power, and Representation* (Boulder, Colo.: Lynne Rienner, 2002), 214.

215. Sheldon Goldman, Elliot Slotnick, Gerard Gryski, and Gary Zuk, "Clinton's Judges: Summing Up the Legacy," *Judicature* 84, no. 5 (March–April, 2001): 244–9.

216. Richard Pacelle, "A President's Legacy: Gender and Appointment to the Federal Courts," in *The Other Elites: Women, Politics, and Power in the Executive Branch*, ed. MaryAnn Borrelli and Janet Martin (Boulder, Colo.: Lynne Rienner, 1997), 147–66.

217. Kenneth M. Davidson, Ruth Bader Ginsburg, and Herma Hill Kay, *Sex-Based Discrimination* (St. Paul, Minn.: West, 1974).

218. Karen O'Connor, "The Next Thurgood Marshall?" *Atlanta Journal and Constitution*, June 15, 1993, A23.

219. John Leo, "Politics of the Bench: Would Bush's Supreme Court Picks Make a Difference?" *U.S. News & World Report*, November 6, 2000, 14.

220. "Women Appointed to the Carter Administration" (New Brunswick, N.J.: Center for the American Woman and Politics, n.d.); Susan J. Carroll and Barbara Geiger-Parker, *Women Appointed to State Government* (New Brunswick, N.J.: Center for the American Woman and Politics, 1983). See, however, McGlen and Sarkees, *Women in Foreign Policy*, chap. 4, for some contrary data about Reagan appointees.

221. Vital Voices, http://www.vital voices.org.

222. Elaine Martin, "The Representative Role of Women Judges," *Judicature* 77 (November/December 1993): 166–73; Sue Davis, Susan Haire, and Donald R. Songer, "Voting Behavior and Gender on the U.S. Court of Appeals," *Judicature* 77 (November/December 1993): 129–33.

223. Karen O'Connor and Jeffrey A. Segal, "The Supreme Court's Reaction to Its First Female Member," *Women & Politics* 10 (1990): 95–104.

224. 112 S.Ct. 2791 (1992).

225. 410 U.S. 113 (1973).

226. Quoted in Rep. Patricia Schroeder, "Viewpoint: Why I'm Leaving Congress," *Glamour*, February 1996, 106.

Employment and Educational Rights and Realities

Women's struggle for equal educational and employment opportunities has been a long one. Even before the first woman's movement, feminist writers such as Mary Wollstonecraft argued:

> Mankind should all be educated after the same model, or the intercourse of the sexes will never deserve the name of fellowship, nor will women ever fulfill the peculiar duties of their sex, till they become enlightened citizens, till they become free by being enabled to earn their own subsistence, independent of men.*

Resolutions calling for equal educational, professional, and employment opportunities were regularly passed at women's conventions in the nineteenth century. But women still constitute just over 40 percent of all students receiving professional degrees, and a woman who works outside the home can expect to earn only about 76 cents for every dollar earned by a man.

The efforts to rectify these inequalities and the barriers to success are the topics of the next two chapters. Chapter 3 covers the efforts of various women's movements to expand women's employment and educational rights and opportunities, and Chapter 4 examines the progress made and the barriers that remain.

Employment and educational rights—including equal pay for equal work and the removal of legal roadblocks to women's practice of some professions—affect only a limited number of women. Many laws that equalize employment and educational opportunities are nonthreatening because their effect is not always universal. Women can choose whether or not they wish to work outside the home or get a college degree, and whether or not they wish to take full advantage of antidiscrimination legislation. In the educational area, when barriers to admission are eliminated, only some women will opt for certain kinds of training. Owing to the nonuniversal and

---

*Quoted in Alice S. Rossi, ed., The Feminist Papers: From Adams to de Beauvoir
(New York: Columbia University Press, 1973), 76.

therefore "non-lifestyle-endangering" nature of rights in these areas, strong opposition groups have not emerged to lobby against or challenge in court any of the recent employment and educational rights laws.

For the most part, conservative women's groups have not challenged specific laws designed to improve women's employment or educational status. In fact, these groups have viewed some pieces of antidiscrimination legislation, most notably the Pregnancy Discrimination Act, as fostering motherhood roles. Most objections to expanded rights for women have come from men. Men's hostility toward equal educational and professional opportunities for women continues to be a significant barrier to full equality.

"*And I'm sure no one will mind if we fold a few clothes while we talk.*"

WEB EMPOWERMENT TOOLS

U.S. Department of Education
  http://www.ed.gov

Bureau of Labor Statistics
  http://www.stats.bls.gov

American Association of University Professors
  http://www.aaup.org

Working Mother's Resource for Negotiating Flexible Work
  http://www.workoptions.com

United States Department of Labor
http://www.dol.gov

National Partnership for Women
and Families
http://www.nationalpartnership.
org

Women's Work
http://www.wwork.com

National Committee on Pay Equity
http://www.feminist.com/fairpay

National Center for Education
Statistics
http://nces.ed.gov/

Association for Women in Science
http://www.awis.org/

Institute for Women and
Technology
http://www.iwt.org

Girl Geeks: The Source for Women
in Computing
http://www.girlgeeks.com

Business Woman's Resource
(plus *Working Mother* magazine)
http://www.workingwoman.com

Catalyst Advancing Women Into
Business Leadership (Catalyst
Census of Women Corporate
Officers and Board Members)
http://www.catalystwomen.org

CHAPTER

3

The Struggle for Employment and Educational Rights

Distinct eras of women's gains in employment and educational rights and opportunities closely parallel (but are not identical to) the periods of women's movement activity noted in the Introduction. From 1820 to 1900, young, white, primarily unmarried women left their homes in increasing numbers to seek employment in the growing textile industry. Other more privileged women, often closely allied with the woman's rights activists, sought entrance into higher-prestige occupations, particularly medicine and law. Many of them were forced to break legal and social barriers to gain admission to professional schools and again later to earn even minimal acceptance in their chosen fields. During this period, and even earlier, a large number of women's colleges were founded, and some formerly "male-only" universities opened their doors to female students.

A second period of change—from 1900 to 1930—can be delineated. In those years, the composition of the female labor force was altered dramatically both by the influx of immigrant women into the labor force and by the growth of white-collar jobs for unmarried, middle-class women. These changes were accompanied by an alteration in the ideology of white middle-class women active in the drive for woman suffrage. Generally, they were less concerned with eliminating all legal, social, and economic barriers for women. Instead they worked to protect working women and children from unsavory working conditions. Employment legislation promoted by those active in the suffrage and progressive movements tended to be based on the same logic as their arguments for the vote—namely, that a woman's proper role in life was that of devoted wife and mother. The dominant ideology of the time also was evident in the substandard preparation given to women in American colleges and in the lifestyles of female professionals.

World War II and the period of the 1950s and 1960s saw yet another radical alteration in the kinds and number of women working outside the home. Substantial legal changes designed to improve women's economic status, however, did not occur until passage of the Equal Pay Act in 1963. The period since then has been marked by the activity of women's groups and by the enactment of sweeping antidiscrimination legislation designed to improve women's employment status and educational opportunities. Many of these new laws, however, suffer from uneven enforcement. Thus, efforts to force compliance and to eliminate other barriers to economic and educational opportunity still occupy a good deal of the energies of members of the current women's rights movement.

New issues also continue to emerge. In the 1980s, women's rights activists took up the fight for comparable worth. As women have traditionally been channeled into low-prestige, low-paying positions, activists argued that women's jobs should be reevaluated. In 1993, during the Clinton administration, women's rights groups were able to secure passage of the Family and Medical Leave Act. Throughout the 1990s, the number of women in the labor force increased as a good economy and changes in public policy led more women to work outside the home. In 1996, President Clinton signed the Personal Responsibility and Work Opportunity Reconciliation Act, aimed at reforming welfare programs by limiting the amount of time an individual could receive benefits. Across the nation, states enacted a series of programs to provide job training and child-care services to former welfare recipients. At the national level, activists continued to pressure Congress and the Clinton administration to pass legislation guaranteeing equal pay, to provide tax credits for child care and adult training programs, and to increase the earned income tax credit for America's poorest workers. Americans were confronted with new political and economic challenges following the terrorist attacks on September 11, 2001. While the George W. Bush administration rallied global support for a "War on Terrorism," the domestic economy weakened and millions of workers lost their jobs. For many women and their families, a fundamental issue for homeland security is the increasing number of Americans who are unemployed and uninsured.

This chapter illustrates the tension between women's employment status and motherhood. Historically, a variety of laws and practices designed to "protect" women (and usually their childbearing functions) at work (or from too much education) have been enacted and then challenged as denying women equal rights. In this chapter, we trace the evolution of those laws and practices.

THE WOMAN'S MOVEMENT

In colonial times, few individuals—male or female—sought employment outside of the home. Wives toiled beside their husbands in the fields, kept house, tended gardens, and raised poultry. Marriage was viewed as an economic necessity, and the contributions of both spouses were valued because the work of each was geared toward the survival of the household as an economic unit. The coming of the Industrial Revolution, however, altered this delicate balance. In the United States, as citizens and immigrants flocked to cities, men entered nonagricultural occupations; most women stayed at home and provided essential but nonremunerative services: cooking, cleaning, and child rearing. For middle-class whites, the business world was perceived as a "dog-eat-dog" existence from

WOMEN AND HIGHER EDUCATION

The first schools of higher education for women were called female seminaries, best exemplified by Troy Seminary, founded in 1821 by Emma Hart Willard, and Mount Holyoke, chartered in 1836 by Mary Lyon.[a] These seminaries offered subjects ranging from the ancient languages to the sciences, mathematics, and history. Indeed, most seminaries offered courses roughly similar to those taught in men's colleges. After the 1850s, many seminaries were replaced by teacher training (normal) schools and public high schools, whereas others came to call themselves colleges.

The first real women's colleges were private: Vassar, founded in 1865, Wellesley and Smith, both chartered in 1875, and Bryn Mawr, begun in 1884. Their goal was to prepare women for their domestic responsibilities and for teaching. Gradually, some public coeducational colleges were developed or created as a result of pressure from women and their tax-paying parents.

Women did so well in college and their numbers grew so rapidly that some universities, most notably Stanford and the University of Chicago, began to limit, restrict, or segregate women students. One problem confronting women seeking education was the prevailing view that women would not be able to absorb an education without encountering physical harm. Until the late nineteenth century, many people believed women's brains were much smaller than men's and would burst if filled with too much learning. Another concern was the "desexing" of educated women. Women who graduated from college, it was argued, either would not marry or, if they did, would disobey their husbands and refuse to have children.

The late 1940s and early 1950s witnessed continued educational setbacks for women, as returning war veterans crowded women out of some college slots. But the number of women in college continued to grow, and by the early 1980s, women outnumbered men in institutions of higher learning. This trend continued throughout the 1990s as women earned more bachelor's degrees than men, and in certain fields, women received more master's and doctoral degrees than their male counterparts. However, a recent study by the U.S. Department of Education indicates that the vast majority of advanced degrees earned by women are clustered within three areas: psychology, education, and English language and literature. In 1997–1998, women earned only 12.2 percent of the doctoral degrees in engineering.[b]

---

[a] See Barbara Miller Solomon, *In the Company of Educated Women* (New Haven, Conn.: Yale University Press, 1985).

[b] http://nces.ed.gov/programs/coe/2001/section3/tables/t30_1.asp.

which a dutiful husband was expected to protect his wife. Thus, from the colonial period to the time of the first woman's movement, females were educated to fulfill their proper role within the home, not to enter the job market. Any type of employment was considered unacceptable unless it was essential for a woman's survival. White women who worked outside the home were often looked upon as inferior and put in a class with prostitutes or indentured servants.[1]

Some women, including widows, unmarried women, and women whose husbands could not earn enough to support the family, found it necessary to work outside the home. Many used their "womanly" skills and became domestics. In the South, slavery held women in bondage to their masters whether they worked in the house or in the fields. Many women, particularly in the Northeast, found work in the fledgling textile industry, which relied heavily on cheap (i.e., female) labor. By 1831, women held 80 percent of the jobs in New England's textile mills. By 1850, more than 225,000 American women were employed in that industry.[2]

The Seneca Falls Convention and the Woman's Movement

As opportunities for men expanded, societal restrictions on women's opportunities increased. These limits caused the women at Seneca Falls to demand equal educational and employment opportunities on the principle "that the equality of human rights results necessarily from the fact of the identity of the race in capabilities and responsibilities."[3]

Although deeply concerned about the economic and educational plight of women, those active in the first woman's movement did little to solve those problems. They were increasingly more concerned with woman's suffrage. Most improvements in this sphere, therefore, came as the result of the efforts of individual women, with only limited help from others in the movement.

Efforts on Behalf of Working Women.   Most jobs open to women in factories and in the textile industry required long hours of work at low pay in substandard conditions. Eleven- or twelve-hour workdays were not uncommon. Hours aside, females were paid less than their male counterparts universally. These depressed wages were the result of a variety of factors. Many men believed that women were inherently inferior and, consequently, their labor was worth less. Moreover, rigid societal values limited the number of jobs open to women, which made competition for even low-paid jobs keen. Even many women employed in the textile industry were not troubled by these inequities. They viewed their jobs as only short term and saw factory employment as an escape route from the farm until a suitable mate was found.

While most women who worked during this period were employed in factories, a limited number held "prestige" occupations. It was from this limited pool of educated women that the woman's movement most frequently drew support. Leaders in the woman's movement often were tutored at home. A few, like Susan B. Anthony, attended female seminaries where women were trained to teach. From the time of the Seneca Falls Convention, in fact, the movement was largely dependent upon these white, educated, middle-class women not only to serve as leaders but also to form the core of its strongest supporters. Few African American women or poor women had the time or energy or, in the case of slave women, the basic freedom to become involved in the movement.

Professionalization and Education. During the 1800s, several roadblocks were erected that affected even educated women's abilities to enter most professions. One noteworthy barrier came in the form of "professionalization"; that is, a college education or advanced training was required before one could attempt to practice certain professions. Since women were routinely denied admission to most colleges and medical and law schools, they had no opportunity to pursue certain careers. Additionally, state licensing of "prestige" professions, most notably law and medicine, was another barrier to women's employment opportunities.

As the number of public elementary and secondary schools increased in this period, the teaching profession opened up to women. Many people believed that women were naturally suited to teaching, given "the greater intensity of the parental instinct in the female sex, their natural love of children, and the superior gentleness and forbearance of their dispositions."[4] Some argued that the more moral and religious nature of women made them better teachers of young minds than men.[5]

Financial considerations, however, constituted the most important factor for allowing women to teach. As the nation committed itself to universal public education (at least for whites), thousands of new teachers were needed. Men could not be counted on to fill these positions because of the numerous, more profitable opportunities open to them. Indeed, because women were expected to teach only until they married, their salaries were often only one-third to one-half those paid to males. Pay differentials were even worse for African American teachers. When economics was combined with the rising number of young women who wanted to work, the result was the massive influx of women into the teaching profession. By 1880, women constituted 57.2 percent of all elementary school teachers.[6]

THE SUFFRAGE MOVEMENT

During the woman suffrage movement, demands for women's educational and employment rights failed to attract even the limited support offered by the woman's movement. Because of the suffrage movement's narrow focus and conservative ideology, only a few of the groups affiliated with the suffrage cause, most notably the National Woman's Party (NWP), continued to work for equal rights for women in every facet of life. Real progress in these areas during this period—indeed, until the 1960s and the rise of the women's rights movement—was accomplished either by individual women or those acting in small groups. As in the earlier movement, this tended to result in severe limits on educational and employment opportunities for all women. Additionally, at least some of the "progress" made during the suffrage era was regressive. Conservative views about women's roles resulted in legislation and court cases that often limited the occupational opportunities available to women.

The narrow focus of the suffrage movement and its more traditional views about women explain much of the difference between it and the woman's movement. Another important difference between the two movements was their respective attitudes toward blue-collar workers. Most suffragists wanted little to do with immigrants, the poor, or African American women who worked in factories (or fields) at the turn of the century. Some suffragists, associating the plight of working women with the rights of foreign-born or uneducated individuals, appeared ready to abandon a whole class of women workers in their new emphasis on educated suffrage (discussed in Chapter 1).

As the twentieth century approached, however, some women, particularly those allied with the growing progressive movement and not necessarily the National American Woman Suffrage Association (NAWSA), saw the need to address the problems of working women. Increasingly during the last decade of the nineteenth century, some middle-class women began to recognize that most employed women were not working for fun but rather to help support themselves and their families. In fact, 43 percent of African American women, 25 percent of immigrant women, and 15 percent of American-born white women were employed outside the home by 1900.[7] Reformers realized that if these women were going to be able to fulfill their paramount roles as mothers and homemakers, the terrible conditions under which they toiled outside the home would have to change.

The Women's Trade Union League (WTUL) was formed in 1903 to organize women laborers into units to bargain for shorter hours and better wages. Its membership was varied and included individuals from the working-class trade union movement and upper-middle-class women from the settlement house movement.[8]

From the very beginning, the WTUL was dedicated to the cause of woman suffrage along with its other goals. It had some early successes in organizing women workers, but after 1909 it increasingly devoted its efforts to securing protective legislation for women workers.[9] The WTUL did not play an active role in the suffrage cause until after 1912, however, when working-class women's potential usefulness was finally recognized by NAWSA leaders.[10]

The Drive for Protective Legislation

The second strategy to improve the status of working women—passage of protective legislation—was also the main goal of another middle-class reform group, the National Consumers' League (NCL). It was dedicated to the improvement of working conditions in retail shops and factories.[11] Most NCL members believed that a woman's proper role in life was to be a good wife and mother. They believed that working long hours was detrimental to women's health and their ability to care for their families. Through education, legislation, and litigation, the

NCL sought to educate the consuming public about substandard conditions in many shops and factories. These concerns were vividly brought home to most Americans in 1911 by the Triangle Shirtwaist Company fire in New York City. As flames trapped workers—mostly young, poor, immigrant women—forty-seven leaped from the upper floors of a tall sweatshop to their deaths. Ninety-nine others died inside behind locked doors that barred their escape.

The NCL's efforts resulted in the passage of several state laws for women. These laws limited the number of hours a day a woman could work in any one establishment. This legislation, however, soon was attacked by employers.[12]

Maximum Hour and Minimum Wage Laws.   In 1907, an Oregon employer was convicted for violating an NCL-backed state law that prohibited women from working more than eight hours a day. The U.S. Supreme Court had recently ruled that a similar New York law regarding the hours of bakers was unconstitutional. Thus, the NCL's lawyer, Louis Brandeis (who later became the first Jewish U.S. Supreme Court justice), submitted a lengthy brief to the Court, containing statistics indicating the negative impact of long hours of work on a woman's health and her reproductive capabilities. In essence, Brandeis's arguments echoed the ideology of the suffrage movement. He argued that women had unique characteristics and therefore were in need of special protective labor legislation.

The Supreme Court was receptive to his arguments. In upholding the constitutionality of the Oregon statute, in *Muller v. Oregon* (1908), the Court noted:

> That woman's physical structure and the performance of maternal functions place her at a disadvantage in the struggle for subsistence is obvious. This is especially true when the burdens of motherhood are upon her. Even when they are not, by abundant testimony of the medical fraternity, continuance for a long time on her feet at work, repeating this from day to day, tends to injurious effects upon the body, and, as healthy mothers are essential to vigorous offspring, the physical well-being of woman becomes an object of public interest and care in order to preserve the strength and vigor of the race. . . .
>
>   . . . Even though all restrictions on political, personal, and contractual rights were taken away, and she stood, so far as statutes are concerned, upon an absolutely equal plane with him [man], it would still be true that she is so constituted that she will rest upon and look to him for protection; that her physical structure and a proper discharge of her maternal functions—having in view not merely her own health, but the well-being of the race—justify legislation to protect her from the greed as well as the passion of men.[13]

Muller v. Oregon established the principle that women workers could be treated differently from their male counterparts under the law. NCL leaders saw this decision as helping women by remedying at least one evil—long hours. In actuality, however, many employers used this decision to justify not hiring women or treating women workers differently from men. In New York City, for example, hundreds of women typesetters lost their jobs at several local newspapers. Their employers claimed that they would be in violation of the law if they forced the women to work long hours on the night shift. The irony of this action was that these were high-paying positions that most of the women desperately wanted to keep. Other available "female" jobs paid far less.

Wages were another concern of the NCL and other progressive organizations. Fearing that low wages forced some women into prostitution, these organizations believed that it was absolutely necessary to secure state minimum wage laws to protect a woman's virtue. Again, little thought was given to the possibility that employers would or could hire men at wages lower than the statutory minimum for women, thereby making it a matter of business sense for employers to replace their female workers with cheaper males.

The NCL successfully lobbied several state legislatures for the adoption of minimum wage laws. These laws, like the maximum hour provisions before them, soon encountered challenges in the courts.

The first major case was *Adkins v. Children's Hospital* (1923), which challenged the District of Columbia's "living wage" standard for women.[14] The NCL again defended the constitutionality of minimum wage protections in court. In sharp contrast, however, the National Woman's Party, which viewed protective legislation as inconsistent with its support of an equal rights amendment, filed a brief in opposition to the NCL's arguments. The Supreme Court appeared mindful of this division. In its decision, the Court declared minimum wage laws for women unconstitutional, noting:

> But the ancient inequality of the sexes, otherwise than physical, as suggested in the *Muller* Case, has continued "with diminishing intensity." In view of the great—not to say revolutionary—changes which have taken place since that utterance, in the contractual, political, and civil status of women, culminating in the Nineteenth Amendment, it is not unreasonable to say that these differences have now come almost, if not quite, to the vanishing point.

Adkins probably accelerated the disintegration of the fragile suffrage movement coalition by presenting a major issue upon which component women's groups could not agree.

Women and Work After Gaining Suffrage

After *Adkins*, women's working conditions in the United States largely remained the same, but the kinds of work women obtained changed considerably. By 1930, 30 percent of the employed women in the United States were engaged in nonmanual occupations—often as clerical workers. In fact, a particularly significant phenomenon occurred during this period—the colonization by women of the new white-collar clerical and sales jobs. From 1890 to 1920, the percentage of all working women who were employed in these fields rose from 5.3 to 25.6.[15] This change in the composition of the female workforce had an impact on the NCL's fight for improved labor conditions. As the proportion of women working in factories and other occupations notorious for their hazardous conditions declined, it became much more difficult to get people to rally for improved conditions. Immigrant women who were employed as factory workers, domestics, and office clerks often feared losing their jobs and resisted attempts at organization.

Lack of organization, occupational segregation of women, and employer intimidation resulted in low wages for women when compared to men, both overall and within occupational categories. Like poor immigrant women, African American women often suffered from low wages, substandard conditions, and very limited job opportunities.

The Great Depression intensified women's problems. Most people believed that men, rather than married women, should get the few available jobs. Some employers adopted policies prohibiting the hiring of married women or calling for a woman's immediate discharge upon marriage. In fact, during the Great Depression, over half of the states had laws specifically barring the employment of married women in some occupations. For example, most public school systems had policies against hiring married women, and a majority fired women upon their marriage. Similar laws were adopted in many states and municipalities. Even the national government passed legislation that prohibited the employment of more than one family member from one household—a practice that had a far greater adverse impact on women than men.[16]

Education and the Professions

The percentage of women with college educations and advanced degrees rose dramatically, as revealed in Tables 3.1 and 3.2. But this apparent progress was in many ways deceptive. The expansion of coeducation to most state colleges

TABLE 3.1 **Percentage of Bachelor's Degrees Earned by Women**

Field of study	1970–71	1997–98
Health profession and related sciences	77%	82%
Education	75	75
Psychology	44	74
English language and literature/letters	66	67
Visual and performing arts	60	59
Communications	35	60
Biological/life sciences	29	55
Business management and administrative services	9	48
Social sciences and history	37	49
Mathematics	38	46
Agriculture and natural resources	4	41
Physical sciences	14	38
Computer and information sciences	14	27
Engineering	1	17
Total[a]	43	56

[a] Includes other fields of study not shown separately.

Source: U.S. Department of Education, NCES, 1970–71 Higher Education General Information Survey (HEGIS), "Degrees and Other Formal Awards Conferred" survey, and 1997–98 Integrated Postsecondary Education Data System (IPEDS) "Completions" survey.

TABLE 3.2 Percentage of Master's and Doctoral Degrees Earned by Women

Field of study	Master's Degrees		Doctoral Degrees	
	1970–71	1997–98	1970–71	1997–98
Total	40.1	57.1	14.3	42.0
Health profession and related sciences	55.3	77.7	16.5	62.5
Education	56.2	76.4	21.0	63.2
Psychology	40.6	73.1	24.0	67.5
English language and literature/letters	60.6	66.1	28.8	59.1
Visual and performing arts	47.4	58.8	22.2	51.3
Communications	34.6	61.3	13.1	52.4
Biological/life sciences	33.6	52.4	16.3	42.5
Business management and administrative services	3.9	38.6	2.8	31.4
Social sciences and history	28.5	46.7	13.9	40.8
Mathematics	27.1	41.0	7.6	25.7
Agriculture and natural resources	5.9	43.0	2.9	27.4
Physical sciences	13.3	35.9	5.6	25.2
Computer and information sciences	10.3	29.0	2.3	16.3
Engineering	1.1	19.0	0.6	12.2

Source: U.S. Department of Education, NCES, 1970–1971 Higher Education General Information Survey (HEGIS), "Degrees and Other Formal Awards Conferred" surveys, and 1997–98 Integrated Postsecondary Education Data System (IPEDS) "Completions" survey.

and many private schools was met with resistance by many college administrators and faculty. Admission of women was often motivated by the economic dependence on students' tuition payments to survive and not by acceptance of the idea that women could and should receive a college education.

In keeping with prevailing stereotypes about women's mental abilities and natural propensities, women students, or *coeds* as they were called, were channeled into liberal arts and other "female" majors. Entire curricula were developed for near-exclusive study by women. Most notable of these were social work, education, library studies, and home economics. Because many people believed that a young woman's ultimate "career" was wife and mother, they also believed she should take college courses concerned with the proper running of a home (sewing, cooking, and child care). This philosophy was, of course, entirely in keeping with the dominant woman suffrage view that a woman should devote her full energies and abilities to being the best possible mother and wife.

As more women sought college entrance, coeducational institutions began to limit the number of female students. In 1925, American medical schools adopted a 5 percent quota for female students (a standard that was to remain in effect until 1945). Moreover, few—40 out of 482—hospitals in the United States accepted women as interns.[17] Not surprisingly, the number of women doctors declined from a high point of 6 percent in 1910. Similarly, the position of women in law remained abysmal. Although by 1916 all states in the Union allowed women to practice law, many law schools denied admission to women, as did many professional legal associations.[18] Moreover, the few women who were physicians and lawyers were relegated to doing what their colleagues viewed as low-status "women's work." Female attorneys generally practiced in the areas of matrimonial law or wills and estates, while female doctors became obstetricians or pediatricians, not surgeons.

While the situation of women in "male" professions improved only marginally, the crowding of women into their "natural" professions continued unabated. Indeed, virtually all of the "progress" women made in the professions during the suffrage era (the percentage of women working as professionals in 1920 was close to 12 percent) can be attributed to the opening of several new "learned" occupations for women.[19] Nurses and teachers, in fact, made up 75 percent of all female professionals.[20] Other women became librarians, home economists, and social workers. Many of these women became leaders in the suffrage movement.

Thus, even though large numbers of white women went to college, their training gave them a perspective largely incompatible with the principle of equal rights. Accordingly, the major legal advances won during this period concerned the legalization of protective legislation—judicial recognition of the fact that women workers needed protection—and were not grounded in notions of equality sought by women in the first woman's movement.

WORLD WAR II

The onset of World War II and the activation of men into the military reversed the economic climate of the 1930s. With men off to war, the U.S. government undertook a massive campaign to recruit women into the paid labor force. This campaign brought about the abolition of many of the employment restrictions affecting women in the 1930s, and women moved into the labor force in large numbers. Between 1940 and 1945, the percentage of employed women rose from 26 to 36 percent. Perhaps the most important aspect of this increase was the rise in the number of married women who joined the labor force. Between 1940 and 1945, the percentage of married women who worked rose from 15 to 24 percent.[21] During the war years, 75 percent of the new women workers were married.

As most prewar discriminatory hiring policies were abandoned, women gained employment in a variety of situations formerly closed to them. They became welders, airplane pilots, and Wall Street analysts, for example.

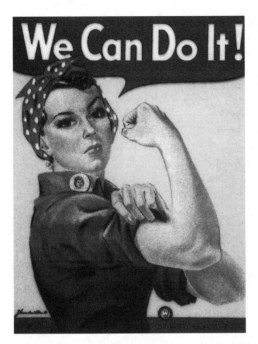

During World War II, the War Production Coordinating Committee commissioned this poster of "Rosie the Riveter" to encourage women to leave their homes, work in factories, and help the war effort.
Source: AP/Wide World Photos.

Liberalization of federal government employment practices resulted in the hiring of thousands of women in jobs vacated by men. The number of female doctors grew as the shortage of male physicians and male students forced the national government, medical schools, and hospitals to relax their previous restrictive practices. One million women were hired as clerical workers by the U.S. government to handle the new bureaucracy brought about by the war.[22]

The national government furthered this progress by endorsing in principle the idea of equal pay for equal work. Unions, too, began to treat women workers more fairly. After congressional passage of the National Industrial Recovery Act in 1933, which recognized labor's right to organize, some unions began to concentrate their energies on mass production industries. In the late 1930s, the Congress of Industrial Organizations began to organize unskilled workers and often had to appeal to women in the factories where unionization attempts were being made. According to Barbara Deckard, the number of union women grew from 800,000 in 1939 to more than 3 million by the end of the war in 1945.[23] Unionization and employer need for women workers resulted in a tremendous improvement in women's earnings.

World War II and the employment conditions it created brought about an expansion of economic opportunity that women, acting alone or in small groups, had previously been unable to produce. These new rights, however, were limited by the fact that the conditions that necessitated them were temporary. The kinds of permanent legal changes required to produce real equal opportunity were not undertaken. For example, the U.S. government failed to adopt a law requiring equal pay for equal work; it simply endorsed the idea. Many employers ignored the equal pay provision or circumvented it by reclassifying jobs performed by women workers. Similarly, it continued to be legal for employers to refuse to hire older or married women. And there were no national legal prohibitions against flat refusals to employ women at all. Thus, many job classifications remained male or were only temporarily staffed by women until a more "appropriate" person—a man—could be hired. Union protection of female members also often lagged behind that afforded to men. Separate seniority lists for each sex, for example, were not illegal or uncommon.

After the war, it surprised many employers as well as the U.S. government that the women wanted to stay on the job. Many women, however, lost their positions to returning veterans, who, by law, were given preference. Within two months after the end of World War II, almost 800,000 women lost their jobs in the aircraft industry alone.[24]

Many corporations quickly moved to reestablish prewar prohibitions against the employment of married women, fearing a postwar recession. Much of the protective legislation concerning the hours, conditions, and kinds of work women could do was reinstituted. These actions clearly reflected a concerted effort to encourage women to return to their homes, husbands, and children. Within a few short years after the veterans' return, however, large numbers of women reentered the workforce but did so by taking traditional jobs at far lower pay than they had enjoyed during the war.[25] African American women generally stayed in the workforce regardless of changing attitudes. Facing pervasive discrimination, their total family income was generally much lower than that of white families, virtually necessitating a two-income household.

The reentry of white women into the workforce was a particularly interesting phenomenon, given the "return to the home" ethos that characterized the postwar period. Although popular magazines proclaimed the benefits and rewards of suburban living and the homemaker role as a rewarding full-time occupation, many married women abandoned this "ideal" for the working world. According to Betty Friedan, while the editors of the *Ladies' Home Journal*, *McCall's*, and *Redbook* magazines created a "feminine mystique" by depicting women as "young, frivolous, almost childlike; fluffy and feminine; passive, gaily content in a world of bedroom and kitchen, sex, babies, and home,"[26] millions of "contented" housewives sought employment outside the home—most out of financial necessity. In 1950, for example, for the first time in American history, married women constituted more than 50 percent of all women workers. Nearly 25 percent of them had school-age children—a dramatic change from the prewar period. These trends continued unabated into the early 1960s.[27]

Changes in the number and kind of working women, however, were not accompanied by an improvement in the economic conditions or rights of women. For the most part, women still were clustered into female jobs. Few held prestigious occupations, while the "professions" open to women— nursing and teaching—continued to be almost totally dominated by females. Additionally, as larger numbers of women sought work outside the home, the concentration of women in certain fields tended to drive wages downward—at least in relation to those of men. From 1940 to 1960, the wage gap increased steadily, largely due to the ghettoization of female employees in low-paying fields and the nonexistence of national equal pay legislation.

Education After World War II

Just as returning veterans reclaimed jobs from women, they also had an effect on the proportion of women in colleges and universities. From 1940 to 1950, the percentage of baccalaureate degrees awarded to women declined precipitously. Part of this dramatic change was a direct consequence of government policy. Even though women helped in the war effort, they did not receive G.I. benefits. Thus, large numbers of returning veterans—most of them male—were able to attend college financed by the federal government. Before 1940, most men and women who enrolled in postsecondary education were from middle-class or well-to-do families. After the war, because of the tuition and living assistance grants available to returning veterans, many men who formerly would have been unable to afford a college education could do so. Without similar benefits for women, even though they had supported the war effort in the only way they were allowed to (by statute women could not be drafted), a large number of women were priced out of a college education.[28] Women who could afford to attend a college or university often met a "veterans first" policy or the stringent kinds of quotas that had been utilized to exclude women before the war.

The women who attended college after the war continued to face discrimination. They were encouraged to major in "women's" fields, especially teaching, where the demand for workers was high. Few tried to obtain professional or higher academic degrees; those who did were often denied admission because of their sex. Additionally, continued curricular emphasis on the rewards of motherhood and marriage led large numbers of women to drop out of school to marry. Even those who graduated almost invariably married soon after and never sought employment.

By the early 1960s, even when women had equipped themselves with the tools necessary for a career, ghettoization and the continuing myths about why most women worked resulted in low wages compared to those of men—even when they did the same work. As late as 1960, it was estimated that a woman with a college degree could only expect to earn the same wages as a man who had completed the eighth grade.[29]

THE WOMEN'S RIGHTS MOVEMENT

As the 1960s approached, some women recognized that gender-based discrimination existed in all spheres. Many of them campaigned for John F. Kennedy, who they believed would support legislation to expand women's rights. When his first major appointees were announced and only two out of 240 were women, his female supporters were outraged. To appease them and, some believe, to avoid the equal rights amendment question, Kennedy signed

Executive Order 10980 on December 14, 1961, creating the President's Commission on the Status of Women. (Mary Anne Baker et al. suggest that Kennedy hoped the commission would find facts to be used against passage of an ERA.[30]) The mandate of the executive order was to analyze and recommend changes to end the "prejudices and outmoded customs that act as a barrier to full realization of women's basic rights." When the commission's report was made public in 1963, perhaps its most concrete recommendations concerned employment and labor standards.

In terms of employment rights and the creation of a women's rights movement, the commission's importance cannot be overstated. It was chaired by former First Lady Eleanor Roosevelt, who had extremely close ties to women active in the progressive movement. The commission brought women together for the first time since the 1930s. Its members were drawn largely from the ranks of business and professional women's clubs, with limited representation from organized labor. These women soon formed the leadership nucleus of the women's rights movement.

In addition to providing the leadership of the fledgling movement, the commission gave women an agenda and publicized that agenda, which helped produce some governmental action. Examples of responses to commission recommendations include several executive orders and passage of the Equal Pay Act (EPA). Only one year after the commission issued its recommendations, the Civil Rights Act of 1964 also was enacted.

The Equal Pay Act

Prior to congressional passage of the Equal Pay Act of 1963, several efforts were made to secure such a law. During World War II, the Women's Bureau, a division within the Department of Labor devoted to the improvement of the state of working women, called for women to be paid equal pay for comparable work. In 1945, legislation calling for equal pay was actually introduced in the House of Representatives but never came to a vote. Similar legislation was introduced during every subsequent session of Congress until 1963, but without presidential backing, equal pay supporters were unsuccessful. Once Kennedy threw his support behind the proposed equal pay amendment to the Fair Labor Standards Act of 1938, it passed quickly.

The Equal Pay Act, however, did not pass in the form advocated by its staunchest supporters. It exempted several classes of workers, and instead of guaranteeing *equal* pay for *comparable* work, it required only that *equal* pay be had for *equal* work. It forbade an employer to "discriminate on the basis of sex by paying wages . . . to employees at a rate less than that which he pays . . . employees of the opposite sex . . . for equal work on jobs the performance of which requires equal skill, effort, and responsibilities, and which are performed under similar working conditions." The act also allowed for four exceptions: (1) if sex differences were part of a seniority system or training program, (2) if earnings were dependent on a merit system, (3) if earnings were dependent on the quantity or quality of production, or (4) if salaries were based on any factor other than sex.

Department of Labor Enforcement.   Initially, the Equal Pay Act's greatest impact was on working-class women. In fact, it was not amended to cover administrative, executive, or professional employees until 1972. The Wage Standards Division of the Department of Labor (DOL) was empowered to bring suits on behalf of women who alleged violations of the law. In general, DOL was very successful in terms of attempting to bring about compliance with the act's provisions. Since the act allows a woman to file a complaint anonymously and, therefore, not fear employer retaliation, many complaints were filed and then thoroughly investigated by DOL. By 1973, more than $200 million in back pay awards were secured by the agency for aggrieved employees, most of them women.[31] In fact, from 1963 to 1979, when DOL was divested of its enforcement powers, although the Equal Pay Act's language is written in terms of equal pay for equal work, DOL was able to convince the courts to interpret this provision to require that work done must be only "substantially equal."[32]

On July 1, 1979, however, over the protest of many women's groups, Equal Pay Act enforcement was transferred to the Equal Employment Opportunity Commission (EEOC). (The EEOC initially was created by Congress to enforce the provisions of the Civil Rights Act of 1964.) This was done as part of President Jimmy Carter's reorganization plan to streamline government. The EEOC has never been a particularly effective enforcement agency, and compliance efforts have lagged.

From 1980 to 1992, during the Reagan and George H. W. Bush administrations (and with Clarence Thomas heading the EEOC), awards dropped to less than $2 million a year, in contrast to the $20 million a year won by the DOL. During the Clinton administration, the EEOC did only slightly better. In 1995, for example, the EEOC won $2.8 million in awards for plaintiffs but resolved only 16.1 percent of the charges filed with it.[33]

Over the years, however, fewer and fewer employers have continued to pay male and female employees blatantly different wages for the same or similar work. Still, as discussed in Chapter 4, women's wages continue to lag behind those of men.

The Civil Rights Act of 1964

Members of the Commission on the Status of Women recognized that employment discrimination was rampant, yet their final report made no specific call for new antidiscrimination laws. Nevertheless, in 1964, Title VII of the Civil Rights Act, which prohibits discrimination based on race, color, religion, national origin, or sex in all terms, conditions, or privileges of employment, was enacted. Like the Equal Pay Act, it also includes an exception: discrimination based on sex, religion, or national origin (but not race) is permissible if it is "a bona fide occupational qualification reasonably necessary to the normal operation of that particular business enterprise." The Equal Employment Opportunity Commission was created to enforce its provisions.

The inclusion of the "sex" prohibition in the Civil Rights Act originally was tacked onto the bill by a southerner to make a joke of the bill, divide supporters, and thereby lead to its defeat. Martha Griffiths (D-Mich.) initially intended to sponsor the addition. Upon hearing of a southerner's plan to include sex in the bill, however, she deferred to him. She believed that his sponsorship, no matter what his intentions, could swing some conservative votes needed to pass the entire bill.[34] Griffiths calculated correctly.

Enactment of this major tool to fight sex discrimination is interesting. Unlike the large number of women's groups that testified in favor of the Equal Pay Act, no organized women's groups spoke on its behalf, although Griffiths and other female representatives lined up solidly behind its passage.

EEOC Enforcement.   Ironically, it was not the actions of existing women's rights groups but, instead, the EEOC's nonenforcement of the Civil Rights Act that provided the catalyst for the formation of the rights branch of the current women's movement. From the beginning, EEOC officials refused to take its sex discrimination provision seriously, noting the absence of legislative history on its sex clause and the mirth that it inspired when it reached the floor.[35] Repeatedly, the agency failed to investigate complaints of sex discrimination, which prompted Griffiths to attack the agency's inaction from the floor of the House of Representatives. Griffiths was not the only person concerned with EEOC negligence. Many women, frustrated by the EEOC's incompetence and the inability of the Commission on the Status of Women to force the EEOC to act, formed the National Organization for Women (NOW) in 1966. One of NOW's first goals was the eradication of sex discrimination in employment, but without EEOC support, it could do little.

Unlike DOL's vigorous enforcement of the Equal Pay Act, the EEOC's enforcement of the Civil Rights Act's sex discrimination clause was totally inadequate. NOW and several other women's rights groups took a number of actions to remedy this problem. First, throughout 1966, they put pressure on the EEOC to initiate the steps necessary to draft regulations to implement the act's ban on sex discrimination in employment.

Second, women put pressure on employers and the EEOC to follow the letter and spirit of the law. New York City NOW members, for example, picketed the *New York Times* offices to protest the newspaper's maintenance of sex-segregated employment advertisements. Later, in December 1967, NOW held what Jo Freeman calls "perhaps the first contemporary feminist demonstration."[36] NOW members and others picketed EEOC offices around the country to draw attention to the agency's inaction. NOW also filed suit against the EEOC for failing to enforce Title VII. In Pittsburgh, in response to a complaint filed by NOW, the city's Commission on Human Relations brought suit against a local newspaper, the *Pittsburgh Press.* It claimed that the paper's publication of sex-segregated advertisements violated Title VII of the Civil Rights Act.[37]

Third, NOW and other women's groups also began to lobby Congress for passage of the Equal Employment Opportunity Act (EEOA). They believed that the EEOC needed powers to bring suit if discrimination was found after an investigation. Without additional legislation, all the EEOC could do was seek voluntary compliance. The EEOA, as ultimately passed in 1972, also widened the coverage of the Civil Rights Act to include employers and unions with eight or more workers, employees of both the state and the federal government, and employees of educational institutions.

Finally, women's rights groups recognized that they would need to litigate to obtain employment rights. Civil Rights Act or Title VII litigation, as it is often called, involves complex issues of fact and the introduction of statistical information, particularly where a pattern and practice of discrimination is alleged. Most aggrieved women do not have the resources necessary to retain attorneys to handle their claims. Thus, many women's rights groups have been extensively involved in both counseling and representing women who claim employment discrimination. In fact, NOW's recognition that political pressure alone might not be sufficient to change the EEOC's inaction concerning sex discrimination complaints led it to form a legal arm to litigate alleged violations of both the Civil Rights and Equal Pay Acts. Shortly after NOW's creation, those unhappy with some of NOW's policies on more controversial issues formed other women's rights organizations concerned with employment and educational discrimination. All, however, agreed that it was imperative to force the EEOC to treat sex discrimination complaints seriously. Thus, other groups such as the Women's Equity Action League also took steps to form legal funds to finance sex discrimination employment litigation.

This strategy was entirely in keeping with the ideology of the emerging rights branch of the movement. Women sought changes in discriminatory practices, some of which would allow them to better pursue motherhood and a career. In keeping with this philosophy, women began to use conventional political and legal pressure to expand employment rights under Title VII by attacking several types of discriminatory practices.

BFOQs, Customer Preference, and Protective Legislation. One of the first actions taken by NOW was an effort to limit the scope of the bona fide occupational qualification (BFOQ) exception of Title VII of the Civil Rights Act of 1964, which allows employers to take sex into account when it is a BFOQ for a particular position. Examples of legal BFOQs include hiring only females as wet nurses or hiring only male actors to play Batman. Interpretation of this vague provision, however, led to controversy. Some argued that an expansive interpretation of the BFOQ provision would allow most protective legislation to remain on the law books, whereas a narrow one would have invalidated most of these laws.

As soon as the potential ramifications of a narrow interpretation of the BFOQ were realized, several groups, including the NCL, the Young Women's Christian Association (YWCA), and the American Association of University Women (AAUW), wrote to the director of the EEOC urging him to construe Title VII to allow "differential legislation" for females, noting that it had beneficial effects on their health and well-being.[38]

In contrast, representatives from the National Woman's Party and from the National Federation of Business and Professional Women's Clubs (BPW) and Representative Griffiths spoke in favor of a narrow construction of the BFOQ, which would necessitate an end to protective legislation for women. Additionally, NOW testified in opposition to state maximum hour laws and laws setting weight-lifting maximums or limiting night work. A NOW representative stressed the fact that many state laws operated to deprive women of jobs they desperately needed to support their families. These sentiments were in sharp contrast to those of the NCL and other more conservative groups. An NCL representative testified, "While men may also require protection from overtime hours, as a group their need is less than that of women, who usually spend more time on family and home responsibilities."[39]

Although there was conflicting testimony from women's rights groups concerning the desirability of protective legislation, the EEOC took two actions signaling its support for women's rights groups. First, in 1968, it submitted a friend of the court brief in a case originally sponsored by NOW, arguing that Title VII invalidated California's laws that prohibited women from lifting certain weights or working overtime. The federal district court adopted the EEOC's position. In 1971, it ruled that a California law (limiting women's work hours and the weights they were permitted to lift, which was cited by a railway as its reason for not hiring women as agent-telegraphers) was a violation of Title VII of the Civil Rights Act.[40]

After the 1971 decision, some employers tried to justify discriminatory employment practices by equating business necessity allowed under the BFOQ with "customer preference." For example, in spite of contrary urgings from women's groups, airline companies had long refused to hire men as flight attendants, citing customer preference. They argued that traditionally women were viewed as the more nurturing and comforting of the sexes, and should an emergency arise in the cabin, male passengers would reject handholding-type overtures from male attendants. Ultimately, the airlines' refusal to hire male attendants was found to be illegal.[41]

In a second action signaling its support for women's rights groups, the EEOC enacted guidelines that interpreted the BFOQ very narrowly, and women's rights groups continued to challenge any kind of "protective" legislation in the courts, which had been very receptive to their activities. In fact, on only one occasion has the U.S. Supreme Court relied on the BFOQ to justify an employer's refusal to hire women. In *Dothard v. Rawlinson* (1977), the Supreme Court upheld Alabama's refusal to hire women as prison guards in the state's correctional facilities.[42] There, the Court, however, narrowly construed BFOQ. In essence, the Court took notice that conditions in Alabama's dormitory-style prisons were so bad that really no one should work in them, but since someone had to, it was reasonable for the state to hire only males.

Comparable Worth.   Another issue that has arisen under Title VII is that of comparable worth. While the Equal Pay Act has been construed as encouraging equal pay for similar work, authors of the act deny that they meant anything other than that. Nevertheless, many women's rights groups have advocated that women be given "equal" or "comparable" wages for "equivalent" or "comparable" work. Such demands involve reassessment of the way that jobs are evaluated and worth assigned in this country. Thus, level of skill, effort, and responsibility are key, not the job itself. For example, using a point system based on four factors—know-how, problem solving, accountability, and working conditions—one employee-benefits firm has compared nurses and "sanitation engineers," also known as garbage collectors. (See Table 3.3.) According to this plan, these employees should earn equal wages.[43]

Comparable worth gained attention in 1981 when the U.S. Supreme Court ruled that female workers could sue for discrimination under Title VII even if they were not performing the same jobs as men. In *County of Washington v. Gunther* (1981), a group of female prison guards, called matrons, earned lower wages and benefits than their male counterparts, known as deputy sheriffs.[44] Their jobs differed in that women were required to guard fewer prisoners and to perform clerical tasks. The Court ruled that they could sue even though the jobs were different.

Although the idea of comparable worth received a lot of attention in the 1970s and 1980s, it received little attention in the 1990s. Given poor EEOC enforcement, some argued that new, national legislation to alleviate wage gaps was imperative. To reduce pay inequities, the Fair Pay Act was introduced in Congress in 1994. It would have prohibited discrimination in equivalent jobs, but the bill did not get far in the Republican-controlled Congress. The continued sexual segregation of the workplace is a major reason for the ongoing wage gap between American men and women. The Fair Pay Act of 2000 did not fare much better than its earlier version. It would have required employers to pay women the same amount for work performed in female-dominated job categories as men receive for work performed in male-dominated job categories if the employer considered the job to be of equivalent value to the business. The results of the nationwide survey "Ask a Working Woman," sponsored by the American Federation of Labor and Congress of Industrial Organizations, reported that pay equity was the most important policy issue for working women in the 2000 election.[45]

There seems to be no quick resolution to the problems of equity faced by women in employment. The failure of legislative efforts such as the Fair Pay Act have resulted in the broadening of the wage gap between the sexes. The National Committee on Pay Equity designated Tuesday, April 15, 2003, as "Equal Pay

TABLE 3.3 A Comparable Worth Point System

	Nurse	Sanitation Engineer
Know-how	150	60
Problem solving	75	40
Accountability	175	165
Working conditions	50	185
Total	450	450

Source: Kenneth Janda, Jeffrey M. Berry, and Jerry Goldman, *The Challenge of Democracy*, 2nd ed. (Dallas: Houghton Mifflin, 1990), 20.

Day" to signify "the point into the new week that a woman must work in order to earn the wages paid to a man in the previous week . . . because women on average earn less, they must work longer for the same pay."[46] In previous years, the National Organization for Women suggested a number of "Action Ideas" to its membership to commemorate Equal Pay Day. The Nebraska Commission on the Status of Women delivered apple pies to state legislators, with the message that "women want their piece of the pie." A Michigan chapter of Business and Professional Women/USA distributed 1,000 red purse pins on Equal Pay Day, reminding the community that women's pay is "in the red."[47]

Progress, however, has been made at the state level. Some states have relatively weak pay equity laws for state employees. Still, those laws encourage employers to rethink their pay scales, and as a result, there has been some equalization of pay between women and men doing different jobs of comparable worth.[48] Figure 3.1 demonstrates that pay equity continues to be a problem throughout the nation, with some states doing much better than others.

Affirmative Action

Affirmative action programs attempt to remedy past discrimination against women, minorities, and others by increasing recruitment, promotion, retention,

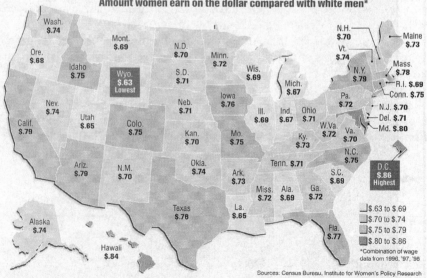

Women of Wyoming, unite: You're really underpaid

On average, U.S. women earn 74 cents for every dollar white men make. While the wage gap has narrowed from 60 cents on the dollar in 1979, this may be partly because of a drop in men's inflation-adjusted wages. Also, many women work part time and in low-paying fields.

Amount women earn on the dollar compared with white men*

FIGURE 3.1   The Wage Gap Across America
Source: © 2001, *U.S. News and World Report*, L.P. Reprinted with permission.

and on-the-job training opportunities and removing barriers to admission to educational institutions. Because there has been a long history of discrimination against women and African Americans in particular, most affirmative action programs are geared toward helping those two groups.

Title VII of the Civil Rights Act of 1964 and presidential Executive Order 11246, as amended by Executive Order 11375 in 1967, provided the initial basis for affirmative action toward women in employment in the United States. Title VII, as already noted, outlaws discrimination by employers or unions. Executive Order 11246, issued by President Lyndon Johnson in 1965, bars discrimination on the basis of race, color, religion, or national origin in federal employment and in employment by federal contractors and subcontractors. This order specifically required all executive agencies to "maintain a positive program of equal opportunities." The order also requires contractors to "take affirmative action to ensure that applicants are employed, and . . . treated during employment without regard to their race, creed, color, or national origin." In 1967, with the issuance of Executive Order 11375, this provision was expanded to include women. Somewhat reminiscent of the EEOC's failure to enforce Title VII, women's groups were unable to secure enforcement of this order until 1973. Title IX, discussed later, also provides the basis for affirmative action in education. It requires educational institutions receiving federal dollars to take "specific steps designed to encourage individuals of the previously excluded sex to apply."

In a series of cases decided in 1978–1980, the U.S. Supreme Court upheld the constitutionality of affirmative action plans, and in one case ruled that Title VII permitted a steelworkers' union and an employer to reserve one-half of all job openings in a training program for black workers. In 1987, in *Johnson v. Transportation Agency*, the Supreme Court relied on these earlier rulings to uphold an affirmative action plan that resulted in the promotion of a woman worker.[49]

In 1978, Santa Clara, California, adopted an affirmative action plan to remedy the effects of past practices and to attain a more equitable representation of women. Sex was to be considered as one factor in choosing among qualified job applicants in fields where women were traditionally underrepresented.

Diane Joyce and Paul Johnson were two of nine applicants who applied for a road dispatcher job, which was classified as a skilled craft position, a position no woman had ever held. Both had worked for the agency for several years and, in fact, had worked as dispatchers without the title or extra salary. After a personal interview in front of two superiors, Joyce and Johnson were rated 73 and 75, respectively. After a second round of interviews, Johnson was recommended for the job, but Joyce was hired after the agency's affirmative action coordinator intervened.

Johnson then filed a complaint with the EEOC, which refused to make a decision. The district court ruled for Johnson but was later reversed by the U.S. Supreme Court; the Reagan Justice Department filed a brief urging the justices to side with Johnson and against affirmative action programs. Women's rights groups lined up on the side of Joyce. In March 1987, the Supreme Court upheld the plan, concluding that Title VII permitted discrimination to end discrimination—even in situations where no showing of past discrimination was made. According to the Court, it was appropriate for the agency to take note of the *total* absence of women from the skilled craft jobs and to use sex as a factor in the appointment process.

The six-person majority was not a strong one. Justice Sandra Day O'Connor, then the lone female on the bench, concurred only because she believed prior intentional discrimination had occurred. In subsequent affirmative action decisions, however, Justice O'Connor has not found intentional discrimination. In fact, a series of seven conservative decisions involving race and sex discrimination decided in 1988 and 1989 led to congressional passage of the Civil Rights Act of 1991 after extensive lobbying by a coalition of women's and civil rights organizations. It eased substantive and procedural requirements on employees seeking to prove discrimination. It also provided new remedies for victims of intentional employment discrimination, including sexual harassment.

There were repeated challenges to affirmative action throughout the last decade. In 1995, the Supreme Court issued a ruling calling affirmative action programs into serious constitutional question. The Republican Party platform in 1996 and 2000 called for an end to all federal affirmative action programs. The Democratic Party platform in 2000 proposed actions aimed at "mending, not ending" the program. The results of the 2000 and 2002 elections raised serious doubts about the future of affirmative action programs, with a Republican president and a Republican-controlled Congress. Yet 80 percent of all working women support strengthening rather than eliminating affirmative action laws. In fact, a mere 4 percent of working women said that affirmative action is not important to them.[50]

Affirmative action is a particularly thorny legal issue for African American women and other women of color. Not only do they often experience discrimination based on their gender, but they often suffer on account of race, too. Proving discrimination then can become much more complex. Even in the wake of legislation such as California's Proposition 209, which banned the use of affirmative action programs across the state, activists continue to emphasize the legal standing of the program across the nation. Attorney and Civil Rights activist Beth Wilson argues, "We are very clearly in the midst of serious challenges to affirmative action. Those of us who believe in its rightness must regain the high ground in framing the debate, in defining the terms, in interpreting what it is and what it is not, and in making a persuasive case for what we think is just." She asserts that the pendulum of public attitudes has swung back and forth on issues such as affirmative action, but that "the backward arcs have never been dramatic—especially in comparison with the wide swings forward."[51]

In June 2003, the Supreme Court issued two rulings that will impact affirmative action programs on college campuses. In two separate cases involving the University of Michigan, the justices redefined how race could be used in college admissions. In *Gratz v. Bollinger*, the Supreme Court ruled that a University of Michigan undergraduate admissions policy that awarded points to applicants

Profiles in Leadership
THE SANCHEZ SISTERS ELECTED
TO CONGRESS

"My daughters know that education is the key to success. How do
I know? Because I taught them."

Maria Marcias Sanchez[a]

On election night in November 2002, Loretta and Linda Sanchez made
history as the first sisters to be elected to the U.S. House of Representatives. Loretta Sanchez (D-Calif.) was reelected to a fourth term in Congress. She had quickly made a name for herself in Washington, D.C., as
an advocate for working people after winning a disputed election against
Republican Bob Dornan in 1996. Her younger sister, Linda Sanchez (D-
Calif.) won an election for an open seat in Orange County with the support of the electrical workers union she had represented for years as a
labor lawyer. "During the general election campaign, Sanchez's opponent dismissed her as little more than the kid sister of a congresswoman,
or in his words, 'a cute novelty act.' Sanchez still bristles at the characteri-
zation, observing that no one similarly likened President George W. Bush
and his brother Jeb Bush to anything other than two successful brother
politicians. 'When I got into the labor movement, it was tough for some
folks to accept that I was young, a woman and a woman of color too. You
have to prove yourself before you get the respect that some people give a
man automatically.'"[b] The Sanchez sisters recognize their importance as
role models for a future generation of women in politics.

The Sanchez sisters are the daughters of Mexican immigrants who
raised their family in California. Their mother, Maria, went back to
school after her children were grown to earn a teaching certificate. The
family represents an important new demographic trend in American politics—the rise of the Hispanic voter. According to data from the 2000 U.S.
Census, Hispanic Americans now represent the largest minority population in the country. The impact of Hispanic voters has been seen in the
electoral politics of many Sun Belt states. Both Loretta and Linda Sanchez
ran campaign advertisements in Spanish to reach Hispanic voters in their
districts. On January 7, 2003, Loretta and Linda Sanchez stood together as
they took the oath of office as United States Representatives. Loretta
Sanchez commented, "The people of my district have entrusted me with
a very important job that I take very seriously. I will continue to work
day and night to address the concerns families wrestle with every day;
preparing for retirement, providing a high-quality education for their
kids, and paying the rising costs of prescription drugs. I am dedicated

(continued)

and committed to winning the war on terrorism, and national security, but real security also encompasses economic, health, education and environmental security for every American."[c]

[a] Eleanor Clift and Tom Brazaitis, *Madam President* (New York: Routledge, 2003), 284.

[b] "First Term Representative Is One of Few IBEW Members Ever Elected to Congress," International Brotherhood of Electrical Workers, January/February 2003, http://www.ibew.org/stories/03journal/0301/page12.htm.

[c] Press Release, Office of Congresswoman Loretta Sanchez, "Rep. Loretta Sanchez, Sister Make History, Take Oath of Office," January 7, 2003, http://www.house.gov/sanchez//news/press01703.html.

on the basis of racial identity was unconstitutional. The justices claimed that the point system amounted to an illegal quota. The Supreme Court in *Grutter v. Bollinger*, however, issued a separate ruling supporting affirmative action as a means of achieving the educational goal of a diverse student body. The case involved a white female who was denied admission to the University of Michigan Law School. Barbara Gutter sued the University of Michigan Law School for racial discrimination, claiming that less qualified applicants were admitted to the program on the basis of their race. Justice Sandra Day O'Connor wrote in her majority opinion.

> "Attaining a diverse student body is at the heart of the Law School's proper institutional mission," and she highlighted the "laudable educational benefits that diversity is designed to produce, including cross-racial understanding and the breaking down of racial stereotypes.[52]"

Some commentators heralded the decision as a sign that the attacks on affirmative action of the previous decade were over for now. "The decision provides what looks like a guarantee that affirmative action in admissions is now safe for another generation. Having it in writing—writing that has the force of law— is always a relief."[53]

Sexual Harassment.   Discrimination clearly continues to exist in the workforce. Of late, however, the issue of sexual harassment in the workplace has garnered more attention than other forms of discrimination.

In some instances, sexual requirements have been placed on women workers as conditions for job retention, advancement, or salary raises. Other less flagrant forms of sexual harassment include verbal abuse, sexist remarks or jokes, and offensive touching, patting, and leering. This kind of treatment makes working conditions difficult for women, causing them a tremendous amount of stress. Harassment often leads victims to seek other positions, thereby causing them to lose seniority and other accrued benefits. Problems of sexual harassment have not been confined to the working world either. In fact, the Legal Defense and Education Fund of the National Organization for Women established a special Sexual Harassment in

WOMEN, SEXUAL HARASSMENT,
AND THE MILITARY

Women are an integral part of the United States military. Enlisted women and officers serve in every branch of the armed forces as the military conducts battles in the War on Terrorism in Afghanistan and Iraq. As the nation fights terror at home and abroad, the percentage of women in the military continues to rise. Women make up one-fifth of all recruits and 15 percent of the active duty armed forces. Many women are rising through the ranks of the officer corps, and five have become three-star generals. Minority women in particular have joined the military. African American women represent almost 50 percent of female recruits enlisting in the armed services. Each branch of the military has seen an increase in the number of women willing to serve their country. The Air Force has the highest percentage of women officers (17.3 percent) and enlisted women (19.6 percent), while the Navy has the lowest percentage of women officers (14.9 percent) and enlisted women (14.0 percent). At 17.3 percent, the number of women officers in the Marine Corps is greater than the number of enlisted women who make up 6.2 percent of this branch of the armed services.[a] Yet sexual harassment scandals such as the Navy's Tailhook incident in the 1980s and at the Army's Aberdeen Proving Ground in the 1990s demonstrate that women are far from receiving equal treatment in the military. A survey released by the Pentagon in 1996 revealed that 55 percent of the 50,000 women who responded believed that they had experienced sexual harassment in the previous year.

All branches of the services are trying to end sexual harassment, not just because it's wrong, but because the military needs all the women it can get. "If a secret blast went off right now, killing all the women, the Army would cease to function," says a spokesperson for its personnel branch. In 1994, the Pentagon opened up all positions to women except those in "direct combat." Some argued that this added to the confusion over women's role in the military, as women "can now participate in roles that seem to be in combat in everything but name." Conservatives on the House National Security Committee had claimed that the Army "has been naïve in training women and men in the same boot camps, and in widening jobs open to women including flying combat jets and serving on warships." In spite of these criticisms, the Army continues to recruit women; at the same time it is instituting new procedures to handle sexual harassment complaints. The Navy, too, has taken positive measures to head off sexual harassment. Training teams were sent to every base to teach personnel about sexual harassment and how to report allegations of abuse.

(continued)

Yet sexual harassment remains a persistent problem in the armed services. E. Cameron Ritchie, program director for mental health and women's issues for the Office of the Assistant Secretary of Defense for Health Affairs, reported in April 2001 on the results of a recent study of sexual harassment in the military. The study found that 23 percent of women treated by the Department of Veterans Affairs for depression and alcohol abuse reported that they have been victims of sexual assault while on active duty. Dr. Ritchie, a lieutenant colonel, underscored the efforts the military is taking to prevent sexual harassment. "It's a readiness issue. It's a medical issue. It's an issue for all of us."[b] The vital roles that women play in the active duty military became increasingly clear as troops prepared to invade Iraq in the spring of 2003. The nation was riveted by the story of the capture and rescue of Private Jessica Lynch, whose story illustrated that women in supposedly "noncombat" roles in the supply line could die on the battlefield. Against the backdrop of women's service in the War on Terrorism, the media and Congress focused attention on allegations that numerous female cadets had been the victims of sexual abuse for years at the Air Force Academy. Congressional lawmakers and military leaders called for policy and personnel changes at the service academy in recognition of the crucial need for women officers to lead the military missions of the new millennium.

---

[a] U.S. Department of Defense, Defense Manpower Data Center, unpublished data, May 31, 1999.

[b] Sargent 1st Class Kathleen T. Rhem, "Services Move to Lower Instances of Rape in the Ranks," American Forces Press Service, April 5, 2001.

Education Project to provide legal assistance for students and faculty members who find themselves victims of harassment.

Public awareness of sexual harassment has evolved slowly. In the late 1970s, radical feminist scholar Catharine A. MacKinnon began to advance the idea that sexual harassment was employment discrimination actionable under Title VII.[54] In November 1980, at the urging of several women's rights groups, the EEOC adopted regulations making sexual harassment an impermissible form of sex discrimination prohibited by Title VII.

When more hearings were held on these guidelines in spring 1981, Phyllis Schlafly, head of the Eagle Forum, testified in opposition. She argued that harassment "is not a problem" and that only those who "ask for it" actually find themselves victims. She asked commission members to rescind the regulations as inconsistent with Title VII.

Schlafly's comments surprised and angered many. Clearly, stringent regulations could be threatening to some men who harass women, but women had little to lose from the regulations. In fact, for conservative women, the regulations guarantee that women have recourse against inappropriate conduct; for women's rights supporters, they provide legal recourse for discriminatory conduct that has a pervasive impact on the employment status of many women.

In 1985, Congress finally codified sexual harassment as a form of discrimination prohibited under Title VII. Basically, two versions of harassment were made illegal: (1) the "quid pro quo" version in which employment terms and benefits are based on or are conditional on sexual favors, and (2) the offensive or hostile work environment that results from harassment, which does not necessarily involve salary or other job benefits.

Meritor Savings Bank v. Vinson (1986) was the first sexual harassment case to reach the U.S. Supreme Court.[55] A unanimous Court found that a bank manager's repeated demands for sexual favors created a "hostile environment" actionable under Title VII. Moreover, such sexual harassment is illegal not only when it results in the loss of a job or a promotion, but also when it creates a hostile work environment.

In spite of *Meritor*, the EEOC was not deluged with complaints. In 1987, the first year the EEOC kept records of complaints, only 5,499 complaints of sexual harassment were filed. It wasn't until 1991, when the nation sat riveted before television sets during the Clarence Thomas confirmation hearings, that sexual harassment as an issue began to get a significant amount of media attention. The issue was debated not only in Washington, D.C., but also in businesses, lunchrooms, and living rooms all over America. More women began to report harassment, and employers began to appear more sensitive to the problem. The EEOC, for example, reported that sexual harassment complaints went up 70 percent the year after the Thomas hearings, and 150 percent by the end of 1995.

The number of sexual harassment complaints filed annually continues to rise in the wake of the U.S. Supreme Court's 1993 decision *Harris v. Forklift Systems*.[56] In *Harris*, the company supervisor admitted asking female employees to fish for coins in his front pants pockets, commenting on the size of a female employee's breasts and buttocks, and suggesting to one woman that they go to a hotel to negotiate her raise. The lower court did not think that this kind of behavior, which forced Teresa Harris to quit her job, was enough to be called sexual harassment actionable under law. A unanimous U.S. Supreme Court disagreed, concluding that for harassment to be actionable, the conduct in question need not "seriously affect [an employee's] psychological well-being" or lead the plaintiff to suffer an injury.[57]

Employment Discrimination and the Consequences of Childbearing

Although the Equal Pay Act and Title VII of the Civil Rights Act are designed to remedy discrimination, from the beginning, the fact that only women bear children has had major consequences on their status in the workforce. Employers have tried to use a variety of tactics to penalize women who opt to have children.

Pregnancy Discrimination. Beginning in the 1970s and continuing today, many forms of pregnancy discrimination—including forced leave, loss of seniority, lack of medical coverage, and outright dismissal—have been challenged by women's rights groups. In a list of demands made at its first conference, NOW listed paid maternity leaves, laws to allow women to return to their jobs with no loss of seniority, and child-care centers. When NOW first decided to target pregnancy discrimination in employment, however, some women, including many in the Women's Equity Action League (WEAL), voiced their concern that the new group should focus its energies on less controversial issues.

The first real schism over how to deal with pregnancy discrimination occurred when the Women's Law Fund (WLF) was founded by some WEAL leaders who disagreed over WEAL's involvement in *Cleveland Board of Education v. LaFleur* (1974), a case challenging the automatic dismissal of school-teachers in their fourth month of pregnancy.[58] WEAL thought that pregnancy discrimination was too controversial to tackle. Nevertheless, both NOW and the ACLU's Women's Rights Project (WRP) filed friend of the court briefs to support the arguments made by WLF, which ultimately sponsored the case. In *LaFleur*, the Supreme Court ruled that it was unconstitutional for the school board to require pregnant women to take unpaid leaves five months before their due dates and prohibit them from returning to the classroom until the semester after their children were three months old.

LaFleur constituted an important victory for women's rights groups, but the Court failed to address whether employers should treat pregnancy like other medical conditions and not as one unique to women. In 1972, based on recommendations of the Citizens Advisory Council on the Status of Women (the new name of the President's Commission on the Status of Women) and women's rights groups, the EEOC adopted regulations that specifically rejected the "pregnancy is unique" argument. But in *Geduldig v. Aiello* (1974), a case challenging California's refusal to pay pregnancy disability benefits to women workers, the justices upheld the constitutionality of a plan that established a medical benefits fund for all workers but excluded any coverage for pregnancy, including normal hospital stays.[59] The justices found that the plan was a reasonable way for the state to limit expenses and that there was "no evidence in the record that the selection of the risks insured by the program worked to discriminate against any identifiable group or class in terms of the aggregate risk protection." Although *Geduldig* was a major loss for the women's rights groups involved, most commentators believed that this decision was grounded not in constitutional theory, but in economic realities—the California plan simply had not been set up to handle these additional claims. Prior to *Geduldig*, in two major cases, *Reed v. Reed* (1971) and *Frontiero v. Richardson* (1973) (see Chapter 1), the Supreme Court struck down laws that treated women differently from men, holding that certain kinds of sex discrimination were prohibited by the Fourteenth Amendment. Because only women get pregnant, the justices found no sex discrimination in *Geduldig*.

Successes of women's rights organizations in litigating *Reed*, *Frontiero*, and *LaFleur* lulled attorneys into believing that the Court was willing to expand the protections of the Fourteenth Amendment to prohibit a wide variety of gender-based discriminatory practices. As *Geduldig* proved, however, this was not the case. Thus, given the Court's opinion in *Geduldig*, feminist lawyers turned to Title VII for possible relief against on-the-job pregnancy discrimination by private employers.

The first test of this strategy came in *General Electric Co. v. Gilbert* (1976).[60] Unlike the situation in *Geduldig*, in which a judicial finding of discrimination might have bankrupted the state's disability system, *Gilbert* involved a private employer's plan that contained a maternity exclusion clause similar to California's. Because *Gilbert* was styled as a Title VII class action lawsuit and involved only one, albeit large, company, many court observers believed that the justices would find in favor of the pregnancy discrimination claim. However, in rejecting the arguments put forth by Gilbert's lawyers that a penalty on the birth process was inherently discriminatory, the Court disregarded EEOC guidelines that interpreted such programs as discriminatory. It also found no Title VII violation, because there was no showing of employer discrimination. Writing for the Court, Justice William Rehnquist adopted the reasoning of the lower court, which had concluded that pregnancy "is not a disease at all and is often a voluntarily undertaken and desired condition."

Women's rights activists were outraged by the *Gilbert* decision and the justices' cavalier attitude toward pregnancy. In droves, they descended on Congress to urge passage of an amendment to Title VII to ban discrimination based on pregnancy.[61] Their efforts resulted in passage of the Pregnancy Discrimination Act (PDA) of 1978 as an amendment to the Civil Rights Act of 1964. It requires employers to treat pregnancy like any other physical condition.

Not surprisingly, the legislation drew strong opposition from employer groups. In contrast, it was an issue that united women's groups on both sides of the ERA controversy. Most women agreed that pregnant women should be entitled to the same benefits as their male counterparts. Women's rights activists believed that the PDA would allow women with children greater career and childbirth options. The Eagle Forum and many conservative women, moreover, believed that the absence of such legislation encouraged abortion. Although the PDA provided a public good, it was not particularly threatening to women. Thus, the absence of opposition from conservative women is not surprising; there is nothing in the law that requires women to work. It simply allows those who wish to work not to be penalized for motherhood—a right strongly advocated by both pro- and anti-ERA camps.

The Difference Debate.   As political scientist Judith A. Baer has noted, "amending the civil rights law has not settled all the difficulties involved, because pregnancy and childbirth are more than physical conditions."[62] Pregnancy makes some women ill, especially in the first trimester, when nausea and fatigue are common. Most women also require some time to recuperate from childbirth. Indeed, a 1993 study concluded that some women take up to a year to recuperate fully from pregnancy.[63] Moreover, pregnancy is a condition unique to women.

Although the PDA requires employers to treat women and men *equally*, some states have opted to require employers to provide "extra" protection or benefits to pregnant workers. A California law passed in 1978, for example, *requires* employers to give employees up to four months of "pregnancy disability leave." But when Lillian Garland attempted to return to her receptionist's position at a California bank, she was told she had no job. She filed a complaint against the bank with the State Department of Fair Employment and Housing. Her employer argued that the California law was in conflict with and was preempted by the PDA because the California law discriminated *in favor of* pregnant workers. The department found in favor of Garland, and her employer filed suit in federal court. The director of the Department of Fair Employment and Housing, Mark Guerra, acted on her behalf in court.

By the time *California Federal Savings and Loan Association v. Guerra* (1987)[64] reached the U.S. Supreme Court, women's rights advocates were weighing in on both sides of the issue, which resulted in a situation that closely paralleled the early split among suffragists over the NWP's support of an ERA and the division that occurred in *Adkins v. Children's Hospital* (1923), described earlier in this chapter. NOW and the ACLU's WRP filed an amicus curiae (friend of the court) brief on behalf of the bank. They argued that application of a policy to women alone (Cal Federal did not guarantee jobs to men who returned from medical leave) would "reinforce stereotypes about women's inclinations and abilities" and "deter employers from hiring women of childbearing age."[65] Other feminists, including Equal Rights Advocates, a California-based public interest law group, argued that this position denied the reality that women alone bear children; that difference, they argued, must be acknowledged.[66]

The Supreme Court never really addressed the debate over equality versus protection. Instead, it concluded that the Pregnancy Discrimination Act was only a floor below which states could not go in treating pregnant workers. Writing for the Court, Justice Thurgood Marshall noted that the purpose of the 1978 act was "to guarantee women the right to participate fully and equally in the work force, without denying them the fundamental right to full participation in family life." Thus, although Garland had already been rehired by the bank, the decision put employers on notice that pregnancy discrimination would not be tolerated.

However, the emphasis on sexual equality in the formation of public policy means that pregnant women in the United States receive far fewer protections and benefits than their counterparts in Western Europe. Many European feminists argue that because only women bear children, government programs and employment policies must create equality of opportunity while recognizing the reality of sexual difference. In France, for example, pregnant women receive generous benefits in the form of free medical care when a child is born, followed by a minimum of four months of paid maternity leave. A woman's job is protected by law until she is ready to return to work, and the maximum legal work week is limited to thirty-five hours. The French government's pro-natalist policies expand the benefits to women for each subsequent birth by increasing the amount of time covered by paid maternity leave and providing families with two or more children with monthly cash stipends. All children are eligible for high-quality child care, with the costs subsidized by the government. If a woman chooses not to return to the workforce after the birth of her child or to work part time, she receives a salary from the state to stay at home.[67] The Global Awareness box provides a comparison of maternity leave benefits around the world.

The Family and Medical Leave Act.   The difference debate was also evident in early attempts to guarantee family and medical leaves for women workers. Representative Howard Berman (D-Calif.), who wrote the California pregnancy disability legislation at issue in the *Cal Federal* case, introduced similar legislation in Congress after Lillian Garland lost in the lower court. Women active in NOW, the Women's Legal Defense Fund (WLDF), the National Women's Political Caucus (NWPC), and the AAUW refused to support Berman's legislation (as they had in *Cal Federal*) because they were uncomfortable with his description of pregnancy as a disability.[68] They then persuaded Berman that parental leave for mothers *and* fathers would be more likely to garner wide support.

Representative Patricia Schroeder (D-Colo.), the cochair of the Congressional Caucus on Women's Issues, soon took up a leadership role on the parental leave bill. She liked the legislation because "it challenged the commitment of conservative family proponents head on while not doing harm to women's rights."[69] Schroeder reasoned that anyone interested in helping families would favor allowing a parent time off to care for a sick child.

The AAUW, ACLU, BPW, NOW, NWPC, WEAL, WLDF, and several labor unions supported the proposed legislation when it was first introduced in the House in 1985. Opposed were the Chamber of Commerce of the United States and the Reagan White House. The legislation soon got caught up in controversial welfare and child-care reform legislation as it was changed and amended. Finally, a watered-down version was vetoed by President George H. W. Bush. Even though polls showed Americans were ready to accept maternity leave, the notion of paternity leave was harder to sell. Gender roles, as discussed in Chapter 4, die hard; and with a president in the White House who was hostile to the idea, supporters held little hope.

The 1992 election of Bill Clinton, who had attacked Bush's veto of the Family and Medical Leave Act, changed the scenario. Congress quickly passed the act in 1993, and Clinton signed it into law with considerable fanfare, noting that it was "a matter of pure common sense and a matter of common decency."[70]

The act gives workers at companies of more than fifty persons the right to take up to twelve weeks of unpaid leave to care for a new baby or to help a family member with a serious health problem. On returning from leave, workers must be given their old job or its equivalent. The highest-paid 10 percent of employees at each company are not fully protected. These "key" employees can lose their jobs if employers can prove their reinstatement would cause "substantial and grievous" harm.

Global Awareness

MATERNITY LEAVE BENEFITS

Country	Length of Maternity Leave	% Wages Paid in Covered Period	Provider of Coverage
Australia	1 year	0%	None
China	90 days	100%	Employer
France	16–26 weeks	100%	Social Security
India	12 weeks	100%	Employer/Social Security
Japan	14 weeks	60%	Social Security or Health Insurance
Kenya	2 months	100%	Employer
Russian Federation	140 days	100%	Social Security
Sweden	14 weeks	450 days paid parental leave: 360 days at 75% and 90 days at flat rate	Social Security
United States	Up to 12 weeks	0%	None
Venezuela	18 weeks	100%	Social Security

Source: "Maternity Leave Benefits, as of 1998," in *The World's Women 2000: Trends and Statistics*, Table 5-C (New York: United Nations Publications, 2000), 140–3.

Women in many nations are able to rely on some form of subsidized maternity leave. Whether the benefit is derived from social security, health insurance, or an employer, women are afforded financial support for their families following the birth of a child. Australia and the United States are the only industrialized nations which do not offer state-sponsored maternity leave benefits. A proposal in 2004 would grant Australian women paid maternity leave at the minimum wage for fourteen weeks following the birth of a child.

Since the act was passed, over 35 million workers have taken advantage of its leave provision. In 2001, the Department of Labor issued the report "Balancing the Needs of Families and Employers," highlighting the results of surveys conducted on the impact of the Family and Medical Leave Act on employers and employees. This study updated survey research conducted in

CHILD CARE: A NATIONAL CRISIS?

According to survey research conducted by the Children's Defense Fund, in 1999 almost 60 percent of mothers with infants, 64 percent of mothers with children under age six, and 78 percent of mothers with children between the ages of six and thirteen are in the labor force. Child care has become a basic necessity for America's working families, yet it remains a need that has not been sufficiently addressed by public policy makers. The CDF survey "Child Care Challenges" found that, across the nation, child care costs more than $3,000 a year per child, and in some states the costs exceed $5,000 per child annually. "In fifteen states, tuition (in-state) for a single year of public college is less than half that of child care tuition." (See Table 3.4.)

For low-wage families, the burden of child-care costs can be financially overwhelming. The report notes that many working families pay more for child care than for their rent or mortgage. "A family with an infant and a four-year-old, with both parents working full time at the minimum wage ($21,400), would spend about 30 percent of their income on child care. In the twenty-three states with the highest child-care costs in urban areas, the same family would spend about 50 percent of their income on child care."[a]

---

[a] Much of the information contained here is derived from the Children's Defense Fund Fact Sheet, "Parent's Face Higher Tuition for Childcare than College," http://www.childrensdefense.org/cc_highcost.htm.

TABLE 3.4 **Child Care vs. College Fund**

Location	Child Care Tuition	Public College Tuition
Wake County, NC	$5,068	$1,841
Honolulu, HI	$6,188	$2,298
Kansas City, KS	$5,200	$2,223
Dane County, WI	$6,240	$2,747
Anchorage, AK	$5,784	$2,552

Source: Children's Defense Fund Fact Sheet, "Parents Face Higher Tuition for Child Care than College," http://www.childrensdefense.org/cc_highcost.htm.

1995 on implementing the federal leave policy. The new report suggests that the Family and Medical Leave Act has successfully enabled millions of workers to take time off the job to recover from illness themselves or to tend to a birth, adoption, or illness within their families. According to the study, "For most employers, the Act had no noticeable effect on their overall productivity, profitability, or growth." The study's authors noted, however, that more than 50 percent of workers who took family or medical leave were worried about "having enough money to pay bills."[71] The majority of workers who were eligible for leave but did not take it claimed they could not afford an unpaid leave of absence from their jobs. The author of the FMLA, Senator Christopher Dodd (D-Conn.), said of the Department of Labor report, "Family leave is like 911—you don't use it unless you truly need it but it's critically important when you do. Thankfully this report indicates that family and medical leave is doing what it should—helping families—but now we need to do more to ensure that even more people can access its benefits."[72]

Reproductive Hazards and Fetal Protection Policies.   The fact that women have children has also been the basis for employer "fetal protection" policies that bar only women of childbearing age from certain jobs. Upon reaching her fiftieth birthday, Virginia Green considered herself done with childbearing, but her employer, Johnson Controls Inc. of Bennington, Vermont, apparently disagreed. The maker of automotive batteries demoted Green from her job as a lead plate stacker to a lower-paying one in the laundry for fear that lead in her blood (absorbed from the batteries) would pose a risk to any fetus she might conceive.

Eight years later, the U.S. Supreme Court finally addressed her demotion and that of three of her female coworkers when it decided its first fetal protection case. Green's lawyers argued that the company's policy resulted in discrimination barred by Title VII. While Johnson Controls argued that its mandatory fetal protection policy was a bona fide occupational qualification permissible under Title VII, the Supreme Court disagreed. In a landmark sex discrimination employment case, the justices ruled that women could not be forced to choose between having a job and having children and that the roles of mother and employee are not mutually exclusive.

Initially, women's rights activists, although unanimous in their agreement that fetal protection policies were illegal, feared that the Court might opt to uphold these policies by construing the BFOQ exception liberally. But in *Automobile Workers v. Johnson Controls* (1991), a unanimous Court protected the rights of millions of workers for whom compulsory sterilization could have been made a legal term and condition of employment by ruling that fetal protection policies affecting women workers violate Title VII.[73] Groups on both sides of the pregnancy litigation in *Cal Federal* supported the decision, as did conservative women's groups, who viewed the company's fetal protection policy as encouraging abortion.

Education

Women have suffered from unequal treatment in education as far back as records have been kept. In the 1960s, women, particularly those in the older branch of the women's rights movement, immediately recognized inequalities in the educational system, their impact on employment opportunities, and the need for concerted action to improve conditions. While many younger-branch women were instrumental in founding women's studies programs, older-branch women pushed for laws to end discrimination. Even before the rise of the older, rights-oriented branch, the National Federation of Business and Professional Women's Clubs long urged abolition of quotas for women in schools (which were used to limit women's access) and actively encouraged women to go back to school. President Kennedy's Commission on the Status of Women even urged government support of continuing education for homemakers. But although commission members recommended "imaginative counseling, which [could] lift aspirations beyond stubbornly persistent assumptions about women's roles and women's interest,"[74] their comments clearly reflected the view that a woman's primary role was motherhood. Instead of criticizing the emphasis many colleges placed on home economics, for example, the commission bemoaned the fact that "even women's colleges have given remarkably little serious thought to the better preparation of their students for the home-making most of them will do."[75]

NOW and later WEAL, however, soon began to call for educational equality for women, as did the few women in the U.S. Congress. Noting, in 1967, that the near absence of women in high-paying, prestige professions and in leadership positions was often a function of limited educational opportunities for women, NOW called for passage of federal and state legislation to ensure that women "be educated to their full potential."[76]

Title IX and the Constitution.   Concern for a woman's right to achieve her full educational potential was a key element in the support that women's rights organizations gave to educational equity legislation. In 1970, with the full support of a wide variety of women's groups, Representative Edith Green (D-Ore.) held hearings that revealed extensive discrimination against women in the nation's schools. Two years later, when Green and Representative Patsy Mink (D-Hawaii), the first Japanese American woman elected to Congress, consequently introduced Title IX as part of the Educational Amendments Act of 1972, they asked women's groups not to testify for the bill, believing chances of passage would be greatly enhanced if less attention were given to its provisions. No women's groups testified, and Title IX was voted into law. As enacted, Title IX prohibits sex discrimination in any elementary, secondary, or postsecondary school if the institution is the recipient of any federal monies. It also extended coverage of Title VII and the Equal Pay Act to educational workers and authorized the U.S. attorney general to instigate lawsuits against educational institutions that fail to comply. The law itself is fairly simple; most of the controversy over it has occurred in the drafting of regulations and enforcement stages.[77]

Drafting regulations to implement Title IX became a battleground for conservative versus liberal women's groups' agendas. When regulations were finally adopted, they prohibited gender bias in three major areas: (1) admissions, (2) student treatment, and (3) hiring and personnel practices.

Women and Politics

CONGRESSWOMAN LOUISE SLAUGHTER FIGHTS FOR TITLE IX

According to Congresswoman Louise Slaughter (D-N.Y.), "It is not by luck that athletic opportunities for women have increased dramatically over the last thirty years, it is because of Title IX. Title IX is now under assault, and my bill reaffirms Congress' commitment to keeping the playing field level for young women athletes across the nation."[a]

Congresswoman Slaughter has been a tireless advocate for women's issues during her eight terms in the House of Representatives. She has championed gender equity in education, health care, and economic development while in Congress and served as Democratic Co-Chair of the Women's Caucus. A microbiologist by training, Slaughter sponsored legislation to establish the Office of Research on Women's Health at the National Institutes of Health. Her focus on women's health issues led Slaughter to be an outspoken opponent of the Department of Education's Commission for Athletic Opportunity, charged by Secretary of Education Rod Paige with reassessing the value of Title IX. In February 2003, the Commission for Athletic Opportunity recommended modifying the classifications that determine whether schools are in compliance with the gender equity provisions of Title IX. Members of the Commission for Athletic Opportunity proposed changing the "three-part test," which required schools to offer athletic opportunities in proportion to the number of women students, with "interest surveys" to assess the level of student support for women's athletic programs on campus. According to the National Organization for Women, "The proposed changes will allow schools to back away from Title IX's goal of equal support for women's and men's sports programs and, in effect, will render meaningless the most important objective of Title IX—that is, to overcome decades of discrimination and neglect of girls' and women's athletic programs."[b]

The National Coalition for Women and Girls in Education estimates that the proposed changes to Title IX would "cost high school girls 305,000 participation opportunities; college women would miss out on 50,000 participation opportunities and 122 million dollars in athletic scholarships."[c]

On March 11, 2003, Congresswoman Louise Slaughter introduced a resolution to protect Title IX. "I hope this resolution sends a clear message to the Administration that Members of Congress and women around the country will not tolerate attempts to weaken Title IX."[d]

---

[a] News Release, Office of Congresswoman Louise M. Slaughter, "Slaughter Introduces Legislation to Protect Title IX," March 11, 2003, http://www.slaughter.house.gov/NR/exeres/BE1B2B78-5951-4EEC-AF61-95ECD79E8424.htm.

[b] Jill Filipovic, "Olympic Athletes Criticize Title IX Recommendations," http://www.now.org/eNews/march 2003/030303titleix.html.

[c] Legislative Update Special Report, "Bush Commission Weakens Title IX in Sports: Phony Study Commission Issues Radical Recommendations," National Organization for Women, February 2003, http://www.now.org/issues/legislat/200302.html.

[d] Office of Congresswoman Louise M. Slaughter, "Slaughter Introduces Legislation to Protect Title IX."

Admissions.   Title IX and its implementing regulations do not outlaw single-sex schools. They simply prevent public institutions that already receive federal money from becoming single-sex institutions. Historically, single-sex education has produced division even among women who advocate full educational equality. According to a 1973 Carnegie Commission report, "various studies have shown that women who attend women's colleges have academic records superior to those of their coeducational sisters, on the basis of such measures as persistence, proportion going on to graduate education, and the proportion receiving Ph.D.'s."[78] Findings of this sort have led many women to support sex-segregated colleges, and many men cling dearly to the concept of male-only institutions. The controversy surrounding Shannon Faulkner's efforts to enter the Citadel and then the treatment of Faulkner and the four women cadets who enrolled there in 1996 dramatically highlight these attitudes.

Some women argue that state maintenance of sex-segregated schools, particularly where *states* maintain superior "male-only" schools, denies them equal educational opportunities and equal protection of the laws as guaranteed by the U.S. Constitution. In June 1982, the U.S. Supreme Court ruled that a state's maintenance of a nursing school that admitted only women was unconstitutional. Writing for the Court in *Mississippi v. Hogan* (1982), Justice Sandra Day O'Connor noted:

> Although the test for determining the validity of a gender-based classification is straightforward, it must be applied free of fixed notions concerning the roles and abilities of males and females. Care must be taken in ascertaining whether the statutory objective itself reflects archaic and stereotypic notions. Thus, if the statutory objective is to exclude or protect members of one gender because they are presumed to suffer from an inherent handicap or to be innately inferior, the objective itself is illegitimate.[79]

Thus, although the Court relied on the Fourteenth Amendment and not Title IX, it was clear that some types of single-sex schools could no longer be maintained.

In the late 1980s and into the 1990s, the issue of single-sex schools again heated up. Some private women's colleges, such as Mills College in California, contemplated admitting men to bolster faltering revenues, while lawsuits were filed to open the doors of all-male, state-supported colleges to women. In 1990, the U.S. Justice Department sued the all-male Virginia Military Institute (VMI) and accused it of violating the Fourteenth Amendment for its policy of excluding women. Governor L. Douglas Wilder of Virginia refused to defend the policy, so the school's board of visitors and alumni took up its defense. They argued that VMI's rigid military-style training was especially beneficial to men, an argument ultimately rejected by a U.S. court of appeals. In taking note of the fact that the U.S. service academies opened their doors to women many years before, the appeals court said VMI must admit women or create a separate "parallel program" for women or forfeit state aid. The state then proceeded to create an alternative program for women, the Women's Institute of Leadership, at Mary Baldwin College, a private women's college close by.

In 1996, the U.S. Supreme Court, in a seven to one vote (Justice Clarence Thomas did not participate in the decision), found that VMI's all-male admissions policy discriminated against women and violated the Equal Protection Clause of the Fourteenth Amendment to the U.S. Constitution. Writing for the majority in *United States v. Virginia,* Justice Ruth Bader Ginsburg dismissed VMI's contention that admitting women would hurt the school. Ginsburg further noted her belief that the program set up at Mary Baldwin was a "pale shadow" of VMI because it lacked the military training, prestige, and tradition of the all-male school. "In myriad respects," said Ginsburg, the Mary Baldwin program "does not qualify as VMI's equal."[80]

The Court's decision did not mean an end to all single-sex public institutions. The Court was clear to point out that single-sex schools could pass constitutional muster so long as states provide opportunities "evenhandedly" to both sexes.[81]

Student Treatment.   Although debate continues over the appropriateness of non-state-supported, sex-segregated schools, most women agree that female students should be treated equally in coed schools. Passage of Title IX was to have accomplished this, but women's groups are still pressing for its full enforcement.

After passage of Title IX, the Department of Health, Education, and Welfare (HEW) (the precursor to the Department of Education and the Department of Health and Human Services) was slow to draft regulations to implement its provisions. Once HEW acted, women's rights groups have been forced, over the years, to try to ward off efforts to undermine the law through amendment, weaker regulations, or judicial decisions. In *Grove City College v. Bell* (1984), for example, the Supreme Court limited Title IX by finding (as urged by the Reagan administration) that it only applied to specific programs within universities that actually received federal aid.[82]

AMERICAN WOMEN'S SOCCER TEAM WINS THE WORLD CUP: A VICTORY FOR TITLE IX?

On July 9, 1999, Brandi Chastain scored the tie-breaking penalty kick to catapult the American Women's Soccer Team to a World Cup victory over China. A joyous Chastain garnered international attention by ripping off her jersey, revealing a sports bra. In the stands that day was President Clinton, who said of the American team's victory, "I think the whole country was caught up in this, not only soccer fans but young girls. In some ways, it's the biggest sporting event of the last decade."[a] Such winning moments propelled women's sports into the media spotlight and launched the Women's United Soccer Association. Mary Jo Kane, director of the University of Minnesota's Tucker Center for Research on Girls and Women in Sports, credits these winning plays to the success of Title IX. "In one generation we have gone from a young girl like me hoping that there is a team, to young girls today who hope that they make the team."[b] In the summer of 2003, however, the Women's United Soccer Association was disbanded due to rising debts and low attendance. The American Women's Soccer Team lost its semifinal match to Germany, the eventual winner of the 2003 World Cup.

Photograph of Brandi Chastain.
Source: AFP/Corbis.

---

[a] "Brilliant Brandi," CNN/SI—Women's World Cup, http://robots.cnnsi.com/soccer/world/1999/women's_worldcup/news/1999/07/10/us_china_ap/.

[b] Elizabeth Crowley, "Title IX Levels Playing Field for Funding Women's Sports," *Wall Street Journal*, June 22, 2000, A12.

Athletic programs, where Title IX has had tremendous impact, are often funded by ticket sales, alumni contributions, or the sale of television rights, and not by federal dollars. In essence, *Grove City* initially gave schools a new license to discriminate. Within six months, numerous Title IX actions were dropped, and charges of discrimination in women's sports programs were no longer being investigated.[83]

Women's rights groups began to lobby Congress to pass legislation that would overrule the Supreme Court decision immediately, but they were not successful until 1988. And although the Department of Education is charged with enforcing Title IX, many women's organizations routinely monitor Title IX compliance, and most universities have their own compliance officers.

Monitoring groups were especially necessary during the Reagan and George H. W. Bush administrations. The Women's Legal Defense Fund and Women's Law Center filed several suits to force equal treatment of women students. Their cause was helped by a 1992 Supreme Court case that allowed monetary damages to be awarded in cases of deliberate discrimination.[84] Numerous Title IX lawsuits were filed involving reinstatement of women's sports programs, upgrading women's club teams to varsity status, and retaliatory firings related to Title IX complaints in reaction to the Court's ruling.[85]

In 1992, the powerful National Collegiate Athletic Association (NCAA) announced that it would pressure its member schools to offer *equal* opportunities to female athletes. In 1972, when Title IX was passed, only 294,000 girls played high-school sports. By 2001, that number had grown—in large part in response to Title IX—to more than 2.7 million.

Thirty years after the introduction of Title IX, young women continue to face significant inequalities in college-level sports. According to data reported in the *Chronicle of Higher Education*, the total dollars allocated to the sports budgets of Division I schools surged from 1997 to 2001, growing from $1.78 billion to $2.70 billion. Yet the funding allocated to women's sports programs has barely increased, from just 30.9 percent to 34.6 percent.[86]

The Women's Sports Foundation estimates that less than 9 percent of Division I universities actually complied with Title IX in 2000.[87] The NCAA Gender Equity Report Card revealed that female athletes received $133 million less in scholarships than male athletes in 2001. Recruiting expenses for women athletes were less than 20 percent of those of men,[88] and for every "$1 a man's basketball coach is paid, the woman's coach is paid 55 cents."[89] This disparity continues in spite of the fact that women constitute the majority of undergraduates in the United States and on most campuses.

Until recently, a major problem with Title IX enforcement has been not knowing how much money a college spends on men's and women's sports programs. In 1994, an amendment to the Elementary and Secondary Education Act was proposed by Senators Carol Moseley Braun (D-Ill.) and Edward Kennedy (D-Mass.). As passed by Congress and signed by President Clinton, the Improving America's Schools Act of 1994 requires universities to disclose to students a variety of information related to gender equity, including funding and participation rates. The Office of Civil Rights in the Department of Education is charged with enforcing the act, as well as Title IX.

Increased emphasis on Title IX enforcement has led many women to file lawsuits to force compliance. In 1991, in an effort to trim expenses, Brown University cut two men's and two women's teams from its varsity rosters. Several women on the downgraded gymnastics team filed a Title IX complaint against the school, arguing that it violated the act by not providing women varsity sport opportunities in relation to their population in the university. The women also argued that cutting two women's programs saved $62,000, whereas the men's cuts saved the school only $16,000. Thus, the women's varsity programs took a bigger hit in violation of federal law.

A U.S. district court refused to allow Brown to cut the women's programs. A U.S. court of appeals upheld that action, concluding that Brown failed to provide adequate opportunities for its female students to participate in athletics.[90] In 1997, in *Brown University v. Cohen*, the U.S. Supreme Court declined to review the appeals court decision. This put all colleges and universities on notice that discrimination against women would not be tolerated, even when, as in the case of Brown University, the university had, since passage of Title IX, tremendously expanded sports opportunities for women.[91]

Test Fairness.   Test fairness is another area in which unequal treatment continues to harm women students. In 1985, an article by Phyllis Rosser in *Ms.* magazine looked at gender bias in educational testing.[92] The National Center for Fair and Open Testing (FairTest) then commissioned a study of the Scholastic Aptitude Test (SAT), and the House Judicial Subcommittee on Civil and Constitutional Rights held hearings. Those hearings and subsequent reports led the ACLU's Women's Rights Project to file suit on behalf of NOW and Girl's Clubs of America to challenge New York State's use of SAT scores to award $8.4 million in college scholarship money. Sole use of SAT scores resulted in girls receiving only 28 percent of Empire State Scholarships for Excellence even though they were 53 percent of the test takers. As revealed in Table 3.5, women score much lower on SATs even though they earn higher grades in high school. Commenting that "SAT scores capture a student's academic achievement no more than a student's yearbook captures the full range of her experiences in high school," a federal judge found that New York's awarding of state scholarships solely on the basis of SAT scores was "in violation of Title IX and the equal protection clause of the U.S. Constitution."[93]

TABLE 3.5   **Women and SAT Score Bias**

Year	Average Verbal Score			Average Mathematical Score		
	Total	Male	Female	Total	Male	Female
1966–67	543	540	545	516	535	495
1971–72	530	531	529	509	527	489
1976–77	507	509	505	496	520	474
1981–82	504	509	499	493	516	473
1986–87	507	512	502	501	523	481
1991–92	500	504	496	501	521	484
1996–97	505	507	503	511	530	494

Data derived from statistics (recentered scale) provided by the College Entrance Examination Board, National Report on College-Bound Seniors, various years. (Copyright U.S. Department of Education, September 1999.)

Colleges, however, still make use of these tests for admissions and scholarship decisions. Although test preparers have been aware of the gender differences in scores, some continue to dismiss them. In 1996, for example, boys made up 61 percent of all National Merit Scholarship semifinalists (girls were 54 percent of the test takers), a designation based on preliminary SAT (PSAT) scores.[94] In response to charges from FairTest about continued bias, a public information officer from the National Merit Corporation said, "We are not convinced that the test is biased. . . . It could be showing a disparity in academic preparation. If girls are getting better grades in home economics or things like that, they're not better prepared."[95] If, indeed, girls are less well prepared for these tests than boys, one could argue that schools are violating Title IX by offering differing opportunities to female students.

Some colleges and universities have added new criteria to admissions policies to maintain a diverse student body in response to charges of test bias and recent initiatives by some states, such as California and Texas, to disallow the use of affirmative action policies in admitting students. According to one report, "continued reliance on test scores makes it hard to sustain previous levels of minority enrollment, so there's been a scramble to race-blind alternatives." Students applying to the University of California who are in the top 4 percent of their high school class and students ranked in the top 10 percent of their high school class applying to the University of Texas will be admitted regardless of test scores.[96]

Hiring and Personnel Practices.   Title IX also prohibits employment discrimination in all educational institutions receiving federal assistance. Although the number of women Ph.D.s continues to grow, as revealed in Table 3.2, the growth has not been reflected in the faculties of most universities, particularly research-oriented universities. Although women make up 36 percent of all college faculty members, these women are often clustered at women's, small Catholic, or community colleges. The American Association of University Professors reports that at the millennium, women "are most well represented at institutions without rank and least well represented at doctoral-level institutions. Women make up 50 percent of faculty at institutions without rank, 48 percent of the faculty at two-year colleges with rank, 40 percent of faculty at general baccalaureate institutions, 38 percent of the faculty at comprehensive institutions, and 31 percent of the faculty at doctoral-level institutions."[97] Despite increases in the number of women faculty in America's colleges and universities, women are most likely to hold no rank or to be assistant professors, while men are most likely to hold the rank of full professor. Across the nation, only 7 percent of women faculty hold the rank of full professor.[98]

Once employed, women often face a variety of forms of discrimination ranging from blatant to the most subtle. Although both Title VII and Title IX prohibit discrimination, the kinds practiced in academia are difficult to prove, owing in large part to the deference most judges give to the judgment of a woman's senior peers (often white men) as to the quality of her teaching and research.

Women's groups and women's studies programs have been instrumental in monitoring university practices. They often serve as a clearinghouse for information and as a support system for women on campus. Volumes of information about women's studies and about Title IX and how to monitor compliance, file complaints, and keep abreast of the latest developments now exist on the Internet to provide a communications network and enhanced monitoring of continued discrimination.[99]

Opposition to Employment and Educational Equity

Phyllis Schlafly spoke out quickly and vigorously against defining sexual harassment as illegal employment discrimination. She also opposed comparable worth legislation. In 1985, appealing to class resentments, she argued that comparable worth "would empower 'bureaucrats' to freeze blue-collar wages, because the so-called 'scientific criteria' used to evaluate job worth mask biases against manual labor."[100] Representatives from Schlafly's Eagle Forum and Concerned Women for America (CWA) also testified against the Family and Medical Leave Act. They argued it was biased against the working poor, who could not afford to take unpaid leaves, and that it would encourage employers to discriminate against women of childbearing age.

Conservative women have also parted ways with other women over issues of educational equity. In 1975, shortly after the first set of Title IX guidelines was announced, a tremendous outcry was raised when HEW officials ruled that father/son breakfasts were prohibited by Title IX. ERA opponents charged that this was a first step toward destruction of the family and unwarranted governmental action.[101] Although this interpretation of Title IX resulted in extensive media coverage and angry letters to HEW from conservative women, conservative women's groups were even more upset about moves being made in the schools and by publishers to remove sex-role stereotyping from textbooks.

In 1979, Phyllis Schlafly, Concerned Women for America, and many Republicans urged passage of the Family Protection Act (FPA), which would have denied "federal funds for purchase of textbooks that 'belittle' women's traditional role in society."[102] Although the FPA died, CWA continues to be influential on the state level, especially in California and Texas, where conservative texts written to glorify women's traditional roles have been adopted in many elementary and secondary schools.

Conservative women's groups enjoyed tremendous access to the White House and the agencies charged with enforcing educational equity during the 1980s. The New Right, in fact, of which conservative women's groups are a part, was instrumental in bringing about the election of Ronald Reagan in 1980, and it was rewarded for those efforts. Since 1992, however, many conservative groups have turned their attentions to local elections. For example, CWA is particularly concerned with what it calls the secular-humanist curriculum taught in many public schools and has taken an active role in trying to ban discussions of feminism and homosexuality in public schools. Since 1992, CWA, along with fundamentalist Christian groups, has supported thousands of candidates for local school board elections to further these interests.

In 2000, CWA came out against the United Nation's Convention on the Elimination of All Forms of Discrimination Against Women (CEDAW). According to CWA, passage of this treaty would undermine the sovereignty of the nation, curtail parental rights, and promote "gender re-education" by requiring schools to use gender-neutral textbooks in the classroom.[103]

CONCLUSION

Women have made enormous strides since they first gathered in Seneca Falls to demand greater educational and employment opportunities. Although the franchise was won in 1920, more than four decades passed before national legislation guaranteeing some semblance of equality in wages and equal opportunity in the workplace was enacted.

Prior to the 1960s, most of the progress made in employment and education came about as a result of individual efforts or employer demand. Neither the early woman's movement nor the woman suffrage movement attempted to attack head-on the problems in either sphere, although each movement supported notions of increased opportunity.

Once the Equal Pay and Civil Rights Acts of 1963 and 1964, respectively, were signed into law, parity did not occur. In fact, the failure of the EEOC to enforce the Civil Rights Act was an important reason for the creation of the National Organization for Women: women were enraged when legitimate complaints of discrimination were not investigated.

Over the years, women's rights groups have pursued several different courses of action in their quest to gain greater educational and employment opportunities free from discrimination. Since passage of the Equal Pay and Civil Rights Acts, women's rights organizations routinely have filed lawsuits to seek compliance with existing law. They have also lobbied the executive branch for better enforcement of existing statutes but, particularly during the Reagan-Bush years, to little avail.

Women's groups have also lobbied for additional legislation and regulations to ban discrimination in the workplace and in schools. The Pregnancy Discrimination Act of 1978, sexual harassment guidelines, and Title IX are examples of these efforts. After years of work, women in Congress, with the aid of women's rights lobbying (as well as popular support), secured passage of the Family and Medical Leave Act.

Gains in this area have been fostered by two factors. First, even some conservative women supported antibias employment legislation. Not only did some of the proposed laws protect motherhood—the Pregnancy Discrimination Act is one example—but also, according to some, the protections found in many of those laws negated any need for the ERA.

Second, there was little organized business opposition to most of these proposals. However, when more threatening, costly changes including comparable worth, affirmative action, and pregnancy disability payments, for example, began to appear in regulations implementing laws or executive orders, a strong backlash arose that was exacerbated by the economic downturn of the late 1980s and early 1990s.

Many employers and white males in particular, threatened by a loss of jobs or lessened chances of promotion, immediately began to lobby, litigate, or simply ignore equal opportunity as well as affirmative action guidelines. They viewed quotas or goals as true public bads that could only hurt their ability to pursue their education or careers.

All of these various statutes, regulations, and judicial rulings combine to make most forms of sex discrimination unquestionably illegal. Yet even with the increased number of females with a college education, women continue to be underrepresented in high-prestige occupations, clustered in low-paying jobs, and frequently subjected to on-the-job abuse.

NOTES

1. Judith Papachristou, *Women Together: A History in Documents of the Women's Movement in the United States* (New York: Knopf, 1976), 126.
2. Mary Frances Berry, *The Politics of Parenthood: Childcare, Women's Rights, and the Myth of the Good Mother* (New York: Viking, 1993), 46.
3. Reproduced in Elizabeth Cady Stanton, Susan B. Anthony, and Matilda Joslyn Gage, eds., *History of Woman Suffrage*, vol. 1, 1848–1861 (Rochester, N.Y.: Charles Mann, 1887), 72.
4. Horace Mann as quoted in Thomas Woody, *A History of Women's Education in the United States*, vol. 1 (New York: Science Press, 1929), 463.
5. Kathryn Kish Sklar, "The Founding of Mount Holyoke College," in *Women of America: A History*, ed. Carol Ruth Berkin and Mary Beth Norton (Boston: Houghton Mifflin, 1979), 185.
6. Woody, *History of Women's Education*, vol. 1, 499.
7. Lois W. Banner, *Women in Modern America: A Brief History*, 2nd ed. (San Diego: Harcourt Brace Jovanovich, 1984), 65–69.
8. James J. Kenneally, *Women and American Trade Unions* (St. Albans, Vt.: Eden Press, 1978), chaps. 5, 6.
9. Ibid., 479.
10. Ibid., 481–86. The union between suffrage forces and the WTUL was an uneasy one born from expediency. The WTUL started working hard for suffrage after its poor treatment at the hands of male unionists and after its change of policy favoring protective legislation. WTUL leaders believed it was necessary for working women to have the vote to get laws passed.
11. See generally Maude Nathan, *The Story of an Epoch-Making Movement* (Garden City, N.Y.: Doubleday, 1926); Karen O'Connor, *Women's Organizations' Use of the Courts* (Lexington, Mass.: Lexington Books, 1980), chap. 4; Vivien Hart, *Bound by Our Constitution: Women, Workers, and the Minimum Wage* (Princeton, N.J.: Princeton University Press, 1994).
12. Clement E. Vose, *Constitutional Change* (Lexington, Mass.: Lexington Books, 1972), chap. 7. For a discussion of the legal arguments made in these cases, see Judith A. Baer, *The Chains of Protection: The Judicial Response to Women's Labor Legislation* (Westport, Conn.: Greenwood Press, 1978); Nancy Woloch, *Muller v. Oregon: A Brief History with Documents* (Boston: Bedford Books, 1996).

13. 208 U.S. 421 (1908).

14. 261 U.S. 525 (1923).

15. Lois Scharf, *To Work and to Wed: Female Employment, Feminism, and the Great Depression* (Westport, Conn.: Greenwood Press, 1980), 10. Also reflecting the changing job opportunities for women was the growth of professional business and commercial schools. Business colleges like Katherine Gibbs Schools mushroomed in response to the demand of business for trained young women to staff the expanding number of clerical and secretarial openings.

16. Data in this paragraph come from Carol Hymowitz and Michaele Weissman, *A History of Women in America* (New York: Bantam Books, 1978), 306.

17. Barbara Sinclair Deckard, *The Women's Movement*, 2nd ed. (New York: Harper and Row, 1979), 317.

18. For example, the New York City Bar Association refused to accept female members until 1937. This kind of discrimination, plus social mores that acted against women seeking careers in the law, resulted in women making up 2 percent or less of all attorneys through 1940.

19. Barbara J. Harris, *Beyond Her Sphere: Women and the Professions in American History* (Westport, Conn.: Greenwood Press, 1978), 104–5.

20. William H. Chafe, "The Paradox of Progress," in *Our American Sisters*, 2nd ed., ed. Jean E. Friedman and William G. Shade (Boston: Allyn and Bacon, 1976), 386.

21. William H. Chafe, *The American Woman* (New York: Oxford University Press, 1972), 144–5.

22. Hymowitz and Weissman, *History of Women*, 312.

23. Deckard, *Women's Movement*, 319.

24. Hymowitz and Weissman, *History of Women*, 314.

25. Harris, *Beyond Her Sphere*, 155.

26. Betty Friedan, *The Feminine Mystique* (New York: Dell, 1963), 30.

27. Additionally, by 1965, 35 percent of all married women with husbands present worked. In fact, 42.7 percent of mothers with school-aged children worked, as did 23.3 percent of those with preschool-aged children. U.S. Department of Labor, Bureau of Labor Statistics, *Perspectives on Working Women: A Databook* (Bulletin #2080) (October 1980), 27.

28. Women's Bureau, 1969 Handbook (Washington, D.C., 1969).

29. Hymowitz and Weissman, *History of Women*, 316.

30. Mary Anne Baker et al., *Women Today: A Multidisciplinary Approach to Women's Studies* (Monterey, Calif.: Brooks/Cole, 1980), 24.

31. Norma K. Raffel, "Federal Laws and Regulations Prohibiting Sex Discrimination," in *The Study of Women: Enlarging Perspectives of Social Reality*, ed. Eloise C. Snyder (New York: Harper and Row, 1979), 106.

32. *Schultz v. Wheaton Glass Co.*, 421 F.2d 259 (3d Cir.), cert. denied, 398 U.S. 905 (1970).

33. Equal Employment Opportunity Commission, "Equal Pay Act Charge Statistics," January 9, 1997. (mimeo)

34. Jo Freeman, *The Politics of Women's Liberation* (New York: David McKay, 1975), 53. Some today downplay the joke angle of the "sex" addition. See Ann N. Costain, *Inviting Women's Rebellion* (Baltimore: Johns Hopkins University Press, 1992), chap. 2.

35. The first director of the EEOC went so far as to say that the law was "conceived out of wedlock" and that "men were entitled to female secretaries." Quoted in Jo Freeman, "Women and Public Policy: An Overview," in *Women, Power, and Public Policy*, ed. Ellen Boneparth (New York: Pergamon Press, 1982), 53.

36. Freeman, *Politics of Women's Liberation*, 77.

37. *Pittsburgh Press Co. v. Pittsburgh Commission on Human Relations*, 413 U.S. 376 (1973). NOW became party to the suit at the Supreme Court level and was supported with amicus curiae briefs from several women's rights groups. Although the EEOC had succumbed to feminist pressures and announced regulations prohibiting male and female help-wanted ads, the Supreme Court upheld the agencies' construction of Title VII by only a one-vote majority.

38. Barbara Allen Babcock et al., *Sex Discrimination and the Law: Causes and Remedies* (St. Paul, Minn.: West, 1975), 262. This book contains an excellent summary of the protective legislation controversy that actually began in the 1920s. See 229–82.

39. Statement by Katherine P. Elickson of the National Consumers' League before the Equal Employment Opportunity Commission, May 2, 1967, 1, reported in Babcock et al., *Sex Discrimination*, 266, n. 60.

40. 444 F.2d 1219 (9th Cir. 1971).

41. See *Diaz v. Pan American Airlines*, 442 F.2d 385 (5th. Cir. 1971), cert. denied, 404 U.S. 950 (1971).

42. 433 U.S. 321 (1977).

43. Kenneth Janda, Jeffrey M. Berry, and Jerry Goldman, *The Challenge of Democracy*, 2nd ed. (Dallas: Houghton Mifflin, 1990), 20.

44. 452 U.S. 161 (1981).

45. To examine in-depth the results of the "Ask a Working Woman" survey, including a chart that highlights the top four legislative priorities of working women by race, income, education, age, and children, go to http://www.aflcio.org/women/survey1.htm. The National Committee on Pay Equity recommends that comprehensive changes be made to ensure economic equity in the workplace. For more information about pay equity issues, visit their website at http://www.feminist.com/fairpay/about.htm.

46. http://www.feminist.com/fairpay/epd.htm.

47. National Organization for Woman Action Alert, http://www.now.org April 1, 2001.

48. Ibid.

49. 480 U.S. 616 (1987).

50. From the "Ask a Working Woman" survey, http://www.aflcio.org/women/survey1.htm.

51. Beth Wilson, "The Pitfalls and the Pendulum," in *Black Issues in Higher Education* 15, no. 1 (March 5, 1998): 104.

52. Grutter V. Bollinger, 02 U.S. 241 (2003)

53. Nicholas Lemann, "A Decision That Universities Can Relate To," *New York Times*, June 29, 2003, 14.

54. Catharine A. MacKinnon, *Sexual Harassment of Working Women* (New Haven, Conn: Yale University Press, 1979).

55. 477 U.S. 57 (1986).

56. *Harris v. Forklift Systems*, 510 U.S. 17 (1993).

57. David Hancock, "End Sexual Harassment, Companies Urged," *Miami Herald*, March 3, 1993, B2.

58. 414 U.S. 632 (1974).

59. 417 U.S. 484 (1972). *Geduldig* was sponsored by Equal Rights Advocates, a California-based feminist public interest law firm. The firm received substantial amicus curiae support from WRP, NOW, and even WEAL, whose leaders by 1974 realized the pervasive consequences of pregnancy-based discrimination.

60. 429 U.S. 125 (1976).

61. Karen O'Connor and Lee Epstein, "Beyond Legislative Lobbying: Women's Rights Groups and the Supreme Court," *Judicature* 67 (1983): 134–43.

62. Judith A. Baer, *Women in American Law* (New York: Holmes and Meier, 1991), 109–10.

63. "Report Says New Mothers Take Longer Than Thought to Recover," Reuters, March 16, 1993, NEXIS.

64. 479 U.S. 272 (1987).

65. Baer, *Women in American Law*, 103.

66. For more information on the difference debate, see Flora Davis, *Moving the Mountain: The Women's Movement in America since 1960* (New York: Simon and Schuster, 1991), 475–83.

67. Judith Warner, "French Benefits," in *Working Mother*, May 2001, 56–60.

68. Berry, *Politics of Parenthood*, 160.

69. Quoted in ibid., 161.

70. "President Clinton Announces New Family-Friendly Workplace Proposals," June 24, 1996, http://www.whitehouse.gov/WH/dispatch/062496.html. The other statistics contained in this paragraph can also be found there.

71. Summary of finding from the Department of Labor 2000 Family and Medical Leave Surveys, http://www.dol.gov/dol/asp/public/fmla/factsheet.htm.

72. Press Release U.S. Department of Labor, "New Survey Results: Millions of Americans Benefit from, support FMLA," January 9, 2001, http://www.dol.gov/dol/opa/public/media/press/opa/opa2001008.htm.

73. 111 S.Ct. 2238 (1991). See Sally K. Kenney, *For Whose Protection? Reproductive Hazards and Exclusionary Policies in the United States and Great Britain* (Ann Arbor: University of Michigan Press, 1993).

74. Commission on the Status of Women, *American Women: Report on the President's Commission on the Status of Women* (Washington, D.C.: U.S. Government Printing Office, 1963), 13.

75. Ibid., 17.

76. "NOW Demands," quoted in Papachristou, *Women Together*, 222.

77. For an excellent account of the lobbying activities that led to passage of Title IX, see Marian Lief Palley and Joyce Gelb, *Women and Public Policies: Reassessing Gender Politics* (Charlottesville: University of Virginia Press, 1996).

78. Quoted in Babcock et al., *Sex Discrimination*, 1014–5.

79. 458 U.S. 718 (1982).

80. 116 S.Ct. 2264 (1996).

81. Douglas Lederman, "Supreme Court Rejects VMI's Exclusion of Women," *Chronicle of Higher Education*, July 5, 1996, A21.

82. 465 U.S. 555 (1984).

83. Baer, *Women in American Law*, 227.

84. *Franklin v. Gwinnett County School District*, 111 S.Ct. 1028 (1992).

85. Carol Herwig, "Colgate Prevails in Title IX Appeal," *USA Today*, April 28, 1993, 9C.

86. Welch Suggs, "Title IX at 30," *Chronicle of Higher Education*, June 21, 2002, A38.

87. "Gender Equity, Creative Solutions: A Case Study," Women's Sports Foundation, July 28, 2000, http://www.womenssportsfoundation.org/cgi-bin/iowa/issues/rights/article.html.

88. Candiss Collins, "Women in Sports: No More 'Wait till Next Year,'" *USA Today*, February 10, 1993, 11A.

89. Mariah Burton Nelson, "In Search of a Level Playing Field," *USA Today*, March 19, 1992, 11A.
90. *Cohen v. Brown University*, 101 F.3d 155 (1996).
91. *Brown University v. Cohen*, 117 S.Ct. 1469 (1997).
92. Phyllis Rosser, "Do SATs Shortchange Women?" *Ms.*, December 1985, 20.
93. Quoted in ibid., 10.
94. "Boys Predominate in a Contest: Fueling Complaint of Test Bias," *New York Times*, May 26, 1993, B7.
95. Data obtained from website that has been discontinued.
96. Ben Wildavsky, "Reining in the test of tests," in *U.S. News & World Report*, March 5, 2001, 47.
97. Marcia Bellas, "Faculty Salary and Faculty Distribution Fact Sheet 2000–2001," American Association of University Professors, http://www.aaup.org/Wbellas.htm.
98. Ibid.
99. For more on Title IX, see http://www.mcs.net/~sluggers/titleixpage.html.
100. Susan E. Marshall, "Who Speaks for American Women: The Future of Antifeminism," *Annals*, May 1991, 58.
101. Joseph A. Califano Jr., *Governing America* (New York: Simon and Schuster, 1981), 223–4.
102. Carol Felsehthal, *Phyllis Schlafly: The Sweetheart of the Silent Majority* (Garden City, N.Y.: Doubleday, 1981), 319. See also Janet K. Boles, "Social Movements as Policy Entrepreneurs: The Family Protection Act and Family Impact Analysis" (paper delivered at the annual meeting of the American Political Science Association, Washington, D.C., 1982).
103. Laurel MacLeod and Catherina Hurlbert, "Exposing CEDAW," Concerned Women for America (September 5, 2000), http://cwfa.org/library/nation/2000-09-pp-cedaw.html.

Women's Economic and Educational Status

As detailed in Chapter 3, the expansion of employment and educational rights for women that occurred during the early woman's and suffrage movements failed to produce full and equal participation. Slow progress was due partly to the absence of any laws guaranteeing equal employment and educational rights for women. In fact, the "protective" legislation that was enacted at the urging of many women's groups during the suffrage era actually *reduced* women's employment opportunities in many fields.

The 1960s and the 1970s saw passage of several laws to improve educational and employment opportunities for women. These laws, however, have yet to be fully enforced. The decade of the 1980s was a particularly difficult time. Both the Reagan and George H. W. Bush administrations actively sought to undermine full enforcement of antidiscrimination legislation. Thus, by the end of the 1990s, it was not surprising that women's gains in the employment and educational spheres, while often impressive, did not produce anything approaching equality in the marketplace.

Paralleling our findings in the political arena, the data in the economic sector show that legal change is a necessary but insufficient condition for equality. Additional legal guarantees and the active enforcement of existing laws are just part of the reason for the continued inequality of women. These changes alone, however, will not bring full parity. Rather, as in politics, additional barriers continue to limit the progress of women. More specifically, the advancement of women in the educational and employment spheres has been hampered by barriers that parallel those that have limited women's progress in politics, namely (1) cultural attitudes about the roles and abilities of women, (2) conflict between women's family roles and marketplace activity, (3) women's lack of preparation and resources for all aspects of marketplace involvement, (4) sex discrimination by employers and associates on the job, and (5) the structure and demands of the economy.

In the sections that follow, we explore how these barriers, both in the past and the present, have limited women's progress. We also examine how these barriers have changed over time, especially during the current women's rights movement. Finally, we try to identify what additional changes must be made before women can take an equal place with men in the marketplace in the twenty-first century.

ATTITUDES TOWARD WORK AND WOMEN

Before the Women's Movement

Many people looked down on the few women who entered the workforce in nontraditional roles during the colonial period. Women workers, however, encountered little resistance, largely due to the shortage of men to perform many jobs—including but not limited to physicians, innkeepers, and shop-keepers. The public was hesitant to condemn women who provided these nec-essary services, especially since many businesses were family owned and it was not unusual for a wife to continue the business upon the death of her hus-band.[1] Some historians argue that in the early years of industrialization, the employment of young, single women in factories was viewed positively by many.[2] Few even questioned the practice of having slave women, married and unmarried, work long hours as field hands, domestics, or nannies.

As industrialization proceeded, the division of sex roles became more pronounced. Increasingly, work that had been done at home was moved to the factory. Men went "out" to work, while women stayed "in" the home. The symbol of the new middle class became the wife of leisure, although there was little real leisure associated with running a home in the mid-1800s. Most poor, African American, or immigrant families could ill afford the luxury of an unemployed wife, yet the common practice even in these groups was for the wife not to seek paid employment if it was economically feasible. While married women were discouraged from working, there is considerable evidence that women participated in family-run businesses located in the home.[3] Moreover, among single women of both native-born and immigrant parents, census data suggest that they worked unless the family could afford otherwise. However, negative attitudes toward women's employment seemed to heighten with the economic recession and massive industrial unemployment of the 1870s and the 1890s, as some women appeared to be "taking jobs from men."[4]

At the dawn of the twentieth century, many new white-collar jobs were developed. It became increasingly acceptable for young, middle-class women to work outside the home. The era of the 1920s and the "new woman" may have been a particularly favorable time for young, white, working women. Attitudes toward the employment of married women, however, were decidedly negative in the first public opinion polls taken in the 1930s. Perhaps in part because of the depression, in 1936 only 15 percent of the public gave an unqualified favorable response to a question concerning the advisability of married women working. The reasons given most frequently by those who objected were: (1) women take men's jobs (36 percent), (2) a woman's place is in the home (35 percent), and (3) one is guaranteed a happier home life or healthier children if women do not work (21 percent).[5] In 1937 and 1938, when the question was rephrased to include the possibility of a married woman working "if she had a husband capable of supporting her," less than a quarter of the public (25 percent of the women but only 19 percent of the men) approved. There also was widespread support for the practice of refusing to hire or actually firing women who could depend on their husbands for support. Over half of all respondents, for example, declared they would favor a law prohibiting employment of a married woman for state or local government if the woman's husband earned $1,000 a year.[6]

World War II radically altered these views. Workers were in tremendous demand to replace men at war. Public support for a married woman working outside the home rose dramatically. Sixty percent of the public said married women should take jobs in the war industries. When the qualifier "without children" was added, this number climbed to more than 70 percent.[7] Polls revealed that women were more supportive of women working.[8] More than three-quarters of those queried also supported the concept of equal pay for equal work.[9]

These views were short lived. By the war's end, fueled in part by the fears of public officials and male workers about a shortage of jobs, the nation embarked on an effort to return women to the home. Popular magazines proclaimed the benefits and rewards of suburban living and caring for the home as a full-time, fulfilling occupation. This change in public sentiment was quickly reflected in the public opinion polls. In the immediate postwar years, only 18 percent of the public in a national sample gave unqualified approval to a married woman working if her husband was capable of supporting her. When the question raised the specter of a "limited number of jobs," 86 percent, a proportion higher than reported during the Depression, disapproved of a married woman working if she had a husband capable of supporting her. Even when no mention was made of a limited number of jobs, and the question focused only on women with no children under age sixteen, only 34 percent of all men surveyed in 1946 gave unqualified approval. In contrast, 42 percent of all women viewed these women workers in a positive light.[10]

Women who worked often justified their employment by claiming economic necessity, an acceptable reason for many people.[11] While economic motives may have made employment more socially acceptable, most women who went to work enjoyed it.[12] As more women went to work, support for women's employment climbed, especially in the high-prosperity years of the 1950s, when jobs were abundant.

Employers also played a catalytic role in attitudinal change. Their expanding demand for women workers (a result of new openings in traditional women's fields) made possible the increased employment of women. Moreover, because demand occurred when there were fewer single women to fill it, employers were willing to discard many of their own prejudices and biases against hiring married women. Thus, the changing practices of women and employers set the stage for the women's movement and its message that women's employment was not only acceptable but also desirable.

The Impact of the Women's Movement

As early as 1969, before the message of the women's rights movement reached many in America, popular support for married women working outside the home had already climbed from its postwar low of 18 percent to a record 55 percent.[13] Figure 4.1 reports the results of a survey from 1977 to 2000 that indicates a steady decline (until 2000) in the belief that women should tend to the home while men work.

There is some evidence that more men than women still have reservations about a married woman working. For example, in the fall of 2002, 28 percent of first-year college men as compared to 17 percent of first-year women agreed "the activities of married women are best confined to the home and family."[14] The specter of women taking jobs away from men also seems to fuel resistances. In 1977, when asked if a married woman should work if there were a limited number of jobs and she had a husband capable of supporting her, 64 percent of the public disapproved of her working, a figure only 20 percent lower than the opposition to a similar question in 1946.[15] Although the question has not been repeated since 1977, the negative shifts in public sentiment toward women working in the late 1800s, the 1930s, and the postwar 1940s, which were tied to strong economic downturns or the prospect of such, raise

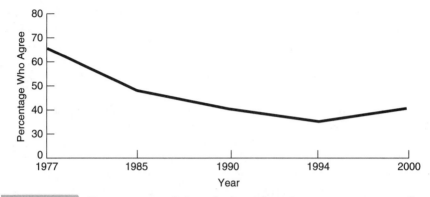

FIGURE 4.1 **Percentage of Population That Agrees It Is Better for Men to Work and Women to Tend to the Home**
Source: General Social Surveys, 1972–2000, http://csa.Berkeley.edu:7502/cgi-bin12/hsda3.

the possibility that these attitudes are highly volatile. Indeed, a headline in 1993 proclaimed "Women Making Job Gains at Expense of Men,"[16] indicating that negative attitudes persist and may actually be behind much of the resistance to affirmative action (see Chapter 3).

Even though approval for a married woman entering the workforce generally seems strong if the scenario does not include a job shortage, many people still believe a wife should place her career second to her husband's. Several questions tap this attitude. The first queries whether "it is more important for a wife to help her husband's career than to have one herself." In 1977, over half of the public (57 percent) agreed with this statement. Steady declines in the 1980s and early 1990s left 18 percent endorsing this view in 1998.[17] Relatedly, a majority of the public (66 percent) agreed in 1977 that it was better for society if the man is the achiever outside the home and the woman takes care of the home and the family.[18] In 2000, less than 41 percent of the public agreed with the statement.[19]

In response to the second more concrete set of questions about whether a woman or a man should give up her or his job if the spouse is offered a transfer, almost two-thirds of all women (62 percent) and more than half of all men (55 percent) surveyed in 1989 said the *wife* should give up her job if her husband is offered a very good job in another city. When the situation is reversed and the wife has the offer, only 29 percent of the women and 28 percent of the men believed the *husband* should quit and move with her.[20] A survey of college-educated men and women in the mid-1990s found that even among those who if forced to choose would prefer a career to marriage, more women (88 percent) than men (67 percent) were willing to move for the sake of their spouse's career. As the authors of this study note, "these women will be prone to experiencing an inner struggle as they weigh their conflicting commitments to their husbands and their own careers."[21] This conflict is even greater for women with children who want to work, as the public is even more adamant about a woman's need to sacrifice her career for her children.

ATTITUDES TOWARD MOTHERS WORKING

Early in the Industrial Revolution, in England and in some parts of the United States, whole families were often hired for factory work, apparently with public approval. By the mid-1800s, however, popular sentiment strongly opposed a mother working, although little thought was given to the hard work done by women in the home or on the family farm. Similarly, few objected to married African American women working. Indeed, in the South after emancipation, it was expected that wives and children of sharecroppers would work alongside the man of the family in the fields.[22] Married African American women who were not sharecropping were expected to fill the housekeeping needs of white women, who generally gave little thought to the domestic concerns of their help. As the century progressed, the evils of factory life and the toll it took on working women (usually white) and their families were an important rationale for the enactment of protective legislation in the early 1900s.

The almost universal practice of white middle-class women leaving their jobs before the birth of their first child was in keeping with the popular notion that the roles of worker and mother were incompatible. Even in the 1920s, an era of relatively high support for women working, the majority of professional women saw their choice as *either* marriage and a family *or* work. During this period, only 19.3 percent of professional women were married, and most viewed a family and a profession as mutually exclusive.[23]

In the 1930s and 1940s, one of the most frequently cited objections to married women working was that the practice posed potential harm to children. Although the period from 1960 to the present has seen a massive increase in the number of mothers working, altering public sentiment toward their employment has been only partially accomplished. In a 1997 poll, 55 percent of the public agreed that it would be better for women to stay home and take care of the house and children even if it may be financially necessary for mothers to be working.[24]

As revealed in Table 4.1, part of the objection to a mother working stems from a feeling that employment harms the mother-child relationship. Thus, in 1977, over half the public (52 percent) disagreed with the notion that a working mother could establish as warm and secure a relationship with her children as a mother who does not work. By the mid-1980s, opinion had shifted rather dramatically on this position, with a majority of the public (61 percent) agreeing with the statement. Although nearly 40 percent of the public still believe that working women make worse mothers, almost a quarter believe they make better moms and a third rate them the same as those who do not work outside the home. A majority of Americans believe that a woman can have a very successful, high-paying career and also be a very good mother (71 percent), while less than a third believe that women must choose between the two roles.[25]

A related question about the impact of a mother's job status on her preschool children produces a similar pattern of responses, but there is much greater agreement that a preschool child is likely to suffer if a mother works, as revealed in Table 4.2. More than two-thirds of all respondents (68 percent) held this view in 1977. Although this belief declined dramatically over the next

TABLE 4.1 **The Mother-Child Relationship If the Mother Works**

Survey question: A working mother can establish just as warm and secure a relationship with her children as a mother who does not work.

Year	Strongly Agree	Agree	Disagree	Strongly Disagree
	(%)	(%)	(%)	(%)
1977	16	33	34	18
1985	21	40	29	10
1986	22	40	30	8
1988	24	39	28	9
1989	22	42	30	7
1990	22	42	29	8
1991	20	45	28	6
1993	20	47	27	6
1994	23	46	26	5
1996	24	42	26	7
1998	22	45	25	7
2000	20	41	29	10

Source: James Allan Davis and Tom W. Smith, *General Social Surveys, 1972–2000*, National Opinion Research Center, distributed by Roper Center for Public Opinion Research, Storrs, Conn.

TABLE 4.2 **The Effect on Preschool Children If Their Mother Works**

Survey question: A preschool child is likely to suffer if his or her mother works.

Year	Strongly Agree	Agree	Disagree	Strongly Disagree
	(%)	(%)	(%)	(%)
1977	21	47	28	5
1985	13	41	36	10
1986	11	40	40	9
1988	11	37	41	11
1989	9	39	42	10
1990	8	41	42	9
1991	9	39	42	10
1993	7	36	47	10
1994	8	35	47	11
1996	9	38	43	11
1998	8	33	46	10
2000	10	38	42	10

Source: James Allan Davis and Tom W. Smith, *General Social Surveys, 1972–2000*, National Opinion Research Center, distributed by Roper Center for Public Opinion Research, Storrs, Conn.

decade, still 48 percent of the people interviewed in 2000 thought this practice was harmful. There was a gender gap of nearly 14 points, with men more likely to agree with the statement. Not surprisingly, working mothers, especially college-educated working mothers, are particularly likely to think that they are able to establish a warm relationship with their children and that working does not harm preschool children.

According to a 2001 Gallup Poll, only 13 percent of Americans say that having two working parents is the ideal family situation. Forty-one percent prefer one parent to work either part time or at home, while the remaining 41 percent believe that it is best for one parent to stay at home solely to raise the children. Although the majority of Americans (55 percent) believe that it does not make a difference which parent stays at home, of those who did think it mattered, 43 percent preferred the mother to stay at home. In contrast, only one percent believed the father should stay home.[26] Thus, even if a woman wants to work, she may find herself in conflict with a spouse who believes a mother should stay home. As Lesley Lazin Novak and David R. Novak point out, many women "are likely to be caught in an internal bind between their personal aspirations and their culturally ingrained need to stay home after they become mothers."[27]

Attitudes toward the employment of women and the place of work in women's lives are not the only attitudinal barriers to the equality of women in the marketplace. One other set of very restrictive cultural views concerns the ability of women to perform certain jobs or to undertake appropriate training or education.

Attitudes About the Abilities of Women

As we saw in Chapter 2, negative attitudes about the abilities of women have stymied their progress in securing high elective office. Many of these same stereotypes translate into similar doubts about the aptitudes of women in the economic realm.

In the nineteenth century, many commentators believed that women simply lacked the mental, physical, and emotional attributes necessary for work outside the home. Often such work, or the preparation for it in school, was seen as disastrous for the health of women. In the 1870s, a major medical text claimed:

> During the epoch of development, that is the age from fourteen to eighteen or twenty . . . the system . . . is particularly susceptible, and disturbances of the delicate mechanism [the menstrual function] . . . , induced . . . by constrained positions, muscular effort, brain work, and all forms of mental and physical excitement, germinate a host of ills. Sometimes these causes, which pervade . . . our . . . schools produce an excessive performance of the . . . function, and this is equivalent to a periodic hemorrhage.[28]

This "knowledge" not only kept middle-class women out of the workplace but was also used as a rationale to prevent them from acquiring an education or skills to prepare them for work outside the home.

Global Awareness

WORKING MOTHERS WORLDWIDE

Comparative Employment/Population Ratio (per 100) of Women With Young Children

	1983	1992	1997
Western Europe			
Belgium	50	62	69
Denmark	—	43	45
France	48	52	51
Greece	27	42	45
Ireland	18	37	48
Italy	38	42	42
Luxembourg	34	37	46
Netherlands	18	42	59
Portugal	—	69	69
Spain	—	31	39
United Kingdom	21	45	55
Other Developed Regions			
Canada	42	54	62
United States	42	49	58

Source: Worlds Women 2000, "Trends and Statistics" (New York: United Nations, 2000).

The employment levels of women with young children have increased dramatically in the last two decades around the world. As women's work experience increases in value, the opportunity costs involved in leaving paid employment to care for a child increase. More women have entered the paid labor force before, during, and after child-rearing than ever before. Although attitudes toward working mothers have changed significantly, women often perform a stressful balancing act. Consequently, family-friendly issues, particularly the availability and quality of child care, have become increasingly salient in many countries. Women's unpaid work in the home and in communities is also gaining attention.

With the growth of women's colleges and the entrance of a few women into the professions, these stereotypes weakened but were far from eliminated. As late as 1891, some women in the suffrage movement believed:

Women cannot maintain the same intellectual standards as men. The claim of the ability to learn, to apply knowledge . . . does not imply a claim to originate, or to maintain . . . the robust, massive intellectual enterprises which . . . are now carried on by masculine strength and energy.[29]

This line of reasoning was the cornerstone of the legal arguments for protective legislation.

Surveys taken in the 1940s show the intervening years did not completely dispel these views. Forty percent of the public continued to believe that men were more intelligent than women. Additionally, a majority believed that men were more creative than women. Pluralities of men and many women also accepted the notion that men were more likely to possess a large range of job-related emotional and mental traits, including the ability to make decisions, handle people, accept new ideas, be even-tempered, and maintain a level head. They also clung to the stereotype that men possessed more common sense than women.[30]

Other clichés facilitated the view that women could not be as productive or as successful as men in many jobs. In the 1970s, for instance, most men and women believed that women had less physical stamina and were more emotional and less logical than men.[31] By the mid-1990s, large numbers of women and men (36 percent and 44 percent, respectively) still believed that "women aren't tough enough for business."[32] Forty-four percent of women and 54 percent of men agreed that few women were in high corporate positions because "men are better suited emotionally for big business than are women."[33]

These attitudes help to explain why women are often viewed as less effective bosses than men, although perceptions have changed dramatically since the 1970s. Whereas a 1975 Gallup Poll indicated that 62 percent of Americans preferred a male boss, with only 7 percent favoring a female boss, by 2002 only a third preferred a male boss, 19 percent favored a female boss, and nearly half of Americans replied that gender made no difference.[34] As revealed in Figure 4.2, overall the public believes that women and men perform equally well as corporate executives. On nine out of ten items, a plurality of Americans believed there would be no difference between the performance of a male and female CEO. However, sizable minorities believed that men would be better able to lead the company during a crisis or downsize the company if necessary. In contrast, women were perceived as more honest, more trustworthy, and better able to understand ordinary people. The business world may be providing a warmer climate for women than politics. Fifty-five percent of women and 48 percent of men agree that "It is more important to have women business leaders in this country than it is to have a female president."[35]

Recent studies show evidence of how women in business are shaping attitudes about women in politics. A 1999 survey revealed significant differences in the attitudes toward women in elective office among those who have experienced a female boss and those who have not worked for a woman. Americans who have experienced a female boss are more likely to say that a female would perform better than a male as president in a number of areas, including moral questions (49 percent vs. 42 percent), personal qualities (29

Survey Question: Whether expect man or woman CEO to do better job

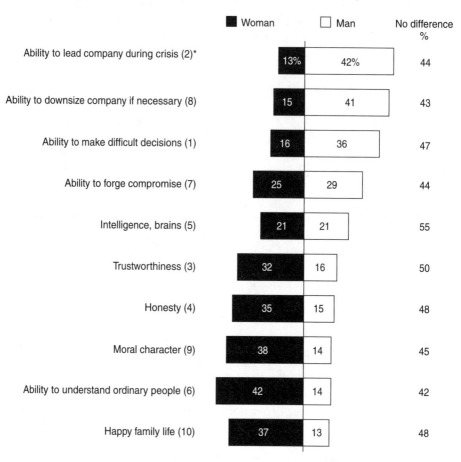

Number reflects "very important" ratings for characteristics

FIGURE 4.2   **Public Perceptions of Male vs. Female CEOs.**
Source: "Women in Elected Office, " report prepared for Deloitte and Touche, January 2002 (Roper Starch Worldwide Inc.). Data provided by Deloitte and Touche.

percent vs. 19 percent), and the economy (24 percent vs. 14 percent). Americans who have worked for a woman also rate women higher on important presidential characteristics, including ability to understand ordinary people (48 percent vs. 37 percent), moral character (42 percent vs. 33 percent), honesty (39 percent vs. 30 percent), and ability to forge compromise (30 percent vs. 21 percent). Americans who have experienced a female boss were also more likely to say there would be "no difference" when it comes to the ability to lead the nation during a crisis (38 percent vs. 28 percent) and preparedness to go to war (30 percent vs. 21 percent). Still, a majority of Americans favor a male president in terms of these characteristics.[36]

The liabilities that women bosses supposedly possess have parallels with the characterizations of women politicians reported in Chapter 2. Women are seen as less effective than men in standing up to competitors and unions in the same way they are expected to be less effective in dealing with the military, enemies, and trading partners. Women's positive attributes are also similar in the political and economic spheres. They are identified as more concerned with "people issues" and more honest. In politics, women's attributes may be a plus in some races. Similarly, women may benefit if they are seen as having the abilities needed to manage the diverse workforce of the twenty-first century. However, for the most important leadership positions of president of the United States or chief executive officer of a major corporation, women are characterized as "not tough enough" in the minds of many citizens. The stereotypes that persist in the political and corporate sectors may help to explain why there has never been a woman president and why very few women head Fortune 500 companies.

Stereotypes, moreover, are linked to deeply held views about the character traits of men and women. In 2000, for instance, a majority of the public agreed that men are more aggressive and courageous, while women are seen as more emotional, more talkative, more patient, more creative, and more affectionate. Neither sex was considered more intelligent, more "easy going," or more ambitious.[37] Other stereotypes about the abilities of women also persist. Perhaps one of the most damaging is the idea that women have lower mathematical and spatial abilities than men. This notion persists even though most research shows the differences to be minimal and probably the function of women taking fewer math courses, or the bias of tests or researchers, discussed in Chapter 3.[38] This stereotype, however, has devastating effects. High school and college teachers and guidance counselors often track women students away from the natural sciences and engineering, the very courses necessary to enter some of today's most high-tech professions. There is suggestive evidence in a report by the American Association of University Women (AAUW) that teachers may even reinforce or produce the stereotype in the classroom, by allowing boys to do science experiments and diluting women's confidence in their mathematical abilities.[39] In a 2002 survey of freshmen college students, 55 percent of males but only 37 percent of females rated themselves as above average or in the top 10 percent in terms of mathematical ability.[40] Public attitudes toward women's abilities also contribute to another barrier, women's preparedness for paid employment.

PREPARATION OF WOMEN FOR EMPLOYMENT OUTSIDE THE HOME

Early Training for Work

The review of the public's attitudes toward the relative importance and place of work outside the home helps us to understand the lower commitment of women, especially in the past, to salaried employment. Quite simply, prior to 1940, employment was looked upon by most women as something to do before they took up their real life's work—being wives and mothers. There is evidence, however, that many women desired to combine work and a family but were unable to do so.[41] Furthermore, married women who did work, notably African American women and women of limited economic means, faced a job market that took little cognizance of the difficulties they faced as they tried to combine both roles.

The absence of laws preventing discrimination in educational programs also contributed to the inability of all but a few women to acquire the educational preparation necessary for high-prestige fields such as law or medicine. In this climate, young women were not encouraged and, as we have seen, were often discouraged from acquiring an education that would have prepared them for well-paying occupations and professions. The gradual expansion of academic opportunities for women, beginning in the late nineteenth century, did not always change the situation. Most women in high school and even some in college took home economics courses under the assumption that these programs were the best preparation for their future occupations as housewives and mothers. Even those who majored in other areas chose or were channeled into traditional fields. As shown in Table 4.3, the top three careers advised for women in 1950 were nursing, teaching, and secretarial/clerical work. While

TABLE 4.3 **Career Advice From Americans**

Supposing a young man/woman came to you for advice on choosing a line of work or career, what kind of work or career would you recommend?

	2001		1950	
	Men	*Women*	*Men*	*Women*
Computers	18%	16%	—	—
Doctor/Medical field	12	15	29	2
Nursing	—	7	—	28
Technology	10	8	—	—
Business/Sales	9	8	8	—
Trades	4	—	—	—
Teaching	3	6	5	16
Secretarial/Clerical	—	2	—	8
Lawyer/Attorney	3	3	8	—
Construction	3	—	—	—
Military	3	1	—	—
Engineering	2	1	16	—
Social work	2	2	—	7
Government	1	1	6	—

Source: Darren K. Carlson, "Career Advice From Americans on 'Take Our Daughters to Work Day,'" Gallup Poll Release, April 26, 2001, http://www.gallup.com/poll/release/pr010426b.asp.

young women and men today are given similar career advice, underlying stereotypes still affect the choices women ultimately make.

In the past, textbooks and schools also played key roles in narrowing the expectations of young women about lifetime work.[42] Recent examinations of children's literature and textbooks show a continued, though diminished, tendency to include more male characters and to portray women and girls in traditional roles with stereotyped characteristics of passivity, dependency, and a need to be rescued by males.[43] The AAUW study indicates that teachers still tend to encourage boys to do well more than girls, giving the former more classroom attention. African American girls and girls from economically impoverished backgrounds apparently get shortchanged the most.[44] This may help to explain the persistence of sex-role stereotyping of some fields and the finding that women are less confident than men about their own achievements.[45] It also may help us to understand why girls experience such a sharp drop in self-esteem in their teen years.[46] Not surprisingly, 56 percent of men and 63 percent of women believe an important reason women have not risen in corporate ranks is because young girls are not encouraged to aspire to careers as managers.[47]

In an effort to help girls learn about the realities of work, employment opportunities, and the education and training jobs require, the Ms. Foundation launched "Take Our Daughters to Work" in 1993. The campaign evolved in response to research indicating that "girls emerge from adolescence with a poor self-image, relatively low expectations from life and much less confidence in themselves and their abilities than boys."[48] In a survey commissioned by the AAUW, adolescent girls were asked how often they felt "happy the way I am"; 60 percent responded "always." By high school, that figure dropped to 29 percent. For boys, the figures dropped from 67 percent to 46 percent.[49] In 2003, the program was changed to "Take Our Daughters and Sons to Work," with a focus on encouraging girls and boys to explore ways to balance family, work, and community. A national study by the Family and Work Institute reported that 81 percent of girls and 60 percent of boys say they will reduce their work hours when they have children.[50]

Although there is little evidence that women fear success, there may be some concern about doing gender-inappropriate activities, which might be tied to childhood socialization.[51] Indeed, research suggests people still continue to characterize jobs by gender. Certain careers, generally those with high pay, are identified as requiring "masculine" personality attributes, whereas others, often those that are less profitable, are seen as requiring "feminine" qualities.[52] A 2001 survey found that a distinction between "women's work" and "men's work" still exists. For example, 75 percent of Americans say most people think men are better suited to be plumbers, whereas 69 percent consider a woman to be a better child-care worker. While a majority (56 percent) of adults say that men and women are equally suited to perform most jobs, 58 percent also say that men and women are naturally suited to do different jobs. The 2000 Virginia Slims Poll also found behavioral differences between men and women in the workplace. Women are more likely than men to perform tasks outside of their job description that have no beneficial effect on career advancement. More than two-thirds of both men and women report that women are more likely to bring food to meetings, get coffee for others, take notes at meetings, buy gifts for the boss to give to other employees, and make copies. In contrast, less than 3 percent say that men are more likely to take on these tasks. Men were significantly more likely than women to volunteer to take on risky projects at work (36 percent say this of men but only 18 percent say the same of women) and to take on responsibility for presenting a group's ideas to the boss (33 percent vs. 20 percent).[53]

The Women's Rights Movement and Preparation for Work

Passage of Title IX and the message of the women's rights movement about the desirability of women having careers began to have a noticeable impact on the preparation of young women for the professions in the 1970s. In 1968, however, before the movement's message was popularized, surveys of white women born between 1944 and 1954, during the baby boom, found only 29 percent of them expected to be employed at age thirty-five. (In reality, more than 60 percent of the married women and 80 percent of the unmarried women were actually working when surveyed again at age thirty-five.) African American women were better at estimating their chances of working, perhaps because their experiences were based on the employment record of their mothers, most of whom worked. Not surprisingly, the women who did not plan on being employed undertook much less job training and formal schooling.[54] These women were queried again about their work plans in 1973, after the message of the women's rights movement regarding women and work had gained prominence. These same young women had much more accurate estimates of their employment prospects then, although because they were older—nineteen to twenty-nine—many had passed the traditional time for acquiring the education that would prepare them for better jobs.[55]

More recently, surveys of first-year college students nationwide revealed that women are adopting many of the same work and status goals as men. Whereas in 1969 women were 22 percent less likely than men to list "being well-off" financially as a life goal, in 2002 they were 4 percent less likely to have this goal than men. Relatedly, in 2002 nearly three-quarters of both men and women identified raising a family as an important goal. Women in their first year of college, however, were considerably less likely than first-year men, even in 2002, to want to become successful in a business of their own,[56] which is an interesting fact, given that more than one-third of all small businesses are owned by women.

Education and Work Readiness.   In 1969, when first-year college women and men were asked about their educational plans, only 42.8 percent of women expected to go beyond the associate's or bachelor's degree. In contrast, 56.8 percent of men expected to continue their education. Twice as many men expected to get a Ph.D., five times as many men planned on law school, and three times as many men planned to become doctors or dentists.[57] In the late 1960s and early 1970s, women's interest in doctoral degrees increased dramatically while men's interest in such degrees decreased. By the early 1990s, the interests of women and men converged and have changed very little since. In 2002, slightly more women than men expected to obtain an advanced degree (77 percent of women vs. 73 percent of men). The largest gender differences have been the increases in women's interest in medical/dental degrees. In 2002, 10.5 percent of women and 6.9 percent of men expressed interest in these degrees.[58]

The educational attainment of women and men is also increasingly similar. In the 1940s, men were slightly more likely to obtain a college degree (6.9 vs. 4.9 percent in 1940), but men were much more likely to become medical doctors. Only 10 percent of all recipients of an M.D. in 1949 were women,[59] as revealed in Figure 4.3. On the eve of the popularization of the message of the women's movement and before Title IX, the gap between the educational attainment of men and women had grown. Of all women age twenty-five to twenty-nine in 1970, only 12.9 percent had completed college, in contrast to 20 percent of similarly aged men.[60] The percentage of medical degrees awarded to women had also declined, to 8 percent. (They had actually slipped even

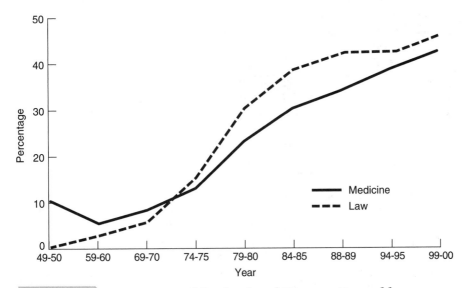

FIGURE 4.3 **Percentage of Professional Degrees Earned by Women in Medicine and Law**
Source: U.S. Department of Education, National Center for Educational Statistics, Higher Education General Information Survey (HEGIS), "Degrees and Other Formal Awards Conferred" surveys, and Integrated Postsecondary Education Data System (IPEDS), "Completions" surveys. Printed in National Center for Educational Statistics, *Digest of Education Statistics 2001* (Washington, D.C.: U.S. Department of Education, 2002), 322.

lower, to 6 percent in 1959–1960.) The percentage of women receiving law degrees was also dismally low, at 5 percent, although this represented a doubling of the percentage from 1959 to 1960.[61]

Since the changes in cultural values and educational practices in the early 1970s, the number of college-educated women has increased dramatically, such that young women are now more likely than men to go to college. Moreover, in recent years more women than men obtained associate's, bachelor's, or master's degrees. The number of women obtaining postsecondary degrees has also increased at three times the rate of men. By 2000, women were earning more than 44 percent of all Ph.D.s. Similarly, more than 40 percent of both medical degrees and law degrees are now earned by women, as revealed in Figure 4.3. Hispanic and African American women, moreover, are more likely to receive a college or professional degree at every level than their male counterparts. As indicated in Table 4.4, women earned the majority of bachelor's, master's, and doctoral degrees conferred to African Americans and Hispanics.[62]

A closer examination of the fields in which women obtain their degrees, however, shows a persistence of some sex stereotyping. A majority of the doctoral degrees awarded in education and psychology go to women (64 and 54 percent respectively), whereas only 15 percent of Ph.D.s in engineering and 31 percent of those in business go to women. Undergraduate degrees also show a concentration of women in the traditional fields of education (76 percent women), home economics (88 percent women), and nursing (90 percent women). The large number of undergraduate degrees earned by women in nontraditional fields such as business is indicative of the changed commitment of young women to the world of work, as noted in Table 4.5. The damaging stereotypes about the mathematical abilities of women are reflected in the small percentage of women getting their bachelor's degrees in engineering (19 percent) and the physical sciences (40 percent).[63]

Compared to women of an earlier generation, young women in college today are more likely to be preparing for a career at rates equal to their male contemporaries, yet their continued concentration in some traditional fields and their lack of parity in some degree programs have important implications for their ability to compete equally with men for the high-tech jobs of the twenty-first century.

TABLE 4.4 Degrees Conferred to Women, by Race, 1999–2000

	White		*African American*		*Hispanic*	
	(N)	*%*	*(N)*	*%*	*(N)*	*%*
Bachelor's degrees	525,645	57	70,919	66	44,708	60
Master's degrees	191,477	60	24,532	69	11,550	60
Doctoral degrees	13,279	48	1,357	61	688	53

Source: National Center for Educational Statistics, *Digest of Education Statistics 2001* (Washington, D.C.: U.S. Department of Education, 2001).

TABLE 4.5 Degrees Conferred to Women, by Field of Study, 1999–2000

Field	% Bachelor's	% Master's	% Doctoral
Business and management	49.7	39.8	31.9
Communications	61.2	63.2	52.9
Computer, information sciences	28.1	33.3	16.9
Education	75.8	76.4	64.6
Engineering	18.5	20.9	15.5
Home economics	87.9	83.9	76.8
Mathematics	47.1	44.9	25.0
Physical sciences	40.3	35.4	25.5
Psychology	76.5	75.4	67.4
Social sciences	51.1	50.1	41.2

Source: National Center for Education Statistics, *Digest of Education Statistics 2001* (Washington, D.C.: U.S. Department of Education, 2002).

Workforce Commitment Attitudes.   Surveys of women in the larger society show increasingly higher levels of commitment to the workforce. Women are as likely as men to say they would continue to work if they did not need to financially, and that they get great or moderate personal satisfaction from working.[64] Today, more employed women say that they need to work to support themselves or their families. In 1970, 48 percent of working women gave "to earn extra money" as their reason for working. By 1999, only 22 percent listed this response; "to support self" (27 percent) and "to support family" (46 percent) were the most common reasons for working.[65] Increasing work hours has become the primary method of raising family incomes, rather than through regular pay increases.

Although the number of families headed by a single woman has grown (representing 17.3 percent of families in 2000), much of the increased workforce commitment of women is due to wives joining the paid labor force and working outside the home.[66] Married women are also more likely to continue working after having children. Public attitudes toward working mothers show considerable conflict between work roles and home roles. Perhaps as a consequence, working mothers report that they "frequently" or "sometimes" feel torn between the demands of their job and wanting to spend more time with their families.[67] Nearly 40 percent of both men and women report that work is always or often stressful, while women are slightly more likely than men to say that they come home from work exhausted (44 percent vs. 38 percent).[68] When surveyed in 1999, 44 percent of working mothers reported they would prefer to stay home rather than work if they were free to do either. Fifty-nine percent of those not employed preferred staying home to working. Women were also more likely than men to prefer more opportunity to work at home. Although many women with dual roles experience stress, most report that they are doing a fairly good job of balancing their jobs and their families.[69] Whether the dual roles limit their prospects at work is a topic we return to later.

Even if women are able to overcome traditional attitudes and prepare themselves to take an equal role with men, equality is not assured. Two important groups have acted, and probably will continue to act, to prevent women from achieving equality with men in the marketplace: employers and male workers.

SEX DISCRIMINATION

Discrimination by Employers

Sex discrimination by employers against women stems from two sources, cultural attitudes and economic self-interest. It is usually impossible to disentangle the two. Take, for example, the custom of employers hiring males for certain positions. Economists refer to this as "preference" or "taste." Preferences, in turn, are often cited as explanations for segregation of occupations and the lower wages paid to women.

A concrete example of this kind of discrimination in the first half of the twentieth century was the widespread practice of refusing to hire married women (referred to as a hire bar) or firing women who did marry (labeled a fire bar). Claudia Goldin's research on the practice of "marriage bars" has found that the practice began in public school systems sometime in the late nineteenth century. By 1928 (before the Great Depression), 61 percent of all school districts refused to hire married women and 52 percent fired women who married. As public sentiment against married women's employment grew during the Depression, these figures rose to 87 percent of schools having hire bars and 70 percent having fire bars.[70] The federal government and nine states also maintained a version of this policy during the Depression.[71] Until 1970, the U.S. State Department continued to fire women in the Foreign Service who married.[72]

A 1931 survey of large firms in seven cities found the practice extended beyond government, as 12 percent of the firms had fire bars, and an additional 25 percent of firms had a discretionary policy that allowed firing of married women if the situation warranted. Additionally, 29 percent had hire bars, again with 50 percent of all surveyed firms having the discretionary ability to not hire married women. A follow-up survey in 1940 showed that the prevalence of the two types of bars increased during the Depression. Collectively, the marriage hire and fire bars affected as many as 50 percent of the employed women in the sampled cities.[73]

The firms most likely to have either policy (the policies usually went together) were those that promoted from within, had fixed salary schedules, and had other benefits that accrued with years. The data, therefore, suggest that employers used societal distaste for married women working as an excuse for not hiring women or firing them so that women employees could be forced out before they qualified for maximum benefits.[74] The cumulative effect of the marriage bars, of course, was to reinforce cultural stereotypes against married women working and to discourage young women from preparing for a lifetime of work. Moreover, those married women who could find work were required to take jobs with considerably lower pay than they might have earned had they been able to seek employment with all businesses.[75]

Profiles in Leadership

RUTH BADER GINSBURG

> Every constitution in the world that was written after World War II says . . . men and women are persons of equal stature or words to that effect. The United States Constitution is now among the minority of constitutions in the world that does not make that clarion statement. I have three granddaughters and I'd like them, when they whip out their pocket Constitution, to see that.
>
> *Ruth Bader Ginsburg*[a]

On August 10, 1993, Ruth Bader Ginsburg took the oath of office to become an associate justice of the United States Supreme Court. Nominated by President Clinton, Ginsburg is the second woman to hold a seat on the Supreme Court, joining Sandra Day O'Connor, who was appointed by President Reagan in 1981. A petite, sometimes shy woman who wears her hair pulled back in a ribbon, Ginsburg has made her mark on history as a leading advocate of women's rights. Inspired by her personal experience, Ginsburg has been instrumental in changing the Court's interpretation of how the Fourteenth Amendment applies to gender discrimination.

Ginsburg graduated from Cornell University in 1954, first among the women in her class. Marriage and the birth of her first child pressured her to reconsider her plans to pursue a career in law, but her father-in-law encouraged her, saying: "Ruth, if you don't want to go to law school, you have the best excuse in the world, and no one would think the lesser of you. But if you really want to be a lawyer, you will pick yourself up, stop feeling sorry for yourself and you will find a way."[b] One of only nine women entering Harvard Law School in the class of 1959, Ginsburg was asked by the dean why she was "taking up classroom space usually reserved for men, particularly when law firms would not hire women."[c] Despite raising a small child and caring for her husband through his diagnosis and recovery from cancer, Ginsburg excelled academically, earning a position on the law review. When her husband accepted a job offer from a New York law firm, she transferred to Columbia Law School, where she made law review again and tied for first in her class at

(continued)

graduation. However, no prestigious offers followed her outstanding academic performance. She recalls that "to be a woman, a Jew, and a mother to boot, that combination was a bit too much. Probably the motherhood was the major impediment. The fear was I would not be able to devote my full mind and time to a law job."[d] Supreme Court Justice Felix Frankfurter refused to interview her for a clerkship because "he was just not ready to hire a woman."[e]

Ultimately, Ginsburg was hired as a law clerk for a U.S. district judge. After the clerkship, she taught at Rutgers University School of Law, where she hid her second pregnancy in fear of losing her non-tenure-track position. She went on to teach at Columbia Law School, where she became the first woman to earn tenure at the institution. It was her personal encounter with barriers faced by women attempting to combine family and career that fueled her passion for fighting gender discrimination. In her view, the Fourteenth Amendment bans gender discrimination, for women *and* men. She joined forces with the American Civil Liberties Union and helped write the brief for *Reed v. Reed* (1971), in which the Supreme Court struck down a state law that preferred men over women as estate administrators. As a founder and counsel to the ACLU's Women's Rights Project, Ginsburg argued six cases involving gender discrimination before the Supreme Court from 1972 to 1978, winning five. Ginsburg used an incremental approach, starting with the least controversial cases and often using men as plaintiffs to show how even laws meant to help women were based on unfair stereotypes. Her strategy was effective, and in *Craig v. Boren* (1976), the Court ruled that gender-based legal distinctions deserved intermediate-level scrutiny.[f]

Ginsburg's achievements won her national recognition, and in 1980, President Carter appointed her to the U.S. Court of Appeals for the District of Columbia. As a judge, Ginsburg earned a reputation as "a sharp questioner and diligent worker," with a "keen eye for detail."[g] She is noted for her sensitivity to the real-world impact of court decisions and has taken her law clerks on tours of local prisons. When Clinton announced his nomination of Ginsburg for the Supreme Court, he described her as a nominee with "a fine mind, good judgment, wide experience in the law and in the problems of real people, and somebody with a big heart," calling her "the Thurgood Marshall of gender equality law."[h] Although some feminists questioned her position on reproductive rights, Ginsburg clarified her commitment during her confirmation hearings, describing a woman's right to choose an abortion "as something central to a woman's life, to her dignity. . . . And when government controls that decision for her, she's being treated as less than a full adult human being responsible for her own choices."[i]

As a Supreme Court justice, Ginsburg is described as "a paragon of judicial restraint," with the exception of cases involving gender discrimination. As Ginsburg wrote in the majority opinion in *U.S. v. Virginia* (1996), "Generalizations about the way women are, estimates of what is appropriate for *most women*, no longer justify denying opportunity to women whose talent and capacity place them outside the average description."[j] Ginsburg describes the case as personally satisfying, viewing it as her "most important contribution to the bench to date."[k] Analyzing Ginsburg's impact on the Clinton legacy, Karen O'Connor and Barbara Palmer write, "Whether it is her compassion for a woman who lost custody of her children, or women excluded from state supported institutions of higher learning, Ginsburg's refusal to limit women or perpetuate stereotypes permeates her decisions."[l] As a result of her struggles to advance women under the Equal Protection Clause of the Constitution, "doors of opportunity have been opened that have benefited not only the women themselves, but their families."[m]

---

[a] "Justice Ginsburg Rueful over ERA," *San Diego Union-Tribune*, May 22, 2002, A14.

[b] Geneva Overholser, "Let Us Now Praise Wise Old Women," *Seattle Post-Intelligencer*, August 21, 2001, B5.

[c] "Ruth Bader Ginsburg," http://www.factmonster.com/ipka/A0772253.html.

[d] Guy Gugliotta and Eleanor Randolph, "A Mentor, Role Model and Heroine of Feminist Lawyers," *Washington Post*, June 15, 1993, A14.

[e] "Ruth Bader Ginsburg," http://www.factmonster.com/ipka/A0772253.html.

[f] "Ruth Bader Ginsburg," *Supreme Court Historical Society*, http://www.supremecourthistory.org/justice/ginsburg.htm.

[g] Joan Biskupic, "Behind the Robes, Songs and Whitewater Rafting," *Washington Post*, October 20, 1994, A19.

[h] "Ruth Bader Ginsburg," http://www.supremecourthistory.org/justice/ginsburg.htm.

[i] "Ruth Bader Ginsburg," http://www.supremecourthistory.org/justice/ginsburg.htm.

[j] *U.S. v. Virginia*, 116 S.Ct. 2264 (1996).

[k] Karen O'Connor and Barbara Palmer, "The Clinton Clones: Ginsburg, Breyer, and the Clinton Legacy," *Judicature* 84, no. 5 (March–April, 2001): 270.

[l] Ibid., 272.

[m] Neil A. Lewis, "Rejected as a Clerk, Chosen as a Justice," *New York Times*, June 15, 1993.

Support for the economic self-interest explanation can also be seen in the hiring practices of firms in the 1950s. When the supply of single women declined, a result of the decline in the birth rate in the 1930s, most firms quickly dropped their hire and fire bars. A 1950 study of school districts found that only 18 percent still retained the hire bar and 10 percent the fire bar. In at least some firms and school districts, the marriage bars were replaced with "pregnancy bars" that mandated the firing of women expecting a child or prohibited hiring of women with young children.[76] Most of these bars would be eliminated as the supply of older married women declined and the practice was found illegal.

More pervasive than marriage or pregnancy hire and fire bars was the practice of most firms to not hire African American women or to limit the type of positions for which they could be employed. Surveys in the 1930s and 1940s, for instance, found that more than half of all firms queried had a practice of not hiring African American women as clerical or professional workers. Evidence suggests these official policies of discrimination persisted until at least the 1960s.[77]

Although most employers today readily employ married women and women with children, they are still influenced by racism and stereotypes about the work commitment and abilities of women. These kinds of attitudes form the basis for hiring practices that keep women out of management and decision-making positions. Francine D. Blau has documented that stereotypes about what women can do persist in some industries even when other industries are successfully using women workers in comparable job categories.[78] Economists trace such hiring practices to stereotypes about the productivity of women, women's supposed lack of certain qualities (strength, rationality, and mechanical ability), and fears that male employees will leave if women are hired.[79]

Whatever their source or rationale, stereotypes clearly affect women and influence the practices of employers. Perhaps as a result of the women's rights movement publicizing such activities, surveys of women show persistent awareness of this discrimination over the past twenty years, as revealed in Table 4.6.

In 1970, only 40 percent of those women surveyed believed women were discriminated against in obtaining top jobs in the professions. By 1994, this percentage was 53 percent, down slightly from its 1989 high of 58 percent. Similar results can be found regarding the problems faced by women in obtaining executive positions, skilled-labor jobs, and top jobs in the government. With respect to leadership responsibilities in groups of women and men, the perception of discrimination remains unchanged after increasing in the last two decades. Awareness of discrimination in the military is up, perhaps because of the wider reporting of myriad sex scandals in the U.S. Navy and Army.

TABLE 4.6 **How Women Fare Compared to Men in the Workplace**

Proportion of women who say they have an equal chance with male coworkers

	1980	1985	1990	1995	2000
Responsibility	68	73	62	64	64
Salary	55	57	55	55	57
Promotion	52	53	50	53	52
Becoming an executive	34	38	41	42	41

Source: The 2000 Virginia Slims Opinion Poll, conducted by Roper Starch Worldwide Inc. Data provided by Philip Morris USA.

Whereas increased awareness of discrimination in the 1970s and 1980s may be a result of greater press attention, the decline in the 1990s may either signal actual decreases in discrimination or simply the perception that things are improving. When asked, most women report that salaries, job opportunities, and chances at top positions in government and in business have improved. Generally, however, that improvement is seen as a "little" and not a "lot." More than a third of women see the need for major change in all four areas to make women's lives better. Most other women see the need for some change. Interestingly, men are much less likely to think major changes are needed.[80] Consequently, as Table 4.7 reveals, there is a growing gap between men's and women's perceptions of gender discrimination.[81]

Poor treatment by employers is not the only discrimination faced by women. The behavior of male employees also often serves as a barrier to some women's entry or success in a chosen job or career. Indeed, some researchers argue that hiring biases are not "economically rational" but reflect the desire of male employers in concert with male employees to retain male power and prestige in the larger society.[82]

Discrimination by Male Employees

The role of male workers in influencing women's job and wage opportunities cannot be ignored. In polls conducted in the 1930s, 1940s, and 1960s, fear that women would take their jobs was the second most commonly cited reason for men's opposition to women working.[83] Even in the 1990s, supporters of organized labor raised the specter of women taking jobs from men.[84]

Historically, male unionists, in particular, have viewed women workers as a threat. Women were barred from joining unions; when they could join, separate seniority lists were sometimes maintained, and some unions even negotiated differential wage scales for women and men. Judicial rulings eventually made these practices illegal. Even in predominantly female unions, women

---

TABLE 4.7   **Areas in Which Women Face Discrimination**

Percent saying women are discriminated against

	2000		1995	
	Women	*Men*	*Women*	*Men*
Leadership in groups of men and women	45	33	47	39
Executive positions	57	49	59	53
Top government jobs	56	44	56	45
Top jobs in the professions	51	41	53	45
Top jobs in the arts	21	13	22	15

Source: The 2000 Virginia Slims Opinion Poll, conducted by Roper Starch Worldwide Inc. Data provided by Philip Morris USA.

have faced discrimination in attaining leadership positions. As late as 1972, the International Ladies Garment Workers Union (ILGWU), whose membership is nearly 80 percent female, had only one woman official.[85] Similarly, a woman was not elected to the executive council of the American Federation of Labor–Congress of Industrial Organizations (AFL-CIO) until 1980.

The absence of union protection continues to help explain why the working conditions and pay scales of women lag behind those of men. Traditionally, union leaders, perhaps wishing to keep women out of certain job categories, have argued that women are difficult to organize. In 2000, only 13 percent of all working women were union members. New interest by union leaders in creating unions for those engaged in the clerical trades and other traditional women's jobs, however, has opened a whole new era in the relationship of women workers and the union movement. Thus, more union members are women today (39 percent) than twenty-five years ago (22 percent).[86] As their membership has increased, women's representation in union leadership has increased as well, although most noticeably in occupations traditionally more open to women. For example, women comprise a majority of the members of the American Federation of Teachers (AFT), the American Nurses Association (ANA), and the Association of Flight Attendants (AFA). These are the only three national unions in which women currently hold leadership positions with decision-making power.[87]

Women breaking into the skilled trades still face a particularly difficult time in spite of recent court rulings. Unions and union apprentice systems seem especially reluctant to allow women entrance. Employers and unions have intentionally failed to notify women of openings, used questionable screening practices and age requirements, and mandated sponsors for entry in an effort to keep women out of the building and construction trades.[88] Even on job sites where employment goals to hire women exist, it is hard to monitor the number of women because jobs often last for only a few days. This makes it possible for companies to use their core (male) employees.

Women who enter the skilled crafts where pay is high often face hostility, which makes success difficult. A comparison of women in the trades with those in clerical positions found that the former were considerably more likely to report sexual harassment and discrimination. Women in the trades were also exposed to more isolation, loneliness, and hostile supervisors and coworkers than women in traditionally women's fields. Not surprisingly, the tradeswomen were more dissatisfied with their jobs. African American tradeswomen appeared to face the most discrimination and ill treatment, reflecting the double influence of sex and race discrimination.[89] (Indeed, many employers whose policies prevented the hiring of African American women clericals claimed their policy followed from the preferences of their white employees, male and female.[90])

Women in other male-dominated professions also report problems with male colleagues. The most common difficulties revolve around being shut out of informal workers' networks. Closed out of the "old-boy" networks, women are denied the information and peer support necessary for success or promotion.[91] In a 1999 interview conducted by Catalyst, a nonprofit research organization that promotes the advancement of women in business, one CEO commented, "I think that, without question, some women have chosen not to pursue certain tracks that might be more attractive to men. I think the larger reason is probably that we, the men of the organization, have built in credentials that we measure people against and that, for one reason or another, probably are biased against women."[92] Women in the upper levels of management, the professions, and academia are particularly likely to encounter actions, whether conscious or unconscious, of male colleagues to thwart their upward mobility. Women of color report greater barriers to advancement in the corporate world. In particular, "not having an influential mentor or sponsor" isolates them within the corporate culture.[93]

The extent of male efforts to keep women coworkers from succeeding is difficult to measure, but women in the workforce report widespread ill treatment. For instance, a 1994 survey found women agreed overwhelmingly (77 percent) that "women who try to rise to the top of major corporations get held back by the old-boy network."[94] In a 2000 poll, more than four in ten women reported that they have experienced discrimination, and more than a third have experienced sexual harassment. As shown in Table 4.8, the percentages of women reporting discrimination and harassment increase with higher levels of education and occupational professionalism. Moreover, the workplace is the primary place where the discrimination and harassment have occurred.[95]

TABLE 4.8 **Women Who Suffered Discrimination and Sexual Harassment**

Percentage of women who have experienced discrimination or harassment

	Discrimination	*Harassment*
All women	44%	31%
Education		
High school or less	31	25
Some college	49	34
College graduates	55	36
Occupation		
Professionals/managers	58	37
White-collar workers	43	29
Blue-collar workers	46	39
Retirees	27	20
Age		
18–34	50	34
35–49	54	41

(continued)

	Discrimination	Harassment
Age		
50–64	41	26
65 and over	22	17
Party Identification		
Democrats	49%	31%
Independents	48	39
Republicans	34	25

Where the discrimination or harassment occurred

	Discrimination	Harassment
The workplace	58%	73%
Shopping as a consumer	38	7
A social setting	27	35
A bank or financial institution	20	2
School	16	20

Source: "American Opinion," *Wall Street Journal,* June 22, 2000, A14.

ECONOMIC AND MARKETPLACE FACTORS

Many economists who study the labor-force participation rates of women focus on the influence of economic and marketplace factors on the propensity of women to work. Valerie Kincade Oppenheimer, for one, has traced the movement of women into the workplace after World War II to a change in the type of jobs available and the corresponding employer demand for women workers.[96] She argued that as the United States moved toward a service economy, women workers who had traditionally filled service jobs were more actively recruited into the labor force by higher wages and a corresponding elimination of the marriage, and later pregnancy, hire and fire bars.

Other economists focus on the role played by the income of other family members. They reason that women will be more likely to work if their spouse's income is low or if there is no other wage earner in the family.[97]

Claudia Goldin tested these propositions with data from 1890 to 1980. She found that the various economic factors did not have a consistent impact on the labor-market activity of working women. In the early years of this century, a husband's income was an important determinant of whether a married woman worked; if his income was low, a woman was more likely to be employed. Later in the century, from 1940 through 1960, the most important variable became the wages paid to women. As wages rose, so too did women's employment levels. Interestingly, from 1960 through 1980, neither income of family nor women's wages were very good predictors of whether a married woman would work.[98] Research by Eileen Trzcinski suggests it may be the uncertainty of the husband's employment or the risk of divorce that explains women's greater workforce commitment,[99] although women's workforce commitments and developments in the workplace are also important.

IMPACT OF BARRIERS ON THE POSITION OF WOMEN IN THE MARKETPLACE

Just as in the case of politics, the barriers to equality for women in the marketplace go beyond legal ones. Thus, we should not expect that simply removing legal barriers will result in women assuming a comparable position with men in the educational and occupational arenas. The persistence of attitudinal stereotypes about the abilities of women and the place of work in women's lives, the lack of preparation on the part of some women for certain types of economic activity, and discrimination all combine to restrict the progress of women in the marketplace.

Attempts to identify how these barriers limit women in the educational and economic arenas and how they might continue to do so in the future are complicated by the interrelationships and interaction of the barriers. Moreover, not all women are equally affected by all of the barriers, or at least are not affected in the same way. Young college-educated women who desire a career may confront quite different problems from what older, high-school-educated women who would prefer to be full-time homemakers would confront. With these caveats in mind, we turn to an examination of the historical progress of women in obtaining job and pay equality with men.

Employment Levels of Women

Early census data about women are somewhat suspect because questions about women's employment were not routinely included. Claudia Goldin's examination of the limited data that exist suggests that as many as a third or more of single women may have been employed in 1850.[100] By the turn of the century, this number rose to over 35 percent for single women age fifteen to twenty-four and 50 percent for women age twenty-five to thirty-four. Foreign-born and African American women were much more likely to be employed than single white women. In 1890, the participation rate of unmarried foreign-born women was 70.8 percent; for nonwhite women, it was 59.5 percent; and for white women, 38.4 percent.[101] Since 1890, official census figures reveal that the participation rate of single white women has continued to climb, so that 68 percent of all single women were employed in 1999. These figures are just marginally lower than the figures for similarly aged single men.[102]

Because of negative attitudes toward the employment of married women, most people assume married women did not work in the past century. However, Goldin found that 44 percent or more of all female heads of households may have worked before 1820. Her reanalysis of 1890 census data, which includes both work at home and in family businesses such as boarding houses and farms, indicates perhaps 12.5 percent of white married women worked, a 10 percentage point increase from the official figures. The situation was dramatically different for African American women. According to 1890 official statistics, 24.5 percent of them worked.[103] The true figure is probably about twice that if women working on family farms and in family businesses are included.

Employment of married women increased only gradually in the next fifty years, probably because of the marriage hire and fire bars and negative public opinion. Thus, in 1940, about 15 to 17 percent of married women under age thirty-four were working. Older married women were even less likely to work outside the home. African American married women of all ages continued to be employed at higher rates than their white counterparts.[104]

World War II dramatically altered the pattern of married women's employment, as illustrated in Figure 4.4. Older married women with children who were grown or of school age entered the labor force in large numbers in reaction to the government's propaganda campaign and the availability of employment opportunities brought about by the war. In 1950, more than a quarter of all married women age thirty-five to forty-four were working.[105] The 1950s and 1960s saw the recruitment of even more older married women into the labor market. As the number and availability of single women declined, employers dropped their marriage bars, and occupations considered to be "women's" in the service and trade sectors grew.[106] Therefore, by 1970, nearly half of all women with school-age children and almost a third of women with preschool children were in the labor market. It should be noted that these employment figures come *before* most women had heard about the women's movement, at a time when support for a working mother was quite low.

Several factors combined to heighten the trend toward married women and women with children, especially young children, working. One was the message of the women's rights movement and its impact on public opinion.

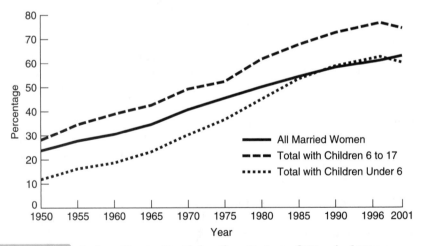

FIGURE 4.4 **Labor-Force Participation Rates of Married Women, Husband Present, by Presence and Age of Children, 1950–2001**

Source: U.S. Department of Labor, Bureau of Labor Statistics, *Perspectives on Working Women* (June 1980), and U.S. Department of Labor, Bureau of Labor Statistics, Marital and Family Characteristics of the Labor Force from the March 1996 Current Population Survey (December 1996); U.S. Census Bureau, *Statistical Abstract of the United States, 2002.*

Another was the downturn in the economy. The 1970s witnessed stagflation (inflation plus low growth), and the 1980s saw declining wage rates, especially for young males.

Historically, women would enter the labor force, leave while their children were young, and then return to work later in life. This created an "M" shape to the labor participation rates of women by age. In contrast, the labor partic-ipation rates of men resembled an inverted bowl as men increased their par-ticipation rates with age until age 44, when participation slowly declines. Today the labor-force participation rates of women and men are nearly iden-tical, in part because many more women do not have children, and those who do have children return to work more quickly.[107] As indicated in Figure 4.4, 61 percent of all married women worked in 2001. Over 74 percent of women with school-age children worked, and nearly 60 percent of women with children under six were employed.

As the value of women's work experience has increased, the cost of leaving the labor force has increased. Women with infants under age one are returning to work faster and in greater numbers. Whereas only 31 percent of mothers with infants worked in 1976, by 2000, 55 percent of new mothers were employed (a slight decrease from 58 percent in 1998).[108] Women who have invested in edu-cation return to work more rapidly after childbirth than women with less edu-cation. In 2000, 64 percent of women with a bachelor's degree or higher were in the labor force, versus 55 percent of those with only a high school degree and 39 percent of those who were not high school graduates. African American women had a higher rate of labor-force participation (66 percent) than whites (53 per-cent) or Hispanics (42 percent).[109] Women with infants were less likely to work full time than other mothers (34 percent vs. 54 percent).

The combination of these trends has resulted in a dramatic increase in the overall labor-force participation rates of women, as illustrated in Table 4.9. The most dramatic changes occurred among white women, whose labor partici-pation rate increased 23.8 percent from 35.8 percent in 1958 to 59.6 in 1999. His-torically, black women have higher rates of participation in the labor force. In 1958, the labor-force participation rate of blacks was 48 percent, 12.2 percent higher than the participation rates of white women. Black women increased their labor-force participation rate to 63.5 percent by 1999, only marginally higher than white women. The labor-force participation rate of Hispanic women continues to lag slightly behind both white and black women, although projections into 2008 suggest that Hispanic women will experience the greatest increases.

Workforce Commitment of Women

In the past, white women who got married or had children dropped out of the labor market, generally permanently. In the 1950s, many firms adopted a pol-icy of offering part-time jobs to mothers and wives to facilitate the combining of multiple roles.[110] Many women took advantage of this practice. Other women opted for less than year-round work, or opted out of the marketplace

TABLE 4.9 **Labor-Force Participation Rates of Women and Men, by Race (in percentages)**

Year	All Women	All Men	White Women	White Men	Black Women	Black Men	Hispanic Women	Hispanic Men
1958	37.1	NA	35.8	NA	48.0	NA	NA	NA
1970	43.3	79.7	42.6	80.0	49.5	76.5	NA	NA
1982	52.6	76.6	52.4	77.4	53.7	70.1	48.2	79.5
1991	57.3	75.5	57.4	76.4	57.0	69.5	52.3	80.1
1996	59.3	74.9	59.1	75.8	60.4	68.7	53.4	79.6
1999	60.0	74.7	59.6	75.6	63.5	68.7	55.9	79.8
2008[a]	61.9	73.7	61.5	74.5	64.6	68.3	57.9	77.9

[a] projection

NA = not available

Source: U.S. Bureau of Labor Statistics, "Employment in Perspective," Report 765, *Statistical Abstract of the United States, 1992,* 381; and Howard N. Fullerton Jr., "The 2005 Labor Force: Growing but Slowly," *Monthly Labor Review* 118, no. 11, 39; U.S. Census Bureau, Statistical Abstract of the United States, 2000, http://www.census.gov/prod/www/ statistical-abstract-us.html.

for several years while they reared their children. These attempts to lessen the conflict between work and family roles were often used by employers as evidence of women's lower commitment to work. Recent evidence suggests these practices are declining. During the 1980s, the proportion of women working full time, year-round rose sharply. By the end of the 1990s, more than half of all working women worked full time.[111]

Many women, especially those with small children, continue to work part time. More than two-thirds of part-timers are women. Part-time work is concentrated in several traditionally "women's fields," notably sales and service occupations, where 40 percent of the women work part time. Professional and managerial women are much less likely to work part time.

With lower wages and more uncertain work schedules, women generally are increasingly likely to be employed at more than one job. In 1970, only 2.2 percent of women held multiple jobs; by 2003, 5.3 percent of all women had multiple sources of income. Most of this increase has occurred since the mid-1980s. Women now constitute almost half (47.8 percent) of persons with two or more jobs.[112] Widowed, divorced, and separated women are actually twice as likely to hold two jobs than are similarly situated men. The need to meet household expenses is the most common reason given for their extensive job market activity.[113]

Another sign of women's increased commitment to the workplace is the short time many professional women now take off when a child is born. In 2001, 51 percent of the 3 million women with infants under age one were employed. Of these new mothers, two-thirds worked full-time.[114] College-educated women and those in well-paying jobs are even more likely to rejoin the labor force shortly after the birth of a child.[115]

Interestingly, as women's commitment to the labor force has increased, men decreased their activity. In the ten-year time period from 1983 to 1993, the percentage of men working or seeking jobs declined 1.4 percent while women's rate of participation in the labor force rose 5.2 percent.[116] The decline for men occurred in all age groups, whereas only women under nineteen were less active in the 1990s, largely because they were spending more time in school preparing for work. Although increased school time may also help to explain some of men's lower participation rates, early retirement and being "unable to work" are the more important factors. What is implied by the latter is not clear, although it is a more common reason given by poorly educated men. Economists expect the decline in workforce involvement by men and the increase by women will continue, largely because the fields in which many men are concentrated are those experiencing the most rapid declines in employment (basically goods-producing jobs such as industrial manufacturing), while occupations in which there is a concentration of women (basically service-producing jobs such as teaching and health services) increase or remain stable.[117]

Even though more women than ever before work full time, year-round, and at multiple jobs, there is evidence that some women are having a difficult time managing their careers and their mother roles. Faced with this conflict, some women choose to delay marriage or children. Others attempt to do it all, often at the expense of their jobs, their families, or their leisure time. These problems are particularly acute for single mothers who lack the support of spouses.

To summarize, the movement of women into the marketplace is a function of five factors. Goldin's work on economic correlates of women's workforce activity over the last century shows quite clearly that attitudes, preparation, family roles, discrimination, and market demands all play a role. In the early years of the twentieth century, when attitudes toward women working highly negative and having a working wife was seen as an indication of the husband's failure to provide, married women worked only if the family's income necessitated it. This helps to explain the relatively high participation rates of African American and foreign-born women whose husbands faced severe discrimination and very low wages. Moreover, because most married women had not readied themselves for work, only the better-educated single women could be drawn into the workforce by the higher wages of the new clerical positions. Later on, in the 1940s and 1950s, as more women obtained an education, they were able to be lured to work by the high wages offered by employers in the war and postwar decades, when the economy needed more skilled women workers. Only more recently have women's decisions to seek employment been weakly shaped by market considerations.

With societal and employer barriers to women working declining, high divorce rates lessening the tie between economic security and marriage, and more women preparing for full-time employment, women's decision to work, like that of men, is less influenced than in the past by economic factors. This is not to say these considerations are completely unimportant. As we shall see in the next section, the 1980s was a period of declining income for young men. This may well help to explain the high employment rates of mothers of young children. But most women today are as committed to work as men. Neither high wages nor inadequate family income are needed to draw them out of the home.

Wages of Women

The dramatic changes in women's employment have been accompanied by somewhat less impressive gains in the relative earnings of women. Although the earnings of women have steadily increased in real dollars since the 1950s, except during recessions, the earnings of women relative to men did not increase until 1980. Part of the gain in women's relative income was a function of the declining wages of men in the 1980s, when an economic recession diminished the numbers of well-paying jobs in traditionally male fields. Whereas the median annual salary of men decreased by 8 percent during the 1980s, women's salaries increased 10 percent during this time period.[118]

As indicated in Figure 4.5, the dramatic gains made by women during the 1980s narrowed the wage gap. Weekly earnings of women compared to men increased from 62.5 percent to 71.9 percent between 1980 and 1990. By 2001, women's weekly wages increased to 76.1 percent of earnings by men. Similarly, the hourly earnings of women climbed from 64.0 percent of male earnings in 1979 to 84.3 percent in 2001.

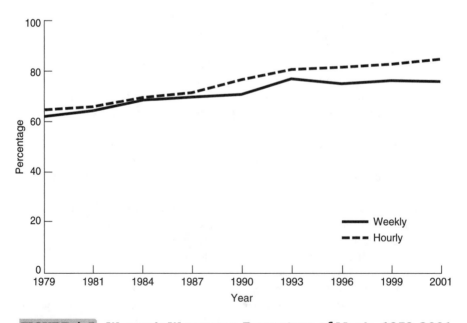

FIGURE 4.5 **Women's Wages as a Percentage of Men's, 1979–2001**
Source: U.S. Department of Labor, Bureau of Labor Statistics, "Highlights of Women's Earnings in 2001," Report 960, May 2002.

An examination of women and men in different age groupings shows the wage gap is narrowest for young men and women under age twenty-four. Those women earn 90 cents for every dollar made by men. Women twenty-five years and over earn 75 percent of men's salaries. White women earn 75 percent of salaries earned by white men, whereas African American and Hispanic women earn 87 percent and 88 percent respectively of the salaries of men of the same race.[119] The difference, of course, is a function of the fact that white men still dominate the high-paying jobs in our society.[120] (See Figure 4.6.)

The overall wage gap in annual income is greater than the gap in hourly or weekly earnings because women are more likely to work only part time or part of the year. In 2001, men worked an average of 42 hours per week versus 36 hours per week worked by women. Married men increased their hours at work to 44, while married women continued to work 36 hours per week. Widowed, divorced, or separated women worked an average of 38 hours per week.[121]

Economists have developed several explanations for the continuing lower earning power of women that parallel and overlap our five barriers to women's marketplace activity. The first focuses on the relative preparedness of women and men for work. Called the human capital theory by economists, the idea is that women invest less in education and training because they view their primary responsibility as taking care of their families.[122] The largest single variable in the human capital theory is education; however, women earn

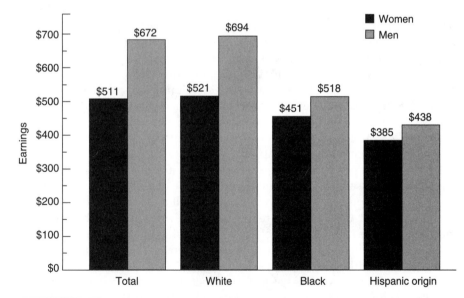

FIGURE 4.6 **Median Usual Weekly Earning of Full-time Wage and Salary Workers by Sex, Race, and Hispanic Origin, 2001 Annual Averages**
Source: U.S. Department of Labor, Bureau of Labor Statistics, "Highlights of Women's Earnings in 2001," Report 960, May 2002.

less than men in every educational level.[123] Other human capital variables include on-the-job training, labor experience, and work effort. Some studies include an even wider variety of personal characteristics.[124]

Women's lack of workforce commitment is also thought to be exemplified by absences from the workplace for days, weeks, or years when family needs require it. Women who take time out from working to be with young children—which lowers their labor experience, on-the-job training, seniority, skills, and professional contacts—do pay a heavy price in terms of their future salaries. One study found that women who had a work gap of a year earned 30 percent less the first year back to work than women who did not leave. Even after twenty years back, they still earned 7 percent less than women who had not taken time off.[125] A 2002 study by economists Elizabeth Caucutt, Nezih Guner, and John Knowles found that women with the lowest wages had more children and had them earlier (starting at age twenty-three) than women with the highest wages (who had their first child at age twenty-six or older).[126] Similarly, sociologist Hiromi Taniguchi determined that the adverse affect of children on women's wages was greater for early childbearers (who first gave birth between ages twenty and twenty-seven) than late childbearers (who first gave birth at age twenty-eight or older).[127] Attempts to control for all the human capital factor differences between men and women generally reduce the wage gap by, at most, 50 percent.[128]

Job segregation of women and men may be included as an explanatory factor in many human capital theory models. Proponents argue that women, because they do not expect to be as committed to the workforce as men, choose occupations that allow them either to do less preparation or to combine working with homemaker duties more easily.[129]

Others argue that the occupational segregation of women's and men's work has as much or more to do with the discriminatory behavior or "preferences" of employers. They propose that such segregation should be treated as a separate explanation. This is often called the crowding hypothesis because women are crowded into a few low-paying jobs by employers' refusal to hire them for a wider variety of occupations. Barbara F. Reskin and Patricia A. Roos posit that employers prefer to hire men workers because they believe they are more productive or because of other prejudiced views about women workers, for instance that they will take time off to meet family commitments. Only if there are not enough men or they can hire women more cheaply for jobs that have often been "de-skilled" will employers hire women.[130] Of course, the socialization of boys and girls that channels each into gender-traditional fields is also at work.

The crowding hypothesis has historical roots in the early occupational profile of women who took jobs as domestics and textile workers for which they could readily transfer their homemaking skills. This crowding of women into a few blue-collar jobs was paralleled in the white-collar occupations and the professions, where women soon constituted the overwhelming majorities of the clerical, teaching, and nursing fields. Economists Stephanie Boraas and William

M. Rodgers offer two interpretations of occupational crowding, suggesting that limited occupational choice may be due to discrimination or personal choices reflecting a desire to balance family and career.[131]

Regardless of the source, occupational segregation is a persistent reality. Table 4.10 gives the proportion of women in some of the more "crowded" and "uncrowded" fields and the average pay in each occupational category. The segregation of women even within broad classifications of workers is notable. Although more than half of all professionals are women, they are found in a few fields (nursing, teaching, social work). Men professionals are similarly concentrated in "their" professions of engineering, dentistry, medicine, and architecture. Because the latter professions pay much better than the former, women professionals earn only 74 cents for every dollar a professional man earns, as the table shows. Similar instances of occupational segregation can be seen in the other job classifications. Notice how some fields are highly sex segregated. A 2003 study reported that females working in predominantly female occupations earned nearly 30 percent less than females working in male-dominated occupations. Males working in female-dominated occupations earned 13 percent less than males in male-dominated occupations. The results showed that males are concentrated in the industries that offer higher salaries.[132]

TABLE 4.10 **Occupational Segregation, 2001**

Occupation	Women in Field (%)	Earnings Ratio, Women's/Men's
Executive, Administrative, Managerial	47	.67
Personnel and labor relations	67	
Administrators, protective services	29	
Managers, medicine and health	76	
Personnel training and labor relations specialists	70	
Managers, marketing, advertising, public relations	38	
Construction inspectors	7	
Professional Specialty	52	.73
Registered nurses	91	
Teachers, pre-kindergarten and kindergarten	98	
Teachers, secondary school	56	
Librarians	83	
Social workers	70	
Teachers, college and university	37	
Health-assessment and -treating occupations	83	
Computer systems analysts and scientists	27	
Physicians	33	
Lawyers	34	
Architects	24	
Clergy	11	

(continued)

Occupation	Women in Field (%)	Earnings Ratio, Women's/Men's
Engineers	10	
Pharmacists	42	
Service Occupations	52	.76
Child-care workers	98	
Private household workers	96	
Cleaners and servants	95	
Protective services	18	
Dental assistants	98	
Nurse's aides	89	
Food servers	71	
Janitors	30	
Cooks	40	
Pest controllers	6	
Firefighters	2	
Police and detectives	18	
Precision, Production, Craft, and Repair	8	.74
Mechanics and repair persons	5	
Automobile mechanics	1	
Construction Trades	2	
Electricians	2	
Tool and die makers	3	
Operators, Assemblers, and Inspectors	35	.72
Textile sewing machine operators	73	
Metalworking and plastic-working machine operators	19	
Welders	3	
Assemblers	42	
Technical and Related Support	50	.74
Dental hygienists	27	
Legal assistants	84	
Engineering and related technologists	20	
Airplane pilots and navigators	3	
Sales	45	.62
Cashiers	78	
Salespersons, motor vehicles and boats	9	
Salespersons, apparel	78	
Salespersons, real estate	52	
Salespersons, securities and financial service	32	
Sales representatives, commodities, except retail	22	
Administrative Support	77	.81
Secretaries	99	
Typists	95	
Traffic, shipping and receiving clerks	29	

Source: U.S. Department of Labor, Bureau of Labor Statistics, "Highlights of Women's Earnings in 2001," Report 960 (May 2002). Percentages and earnings ratio calculated by author.

Occupational segregation helps explain about a quarter to a third of the gap in men's and women's wages, depending on the study.[133] Of course, the gender segregation of jobs in the last two decades has meant that men, clustered in manufacturing jobs, have seen their job openings and wages fall, whereas women, working in the service sector, benefited from increased jobs and wages.

Research suggests that two-thirds of all working women or two-thirds of all working men would have to change jobs to achieve complete occupational integration.[134] Moreover, the most rapid declines in occupational segregation occurred in the 1970s, with more modest changes in the 1980s and 1990s, suggesting a persistent problem. Even in those fields that saw some occupational desegregation, women often made little or no wage gain because of the internal differentiation in men's and women's jobs in the profession or because the salaries of both sexes fell.[135]

A variation on the crowding hypothesis is an argument that women are further pushed into a few jobs by the failure of whole industries or firms to hire women for occupations they are performing elsewhere in the economy.[136] Thus, even if women have good jobs in the industries where they can find work, their incomes are lower than men's in similar positions in industries or firms that have higher pay scales and do not hire women. Economists estimate this industry or firm segregation also contributes to the disparity in women's and men's wages, perhaps as much as 12 to 17 percent.[137]

Three ideas closely related to industrial segregation are the glass ghetto, the glass ceiling, and the glass ladder. The glass ghetto refers to the hiring of women for the same occupations as men but in parts of the profession or field that do not pay as well or have the same prestige or status as the jobs for which men are hired. For instance, women medical doctors often become pediatricians, whereas more men are trained as surgeons. Michael J. Carter and Susan Boslego Carter posit that the problem faced by many women who enter traditionally male fields is that they arrived "too late."[138] The Carters argue that many of these formerly prestigious professions have become two-tiered. One tier consists of prestige jobs with autonomy, opportunities for promotion, and good pay, whereas the other tier involves routinized, dead-end, lower-paying positions. According to the Carters, women are found overwhelmingly in the lower tier, primarily but not exclusively because they arrive late in these professions.

The Carters note, for instance, that although the number of women in academia is increasing, most have entered at a time when the position of university professor is becoming less well paid and offers reduced autonomy. Moreover, the women in academia tend to be concentrated in schools in which these conditions are most pronounced: junior colleges and undergraduate teaching positions. More recent research has also found women professors holding an inordinate number of the positions with the least status: part-time and nontenured slots.[139]

The Carters make a similar argument for the second-tiering of women in law and medicine. They note that the recent increase in the number of graduates from both types of schools has resulted in what is rapidly becoming an oversupply of lawyers and certain types of physicians. Thus, recent women graduates face stiff competition from men for the dwindling number of good jobs. The result is that women lawyers and doctors tend to be found in the most underpaid, routinized, nonautonomous sectors of those professions, namely, positions in the recently created legal clinics, health-care centers, and hospital-based practices. In private law firms, moreover, lucrative partnerships are no longer always available even as tiers of partnerships have been created.

Research by Reskin and Roos, moreover, finds the problem extends beyond the academic, legal, and medical professions. Their study of traditionally male occupations where women made the largest gains in the 1970s found that these tended to be professions men were leaving because of a deterioration in the working conditions. For instance, the traditionally male occupation of pharmacist saw a dramatic increase in the number and percentage of women in the last three decades. This occurred at the very time, and probably because, many men were choosing not to become pharmacists. The male exodus was precipitated by the declining prestige of being a pharmacist. Large chains have eliminated the opportunity to own your own drug store, and computer technology reduced the autonomy of individual pharmacists.[140]

The story is little different in the other occupations that saw large numbers of women enter during the 1970s and 1980s. Indeed, there is considerable evidence that many of these occupations were internally resegregated as women who entered took the less prestigious, often new sectors in the field. A good example is women's admission into the occupation of baker. Most of the new women bakers were hired to bake prepared bread dough sold in grocery stores, whereas male bakers continued to work in the more profitable full-line bakeries.[141] Thus, the glass ghetto often finds women from a wide variety of jobs and professions isolated into the lower-paying sectors of even the most prestigious of occupations.

The glass ceiling operates in almost the same fashion. Women are hired into the lower ranks of a profession but find their paths to the upper levels of the field blocked. This practice seems most notable in the business sector, although it exists in all fields. If we look at the largest U.S. corporations, we find that only a handful of women have made it to the top. In 2002, only 12.5 percent of Fortune 500 corporate officers were women. Moreover, women held only 6.2 percent of the highest titles and comprised only 4.1 percent of the top earners. Only six women were Fortune 500 CEOs.[142] Not surprisingly, the women executives are best represented in the soaps and cosmetics industry, where they are 19 percent of the directors.[143]

The situation was so bad that the U.S. Department of Labor instituted a Glass Ceiling Initiative in 1991 to break the ceiling in firms doing business with the federal government. When the Glass Ceiling Commission issued its report in 1995, it indicated that the barriers to women's and minorities' advancement were considerable. Among its twelve recommendations were calls for more CEO commitment to eliminating the barriers, the establishment of family-friendly programs, more diversity programs, and the implementation of affirmative action plans.[144] Respondents in the 2000 Virginia Slims Poll commented that the glass ceiling today is more about antifamily policies and practices than the belief that women are less capable than men. Women report that they are more likely to share equal responsibility than equal pay with men (64 percent vs. 57 percent). Nearly one-fifth of men believe that there is a good reason women are paid less than men, and one-tenth of women agree.[145]

The work of researchers connected with the Center for Creative Leadership finds several problems facing corporate women.[146] First, women in corporations are often placed in positions with no "path to the top," namely, staff and personnel slots. These specialties (which fit stereotypes about women's management strengths) do not allow the occupants to make "profit-determining" decisions that would show the corporate officers how they could make money for the firm. Second, women in business face many conflicting expectations about appropriate behavior. On one hand, they cannot be too feminine; on the other, they cannot be too masculine. Third, women do not receive the mentoring help of corporate males, nor are they given the same opportunities for on-the-job training. Fourth, women with family demands become exhausted by the burdens of the multiple roles they have to face. In a recent survey by Catalyst, women listed different barriers to their advancement than their superiors. When asked what holds them back from top management, 52 percent of female executives reported "male stereotyping and preconceptions of women," 49 percent said "exclusion from informal networks of communication," and 47 percent said "lack of significant general management/line experience." In contrast, 82 percent of CEO's blamed the lack of experience, while 62 percent said that women "had not been in the pipeline long enough." Those women who have been successful credit their success to "consistently exceeding expectations" (77 percent), "developing style with which male managers are comfortable" (61 percent), "seeking out difficult assignments" (50 percent), and "having an influential mentor" (37 percent).[147]

For many women, however, the task is too daunting and they start their own business. Indeed, women in the 1990s were starting businesses at twice the rate of men. These firms, which are less prone to failure than new enterprises started by men, constitute one-third (36 percent) of small businesses, employ more than 18 million persons (one out of every four U.S. workers), and produce revenues of nearly $2.3 trillion.[148]

The glass ladder (or glass elevator) is the reverse of the glass ghetto. It is the tendency of employers to move men in women-dominated jobs to higher positions with better pay. Evidence of this phenomenon can be seen in the pay differentials of men and women in fields dominated by women. In 2001, for instance, male registered nurses earned $933 per week; women earned $820. The gap between what men and women elementary school teachers earned per week was $40; for cashiers, $35; for social workers, $47; and for health aides, $234.[149]

The last explanation for the wage gap is employer discrimination or, in the terms of economists, employer preference. This is difficult to measure and is often assumed to equal the percentage of the wage gap that is not explained after human capital and occupational and industry controls have been introduced. Of course, some of these latter factors, particularly occupational and firm differences in the employment of women and men, and the glass ghetto, glass ceiling, and glass ladder, also contain elements of employer-based discrimination if women are not being hired for certain jobs or by certain firms or are not being promoted because of stereotyped views about the work qualifications of all women. Generally, as much as 22 to 43 percent of the wage gap remains "unexplained" once human capital, occupational, and industry factors are accounted for. As we noted, this may actually underestimate the amount of the wage gap that is attributable to sex discrimination by employers.

Women and Politics

RAISING CONSCIOUSNESS ABOUT SEXUAL HARASSMENT

No boss should get away with making unwelcome sexual advances and threatening a woman's job status, even if he doesn't actually carry out his threats when she refuses. Sexual misconduct hurts women in the workplace; the boss who paws, propositions and warns of retaliation takes away a woman's dignity . . . even if he doesn't take away her job. He denies her respect . . . even if he doesn't deny her a promotion or a raise.

Patricia Ireland, former president of NOW[a]

The 1991 confirmation hearings for Supreme Court Justice Clarence Thomas mark a turning point in public awareness of sexual harassment. When the Senate Judiciary Committee initially failed to investigate allegations that Thomas sexually harassed law professor Anita Hill as her former supervisor at the Equal Employment Opportunity Commission, the women of Congress stormed the Senate and demanded action. Publicized hearings conducted by an all-male, all-white committee revealed insensitivity to the issue of sexual harassment, as Thomas was handled with velvet gloves while Hill's credibility was attacked. In the aftermath of the hearings, surveys found that most of the public believed sexual harassment was a serious problem. Thus, a December 1992 poll found that 85 percent of women and men cited sexual harassment as a problem in the workplace, up from 74 percent a year earlier.[b] Nearly a decade later, polls indicate that more than seven in ten women and eight in ten men agree that most men know better than to make overt sexual comments or passes at female employees. However, 82 percent of women and 76 percent of men agree that while sexual discrimination is more subtle and less open than in the past, it remains a serious problem today.[c] While more women than ever are filing complaints of sexual harassment, there is still a hesitancy to do so for fear of losing one's job.

To continue raising awareness of sexual harassment, the National Organization for Women launched the Women-Friendly Workplace Campaign. NOW's initiative to stop sexual harassment targets all levels and branches of government, as well as the private sector. Key components of the NOW campaign focus on electing feminist candidates to public office, strengthening EEOC regulations, allowing full compensation for damages and extending the statute of limitations in sexual harassment cases, and strengthening state and local antiharassment laws. NOW offers Women-Friendly Workplace Pledges for consumers who agree to support businesses that are women-friendly and for employers who adhere to minimal standards for a Women-Friendly Workplace. NOW exposes businesses with bad track records on sexual harassment through a "Merchant of Shame" list. NOW also provides an online speak-out for women to share their experiences.[d]

---

[a] "NOW Takes Action Against Sexual Harassment," http://www.now.org/not/05-98/sexharass.html.

[b] Richard Morin, "Sex-Harassment Issue Is Gaining Consensus," *Buffalo News*, December 19, 1992, A5.

[c] Data from the 2000 Virginia Slims Opinion Poll conducted by Roper Starch Worldwide Inc. Data provided by Philip Morris USA.

[d] To review the current "Merchants of Shame," and learn more about the Women-Friendly Workplace Campaign, visit http://www.now.org/issues/wfw/.

Solutions to Pay Inequity

Examination of historical data by Claudia Goldin suggests that there have been two eras when women's earnings grew at a relatively rapid rate compared to those of men. From 1815 to 1850, women's wages rose from 28 to 50 percent of what men earned in the manufacturing sector. And from 1890 to 1930, women's earnings continued to grow as they entered the clerical fields and the traditional women's professions.[150] Goldin argues that both of these previous eras were tied to the better fit between women's skills and the new jobs that were opening to them, a modified version of the human capital theory. She argues further that the period starting from the 1980s may be a third epoch of greater wage equity, especially as women who were socialized to, and prepared for, a lifetime of work enter the labor force.

Our review of the components of the wage gap suggests that although the increased supply of human capital by young women has led to a narrowing of the gap, the other factors producing the gap show only small signs of declining. Moreover, some of the factors contributing to wage disparity may actually be increasing as women find themselves hampered by occupational segregation, the glass ghetto, the glass ceiling, the glass ladder, and employer discrimination.

Comparable Worth

Most recent discussions of the wage gap have focused on the factor of occupational segregation. In part, this is because of the persistence and importance of the disparity between men and women. Indeed, there is even some evidence that the wage gap between men's and women's occupations is actually growing.[151] The solution that has been proposed to eliminate or reduce that part of the wage gap attributable to occupational segregation is known as comparable worth or pay equity, which Rita Mae Kelly and Jane Bayes define as "having comparable salaries for jobs requiring comparable effort, skill, responsibility, and working conditions."[152]

Implementation of comparable worth involves two steps. First, all jobs in a business or government are evaluated by a weighted set of compensatable factors, including qualifications and responsibilities. All jobs are then assigned a total "job value" based on the evaluation. The second step is to recalculate wages so that positions with the same "job value" are accorded equal pay.

Studies using comparable worth evaluation systems (the first step) have found that female-dominated jobs pay about one-third less than male-dominated jobs of the same "job value." For instance, a 1982 study of state government jobs in Minnesota found that (mostly female) registered nurses' jobs rated 275 points, as did (mostly male) vocational education instructors' jobs. However, the registered nurses were being paid $1,732 a month, while the vocational education instructors were being paid $2,260 a month, or $6,000 more a year.[153]

Comparable worth schemes have mostly been implemented (the second step) in state and local governments, in part because of the relative political ease of convincing governments as compared to businesses to adopt comparable worth studies and because wages and job descriptions are more readily accessible in government than in private industry. The Women's Bureau Fair Pay Clearinghouse reports that half the women in two-thirds of the states that have undertaken such a study have seen wage increases.[154] Public service unions also have put pressure on governments and some private industries.[155]

Most studies of the process of implementing these pay schemes, however, indicate they generally are far from completely successful in eliminating the wage gap due to unequal pay for jobs of comparable worth. Unions, professional organizations, administrators, state legislators, and women's groups all attempt to influence the final package, and the women workers often appear not to get their full pay adjustment. A study of the implementation process in Iowa found that the 8.8 percent potential gain to women employees determined by the job evaluators was reduced to a 1.4 percent gain by the time all the participants had their say and the plan was fully in place.[156] On university campuses, pay equity studies have become especially controversial, with male professors claiming such studies fail to adequately measure research productivity, which they claim explains men's higher salaries.[157]

Even if comparable worth plans did equally reward men's and women's jobs, they would not eliminate the problem of occupational segregation, mainly because the plans have been restricted to the public sector. More importantly, comparable worth schemes do not tackle the other problems that we have identified as contributing to the wage gap.

Affirmative Action

Few firms adopt affirmative action policies unless they are mandated to do so by the government or by a court. When such plans are implemented with the express purpose of increasing the number of women and minorities, however, the research suggests they can be quite effective in increasing both the number of women and their positions within the business.[158] Business and public resistance to affirmative action, especially among men, is growing stronger, however. A 2002 poll, for instance, found that 57 percent of women but only 49 percent of men support affirmative action programs targeted to help women. Women are also more likely than men to believe that minorities face discrimination and need the help of affirmative action.[159]

Family Leave, Day Care, and Flexible Jobs

Most other attempts to assist women workers have focused on helping women manage the multiple roles of wife, mother, and worker. In this way, these other reforms are indirectly designed to reduce the wage gap by increasing women's commitment to work, that is, by reducing human capital differences between women and men. The need for change is critical. A 1999 survey reported that 76 percent of women say employers do not make it easy for women who have to juggle motherhood and jobs. As Table 4.11 shows, a majority of full-time, working mothers report that an on-site day-care center (58 percent), flexible hours (59 percent), better benefits (63 percent), and the opportunity to work from home (54 percent) would increase their job satisfaction. Working mothers are also more likely than other working women to mention that less pressure and a more understanding boss would make them more satisfied at work. The expectations that companies should provide family-friendly benefits have increased over the past decade.[160]

One solution that has engendered much political debate is allowing women and men time off to take care of a sick child or elderly parent. In 2000, the absence rate and the lost work time rate for women workers in all age groups was higher than for men. The disparity between women and men workers was greatest for those who are most likely to have young children, those age twenty to twenty-four. Among this group, women had an absence rate for reasons other than illness or injury that was nearly three times higher than men of the same age.[161]

TABLE 4.11 **What Would Increase Job Satisfaction for Employed Women?**

Percentage saying each would make them much or somewhat more satisfied

	2000		1990	
	All employed women	*Employed full-time with children*	*All employed women*	*Employed full-time with children*
Incentive or bonus programs for higher productivity	62	68	55	62
Better health benefits (HMOs, more medical coverage, dental coverage)	56	63	53	58
Being under less pressure at work	55	66	46	53
More rewarding tasks/ responsibilities	51	58	43	47
Having a more understanding boss	51	59	38	41
More feedback from boss/ manager	50	57	42	45
More flexible work hours (flextime, voluntary part-time, job sharing, leaves)	49	59	42	52
More opportunity to work at home	42	54	27	36
A company-run, on-site day-care center	39	58	31	46
Better maternity leave/ parental leave option	36	52	28	42

Source: The 2000 Virginia Slims Opinion Poll, conducted by Roper Starch Worldwide Inc. Data provided by Philip Morris USA.

As discussed in Chapter 3, the Family and Medical Leave Act was passed in 1993. Before its passage, only a third of all employees had unpaid maternity leave.[162] By 2000, 8.3 percent of workers were covered under the new act. The bipartisan commission to review the law's impact found that 35 million workers had taken leaves under the act by 2000. The figure sounds impressive, but because the legislation requires only unpaid leave (a luxury few working women can afford), this law alone will not eliminate the difficulty of conflicting roles. As reported in Table 4.12 the most common reason for not taking leave is financial. Almost nine in ten (88 percent) of those who needed leave but did not take it said they would have taken leave if they could have received more, or at least some, compensation. In the 2000 bipartisan commission survey, approximately two-thirds of those who took leave received some pay during their leave; however, women were less likely to receive pay than men (62.5 percent vs. 70.4 percent). Moreover, less than half of those who were young (eighteen to twenty-four), never married, with less than a high school education, and a household income of less than $20,000 received pay during their leave. Overall, more than half of those taking leave worry about the financial impact of their leave.[163]

Although the majority of leave-takers in the 2000 survey were women (58.1 percent female vs. 41.9 percent male), maternity was not the primary reason for the leave. As revealed in Table 4.13, the most common reason for taking leave among both men and women is one's own health. Use of FMLA for care of a newborn peaks with the twenty-five to thirty-four age group, whereas use for health reasons increases with age. Of those who took leave, the overwhelming majority were white (76.2 percent), 10.6 percent were African American, 8.2 percent were Hispanic, and 2.2 percent were Asian.

FMLA continues to have widespread support. In the 2000 survey, more than four out of every five employees supported twelve weeks leave per year

TABLE 4.12 **Reasons for Not Taking Leave, 1995 and 2000 Surveys**

	Percentage of Leave-Needers	
Reason for Not Taking Leave	*1995 Survey*	*2000 Survey*
Thought job might be lost	29.7%	31.9%
Thought job advancement might be hurt[a]	22.8%	42.6%
Did not want to lose seniority[a]	15.1%	27.8%
Not eligible—worked part-time	14.3%	12.3%
Not eligible—had not worked long enough for employer	N/A	18.4%
Employer denied request[a]	9.9%	20.8%
Could not afford to take leave[a]	65.9%	77.6%
Wanted to save leave time	28.5%	34.3%
Work is too important[a]	40.8%	52.6%
Some other reason	N/A	13.2%

[a] Difference between 1995 and 2000 is significant at p < .05

N/A Indicates reason not asked about in 1995 survey

Note: Percentages sum to more than 100% due to some persons reporting multiple reasons for not taking leave.

Source: U.S. Department of Labor, "Balancing the Needs of Families and Employers," January 2001, http://www.dol.gov/dol/asp/public/fmla.

TABLE 4.13 Reasons for Taking Leave

	Percentage of Leave-Takers	Males	Females
Own health	52.4%	57.6	48.6
Maternity-disability	7.9	na	13.6
Care for a newborn, newly adopted, newly placed foster child	18.5	22.8	15.3
Care for ill child	11.5	10.4	12.2
Care for ill spouse	6.4	7.5	5.5
Care for ill parent	13.0	11.0	14.5

Note: Percentages sum to more than 100% due to some persons taking more than one leave.

Source: U.S. Department of Labor, "Balancing the Needs of Families and Employers," January 2001, http://www.dol.gov/dol/asp/pblic/fmla.

for every employee, and two out of three did not consider the policy burdensome on coworkers.[164] Many states now offer benefits that are more expansive than FMLA. In 2002, California became the first state to enact a comprehensive paid family leave program. The new law expands the state's existing disability insurance program to provide eligible employees 55 percent of their wages for six weeks to care for a newborn, a newly adopted child, or an ill family member. At least twenty-eight additional states have introduced proposals to provide unemployment compensation for parental leave. Montana established an At-Home Infant Care program to provide subsidies in lieu of child-care vouchers to parents who choose to stay home with their infants. Since 2000, a new rule under the Department of Labor allows states to expand disability or unemployment insurance to provide paid family leave. Surveys show that over 80 percent of the public supports such proposals. States are also experimenting with additional extensions to FMLA, including allowing leave for different reasons, and redefining eligibility to increase coverage. Massachusetts, for example, provides twenty-four hours of leave during a twelve-month period to participate in school-related activities or to take family members to routine medical appointments.[165]

A more pressing need is affordable, quality child care for children of working mothers. A majority of the working women with young children who responded to a survey by the Women's Bureau in 1995 were concerned about their ability to find quality child care.[166] Other surveys find that when women's day-care arrangements fail, it causes problems at work; relatedly, if women have to work late, it creates conflict at home.[167] William T. Gormley Jr. argues that inadequate or poor-quality day care also has negative repercussions for businesses in the form of lowered productivity and for our nation's children.[168]

As indicated in Table 4.14, working mothers with children under five are most likely to rely on day-care centers, relatives, or alternate working schedules

TABLE 4.14 Child-Care Choices

Primary child-care arrangements for children under five with employed mothers

Day-care center (workplace or community)	28%
Parent care	27
Other family member	27
Family day care	14
Nanny or babysitter	4

Source: Freya L. Sonenstein, Gary Gates, Stefanie R. Schmidt, and Natalya Bolshen, "Primary Childcare Arrangements of Employed Parents: Findings from the 1999 National Survey of America's Families," Urban Institute (2002), http://www.urban.org/url.cfm?ID+310487.

as their primary child-care arrangements. The cost of these day-care services for a working mother can be sizable. The average annual cost for child-care centers ranges from $4,000 to $6,000. These costs can be significantly greater in metropolitan areas, where costs can be as high as $10,000, exceeding the average cost of tuition in public colleges in all but one state.[169] A third of families with young children earn less than $25,000 per year. Although subsidies are available to low-income families, only 10 percent of eligible children receive assistance, due to limited funds.[170]

Employers in the last two decades have become increasingly involved in helping their employees with child care. They have undertaken this assistance largely because of the increasing number of working mothers. Research shows that such assistance reduces turnover of employees and increases productivity. It is estimated that fewer than 10 percent of businesses that employ one hundred or more workers provided some kind of child-care assistance.[171] This help includes work-site day-care centers, sponsorship or cosponsorship of day-care centers, referral services, and some financial help for child care. The latter ranges from outright money grants to help in locating care.

More recently, a few firms have developed some form of help for the increasing number of women who have to care for elderly relatives. Only a handful of employees currently have elder-care assistance, but it may become more common in the next decade as baby boomers begin to have to care for ill and aged parents.

Employers have also developed a number of other programs to assist women (and to a lesser extent men) who wish to combine work and family responsibilities. The most common is flextime, which allows employees to clock in early or work late in any configuration as long as they work forty hours per week. Thus, one parent can stay home until the children go to school and the other, by starting early, can be home when the children return. The practice helps to increase worker productivity and reduce turnover.

Other employer practices that may help working women combine their roles are the availability of part-time work and the related practice of job sharing. The former, as already discussed, has been used extensively by women since the 1950s to ease the burden of dual roles. It is a practice, however, with heavy costs for the employees, who may find themselves without health insurance or other employer benefits. It is also not very conducive to developing human capital, as few part-timers have access to on-the-job training or promotion. Job sharing is designed to overcome some of the problems of part-time work. With job sharing, two individuals agree to jointly undertake a single position.

Other employers have begun to modify company practices that harm dual-career families. Some employers, for example, limit transfers or help find jobs for spouses of transferred employees. With almost all of these employer assistance packages, the number of employees covered is small. Moreover, with the exception of part-time work, the programs generally are most often accessible to the professional and administrative staff. Production and service employees, jobs where an inordinate number of women are employed, are much less likely to have the full range of options.[172] To acknowledge the companies that are offering the best work-life benefits, *Working Mother* magazine publishes an annual list of the one hundred best companies for working mothers.[173]

Not all women or women's rights activists are convinced that these employer benefits are beneficial. Many worry that women who take advantage of them will jeopardize their chances to make it in the business world. Other feminists reason that without these programs, women will have to make a choice between work and family. The controversy over the "Mommy track" exemplifies the debate. The Mommy track, an idea first proposed by Felice N. Schwartz, would allow women who planned on having children to be hired for separate career tracks that are less demanding than those of men and women who would not have the same family demands. Many believe this would permanently ghettoize women workers and prevent them from ever reaching equality with men.

CONCLUSION

Although barriers facing women in the marketplace have diminished over the past few decades, women still face some serious hurdles in their effort to achieve equality. Although the public no longer objects to married women working, vestiges of the traditional notions about the secondary place of work in the lives of mothers and wives continue to hamper women's full integration into the marketplace. Even today, the influence of stereotypes about women's abilities results in women not being hired in leadership positions and the lack of readiness even of young women for the technical jobs of the twenty-first century. Discrimination by employers and male employees also continues to restrict the hiring and promotion opportunities of women.

The parallels with what we uncovered in the political realm are striking. In both, the barriers facing women are greatest for those positions with the most prestige and power. Additionally, in politics and the marketplace, some of the most pressing problems involve conflict between the domestic roles of women and their efforts to assume equal positions with men. Thus, many of the changes that are needed before all the barriers are eliminated are tied to traditional notions of child care and women's place in the family.

NOTES

1. Sharlene J. Hesse, "Working Women: Historical Trends," in *Working Women and Families*, ed. Karen Wolk Feinstein (Beverly Hills, Calif.: Sage, 1979), 38–9; Claudia Goldin, *Understanding the Gender Gap: An Economic History of American Women* (New York: Oxford University Press, 1990), 48–9.

2. Gerda Lerner, "The Lady and the Mill Girl: Changes in the Status of Women in the Age of Jackson," in *A Heritage of Her Own*, ed. Nancy F. Cott and Elizabeth H. Pleck (New York: Simon and Schuster, 1979), 182–96; Goldin, *Understanding the Gender Gap*, 50–3.

3. Goldin, *Understanding the Gender Gap*, 43–6.

4. Ibid., 53.

5. Reported in Valerie Kincade Oppenheimer, *The Female Labor Force in the United States: Demographic and Economic Factors Governing Its Growth and Changing Composition* (Berkeley, Calif.: Institute of International Studies, 1970), 53.

6. Hazel Erskine, "The Polls: Women's Role," *Public Opinion Quarterly* 35 (Summer 1971): 282.

7. Ibid., 284.

8. Leila J. Rupp, "Women's Place Is in the War: Propaganda and Public Opinion in the United States and Germany," in *Women of America: A History*, ed. Carol Ruth Berkin and Mary Beth Norton (Boston: Houghton Mifflin, 1979), 351.

9. Erskine, "The Polls," 286–7.

10. Ibid., 283–5.

11. Ibid., 285.

12. Alfreda P. Ingelhart, *Married Women and Work* (Lexington, Mass.: Lexington Books, 1979); William H. Chafe, *The American Woman: Her Changing Social, Economic, and Political Role, 1920–1970* (New York: Oxford University Press, 1972), 178–9, reports that in New York 80 percent and in Detroit 75 percent of working women interviewed by the Women's Bureau wanted to continue work at the end of the war.

13. Erskine, "The Polls," 283.

14. L. J. Sax, A. W. Astin, W. S. Korn, and K. M. Mahoney, *The American Freshman: National Norms for Fall 2002* (Los Angeles: Higher Education Research Institute, UCLA, 2002).

15. James Allan Davis and Tom W. Smith, *General Social Surveys, 1972–1996*, National Opinion Research Center, distributed by Roper Center for Public Opinion Research, Storrs, Conn.

16. Joseph P. Ritz, "Women Making Job Gains at Expense of Men," *Buffalo News*, April 10, 1993, A6.

17. Susan Mitchell, *American Attitudes*, 3rd ed. (Ithaca, New York: New Strategist Publications, 2000), 400–3.

18. Ibid., 392.

19. *General Social Surveys, 1972–2000* http://csa.Berkeley.edu:7502?cgi-bin/hsda3.

20. Data from the 1979 and 1990 Virginia Slims Polls. Made available by the Roper Center for Public Opinion Research, Storrs, Conn.

21. Lesley Lazin Novak and David R. Novak, "Being Female in the Eighties and Nineties: Conflict between New Opportunities and Traditional Expectations among White, Middle Class, Heterosexual Women," *Sex Roles* 35 (1996): 66–7.

22. Susan A. Mann, "Slavery, Sharecropping, and Sexual Inequality," *Signs* 14 (Summer 1989): 779–86.

23. This, however, was an increase from the 12.2 percent of all professional women who were married in 1910. Frank Stricker, "Cookbooks and Law Books: The Hidden History of Career Women in Twentieth-Century America," in *A Heritage of Her Own*, ed. Cott and Pleck, 486.

24. "Living Female: A Roper Center Data Review," *Public Perspective*, July/August 2000, 23. Survey by the Washington Post/Kaiser Family Foundation/Harvard University, November 17–23, 1997.

25. "Living Female: A Roper Center Data Review."

26. Chris McComb, "Few Say It's Ideal for Both Parents to Work Full Time Outside the Home," *Gallup Poll Release*, May 4, 2001, http://www.gallup.com/poll/releases/pr010504.asp.

27. Novak and Novak, "Being Female in the Eighties and Nineties," 67.

28. Edward H. Clarke, *Sex in Education*, a book written during the 1870s and quoted in Robert W. Smuts, *Women and Work in America* (New York: Columbia University Press, 1959), 114.

29. Ibid., 112, quoting Mary Putnam Jacobi, a prominent woman physician, in 1891.

30. Erskine, "The Polls," 387–8.

31. The 1972 Virginia Slims Poll, data made available by the Roper Center for Public Opinion Research, Storrs, Conn.; and Connie De Boer, "The Polls: Women at Work," *Public Opinion Quarterly* 41 (Spring 1977): 275.

32. Ibid.; the 1979 Virginia Slims Poll. Data made available by the Roper Center for Public Opinion Research, Storrs, Conn.

33. The 1995 Virginia Slims Poll. Data made available by the Roper Center Research, Storrs, Conn.

34. David W. Moore, "Americans More Accepting of Female Bosses," *Gallup News Release*, May 10, 2002, http://www.gallup.com/poll/releases/pr020510.asp.

35. "Women in Elected Office," Executive report to Deloitte and Touche prepared by Roper Starch Worldwide Inc. Data provided by Deloitte and Touche (2002).

36. Ibid., p. 52.

37. Frank Newport, "Americans See Women as Emotional and Affectionate, Men as More Aggressive," Gallup Poll Release, February 21, 2001, http:www.gallup.com.

38. Janet Shibley Hyde, "Meta-analysis and the Psychology of Gender Differences," *Signs* 16 (Autumn 1990): 55–73. See also Epstein, *Deceptive Distinctions*, generally on the question of biological differences between women and men and the absence of data to sustain the stereotypes.

39. Wellesley College Center for Research on Women, *The AAUW Report: How Schools Shortchange Girls* (Washington, D.C.: American Association of University Women, 1992), 27–8, 70; Sheila Tobias, "The Mathematics Filter," *National Forum* (Fall 1981): 17–8.

40. Linda J. Sax, A. W. Astin, W. S. Korn, and K. M. Mahoney, *The American Freshman: National Norms for Fall 2002* (Los Angeles: Higher Education Research Institute, UCLA, 2002).

41. Stricker reports that professional women were much more eager to combine roles than the percentage of them who were married suggests; "Cookbooks and Law Books," 486. Goldin's work, using old census data and surveys, finds evidence

that, for the generations of women born around 1900 to 1910, the desire to work and be married was particularly strong and may be reflected in the high percentage of this cohort who went to work as married women in the 1950s; *Understanding the Gender Gap*, 148–9.

42. Judith Stacey, Susan Bereard, and Joan Daniels, eds., *And Jill Came Tumbling After: Sexism in American Education* (New York: Dell, 1974).

43. Piper Purcell and Laura Stewart, "Dick and Jane," *Sex Roles* 22, nos. 3/4 (1990): 177–85; Carole M. Kortenhaus and Jack Demarest, "Gender Role Stereotyping in Children's Literature: An Update," *Sex Roles* 28, nos. 3/4 (1993): 219–42; Diane M. Turner-Bowker, "Gender Stereotyped Descriptors in Children's Picture Books: Does 'Curious Jane' Exist in the Literature?" *Sex Roles* 35, nos. 7/8 (1996): 461–88.

44. Center for Research on Women, *The AAUW Report*, 68–71.

45. Ibid., 28–30.

46. Ibid., 12; Emily Hancock, *The Girl Within* (Cambridge, Mass.: Harvard University Press, 1993).

47. The 1995 Virginia Slims Poll.

48. Suzanne Daley, "Little Girls Lose Their Self-Esteem on Way to Adolescence, Study Finds," *New York Times*, January 9, 1991.

49. Wellesley College Center for Research on Women, *The AAUW Report: How Schools Shortchange Women* (Washington, D.C.: American Association of University Women, 1992).

50. Carrie Fernandez, "Making Work a Family Affair," Ms. Foundation Press Release, January 6, 2003, http://daughtersandsonstowork.org.

51. Cecilia Ann Northcutt, *Successful Career Women: Their Professional and Personal Characteristics* (New York: Greenwood Press, 1991), 31–5; Hugh Lytton and David Romney, "Parent's Differential Socialization of Boys and Girls: A Meta-Analysis," *Psychology Bulletin* 109, no. 2 (1991): 267–96.

52. Peter Glick, "Trait-Based and Sex-Based Discrimination in Occupational Prestige, Occupational Salary, and Hiring," *Sex Roles* 25, nos. 5/6 (1991): 351–64.

53. "Women Are Still Treated Differently in the Workplace," Ms. Foundation Press Release, March 20, 2003, http://www.daughtersandsonstowork.org; and the 2000 Virginia Slims Poll conducted by Roper Starch Worldwide Inc., data provided by Philip Morris USA.

54. Goldin, *Understanding the Gender Gap*, 155–6.

55. Ibid., 156.

56. Linda J. Sax, A. W. Astin, W. S. Korn, and K. M. Mahoney, *The American Freshman: National Norms for Fall 2002* (Los Angeles: Higher Education Research Institute, UCLA, 2002).

57. Robert Fiorentine, "Increasing Similarity in the Values and Life Plans of Male and Female College Students? Evidence and Implication," *Sex Roles* 18, nos. 3/4 (1988): 151.

58. Linda J. Sax, A. W. Astin, W. S. Korn, and K. M. Mahoney, *The American Freshman: National Norms for Fall 2002* (Los Angeles: Higher Education Research Institute, UCLA, 2002).

59. National Center for Education Statistics, *Digest of Education Statistics 2001* (Washington, D.C.: U.S. Department of Education, 2002), 322.

60. U.S. Bureau of the Census, Population Reports, Series P-23, no. 173, *Population Profile of the United States, 1991* (Washington, D.C.: U.S. Government Printing Office, 1991), 5.

61. National Center for Education Statistics, *Digest of Education Statistics 2001*, 239.
62. National Center for Education Statistics. *Digest of Education Statistics 2001*.
63. Ibid.
64. The 1985, 1990, and 1995 Virginia Slims Polls. Data made available by the Roper Center.
65. The 2000 Virginia Slims Poll.
66. Lawrence Mishel, Jared Bernstein, and Heather Boushey, *The State of Working America 2002/2003* (Ithaca, N.Y.: Cornell University Press, 2003), 50.
67. 1989 *New York Times* Poll, "Women's Lives: A Scorecard of Change." Data made available by the *Times.*
68. Susan Mitchell, *American Attitudes*, 482–7.
69. Forty-six percent of all working women and 35 percent of men agreed strongly to a certain extent with the statement "The conflicting demands of family and job put me under a lot of stress." To the statement "All in all, I do feel that I do a good job of balancing my job and my family life," 72 percent of women and 70 percent of men agreed. The 2000 Virginia Slims Poll.
70. Goldin, *Understanding the Gender Gap*, 161–3.
71. Ibid., 165–6. Twenty-six states had proposed the legislation to bar married women from state government jobs.
72. Nancy E. McGlen and Meredith Reid Sarkees, *Women in Foreign Policy: The Insiders* (New York: Routledge, 1993), chap. 3.
73. Goldin, *Understanding the Gender Gap*, 171–8.
74. Ibid., 171–4.
75. Ibid., 163.
76. Ibid., 163, 176.
77. Ibid., 147.
78. Francine D. Blau, *Equal Pay in the Office* (Lexington, Mass.: Lexington Books, 1977), chap. 4.
79. Barbara F. Reskin and Patricia A. Roos, *Job Queues, Gender Queues: Explaining Women's Inroads into Male Occupations* (Philadelphia: Temple University Press, 1990), 35–7.
80. The 1995 Virginia Slims Poll.
81. Data from the 2000 Virginia Slims Opinion Poll conducted by Roper Starch Worldwide Inc. Data provided by Philip Morris USA.
82. Reskin and Roos, *Job Queues, Gender Queues*, 37–8, 309–10.
83. Smuts, *Women and Work*, 119–20; Oppenheimer, *Female Labor Force*, 51–5.
84. Ritz, "Women Making Job Gains," A6.
85. Sally Hilsman Baker, "Women in Blue-Collar and Service Occupations," in *Women Working: Theories and Facts in Perspective*, ed. Ann H. Stromberg and Shirley Harkess (Palo Alto, Calif.: Mayfield, 1978), 352.
86. U.S. Department of Labor, Bureau of Labor Statistics, "Highlights of Women's Earnings in 2001," Report 960 (May 2002).
87. Lois Gray, "Women in Union Leadership," in *The American Woman 2001–2002: Getting to the Top*, ed. Cynthia B. Costello and Anne J. Stone (New York: W. W. Norton, 2001), 107–38.
88. Baker, "Women in Blue-Collar Occupations," 355–63; studies of women receiving vocational education in the trades find that they face greater unemployment problems. Center for Research on Women, *The AAUW Report*, 42.

89. Phyllis Kernoff Mansfield, Patricia Barthalow Koch, Julie Henderson, Judith R. Vicary, Margaret Cohn, and Elaine W. Young, "The Job Climate for Women in Traditionally Male Blue-Collar Occupations," *Sex Roles* 25, nos. 1/2 (1991): 71–3.

90. Goldin, *Understanding the Gender Gap*, 147.

91. Roberta T. Anderson and Pauline Ramey, "Women in Higher Education: Development through Administrative Mentoring," in *Women in Higher Education*, ed. Lynne Welch (New York: Praeger, 1990).

92. Sheila Wellington and Katherine Giscombe, "Women and Leadership in Corporate America," in *The American Woman 2001–2002: Getting to the Top*, ed. Costello and Stone, 91.

93. Ibid.

94. The 1995 Virginia Slims Poll.

95. Albert R. Hunt, "Major Progress, Inequities Cross 3 Generations: Grandmother, Mother, Daughter Reveal a Tempered Optimism Amid 'Universally Held Views'" *Wall Street Journal*, June 22, 2000, A9.

96. Oppenheimer, *The Female Labor Force.*

97. Eileen Trzcinski, "Effects of Uncertainty and Risk on the Allocation of Time of Married Women," *Journal of Family and Economic Issues* 17, nos. 3/4 (Winter 1996): 343–4; Goldin, *Understanding the Gender Gap*, 124–6.

98. Goldin, *Understanding the Gender Gap*, 136–8.

99. Trzcinski, "Effects of Uncertainty, 343–5.

100. Goldin, *Understanding the Gender Gap*, 17.

101. Ibid.

102. U.S. Department of Labor, Bureau of Labor Statistics, "Median Weekly Earnings of Full-Time Wage and Salary Workers by Selected Characteristics" (Washington, D.C.: U.S. Department of Labor), http://stats.bls.gov/news.release/wkyeng.t06.htm.

103. Goldin, *Understanding the Gender Gap*, 18, 44–9.

104. Ibid., 25, 38.

105. The figures were almost as high for the youngest group of married women, age fifteen to twenty-four. Ibid., 18.

106. Oppenheimer, *The Female Labor Force*, 136–9.

107. U.S. Department of Labor, "Facts on Working Women," *Women's Bureau Fact Sheet*, March, 2000, http://www.dol.gov/dol/wb/public/wb_pubs/millennium52000.htm.

108. "No Rest for New Moms," *U.S. News & World Report*, November 6, 2000, 10.

109. "Labor Force Participation for Mothers With Infants Declines for First Time, Census Bureau Reports," U.S. Census Bureau Press Release, October 18, 2001, http://www.census.gov/Press-Release/www/2001/cb01-170.html.

110. Goldin, *Understanding the Gender Gap*, 180–3.

111. Paul Ryscavage, "Gender-Related Shifts in the Distribution of Wages," *Monthly Labor Review*, 117, no. 7 (1994): 7; *The American Woman 2001–2002.*

112. U.S. Department of Labor, "Household Data," Bureau of Labor Statistics, May 2, 2003, http://www.bls.gov/news.release/empsit.tl3.htm.

113. John F. Stinson Jr., "Multiple Jobholding Up Sharply in the 1980s," *Monthly Labor Review* 113, no. 7 (1990): 3–5.

114. U.S. Department of Labor, Bureau of Labor Statistics, "Employment Status of Mothers With Own Children Under 3 Years Old by Single Year Age of Youngest Child, and Marital Status, 2000–01 Annual Averages," http://www.bls.gov/news.release/famee.t06.htm.

115. Meredith K. Wadman, "Mothers Who Take Time Off Find Their Careers Pay a Heavy Price," *Wall Street Journal*, July 16, 1992, B1.

116. Howard N. Fullerton Jr., "The 2005 Labor Force: Growing but Slowly," *Monthly Labor Review* 118, no. 11, 33–4.

117. William Goodman, "Women and Jobs in Recoveries: 1970–93," *Monthly Labor Review* 117, no. 7 (1994): 28–36.

118. "Closing the Gender Gap," *Society* 30, no. 3 (1993): 3.

119. U.S. Department of Labor, Bureau of Labor Statistics, "Highlights of Women's Earnings in 2001," Report 960 (Washington, D.C.: Department of Labor, 2002).

120. *Employment and Earnings*, January 1997, 204.

121. U.S. Department of Labor, Bureau of Labor Statistics, "Household Data: Annual Averages" (2002), http://www.bls.gov/cps/cpsaat22.pdf.

122. Margaret Mooney Marini, "Sex Differences in Earnings in the United States," *American Sociological Review* 26, no. 15 (1989): 352.

123. In 1994, college-educated women earned almost $12,000 less than college-educated men. U.S. Department of Labor, Women's Bureau, "Facts on Working Women."

124. Ibid.

125. Joyce P. Jacobsen and Laurence M. Levin, "Effects of Intermittent Labor Force Attachment on Women's Earnings," *Monthly Labor Review* 118, no. 9 (1995): 16–8.

126. Elizabeth Caucutt, Nezih Guner, and John Knowles, "Why Do Women Wait? Matching, Wage Inequality and Incentives for Fertility Delay," Unpublished Manuscript quoted in "Marriage, Motherhood and Money: How Do Women's Life Decisions Influence Their Wages?" *Regional Economist* (April 2003): 7.

127. Hiromi Taniguchi, "The Timing of Childbearing and Women's Wages," *Journal of Marriage and the Family* 61 (November 1999): 1008–19.

128. Marini, "Sex Differences in Earnings," 352–6; Elaine Sorensen, "The Crowding Hypothesis and Comparable Worth," *Journal of Human Resources* 25, no. 1 (1990): 62–6. Most economists doubt the validity of studies that include hundreds of "human capital" variables that "explain" all of the gender gap.

129. Marini, "Sex Differences in Earnings," 351–2; Jacobsen and Levin, "Effects of Intermittent Labor Force Attachment," 14–6.

130. Reskin and Roos, *Job Queues, Gender Queues*, 35–8.

131. Stephanie Boraas and William M. Rodgers III, "How Does Gender Play a Role in the Earnings Gap? An Update." *Monthly Labor Review* (March, 2003): 9–15.

132. Boraas and Rodgers, 14.

133. Sorensen, "The Crowding Hypothesis," 62–3.

134. Mary C. Icing, "Occupational Segregation by Race and Sex," *Monthly Labor Review* 115, no. 4 (1992): 30–6.

135. Reskin and Roos, *Job Queues, Gender Queues*, 81–4.

136. Ibid., 60–1.

137. Erica L. Groshen, "The Structure of the Female/Male Wage Differential: Is It Who You Are, What You Do, or Where You Work?" *Journal of Human Resources* 26, no. 3 (1991): 457–72; Sorensen, "The Crowding Hypothesis," 73.

138. Michael J. Carter and Susan Boslego Carter, "Women's Recent Progress in the Professions or, Women Get a Ticket to Ride After the Gravy Train Has Left the Station," *Feminist Studies* 7, no. 3 (1981): 475–92.

139. Nancy E. McGlen and Meredith Reid Sarkees, "Political Science: A Hostile or Friendly Institution for Women" (paper delivered at the annual meeting of the American Political Science Association, Washington, D.C., 1997).

140. Reskin and Roos, *Job Queues, Gender Queues*, 111–27.

141. Ibid., 257–74.
142. "Catalyst Celebrates 40th Anniversary and Releases Latest Measure of Women on Corporate Boards," *Perspective* (January 2002), http://www.catalystwomen.org.
143. *1996 Catalyst Census of Women Board Directors of the Fortune 500 Companies.*
144. U.S. Federal Glass Ceiling Commission, *A Solid Investment: Making Full Use of the Nation's Human Capital: Recommendations of the Glass Ceiling Commission* (Washington, D.C.: Government Printing Office, November 1995).
145. The 2000 Virginia Slims Poll.
146. Ann Morrison, Randall P. White, Ellen Van Velsor, and Center for Creative Leadership, *Breaking the Glass Ceiling* (Reading, Mass.: Addison-Wesley, 1992), 139–54.
147. "Women in Corporate Leadership: Progress and Prospects," Catalyst, 1996, http://www.catalystwomen.org/press/infobriefs/infobrief1.html.
148. Pat Swift, "Opportunity Abounds, and It's There for the Taking," *Buffalo News*, January 25, 1997, C7; National Federation of Women Business Owners, "Women-Owned Businesses in the United States: 1996, A Fact Sheet" (Washington, D.C.: Author, 1996). Linda N. Edwards and Elizabeth Field-Hendrey, "Home-Based Workers: Data from the 1990 Census of the Population," *Monthly Labor Review* 119, no. 11 (1996): 26–34.
149. U.S. Department of Labor, Bureau of Labor Statistics, "Highlights of Women's Earnings in 2001," Report 960, 2002.
150. Goldin, *Understanding the Gender Gap*, 58–73.
151. Sorensen, "The Crowding Hypothesis," 72.
152. Rita Mae Kelly and Jane Bayes, *Comparable Worth, Pay Equity, and Public Policy* (Westport, Conn.: Greenwood Press, 1988), 4.
153. Sara M. Evans and Barbara Nelson, *Wage Justice: Comparable Worth and the Paradox of Technocratic Reform* (Chicago: University of Chicago Press, 1989).
154. U.S. Department of Labor, Women's Bureau, "Worth More Than We Earn: Fair Pay for Working Women," *Fair Pay Clearinghouse*, September 1996.
155. U.S. Department of Labor, Women's Bureau, "What Works: Fair Pay for Working Women," *Fair Pay Clearinghouse*, September 1996.
156. Peter F. Orazem and J. Peter Mattila. "The Implementation Process of Comparable Worth: Winners and Losers," *Journal of Political Economy* 98, no. 1 (1990): 149; Joan Acker, *Doing Comparable Worth: Gender, Class, and Pay Equity* (Philadelphia: Temple University Press, 1989).
157. Robin Wilson, "Equal Pay, Equal Worth?" *Chronicle of Higher Education*, November 24, 1995, A15–16.
158. Alison M. Konrad and Frank Linnehan, "Formalized HRM Structures: Coordinating Equal Employment Opportunity or Concealing Organizational Practices?" *Academy of Management Journal* 38, no. 3 (1995): 787–803.
159. Lydia Saad, "Pondering Women's Issues, Part II," Gallup Poll, February 18, 2003, http://www.gallup.com/poll/tb/goverpubli/20030218b.asp.
160. The 2000 Virginia Slims Poll.
161. U.S. Department of Labor, Bureau of Labor Statistics, "Absences From Work of Employed Full-Time Wage and Salary Workers by Age and Sex," ftp://ftp.bls.gov/pub/special.requests/lf/aat46.txt.
162. Stephanie L. Hyland, "Helping Employees with Family Care," *Monthly Labor Review* 115 (1990): 23.
163. U.S. Department of Labor, "Balancing the Needs of Families and Employers: The Family and Medical Leave Surveys 2000 Update," http://www.dol.gov/dol/asp/public/fmla/main2000.htm.
164. Ibid.

165. "State Family Leave Benefit Initiatives in the 2001–2002 State Legislatures: Making Family Leave More Affordable," *National Partnership for Women and Families*, http://www.nationalpartnership.org; "State Family and Medical Leave Laws," *National Conference of State Legislatures*, http://www.nscl.org/programs/employ/fmlachart.htm.

166. U.S. Department of Labor, *Working Women Count*, 20.

167. The 2000 Virginia Slims Poll.

168. William T. Gormley Jr., *Everybody's Children: Child Care as a Public Problem* (Washington, D.C.: Brookings Institution, 1995).

169. "Children's Defense Fund Report Finds the High Cost of Child Care Puts Quality Care Out of Reach for Many Families," Children's Defense Fund Press Release, December 11, 2000, http://www.childrensdefensefund.org.

170. "Child Care and Early Education Basics," Children's Defense Fund Fact Sheet, April 2000, http://www.childrensdefensefund.org.

171. Marcia Eldridge, "The State of Dependent Care," *National Business Women* (Spring 1993): 11–4.

172. Hyland, "Helping Employees," 23.

173. http://www.workingmother.com.

Familial and Reproductive Rights and Realities

The changes sought in familial and reproductive rights are the most controversial of all the issues discussed thus far. More than political or employment rights, familial and reproductive rights are most likely to be universal in application and therefore perceived as threatening to the greatest number of people.

Efforts to change traditional practices in this arena had to be postponed until greater political and economic rights were obtained.* Without political rights, women had little chance of gaining or maintaining economic and social rights. Without economic opportunities to earn wages outside the home, few women had any options in life other than to marry and remain at home under the "protection" of their husbands. This was especially true when women had little or no control over reproduction. Without the ability to limit the number or timing of the arrival of children, women were made even more dependent on men for their livelihood.

Because of their inferior political and economic status, women were reluctant to challenge the institution of marriage or to make demands for significant changes in its structure. Without alternative lifestyle options, loss of this institution would have plunged most women into the depths of poverty and to the bottom of the political underclass. Early efforts in this arena were therefore limited to gaining control over reproduction—a prerequisite for any other changes in family structure.

The achievement of political and economic rights eventually made possible attempts to reform the traditionally male-dominated institution of marriage. Parallel to these efforts were ones centering on a woman's right to control reproduction.

*The ideas of much of the following discussion draw heavily on Barbara Easton, "Feminism and the Contemporary Family," in *A Heritage of Our Own: Toward a New Social History of Women*, ed. Nancy F. Cott and Elizabeth H. Pleck (New York: Simon and Schuster/Touchstone Books, 1979), 555–77. See also Betty Friedan, *The Second Stage* (New York: Summit Books, 1981), 83–123.

"Yes, I realize that we are free agents, but I have to take on the additional risk of pregnancy and am more susceptible to certain sexually transmitted diseases, so I think you should pay for the movie."

As we have seen, women's economic opportunities and political power still are unequal to men's. Some women thus remain dependent on the institution of marriage. Real or even imagined threats to marriage can be very disturbing to women who believe they have little chance to support themselves or their families without it.

Sexuality is an additional complication. Sexual identity has been linked to gender, and gender roles have been linked to roles within the traditional family. In turn, family roles have defined gender-role behaviors. Thus, for some, challenges to the traditional family pose a serious threat to sexual identity.

A vocal, well-organized, well-financed, and politically powerful counter-movement arose to prevent changes in familial and reproductive rights. This movement, threatened by changes in family and gender roles, appears to recognize the connection between economic and political power and change in the family. Thus, the "New Right" wants to roll back rights in all three areas, and especially abortion rights. The outcome of this struggle may hold the key to the future of the women's movement.

WEB EMPOWERMENT TOOLS

U.S. Census Bureau
http://www.census.gov

NARAL Pro-Choice America
http://www.naral.org

Urban Institute (nonpartisan economic and social policy research organization)
http://www.urban.org

National Center for Health Statistics
http://www.cdc.gov/nchs

Children's Defense Fund
http://www.childrensdefense.org

Statistical Abstract of the United States
http://www.census.gov/prod/www/statistical-abstract-us.html

U.S. Department of Justice Violence Against Women Office
http://www.ojp.usdoj.gov/vawo/

Families and Work Institute
http://www.familiesandwork.org/

U.S. Department of Labor Women's Bureau
http://www.dol.gov/dol/wb

Welfare Information Network
http://www.financeprojectinfo.org/win/

Vital Voices (supporting and accelerating economic, social, and political progress of women globally)
http://www.vitalvoices.org

Center on Budget and Policy Priorities
http://www.cbpp.org

National Gay and Lesbian Task Force
http://www.ngltf.org

Planned Parenthood
http://www.plannedparenthood.org

National Child Care Information Center
http://nccic.org/

The American Federation of Labor–Congress of Industrial Organizations (AFL-CIO)
http://www.aflcio.org

Leadership Conference on Civil Rights
http://www.civilrights.org/

Economic Policy Institute
http://www.epnet.org

Brookings Institution
http://www.brookings.org

Mothers Ought to Have Equal Rights
http://www.mothersoughttohaveequalrights.org

Institute for Women's Policy Research
http://www.iwpr.org/

The Struggle for Familial and Reproductive Rights

According to noted historian Carl N. Degler, the period around 1830 signaled the development of what he terms the modern family.[1] Changes in the institution of marriage and thus the family were characterized by

1. Marriages based on mutual affection and not parental arrangement.
2. "Separate spheres" for the sexes in which "a woman's life was physically spent in the home and with the family, while the man's life was largely outside the home, at work."
3. A focus on the importance of child rearing.
4. Smaller families.[2]

In this modern family, a woman's place was indisputably in the home. As the keeper of the family, a wife was regarded as the moral superior of her husband, although this "superiority" did not necessarily carry over into their interpersonal relations or into laws concerning a woman's place in the family. Relegation of women to the home also put married women in the position of near-complete economic dependence on their husbands, which was further exacerbated by laws that treated women, at best, as no better than children.

In this chapter, we examine the laws and social policies relating to marriage, the family, and reproduction that have affected women. Major societal changes have occurred. Most women now work outside, as well as within, the home, and few individuals live in "traditional" families as defined by television's *Leave It to Beaver* or even *The Brady Bunch*. Recent changes in family structure are reflected in television programs that depict a blended family or a single parent, as in *Judging Amy*. Yet the disappearance of working mothers from television sitcoms has led one writer to assert: "TV just doesn't get it when it comes to portraying real-life women."[3] We focus on how each of the women's movements pursued changes in a woman's place in the family and the choices open to her. As family roles and values have changed, many of the struggles for women's rights have been closely tied to a woman's role—and expectations about that role—in the family, especially her motherhood role.

In 1996, President Bill Clinton was assured the support of many women when he enthusiastically endorsed forcing health care plans to stop requiring new mothers to leave the hospital immediately after delivery. Women who had "drive-through deliveries" were shown to have higher rates of infection and their babies required more emergency room visits than mothers and babies who were allowed to stay in the hospital for longer periods of time.

Source: Toles © 1995, *The Buffalo News*. Reprinted with permission of Universal Press Syndicate. All rights reserved.

Deep-rooted notions about women's "proper" role continue. Thus, opposition to a woman's equality in the family or concerning her reproductive rights continues to rage.

THE WOMAN'S MOVEMENT

During the 1848 Seneca Falls Convention, participants were very concerned about the laws and practices that made women inferior to men in family matters. The Declaration of Sentiments included accusations that men had

- made [a woman] if married, in the eye of the law, civilly dead.
- taken from her all right in property, even to the wages she earns.

- compelled [her] to promise obedience to her husband, he becoming, for all intents and purposes, her master—the law giving him power to deprive her of her liberty, and to administer chastisement.

- framed the laws of divorce, as to what shall be the proper cause.

- [assigned] guardianship of the children . . . upon a false supposition of the supremacy of man, and giving all power into his hand.

- created a different code of morals for men and women.

Effects of the Common Law

Historically, many of the problems described previously stemmed from women's legal inferiority, which was directly traceable to the English common law, adopted by the colonists. One common-law doctrine, termed *coverture*, provided that women lost all legal capacity upon marriage. Married women ceased to be persons in the eyes of the law because their legal identities merged with those of their husbands, who represented them in the public sphere. In essence, behind Mary Jones's new name, Mrs. John Smith, Mary Jones ceased to exist. Married women had no right to contract, to sue (or be sued) in their own names, or to own property. English feminist Mary Wollstonecraft argued that married women were "civilly dead" under the code of coverture, and that for a republic to be truly just, women must exercise civil rights whether single or married.[4] Perhaps the greatest effect of coverture was in the simple issue of control. As it evolved, coverture produced and legitimized almost total male domination over women. A married woman lost claim to her name, her assets, and even her children. As the sole legal guardian of his offspring, a man could, by will, transfer custody of his children to someone other than his wife. Slave women had even fewer rights. They were chattels to be bought and sold, and their marriages were not even legal.

To remedy these inequities (as they affected white women, at any rate), many women lobbied various state legislatures for reforms. In 1848, for example, New York passed a Married Woman's Property Act, which gave women the right to control property acquired by "inheritance, gift, bequest, or devise." Women continued to be denied control over their wages and earnings, and still were denied custody of their children and the right to divorce drunken or abusive husbands.

Their successes, however, led women to lobby for similar and more extensive changes. For example, New York passed additional legislation in 1860 expanding women's control of their inheritances and wages and allowing them to make contracts and sue in their own names. Women were given joint custody of their children for the first time. A widow was also permitted to inherit at least a third of her husband's estate, regardless of whether he left a will to the contrary.

Divorce Reform

As early as 1852, Elizabeth Cady Stanton, as president of the New York Woman's Temperance Society, shocked many of its members when during its convention she urged:

> Let no woman remain in the relation of wife with a confirmed drunkard. Let no drunkard be the father of her child. . . . Let us petition our State government so to modify the laws affecting marriage and the custody of children that the drunkard shall have no claim on his wife or child.[5]

The radical nature of Stanton's demand—at the time only one state allowed a woman to divorce her husband for drunkenness—led supporters of temperance to distance themselves from Stanton's demands and the woman's movement. It appears that even temperance supporters did not want to complicate the drinking issue with a more controversial one—divorce—although it was clear that many unhappy marriages resulted from drinking problems. A drunken husband could spend all of his wages, sell his or his wife's property, or apprentice his children to work for others without consulting his wife. Even so, many temperance workers feared that their goals would be harder to achieve if they were allied with calls for other, more radical reforms.

Undaunted, Stanton continued to press for sweeping reform. In 1853, she wrote to Susan B. Anthony, "It is in vain to look for the elevation of woman so long as she is degraded in marriage."[6] At the 1860 National Woman's Rights Convention, Anthony noted, "By [marriage] man gains all; woman loses all; tyrant law and lust reign supreme with him."[7]

These comments horrified many women in attendance. In her autobiography, Stanton wrote, "So alarming were the comments on what had been said that I began to feel that I had inadvertently taken out the underpinning from the social system."[8]

Divorce reform, like domestic violence reform today, was viewed by many as a basic threat to the stability of the family. In contrast, married women's property acts, especially those that gave women joint custody of their children, were generally viewed as strengthening women's proper role—motherhood. Also, on a more practical level, some legislators believed that their daughters needed protection from wandering or shiftless husbands. Under coverture, a man could dispose of all assets that a woman received from her family. Changes in divorce laws, however, were not without critics. In 1870, for example, Horace Greeley predicted that "easy divorce would destroy America blasted by the mildew of unchaste mothers and dissolute homes."[9]

Birth Control

While divorce reform was viewed by many as radical, at least some women spoke out in favor of reform. This was not the case with birth control. As early as 1856, Lucy Stone aptly captured women's consensus about the issue: "It is very little to me to have the right to vote, to own property, etc., if I may not keep my body and its use my absolute right. *But we are not ready for that question*"[10] (emphasis added).

Some reformers did, however, try to discuss controversial issues. *The Revolution*, for example, published by Anthony and Stanton, often included discussions of prostitution, free love (see Chapter 1), rape, and even spousal abuse. But views such as these, declining birth rates (indicating that some form of family planning was being used by some), and a general concern with declining morals led to the passage of a series of laws banning abortion and obscenity. In 1873, for example, the U.S. Congress passed the Comstock Act. It prohibited the use of the U.S. mail for distribution of any "obscene" materials. It specifically labeled as obscene "the dissemination of any pornography, abortion devices, and any drug, medicine, article or thing designed, adapted, or intended for preventing *conception*"[11] (emphasis added). It also branded as "smut" and therefore "obscene" many essays that urged abstinence as a method of family planning.[12] Proponents of the act, including its sponsor Anthony Comstock, believed that this kind of information could lead only to moral decay and more abortions. Nevertheless, an 1871 American Medical Association report found that 20 percent of all pregnancies were deliberately terminated.[13]

BIRTH CONTROL IN THE 1800s

Ironically, much of the information concerning birth control that Anthony Comstock and others tried to stop was woefully inaccurate. As early as the 1830s, for example, a number of handbooks and guides written by physicians contained instructions for family planning. Many authors advocated periodic abstinence but misjudged the safe period. One author advised, "If intercourse is abstained from until ten or twelve days after cessation of the menstrual flow, pregnancy will not occur." (We now know that information is totally incorrect.) In the 1850s, women used the rhythm method, douches, and intrauterine devices to prevent conception, often without much success. When such family planning failed, some women risked their lives to end a pregnancy." In 1858 the price of an abortion ranged from twenty-five to sixty dollars, an exorbitant price for working women barely able to make ends meet on a salary of three or four dollars a week."[a] Many died after the high cost of an abortion led them to try to perform the procedure themselves. Condoms did not become readily available for men until the 1880s. Throughout the century, women struggled for information about and access to birth control. Even restrictive legislation such as the Comstock Act did not stop the decline in the birthrate in America. In 1900, the birth rate was half what it had been in 1800, with an average of three-and-a-half children versus seven children per married woman.[b]

---

[a] Harriet Sigerman, "An Unfinished Battle," in *No Small Courage: A History of Women in the United States*, ed. Nancy Cott (New York: Oxford University Press, 2000), 247.

[b] Harriet Sigerman, "Laborers for Liberty," in *No Small Courage*, 347.

Voluntary Motherhood.   During this period, many moral reformers and most woman's rights advocates supported the idea of "voluntary motherhood," a woman's right to limit her family size by natural means. They and even radical "free lovers," such as Victoria Woodhull, believed that contraceptive devices were "a standing reproach upon, and a permanent indictment against American women." Distaste for artificial birth control, "the washes, teas, tonics, and various sorts of appliances known to the initiated," stemmed from two sources. First, in keeping with notions of romantic love that pervaded this era, women believed that the use of contraceptives somehow destroyed the love act. Second, many married women feared an increase in marital infidelity.[14]

In an era when a woman's identity, livelihood, and status depended on a stable marriage, threats to that institution were avoided at all cost. This is not to say, however, that these women wished to have children every year. Stanton, who herself had seven children, believed that before women could gain full equality, they had to have control over their bodies. A staunch supporter of voluntary motherhood, Stanton frequently addressed all-women audiences during the suffrage campaign. At those meetings, she regularly talked about the need for women to limit the size of their families to improve their overall status as well as their health.[15]

Cries for divorce reform and voluntary motherhood brought condemnation from the press and the pulpit. It seemed that the controversial changes sought by Stanton and some of her followers were never likely to be adopted. Women did secure positive changes in property and divorce laws before and during the Civil War. But once morals and birth control became issues, the passage of restrictive laws virtually stopped any additional moves for change. It was not until the suffrage movement that significant new advances were made in women's status in the family.

Women and Politics
VICTORIA WOODHULL FOR PRESIDENT

Victoria Claflin Woodhull was born in Homer, Ohio, in 1838, the sixth of ten children. Her family's poverty meant that Victoria's childhood was marked by neglect and exploitation. From the age of five, she worked outside the home, washing laundry and floors. Her parents soon found a more lucrative way for their daughter to contribute to the household income. Both Victoria and her sister Tennessee performed as psychic mediums, charging a dollar for communicating with the dead. At fifteen, Victoria married Canning Woodhull, a doctor who, like her father, suffered from alcoholism. The couple moved around the country with

(continued)

their young children while Victoria made money acting, using her psychic powers, and engaging in prostitution. At twenty-six, Victoria met Colonel James Harvey Blood, a Civil War veteran who was active in abolitionist and suffragist movements. The two began an affair and later married after each had divorced. In 1868, the couple moved with their extended family to New York City, where Victoria became a spiritual advisor to Commodore Vanderbilt, who bankrolled a financial venture that made her the first woman to run a brokerage house on Wall Street. Woodhull also started a weekly paper to disseminate her ideas about free love and women's rights. In the pages of the *Woodhull and Claflin Weekly*, she proclaimed her radical message of sexual liberation. "I have an inalienable, constitutional and natural right to love whom I may . . . to change that love every day if I please."[a]

In 1870, Woodhull became the first woman to testify in front of a congressional committee. She became a national figure by demanding equal rights for women of the men serving on the House Judiciary Committee. Her efforts on Capitol Hill led her to announce her candidacy for the nation's highest office. In 1872, Victoria Woodhull became the first woman to run for president of the United States, campaigning on a women's rights platform supporting divorce and free love. Her feminist politics made perhaps their greatest impact through a speech she delivered to the National Woman Suffrage Association in February 1871. Speaking at the invitation of Susan B. Anthony and Elizabeth Cady Stanton, Woodhull encouraged members of the women's rights organization to revolutionary activism to achieve constitutional equality with men. "We are plotting revolution; we will overslough this bogus republic and plant a government of righteousness in its stead." Almost a century earlier, Abigail Adams had warned her husband, John, that if founders did not "Remember the Ladies" in the new constitution they were writing, the women would rise in rebellion against the tyranny of patriarchy. However, the time was not right for Victoria Woodhull's call for women's liberation and sexual revolution. While suffragists were divided over strategies for achieving their goal, the nation united in its opposition to the radical message of Woodhull's sexual politics. In the years that followed, controversy would distance her from Anthony and Stanton, and a series of scandals that ended with her brief imprisonment would deprive her of a public platform. In 1877, Woodhull emigrated with her family to England, where she died in 1927 at the age of eighty-eight.[b]

---

[a] Quoted in Harriet Sigerman, "Laborers for Liberty," in *No Small Courage: A History of Women in the United States* (New York: Oxford University Press, 2000), 312.

[b] For more information about Woodhull's life and politics, see Mary Gabriel, *Notorious Victoria: The Life of Victoria Woodhull* (New York: Algonquin Press, 1998), and Barbara Goldsmith, *Other Powers: The Age of Suffrage, Spiritualism, and the Scandalous Victoria Woodhull* (New York: Knopf Publishers, 1998).

THE SUFFRAGE MOVEMENT

Like women in the movement before them, most women in the suffrage movement eventually came to view divorce reform as possibly strengthening the family. Although divorce laws generally held men and women to the same moral
standard, suffragists did not take a public stand on the reform issue. Advocates
of divorce reform generally were associated with the several smaller, radical
movements that developed during the suffrage era. From 1895 to World War I,
for example, the philosophies of Charlotte Perkins Gilman, an early radical feminist, were the most widely reported. In *Women and Economics* (1898), she urged
radical changes in the family and child care. Gilman recognized that broadening women's roles in the economy and society meant challenging traditional
notions of motherhood that restricted women to the household. "In recon-
structing in our minds the position of women under economic independence, it
is most difficult to think of her as a mother."[16] She called for professional day
care and communal living arrangements with central kitchens, which would
allow women the freedom to advance in the economic arena. Critics took these
calls as the logical consequences of woman suffrage. Even most suffragists
rejected Gilman's radical views. Yet Gilman anticipated the concerns of modern
feminist theorists that women's duties as primary care givers of children prevent them from fully exercising their rights as citizens.[17]

Educated Motherhood

While rejecting most of the reforms suggested by Gilman and others, women
in the suffrage and progressive movements worked for some changes that
would benefit the position of women in their role as mothers. After woman
suffrage was won, the seriously high infant and female childbirth mortality
rates in the United States were some of the first problems sought to be remedied. Concern for the high number of birth-associated deaths was a natural
response for the women who had sought the vote based on their claims as
mothers. Stressing the idea of "educated motherhood,"[18] they called for federal legislation to give money to the states to set up clinics where expectant
women and young mothers could be taught preventive health care. In many
ways, these proposals perpetuated the idea of a woman's "separate sphere"
by aiding her efforts to be a better mother.

During 1920 and 1921, the Women's Joint Congressional Committee
(WJCC) and each of its constituent organizations lobbied for passage of the
Sheppard-Towner Maternity Act (STMA), a bill that embodied many of the
proposals behind the ideas of educated motherhood. It called for money to be
paid to states to promote welfare and hygiene in maternity and infancy.

Not all women who supported suffrage favored the STMA. Just as the
National Woman's Party (NWP) clashed with the dominant suffrage groups
over strategy for the vote, it also strongly opposed the ideology behind the
STMA.[19] Though never challenging traditional marriage itself—in fact, the
NWP was on record as "dedicated to finer homes and better marriages"[20]—it
believed passage of this law would legally sanction the treatment of women

as "mothers not persons." This categorization of women, according to their capacity to bear children, is called *functionalism*. Historically, functionalist arguments in political theory have limited women's life choices by excluding them from education, economic advancement, and political rights.[21] NWP leaders believed that the functionalist arguments behind the STMA would reinforce the entire notion of separate spheres, as women would be singled out for special treatment solely on account of their reproductive capacity.

Although the STMA was passed and became the first dividend of universal suffrage for women,[22] it did so over vigorous opposition. Many of its strongest opponents had lobbied against the Nineteenth Amendment. Now, they viewed the STMA as an unwarranted invasion of the family by the federal government. Nevertheless, frightened legislators believed women would vote against those who opposed the act; eight years later, when it became clear to members of Congress that women did not vote in a bloc, the law failed to win an extension.

Birth Control in the Suffrage Era

Birth control was an exceptionally controversial issue during the suffrage era. The Comstock Act barred dissemination of birth control information through the mail. Nevertheless, many educated, middle-class women clearly used artificial forms of contraception or somehow restricted their fertility. Poorer and immigrant women, however, continued to have very large families. Soon Margaret Sanger and a growing number of women active in the progressive movement began to believe that family planning was the only way out of poverty for many.

Sanger traveled to Europe to learn more about contraceptive devices, since there was no ban on their dissemination there. On her return, she began publication of *The Woman Rebel*, in which she explained available contraceptive devices, called on women to limit the size of their families, and urged them to revolt against "patriarchal society."[23] Sanger was indicted for violating the Comstock Act, but charges were dropped. Sanger then sought legal changes to allow physicians to fit birth control devices. This move made her goals more acceptable to physicians, a powerful political group, and to many suffragists.

Sanger's arguments for birth control closely paralleled those made earlier by suffragists during their educated motherhood phase. She presented birth control as a social reform, not a woman's issue. Sanger faced an uphill battle, however; birth control was far more controversial than suffrage. Even after ratification of the Nineteenth Amendment, Sanger was unable to attract the support of many women's organizations to her largely separate movement.[24]

Hostility to Sanger and public discussion of birth control was evidenced by the refusal of the General Federation of Women's Clubs to even discuss a birth control resolution at its national meeting. A similar position was also taken by the League of Women Voters. In fact, the only women's organization to go on record publicly in support of the activities of Sanger's National Birth Control League (NBCL) was the National Women's Trade Union League. Even the liberal National Woman's Party refused to adopt a resolution favoring birth control, fearing it would confuse public perceptions of its lone goal—passage of an equal rights amendment—which had nothing to do with birth control. In fact, NWP leaders took great pains to disassociate their goals from any ideas that could be considered antifamily.

The failure of many of the major women's groups to support the birth control movement is not surprising. It was vehemently objected to by many ministers and priests and even suffragists. In declining to be a sponsor of the NBCL, Carrie Chapman Catt, president of the National American Woman Suffrage Association, wrote to Sanger, "Your reform is too narrow to appeal to me and too sordid."[25] Even many socialists believed that an association with birth control made their economic radicalism less acceptable. In fact, many rejected birth control, and some even adopted the argument put forth in the first woman's movement, namely, that artificial contraception only reinforced the moral double standard.[26] Thus, declining support from conservative feminists and isolation from many radicals and socialists largely account for the relative lack of progress by the birth control movement during this period.

The suffrage movement was well defined by its name. A wide variety of groups, often diverse in purpose, came together to secure passage of the Nineteenth Amendment. Few were interested in marriage reform or other reforms affecting families. Some, like Sanger, however, believed that women would be better off if they could limit their families. But she and many others preferred to cast birth control as a social issue and not as a woman's issue.

THE CURRENT WOMEN'S RIGHTS MOVEMENT

Women from both branches of the women's rights movement have been active in the areas of family rights and reproductive freedom. In fact, those in the younger branch probably did more to change the institution of marriage and the family than women in the older branch. They also urged a reexamination of women's sexuality and often were at the forefront of moves for lesbian rights. Younger-branch women enthusiastically embraced many of the reforms sought during the first woman's movement, as well as those pursued by radicals such as Charlotte Perkins Gilman during the suffrage movement.

Another phenomenon that has occurred concerns the older branch's growing acceptance, and indeed advocacy, of changes first advanced by those in the younger branch, including marriage reform, better birth control, and legal abortion. Indeed, Flora Davis and others have speculated that by 1975, the two branches had actually merged.[27] This has led to a movement fairly united in purpose although not necessarily in tactics. However, because the combined forces of both branches of the movement lobbied and continue to lobby for change in the family and for reproductive freedom, a strong countermovement arose to fight for the status quo and against what its followers believe to be the pure public bads advocated by the women's rights movement. Phyllis Schlafly's Eagle Forum and Beverly LaHaye's Concerned Women for America (CWA) were the major groups formed in reaction to these efforts.

Marriage

With the call "the personal is political," women in the younger branch initially challenged all aspects of the sexual relationship between men and women. Groups including the Redstockings, a New York–based, militant activist group, tried to develop a female class awareness among all women. This was often done through consciousness-raising groups. In them, women were expected to see how their individual and common experiences were the product of the same patriarchal system.

The Redstockings and many other groups demanded the elimination of the institutions that perpetuated male and female roles—including marriage. Shulamith Firestone, for example, a leading New York City feminist and author of *The Dialectic of Sex*, painted a future of cybernetic socialism. In it, reproduction was to be done by artificial means, the nuclear family would be replaced by communelike "households," and both men and women would share parenting and other domestic roles, although most tasks would be performed by machines[28]—a future very similar to the one proposed earlier by Charlotte Perkins Gilman.

Most women in the older branch initially tried to disassociate themselves from the tactics and ideology of the younger branch. The women who founded the National Organization for Women (NOW) in 1966 strongly supported both marriage and the family but thought that some legal changes needed to be made so that women could more easily pursue careers while continuing to be good wives and mothers.

Demands for reasonable pregnancy leaves without loss of seniority, tax deductions for child-care expenses, and establishment of child-care centers all reflect concern with the family. Although women in the younger branch also advocated the creation of more child-care centers, they viewed them as but a first step toward eliminating sex-role stereotypes about parenting. In contrast, NOW members and other older-branch women saw them as simply facilitating women's entrance into the workforce and allowing them to combine their worker and motherhood roles more easily.

Older-branch women also were very concerned with the position of women more generally within the marriage institution. While unswerving in their belief in the family, they agreed that wives should be treated as equal partners within the institution of marriage. Like Elizabeth Cady Stanton, they viewed inequalities in marriage as the root of the problems faced by women. Thus, they called for reforms both in marriage and in the legal treatment of married women, both during and upon the dissolution of a marriage.

Marriage and the Loss of Identity

Under the common-law notion of coverture discussed earlier, a woman technically ceased to exist legally upon marriage.[29] Today, this no longer happens, but a woman can lose some of her identity if she takes the last name of her husband.

Names. Since Lucy Stone's marriage to Henry Blackwell in 1855, a small number of women have followed her lead and not adopted their husband's surname.

Like most practices involving marriage, laws and requirements for name changes have been left to the states and thus vary from state to state. Laws in Kentucky and Alabama that require a woman to obtain her driver's license in her husband's surname, regardless of the name she uses in other situations, were upheld by the U.S. Supreme Court in the 1970s.[30] Until the mid-1970s, the U.S. Passport Office refused to issue passports in a married woman's birth name—even if it was the only name by which she was known. Eventually, pressure from a variety of women's rights groups forced the office to end this practice.

This kind of lobbying was also exerted in most states to gain passage of laws that allow women (and men in some states) to choose the name they would like to be known by after marriage. Thus, a woman may choose to retain her birth name, she may hyphenate her last name with that of her husband, or she and her husband may choose to be known by a new name altogether.

Profiles in Leadership
HILLARY RODHAM CLINTON

"We were living in an era in which some people still felt deep ambivalence about women in positions of public leadership and power. In this era of changing gender roles, I was America's Exhibit A."

Hillary Rodham Clinton, Living History[a]

In November 2000, Hillary Rodham Clinton made history as the first First Lady to be elected to the United States Senate. Her autobiography, *Living History*, offers students of women and politics a primer on activism, elected office, and leadership, as well as a portrait of the changing roles of women. Hillary Rodham was a product of America's post–World War II baby boom. She was raised in suburban Illinois, the daughter of a conservative Republican businessman and a Depression Era Democrat homemaker. Through Methodist youth groups and school organizations, she became involved in a variety of social causes and actively campaigned for greater racial understanding and civic participation. Hillary Rodham was featured in a *Life Magazine* profile in 1969 for her commencement speech at Wellesley College in which she challenged her classmates to fully engage in the politics of America's military involvement in Vietnam, the struggle for civil rights, and the emerging movement for women's rights. The following autumn, she enrolled in Yale University Law School, where she focused on family law and children's issues, working over the

(continued)

summers for Marian Wright Edleman in what would become the Children's Defense Fund. At Yale she met a fellow law student who would later become her husband, a former Rhodes scholar from Arkansas named William Jefferson Clinton.

In the wake of the women's rights movement, some women decided to retain their birth names upon marriage. Others combined their name with that of their husband. When Hillary Rodham married Arkansas Attorney General Bill Clinton, she kept her own name, much to the chagrin of her mother-in-law and her husband's political advisors. Soon after, Bill Clinton was elected governor of Arkansas. In Little Rock, where she practiced law, the governor's wife was known as Hillary Rodham. It was only after Bill Clinton failed to win reelection as governor in 1980 that she began to go by Hillary Rodham Clinton, and her husband was reelected the next time he ran for governor. During Bill Clinton's 1992 presidential campaign, Hillary's name seemed to be as great a national fixation as her changing hair styles. Through much of 1992, press accounts of her activities referred to her as "Mrs. Clinton" or "Hillary Clinton." After the 1993 inauguration, however, she quickly reestablished herself as "Hillary Rodham Clinton." What was the public's reaction? Although a *Wall Street Journal*/NBC poll found that 74 percent of those polled believed she was a "positive role model for women," only 6 percent favored her using "Rodham" in her name, with 62 percent opposing her use of her birth name.[b]

In *Living History*, she discusses the controversy surrounding her name during the presidential campaign. "I had ordered new stationary to answer all the campaign mail I was receiving. I had chosen cream paper with my name, *Hillary Rodham Clinton*, printed neatly across the top in navy blue. When I opened the box I saw the order had been changed so that the name on it was *Hillary Clinton*. Evidently someone on Bill's staff decided that it was more politically expedient to drop "Rodham," as if it were no longer part of my identity. I returned the stationary and ordered another batch."[c] The lessons she learned from this incident and others taught her that she "embodied" the changing status of women in the nation. "While Bill talked about social change, I embodied it. I had my own opinions, interests, and profession. For better or worse, I was outspoken. I represented a fundamental change in the way women functioned in our society."[d] Hillary Rodham Clinton became a lightening rod for negative and positive public opinion during her husband's first term in office as she spearheaded an unsuccessful campaign for a universal national health care system.

In 1998, Hillary Rodham Clinton was the keynote speaker at the celebration to mark the 150th anniversary of the Seneca Falls Convention on women's rights. In her years as First Lady, she had traveled the globe to advance the educational, economic, and political rights of women—often taking her daughter Chelsea to emphasize the value of girls to cultures that prize sons over daughters. She relied on faith to heal her family in the wake of the revelations of her husband's affair with a White House intern. In this time of personal and political crisis, the First Lady was approached by New York politicians and citizens to run for the Senate seat that would be vacated by soon-to-retire Senator Daniel Patrick Moynihan. Many have questioned why she decided to run against the advice of her dearest friends and most trusted advisors. "All over the United States and in scores of countries, I had spoken out about the importance of women participating in politics and government, seeking elective office and using the power of their own voices to shape public policy and chart their nation's futures. How could I pass up an opportunity to do the same?"[e] On election night, she shared the spotlight with her daughter and her husband. Hillary Rodham Clinton was ready to write another historic chapter in women's rights. Will that chapter include a run for president? Respondents to the White House Project's 2001 online survey of support for possible women candidates for the presidency ranked Hillary Rodham Clinton as their first choice (39 percent) followed by Oprah Winfrey (25 percent).[f]

---

[a] Hillary Rodham Clinton, *Living History* (New York: Simon and Schuster, 2003), 141.

[b] Jeanne Freeman, "What's in a Name? Lots, When It Is First Lady's," *San Diego Union Tribune*, February 12, 1993, E1; "62% Say First Lady Should Drop 'Rodham,'" *USA Today*, January 29, 1993, 4A.

[c] Clinton, *Living History* (New York: Simon and Schuster, 2003): 111–12.

[d] Ibid., 110

[e] Ibid., 501–2.

[f] Dianne Bystrom, "On the Way to the White House," in *Anticipating Madam President*, ed. Robert P. Watson and Ann Gordon (Boulder, Colo.: Lynne Reinner Publishers, 2003), 101.

Marriage and Divorce Law

Laws governing marriage and its dissolution have long discriminated against women. Women's rights activists recognized that discriminatory state laws needed change, but women's groups were often weak organizationally at the state level. Some organizations with strong state affiliates such as NOW, the National Federation of Business and Professional Women's Clubs, and the League of Women Voters have made considerable inroads to reform, but progress in individual states has not been uniform.

In the 1970s and 1980s, the Eagle Forum and CWA mobilized at the state and local levels. These groups drew supporters from a conservative religious base that saw an easy accommodation between religion and politics. In 1972, Phyllis Schlafly founded STOP ERA to do just what its name implied. Schlafly labeled feminists supporting the equal rights amendment "the unkempt, the lesbians, the radicals, the socialists."[31] She claimed that

ERA supporters had abandoned their God-given roles of wife and mother. Schlafly and her supporters created the Eagle Forum as an outgrowth of STOP ERA in 1975 to represent the interests of conservative women in a variety of issue areas. From the beginning, its state affiliates and strong ties to the religious right have allowed it to lobby effectively against family law changes on the state level.

To get around the "state problem," several national liberal women's organizations have concerned themselves with national solutions to issues including violence against women, divorce, alimony and child support enforcement, child custody, and homemaker rights. As early as 1963, the Commission on the Status of Women suggested the elimination of laws discriminating against women in the marriage relationship and in the dissolution of marriage.[32] Later, NOW drafted an Equal Rights Divorce Reform bill, which called for a greater recognition of a woman's economic contribution to marriage and a right to an equal division of the couple's property.

In 1977, the National Women's Conference, which was supported by the U.S. government as part of the United States International Year of the Woman observance, met in Houston, Texas. More than twenty thousand women came together (two thousand of them as state delegates) to adopt a twenty-six-plank National Plan of Action, which they submitted to President Carter in March 1978. Federal and state lawmakers were urged to enact the economic provisions contained in the Uniform Marriage and Divorce Act, a proposed law supported by the American Bar Association. In documenting the need for such provisions, the conference report noted that in 1977, in Georgia, if a house was titled in a husband's name, it "belonged only to him, even if the wife was the wage earner and made all payments." Further, "in Arkansas, a husband could dispose of all property, even jointly owned, without his wife's consent."[33]

To protest the use of government funds, Phyllis Schlafly held an alternative conference to create a new conservative coalition called the Pro-Family Movement.[34] This brought unwanted controversy to a meeting where women's rights groups failed to foresee one. Not only did the National Women's Conference reveal divisions among women as a group, but it also fostered the creation of another conservative women's group, Concerned Women for America. Deriving its base more from the religious right than the political right (where Schlafly had originally found many supporters), CWA's founder, Beverly LaHaye, created the group after the Houston conference. Unlike the Eagle Forum, it has a legal staff that tries to file lawsuits in what it calls "profamily" cases.[35] As discussed in Chapter 1, it also has a political action committee.

It is not surprising, then, that liberal reform in family law has been slow, as reform has largely had to proceed on a state-by-state basis. The U.S. Supreme Court, however, which rarely involves itself in state domestic disputes, ruled that laws like Arkansas's that allow husbands to dispose of property without spousal consent are unconstitutional.[36]

DOMESTIC PARTNERSHIPS
OR GAY MARRIAGES?

The move for legal recognition of lesbian and gay marriages gained momentum in the 1990s. Early in the decade, many city councils enacted "domestic partnership laws." These laws come in a variety of versions. Most generally allow adults who live together but who cannot legally wed to register at city hall as domestic partners. Registration then provides the couple with certain legal rights that they would not otherwise enjoy. Domestic partners often gain access to family health, dental, and even life insurance plans, which generally cover only married persons. Domestic partnership provisions are especially useful should one partner die or become ill.

The issue of same-sex marriages received a great deal of publicity in 1993 when a decision of the Hawaiian Supreme Court called that state's ban on homosexual marriages into constitutional question. Three homosexual couples that were denied marriage licenses by the state Department of Health in 1990 filed suit in 1991, alleging that the state violated their rights to equal protection under the Hawaiian Constitution, which prohibits discrimination based on sex. In 1993, the state supreme court ruled that the homosexual couples' rights appeared to have been violated and sent the case back to the lower court with instructions that the state must show a "compelling state interest" to continue to deny marriage licenses to same-sex couples. In June 1994, the governor signed a law stating that marriage licenses could only be for male-female couples and stipulating that state policy can be changed only by the legislature, not the courts. The bill also called for the creation of a Commission on Sexual Orientation and the Law. On December 9, 1995, the commission recommended that Hawaii legalize marriage between same-sex couples or set up comprehensive domestic partnership laws.

In 1997, the Hawaiian supreme court issued its final decision denying the constitutional right of homosexuals to marry within the state. Because this case was litigated under the Hawaiian Constitution, no appeal to the U.S. Supreme Court is possible. This decision ended legal challenges by Hawaii citizens, including a movement to hold a constitutional convention to amend the state constitution to ban gay marriages, a tactic that would have negated any judicial action. In 1998, the Hawaiian legislature passed a bill that the governor signed into law that prohibited same-sex marriages.

The U.S. Constitution requires that all states give "full faith and credit" to the laws of and contracts made in the other states. Thus, if a

(continued)

couple gets married in Texas, they are still recognized as being married in California if they move or vacation there. The specter of Hawaii's legalization of same-sex marriages has therefore thrown many state legislatures into a tizzy. Many conservative legislatures quickly passed legislation specifically banning homosexual marriage. The federal government even weighed in on the issue in 1996 as Congress passed, and President Clinton signed into law, the Defense of Marriage Act, a statutory attempt to allow states not to recognize same-sex marriages performed in other states. Currently, thirty-five states have laws prohibiting same-sex marriages.

Gay or lesbian partnerships are legally recognized in a number of European nations, including Sweden, Denmark, and Norway, and in some cities in France and Belgium.[a] In the summer of 2003, the Canadian high court cleared the way for the legal recognition of gay marriage. Yet in the United States, only Vermont has enacted legislation legalizing domestic partnerships. On July 1, 2000, a Vermont law went into effect allowing homosexual couples to be joined in a "civil union." This new law "allows lesbian and gay couples to 'certify' their relationships with the county clerks' offices in Vermont. Once certified, they will receive the exact same benefits, rights, and privileges, and will be beholden to the same responsibilities and burdens, as any heterosexual married couple."[b] Because a civil union is not a marriage, it is unclear what the legal rights couples joined in this ceremony will have outside of Vermont.

---

[a] Jeffrey G. Gibson, "To Honor, Love, and Build a Life: A Case for Same-Gender Marriage," in *Human Rights: Journal of the Section of Individual Rights and Responsibilities*, 23, no. 3 (Summer 1996): 92–5.

[b] Paula Ettelbrick, "Stabilizing Family Through Civil Union Laws," November 1, 2000, www.ngltf.org/library/unions.htm.

Divorce and Custody Laws.   Women still experience legal inequality within marriage under some state laws. They also often fare even more inequitably upon the dissolution of marriage. The 1970s and 1980s brought dramatic changes in state divorce laws. Not only did divorce become easier to get, but the process also became nearly impossible for one spouse to block, even if he or she didn't want a divorce. Guilt no longer became an issue, and "no-fault" divorces are now available in all fifty states.[37]

Many argue that divorce reform has been disastrous for women, although no-fault divorce accompanied by a state-level ERA actually may prove advantageous to women. In the absence of state ERAs, women's and children's standards of living often drop dramatically after divorce. The Uniform Marriage and Divorce Act of 1974—a model law suggested for states—is written in terms of women's needs. Nevertheless, women often get low financial awards from state judges. In the 1980s and 1990s, for example, numerous state commissions on gender bias in the judicial system concluded that women fail to receive adequate alimony, child support, and equitable distributions of marital property. All states have laws allowing for awards of alimony, but few women actually receive it.

For several years, NOW, other women's groups, and the Children's Legal Defense Fund (founded by Marian Wright Edelman, who is profiled in this chapter) repeatedly asked Congress to pass a comprehensive Women's Economic Equity Act (WEEA). The act was initially composed of twenty-six separate bills when it was introduced in 1981; several dealt with alimony, child support, and property settlement enforcement. Many of those provisions have yet to win legislative approval, but Congress did pass tougher enforcement of child support laws. During the Clinton administration, U.S. Attorney General Janet Reno made their enforcement a priority.

Child custody, too, has been another area of concern to women's rights activists. At the time of the Seneca Falls Convention, laws favored fathers in custody disputes. Over time, however, laws changed, reflecting consideration of the best interest of the child. As a result, by the 1930s, most state courts awarded custody of children to their mothers unless the mothers were deemed unfit.

By the 1980s, however, as more fathers began to seek custody, most state courts abandoned the presumption that children were best left in the care of their mothers. Fathers often present courts with promises of higher economic standards for their children. One study found that as many as 90 percent of fathers who sought custody actually won.[38]

Just as troubling of late are the actions of some state court judges who have actually taken away child custody from biological mothers who are lesbians. Although some states such as Massachusetts allow the nonbiological mother in a lesbian couple to adopt the child, in 1993 a Virginia judge terminated a lesbian mother's legal custody of her child because the court found her to be, as a lesbian, "unfit" and "immoral." Custody was awarded to the child's grandmother although it is estimated that there are between 4 and 6 million gay and lesbian parents.[39]

One new area of concern to feminist legal scholars has been the trend to remove divorce and child custody proceedings from courtrooms to less formal alternative dispute resolution (ADR) processes. Several state commissions on gender bias document that women often fare unequally before male judges in terms of alimony, property distribution, and even child custody awards.[40] To remedy this, some advocate use of ADR. Some states require court-connected conciliatory services.[41] Mediation, however, assumes that both parties approach the bargaining table on equal footing. As our discussion in Chapter 6 reveals, women are rarely equal in any marriage. Thus, ADR has been criticized by some as simply perpetuating inequalities.[42]

Women and Politics

MARIAN WRIGHT EDELMAN

"The greatest threat to our national security and future comes from no external enemy but from the enemy within—in our loss of strong, moral, family, and community values and support."

Marian Wright Edelman, 1992[a]

"September 11th beckons us to think differently about the kind of nation and world we want to build for our children."

Marian Wright Edelman, 2002[b]

Almost a decade before the United States was attacked by terrorists, Marian Wright Edelman argued that real national security required economic equity and social support for America's poorest children. Edelman founded the Children's Defense Fund in 1972 to champion the millions of children living in poverty in the world's wealthiest country. The daughter of a Baptist minister in rural South Carolina, Marian Wright Edelman was taught to serve those in need by her parents' examples of caring and conscience. She was educated at Spelman College and earned a law degree from Yale University. Working as a civil rights lawyer in Mississippi, she met her husband, who was also an activist in the struggle for equal citizenship. The mother of three sons, Edelman offered them the gift of life's lessons in her best-selling book *The Measure of Our Success: A Letter to My Children and Yours*. Here she outlined a program for social and political change to ensure that "no child is left behind" in America.

In 2002, in his State of the Union speech, President George W. Bush adopted Marian Wright Edelman's phrase, "Leave No Child Behind," to exemplify his commitment to educational reform in the nation's public schools. In response, the Children's Defense Fund published "The State of Children in America's Union—A 2002 Action Guide," to analyze how the Bush administration's tax-cut policy and budget recommendations failed to adequately fund the programs necessary to ensure the well-being of children. The report examined how poverty impacts one in five children in our nation through hunger, illness, lack of quality affordable child care, and poor housing or homelessness. In the foreword to the report, Edelman challenged the president to match his words with deeds to protect the weakest members of our society. "The Bush administration's budget choices before and after September 11th leave millions of children behind; favor powerful corporate interests and the wealthiest taxpayers over children's urgent needs; widen the gap between rich and poor—already at its largest recorded point in over 30 years; and repeatedly break promises and fail to seize opportunities to leave no child behind."[c] As Congress allocates more funding for military missions overseas and homeland security measures, Marian Wright Edelman reminds us that "National security is far more than military security. It is family and child security. It is economic security."[d]

---

[a] Marian Wright Edelman, *The Measure of Our Success* (Boston: Beacon Press, 1992), 19.

[b] Children's Defense Fund, "The State of Children in America's Union—A 2002 Action Guide to Leave No Child Behind," xiii.

[c] Ibid., v.

[d] Ibid., x.

Motherhood and New Issues of "Family"

Today, many women face several dilemmas regarding motherhood. Should they have children? Must they be married to have children? Will they be able to conceive or adopt? If they have children, how can they reconcile motherhood roles and jobs or careers?

The Decision to Have Children.   Few question the decision of a married woman to have a child. Many, however, often look unfavorably on those who choose to have children without the benefit of marriage. Nevertheless, teenage pregnancy rates are high, as are the pregnancy rates of older, unmarried women. Some career women opt to bear children or to adopt without the benefit of a traditional marriage, as illustrated by the case of fictional television character Murphy Brown or real-life people such as Rosie O'Donnell. No state laws prohibit an unmarried woman from bearing her own child. But some states prohibit adoption by unmarried women, and many women's groups have lobbied to repeal those laws. Even in the absence of restrictive state laws, some state social service adoption agencies rarely place children in the homes of unmarried women.

Childbearing and adoption have been especially crucial areas to lesbians who cannot legally marry. Many states prohibit the placement of children in lesbian homes. Moreover, lesbians who choose to bear their own children often encounter discrimination from physicians when they seek donor insemination services or in vitro fertilization. Women in the younger branch of the women's movement, particularly those associated with the Federation of Feminist Women's Health Centers, have tried to alleviate this problem by expanding their health services to include donor insemination programs. Usually, a majority of their clients are lesbians who were refused artificial insemination elsewhere.

Artificial insemination, the process by which sperm from a donor is injected into a woman, has been in use since the 1890s.[43] In vitro fertilization, a process by which a woman's ova are removed from her body, fertilized (*in vitro* means "in a glass" in Latin), and frozen for later implantation, is a much newer process. It is much more expensive, less commonly used, and less successful than artificial insemination. The development of these technologies and their potential was not lost on lesbians. Many women from the younger branch viewed these technologies as a mechanism by which to further separate themselves from a patriarchal society.

Feminist health centers have taken the lead in donor insemination services as well as in dealing with other specialized health care concerns of lesbians. Conservative women and the New Right have attacked the idea of lesbian parenting, and many have even opposed in vitro fertilization of married women who have been unable to conceive.

There is much concern in the feminist and women's health communities about new reproductive technologies and pregnancy medicalization and their impact on women. Laura Woliver, for example, among others, argues that these new technologies actually decrease women's control and options over maternity.[44]

Surrogacy.   Artificial insemination, egg donation, and in vitro fertilization resulted in the emergence of another issue—surrogate parenthood. There are four types of surrogacy: (1) gestational surrogacy, in which both partners can produce viable embryos that are carried in another woman's uterus; (2) egg donation fertilized with a husband's sperm and implanted in his wife through in vitro fertilization; (3) egg donation with implantation in a third woman; and (4) traditional surrogacy in which the woman who donates her egg also carries the child to term.[45] Surrogacy often questions our traditional definitions of the terms *mother* and *motherhood*. In 1986, surrogate parenting became a media sensation when Mary Beth Whitehead was paid $10,000 to be artificially inseminated with William Stern's sperm. Whitehead signed a contract agreeing to bear the child and then give it to Stern and his wife, a pediatrician. Whitehead, however, changed her mind after the birth. A judge ordered her to give the baby to the Sterns. Both parties then went to court. After a well-publicized trial, the Sterns were awarded custody, and Whitehead, the natural mother, was deprived of all parental rights. The judge insisted that his ruling was based on the best interests of Baby M (as the child had come to be known).

In 1988, the New Jersey Supreme Court upheld the custody award to William Stern but reinstated Whitehead's parental rights, which then allowed her visitation rights. Most important, the court ruled that surrogate parenting was illegal in New Jersey because it violated state adoption laws that banned baby selling.[46]

Since 1980, nearly 10,000 babies have been born through surrogates.[47] Still, surrogacy brings up troubling questions for the courts and feminists. In 1989, the American Bar Association endorsed a model state law that had two options: (1) states could make surrogate contracts illegal (and, therefore, unenforceable), or (2) states could regulate surrogate contracts like adoptions. The model law also suggested that surrogate contracts be limited to married couples with one person having a genetic link to the child. The legal community appears to be leaning toward genetic bonds as a prerequisite for legal surrogacy. In cases where women have simply carried another woman's fertilized eggs, courts have been uniform in their decisions against the surrogates.

In spite of thorny legal, moral, and philosophical issues, some women's rights advocates argue that women should be allowed to do what they want with their bodies.[48] Others fear that surrogacy contracts simply reinforce the stereotype "woman as womb."[49] Surrogacy arrangements also have a deep class dimension; they disproportionately affect poor women, who are more likely to use their reproductive capacities out of simple economic need.[50]

REPRODUCTIVE FREEDOM

The current women's rights movement is also concerned with issues of reproductive rights. According to Gloria Steinem, "reproductive freedom signifies an individual's basic human right to decide whether or not to have children," whereas the phrase rejected by feminists, "population control," "legitimizes some external force or power over women's lives."[51] To remove this external force, women continue to press for improved methods of contraception to allow them greater control over their lives. They also lobby for improved sex education and access to contraceptives to remedy teenage pregnancy. Additionally, younger-branch women have not only started feminist-run health clinics to avoid reliance on male physicians but have also written self-help books, including *Our Bodies, Ourselves*, with the goal of giving women information about, and therefore more control over, their bodies.[52]

Birth Control

By the dawn of the women's rights movement, groups such as Planned Parenthood, created during the second movement, were well established. Still, by the 1960s, two states (Connecticut and Massachusetts) had Comstock-like laws that banned the sale or use of birth control devices or information, although these laws were not well enforced. Elsewhere, women could get prescriptions for diaphragms. By 1960, birth control pills were available from private physicians. No public clinics were available, however, to provide poor women with these types of birth control. After efforts to change these state laws failed, Planned Parenthood opened a clinic in New Haven, Connecticut, specifically to challenge the law. After its director and doctor were tried, convicted, and fined for violating the state law prohibiting dissemination of birth control devices, its challenge to the Connecticut law was ultimately heard by the U.S. Supreme Court. In *Griswold v. Connecticut* (1965), the Court ruled that the Connecticut statute was unconstitutional.[53] In *Griswold*, the Court concluded that the U.S. Constitution contained a broad right to privacy, which was created by "penumbras emanating" from several specific guarantees in the Bill of Rights. These include the First Amendment, which protects association; the Third Amendment, which bars the quartering of soldiers in private homes in peacetime without consent; the Fourth Amendment, which protects Americans from unreasonable searches and seizures of their homes and property; the Fifth Amendment, which guarantees the freedom from self-incrimination; and the Ninth Amendment, which gives to citizens rights not specifically enumerated in the Constitution. Once this right to privacy was established, the Court went on to conclude that a married couple's right to privacy included the right to have access to and use of birth control.

Adolescent Access to Birth Control.   Although *Griswold* upheld the right of a married woman to use birth control—and in 1972 the Supreme Court again used the privacy doctrine to invalidate a state law barring unmarried women from access to birth control[54]—during the 1980s, the Reagan administration tried to limit teenage women's access to birth control. In 1981, for example, the first federal legislation specifically designed to deal with teenage pregnancies was passed.[55] The Adolescent Family Life Act placed emphasis on encouraging self-discipline rather than contraceptive services as a method of birth control. It also banned the use of any federal funds for abortion counseling in spite of the fact that the United States has the highest teen pregnancy rate in the Western world. Although many of the providers of counseling were religious groups that counseled teens that "God wants us to be pure,"[56] in 1989 the U.S. Supreme Court upheld what many called "the gag rule."[57]

Parental consent policies, heavily lobbied for by the Eagle Forum and CWA, have reflected similar conservative values. In 1981, for example, a Department of Health and Human Services regulation required parental notification for adolescents seeking birth control devices in all federally funded clinics.

Women's rights groups have objected to both types of programs. Representative Patricia Schroeder (D-Colo.), for example, spoke out loudly against the Reagan and George H. W. Bush administrations' exclusion of funding for most programs except those that teach abstinence. Most women's rights activists believe that teenagers must be given access to birth control information and devices as an important step not only in stopping teen pregnancies but also in stopping the spread of AIDS. Joycelyn Elders, the first African American woman to serve as U.S. surgeon general, had long espoused this view, which she steadfastly defended during her Senate confirmation hearings in 1993, during the Clinton administration. Eventually, however, after she suggested, during a speech on AIDS prevention, that masturbation is "part of something that perhaps should be taught" in school, President Clinton demanded her resignation.[58]

AIDS continues to be a particularly threatening issue for women of color. In the United States, the incidence of AIDS in Hispanic women is nearly eleven times that in white women. More than half of all women with AIDS are African American, and 80 percent of all pediatric cases are Latino or African American.[59] Thus, feminist women's health centers, the Coalition of Women of Color for Reproductive Health, and the National Black Women's Health Project have been at the forefront of education on this issue.

Global Awareness

REPRODUCTIVE HEALTH CARE FOR TEENAGERS

U.S. teenagers have higher pregnancy, birth, and abortion rates than adolescents in other developed countries. The cost of reproductive health care for teenagers varies by country and by type of service. The table shows costs in several of the industrialized nations.

TABLE 5.1 Reproductive Health Care Costs for Teenagers in Selected Countries

Country	Clinic visit	Private physician visit	Pill prescription
Sweden	Free	Free	Initial cycles free, then $1–3 per cycle
France	Free	Pay full cost; insurance will reimburse 80%	Free at clinic; $1–7 at pharmacy
Canada	Free	Free	Initial cycles free; then $3–11 per cycle
Great Britain	Free	Free	Free
United States	Mostly free	Pay full cost; insurance may reimburse at varying levels	Free or discounted at clinics; $6–35 per cycle at pharmacy

Source: Alan Guttmacher Institute, *Teenage Sexual and Reproductive Behavior in Developed Countries: Can More Progress Be Made?* (2001).

Abortion

Whereas birth control, especially as it concerns teenagers, has been controversial, abortion has been even more so. States first began to enact statutes outlawing abortion except when necessary to protect the life and health of mothers around 1820. During both early women's movements, women procured abortions. But even progressive women such as Elizabeth Cady Stanton and Margaret Sanger preferred not to get involved in any move to change existing abortion laws. Sanger even publicly denounced abortion.

Not until the 1960s did many individuals come to recognize the need for changes in restrictive state abortion laws. In 1959, the influential American

Law Institute (ALI) suggested that state laws be revised to decriminalize abortion in three circumstances:

1. When continuation of the pregnancy would gravely impair the physical or mental health of the mother.
2. When the child might be born with a grave physical or mental defect.
3. When the pregnancy resulted from rape, incest, or other felonious intercourse, including illicit intercourse with a girl below the age of sixteen.

Soon after the ALI-proposed change, a number of events occurring almost simultaneously led to an abortion movement in the United States. Physicians began to lobby for reform. In 1962, abortion became an issue of heated public debate when Sherri Finkbine, a children's television-show host, sought an abortion after she realized that she had taken thalidomide, a drug proven to cause fetal abnormalities. For the first time in history, abortion received prominent national attention. Finkbine was forced to fly to Sweden to get an abortion because she was unable to secure a legal one in the United States. Her plight was broadcast in minute detail. Attention also turned to scientific advances that lessened the medical risks associated with abortion.

Soon after the Finkbine incident, a German measles epidemic swept the United States in 1963 and 1964. If a woman contracts German measles during the first three months of her pregnancy, there is a high probability that the fetus will suffer from interrupted development. As more and more pregnant women found themselves exposed to German measles and unsuccessfully sought legal abortions, public concern over abortion reform increased. Even though more than twenty thousand children were born with various developmental problems directly traceable to German measles, concern and publicity were still inadequate to forge an abortion movement.

Taken together, however, these factors prompted several individuals to become increasingly concerned with abortion reform. By the mid-1960s, Lawrence Lader, the author of a book about Margaret Sanger, began to advocate abortion reform in public speeches and to refer women to physicians who would risk performing the illegal procedure.[60] Around the same time, Patricia Maginnis, a California woman who had undergone three illegal abortions, began publicly to advocate total repeal of all abortion laws—a radical proposal that went far beyond the ALI proposals.

These isolated actions of Lader and Maginnis, even when coupled with news accounts of the horrors of illegal, back-alley abortions and the birth of abnormal children, were not enough to start a movement. It took the infusion of potential supporters provided by both branches of the women's rights movement to forge a pro-choice submovement within the existing movement. In fact, the first formal call for the repeal of restrictive abortion laws can be traced to the Bill of Rights for Women adopted by NOW at its first annual convention in 1967. The last section demanded:

> The right of women to control their own reproductive lives by removing from
> the penal codes laws limiting access to contraceptive information and devices
> and by repealing penal laws governing abortion.[61]

The provision was passed over strong opposition. Some members believed
that abortion was not a civil rights issue; others argued that NOW's association with abortion would bring unfavorable publicity that would make other
more attainable goals increasingly difficult to achieve.[62]

NOW's public support of abortion attracted additional members and even
some of the leaders necessary to start a real move for change. Soon after
NOW's call for repeal, for example, other rights-oriented organizations followed suit. In 1968, the Citizens Advisory Council on the Status of Women
called for the repeal of all restrictive abortion laws, as did the ACLU.

Women from both branches of the women's rights movement became
increasingly active in campaigns to repeal restrictive state laws. In 1969, the
National Association for the Repeal for Abortion Laws was formed (NARAL).
Lawrence Lader helped establish NARAL, as did many NOW members,
including Betty Friedan. Over time, this organization underwent several name
changes, becoming the National Abortion Rights Action League, then the
National Abortion and Reproductive Rights Action League, and most recently
NARAL Pro-Choice America.

NARAL, Planned Parenthood, the YWCA, and other groups used conventional lobbying methods to pressure state legislatures for abortion reform.
The more radical, younger-branch Redstockings held a "speak out" where
prominent women spoke out about their own abortions. In spite of pressure
from the Roman Catholic Church not to do so, in 1970, New York State passed
the most liberal abortion law in the United States. This victory fueled the pro-
choice movement; it also provided the catalyst for a fledgling antiabortion
movement. Thus, by 1972, pressure from right-to-life forces, heavily supported
by the Catholic Church, led the New York legislature to repeal the 1970 law.
This action was vetoed, however, by Governor Nelson A. Rockefeller.

Advocates of repeal of restrictive abortion laws also had other legislative
setbacks because of the efforts of the growing right-to-life movement. In Michigan and North Dakota, for example, proposals for abortion law reform were
put to the voters and were overwhelmingly rejected. Increasingly, those
women in the older branch in particular, but not exclusively, began to believe
that the courts were their best chance for change.

Consequently, between 1969 and 1973, scores of cases were brought by attorneys and abortion rights groups generally on behalf of physicians who performed abortions and later on behalf of women who sought abortions but were
unable to secure them legally. Within this setting and amid growing support for
change among women's rights groups, the U.S. Supreme Court agreed to hear
two more cases involving abortion rights. *Roe v. Wade* (1973) involved a pregnant woman's challenge to a Texas law that prohibited abortions except to save

a mother's life.[63] Because "Jane Roe's"* pregnancy was not life threatening (which would have made her eligible to get a legal abortion in Texas), she was advised to seek one out of state. She did not have the money to do so. After seeking legal counsel, she went to court to challenge the constitutionality of the Texas law. Her lawsuit alleged that the Texas law deprived "women and their physicians of rights protected by the 1st, 4th, 5th, 9th, and 14th Amendments" and that she was deprived of the "fundamental right . . . to choose when and where to have children." Her lawyers relied heavily on the right to privacy enunciated by the U.S. Supreme Court in *Griswold v. Connecticut.*

Unlike the Texas law, the Georgia statute challenged in *Doe v. Bolton* (1973), the companion case to *Roe*, was based on the ALI's Model Penal Code. Doe's lawyers (acting on behalf of Planned Parenthood and several doctors, nurses, clergy, and social workers) alleged that the Georgia law was an undue restriction of personal and marital privacy and a denial of equal protection of the laws.[64]

These abortion cases marked the first major direct national confrontation of pro-choice and antiabortion forces. Amicus curiae (friend of the court) briefs in support of Roe and Doe were filed by several physicians' groups and organizations representing the older branch of the women's movement (including the YWCA, NOW, and Planned Parenthood) as well as the younger branch. While not as numerous, antiabortion groups including Americans United for Life, Women for the Unborn, and Women Concerned for the Unborn Child also filed friend of the court briefs in large numbers.

On January 22, 1973, the Supreme Court handed down its momentous decision. While the justices did not adopt the view that abortion was totally a private matter not to be regulated, as urged by younger-branch women, seven justices concluded that a woman's constitutional right to privacy was more important than a state's right to regulate abortions.

Thus, going further than simply finding the two state laws unconstitutional, the justices effectively invalidated the abortion laws of nearly all the states. In *Roe*, the justices divided pregnancy into trimesters and found different rights in each. The Court held that during the first trimester, a woman had an absolute right to obtain an abortion free from state interference. In the second trimester, the Court found that the "state, in promoting its interest in the health of the mother, may, if it chooses, regulate the abortion procedure in ways that are reasonably related to maternal health." In the last trimester of pregnancy, the justices concluded that the state, to promote its interest in "potential human life," could regulate or prohibit abortions, except when they were necessary to preserve the "life or health of the mother."

This decision was met with enthusiasm by women in the abortion and women's rights movements, but it provided the catalyst for major organizational efforts on the part of the antiabortion movement. In fact, in the aftermath of the abortion cases, several antiabortion organizations were formed or

---

*Most abortion cases involving individuals use pseudonyms for the women.

reformulated. For example, the National Right to Life Committee (NRTLC), which originally was only a small coordinating unit within the National Conference of Catholic Bishops, became an independent organization in 1973 directly "in response to" the Court's abortion decisions."[65] From its inception, NRTLC's ultimate goal has been a constitutional amendment that would give full legal rights of personhood to the fetus from the moment of conception.[66] It is closely allied with the Roman Catholic Church, which has provided it with an important source of members and considerable financial support.

The moral issues underlying the abortion debate and opponents' depiction of abortion as murder immediately made the controversy front-page news across the country, providing free publicity to the growing movement. In addition, just as the women's rights movement had provided an organizational base for pro-choice forces, antiabortion advocates benefited when Phyllis Schlafly, a Catholic, publicly attacked the Court's decision. For example, shortly after *Roe*, she effectively linked abortion rights to the ERA. Schlafly charged that *Roe* was an example of the havoc that would be wreaked on traditional values if the ERA was ratified. Antiabortion advocates blamed the Court's decision for the increasing decline of morals and the destruction of the family.

Within months after *Roe*, state legislatures were deluged with antiabortion bills. These proposed laws included provisions regulating clinics and requiring parental or spousal consent, waiting periods, and the description of the physical and psychological development of the particular fetus before a patient could give her consent for the procedures. Generally, these laws or regulations were enacted at the suggestion of or with the support of NRTLC members. The enactment of this kind of legislation immediately placed pro-choice advocates on the defensive. All around the country, they were forced to expend large sums of money and considerable energy to challenge the constitutionality of these laws.[67] While pro-choice advocates were defending the rights guaranteed by *Roe*, right-to-lifers continued to lobby Congress for a constitutional amendment to ban abortions.

Although early efforts to secure a constitutional amendment were unsuccessful, in 1976 Congress passed legislation (generally referred to as the Hyde amendment for its sponsor Henry Hyde, R-Mo.) that prohibited the use of federal funds such as Medicaid for abortions for poor women in all but three circumstances:

1. When the mother's life was in danger.
2. When two physicians certified that a woman would suffer "severe and long lasting damage."
3. When the pregnancy was the result of rape or incest as reported to the proper authorities.

Although the ACLU had specifically created a Reproductive Freedom Project (RFP) in 1974 to ensure compliance with *Roe*, most pro-choice activists were caught off guard by Henry Hyde and well-organized state groups that lobbied to see restrictions and conditions placed on women's access to abortion. For example, although the RFP, supported by an amicus curiae brief from NOW, successfully challenged a Missouri law that required women to sign detailed consent forms prior to an abortion, the Supreme Court upheld various record-keeping requirements of the law.[68]

With the passage of the Hyde amendment, however, some women's rights groups turned their attentions to Medicaid funding and went to court to block the amendment's implementation. Initially, they charged that Medicaid's refusal to pay for abortions was unconstitutional because it discriminated against poor women.

A series of Supreme Court decisions, however, dealt this argument a stunning blow in 1977. In three separate challenges by women's rights groups and Planned Parenthood to state Medicaid programs that financed childbirths but not abortions, the Court concluded that these practices did not violate a woman's constitutional right to secure an abortion even though some women could not afford them.[69] As a result, the number of publicly funded abortions declined precipitously.

These losses in 1977 mobilized women's rights groups just as *Roe* and *Doe* had done for the right-to-life movement. Although new groups were not created, the ACLU, RFP, and NARAL immediately launched a "Campaign for Choice," which was supported by most other women's rights groups. At the 1977 National Women's Conference in Houston, delegates passed a resolution opposing "the exclusion of abortion . . . from Federal, State, or local funding of medical services," over the strenuous objections of right-to-life delegates.[70]

To implement this resolution, NARAL began a grassroots campaign and founded NARAL-PAC to raise money for pro-choice candidates. Again, however, this was a reactive move designed to counter the growing political forces of the antiabortion movement. But the political winds were blowing in another direction. In 1980, Ronald Reagan, bolstered by the New Right and the Moral Majority, ran a successful campaign for the presidency. He was avowedly against abortion and ran on a campaign platform that contained a plank calling for him to appoint to the federal courts only judges who supported strong family values and who opposed abortion. In fact, his first appointment to the Supreme Court, Sandra Day O'Connor, was criticized because pro-life forces feared that she would not be a vote to overrule *Roe*.

Right-to-life activists' fears were somewhat assuaged in *Akron v. Akron Center for Reproductive Health* (1983).[71] Although *Akron* became the first case in which the Justice Department advanced a pro-life position before the Court (claiming that "the time has come to call a halt" to judicial limitation on state regulation of abortion), the Court struck down a vast majority of the restrictions at issue, including those preventing second-trimester abortions in outpatient clinics and requiring a twenty-four-hour waiting period. Justice O'Connor, Reagan's lone appointment to that date, joined the dissenters, noting her belief that *Roe* "was on a collision course with itself" because the trimester approach was "unworkable" in light of changing medical technology.

Over and over again, well-organized right-to-life groups convinced state legislatures to pass restrictive state abortion laws, sensing that the Court—especially if Reagan could make more appointments to it—was close to overruling *Roe*. And eventually, through Reagan's appointment of new justices to the Supreme Court plus the elevation of Associate Justice William Rehnquist (one of the two dissenters in *Roe*) to the position of chief justice, the scope of *Roe* was slowly limited.

The move to overrule *Roe* judicially picked up during the administration of George H. W. Bush (who had served as Reagan's vice president). During Bush's 1988 campaign for the presidency, he urged "adoption not abortion" as a solution to unwanted pregnancies and resurrected the call for passage of a constitutional amendment to ban abortions. Also adding fuel to the fire was the formation of Operation Rescue, a national group that used more aggressive methods to stop abortions, including trying to bar access to clinics where they were performed. It first made its presence felt at the 1988 Democratic National Convention in Atlanta, Georgia, when it blockaded several local clinics and a feminist health center.

In response to these growing threats to abortion rights, Kate Michelman, the executive director of NARAL, decided to launch a major national campaign to let women know that *Roe* was in jeopardy. Working closely with other groups, including Planned Parenthood, NOW, and the Coalition of Women of Color for Reproductive Health, NARAL designed a two-part strategy. The first was to let women know that *Webster v. Reproductive Health Services*, a case that was pending before the Supreme Court, might be used by the Court to overturn *Roe*.[72] The second part of the strategy was to educate the public to understand that even if *Roe* was not overturned, *Webster* could be a major setback if the Supreme Court was no longer willing to preserve a woman's right to an abortion using the *Roe* framework. NARAL's plan was to get Americans to ask, "Who decides?"

During George H. W. Bush's administration, abortion became an even more publicized issue. When *Webster* was finally announced in July 1989, four justices—Reagan appointees Antonin Scalia and Anthony Kennedy and Chief Justice William Rehnquist and Byron White (who was the second dissenter in *Roe*)—seemed willing to overrule *Roe*. They were unable to muster the support of a fifth justice, however. Thus, *Roe* was not overturned. But Missouri's restrictions on abortions in public hospitals and tests required for fetal viability were upheld. The opinion also read like an invitation to the states to pass additional restrictions. After *Webster*, Michelman warned, "The Court has left a woman's right to privacy hanging by a thread and passed the scissors to the state legislatures."[73]

Webster mobilized forces on both sides as marches were held around the country, and even sitting justices began to voice their fears about a post-*Roe* nation. In the wake of *Webster*, pro-choice groups including NARAL, NOW, the Fund for the Feminist Majority, and Planned Parenthood met to devise a strategy to use at the state and national levels. At the same time, the National

Right to Life Committee moved to get more restrictive state laws passed throughout the country. One of the first states to act was Pennsylvania.

In 1989, Pennsylvania passed the Abortion Control Act. It included, among other things:

1. Lectures by doctors on fetal development (informed consent).
2. A mandated twenty-four-hour delay after the lecture.
3. Reporting requirements that subjected providers to harassment.
4. Spousal notification.
5. More stringent parental consent rules requiring parents to come to a clinic with the minor or, if the parents wouldn't come, judicial approval.[74]

As the challenge to the Pennsylvania law was working its way through the judicial system, George H. W. Bush appointed David Souter to the Court in 1990 to replace Lewis Powell. Pro-choice forces lobbied hard against his appointment, but to no avail. In the first abortion-related case Souter participated in, he sided with the conservative majority. In *Rust v. Sullivan* (1991), the Court upheld regulations promulgated by the Reagan administration that barred family planning clinics receiving federal funds from discussing abortion. In spite of arguments that this gag rule violated physicians' rights to free speech, five justices voted to uphold the regulations.[75]

Pro-choice activists then tried again to raise public awareness of the direction in which the Court was going. Soon after *Rust* was announced, on the last day of the 1990–1991 term of the Court, the pro-choice Justice Thurgood Marshall resigned and Bush nominated the conservative African American federal judge Clarence Thomas to replace him. In spite of concerted lobbying by women's rights groups and questions about Thomas's alleged sexual harassment of Anita Hill, Thomas took the liberal Marshall's place on the Court.

In keeping with their strategies announced earlier, pro-choice groups opted to raise the stakes politically. At a joint press conference, the heads of Planned Parenthood, NARAL, and the ACLU, and Kathryn Kolbert of the RFP, who was set to argue against the constitutionality of Pennsylvania's Abortion Control Statute before the Supreme Court, decided to intensify the abortion debate before the 1992 elections. Thus, they asked the Court to come right out and either reaffirm that abortion was a fundamental right or to overrule *Roe* if that was what it was going to do. Said Faye Wattleton of Planned Parenthood:

> Even if [the Court's ruling] does not come before the election, it will still be a major issue in this election. This is not whether it's better for us politically, but what is better for women. We will not permit the courts to have the last word ever again, and we will show our strength in the polls because we simply will not go back.[76]

In an amicus curiae brief in *Planned Parenthood of Southeastern Pennsylvania v. Casey*, as the challenge to the Pennsylvania law had come to be known, the Bush administration urged the Court to overrule *Roe*. Joining the U.S. government in support of Casey (the governor of Pennsylvania) were groups including Feminists for Life, the U.S. Catholic Conference, and the National Right to Life Committee. Lining up in opposition to the regulations were 178 organizations, including the National Council of Negro Women, the Women's Legal Defense Fund, NOW, NARAL, the YWCA, the National Women's Health Network, the Federation of Feminist Women's Health Centers, and the National Women's Political Caucus.

Given the close nature of *Webster* and *Rust* and the addition of the two Bush appointees, many Court watchers expected that the Court would use *Casey* to overturn *Roe*. In addition to filing briefs, women's groups sponsored the March for Women's Lives on April 5, 1992, to attract more public and media attention to the issue. Drawing between 500,000 and 700,000 marchers, it was the largest pro-choice march ever.

Nearly four months after oral arguments, as tensions on both sides mounted, Justices O'Connor, Kennedy, and Souter announced a joint opinion that, while upholding a woman's right to an abortion, gave the states even greater leeway than *Webster* to limit abortions. In redefining what *Roe* stood for, the plurality opinion rejected *Roe*'s trimester approach to balancing the interest of women and the state. The Court also overturned portions of several other abortion rights cases that had struck down informed consent, parental consent, and abortion counseling requirements as unconstitutional infringements of *Roe*. But most critically, seven justices rejected the idea that a woman's right to an abortion was a fundamental right. Instead, the plurality opinion of O'Connor, Kennedy, and Souter redefined that "central principle" of *Roe* and replaced it with a lesser standard. According to them, states could enact abortion restrictions so long as they did not place an "undue burden" on a woman's right to an abortion. In *Casey*, none of the state's impediments to abortion noted earlier, except the one requiring spousal consent, was deemed an "undue burden."

Casey meant "full employment for reproductive rights lawyers," said Kathryn Kolbert, because it pushed the question back to the states. Said one National Right to Life Committee official, "We're back to where we were in the 1970s and 1980s, testing limits of what the Court will allow."[77]

Recognizing their historic weaknesses at the state level, pro-choice forces renewed efforts for a federal Freedom of Choice Act and focused on the outcome of the 1992 presidential campaign. In 1992, both major candidates—the Republican Party's George H. W. Bush, and the Democratic Party's Bill Clinton—made much of their respective views on abortion, which differed widely. The Democratic Party platform called for a strict adherence to the standards originally set out in *Roe v. Wade* and support for public funding of abortions. In contrast, the Republican Party platform supported a constitutional amendment to ban abortions except in cases where a mother's life is in danger. In that regard, it went even further than the views of George H. W. Bush, who argued that exceptions should be made for cases of rape and incest.

A Pro-Choice Administration

The election of Bill Clinton in 1992 and a large number of new female pro-choice national and state legislators sharply altered the abortion horizon. Just two days after his inauguration, Clinton issued an executive order repealing the Reagan-Bush gag rule on abortion counseling. He also lifted bans on fetal tissue research, abortions on military bases, and the testing of RU-486, an abortion pill. He also nominated Dr. Joycelyn Elders, a strong proponent of *Roe v. Wade*, to be the surgeon general, further trumpeting a change in administrative policy. Perhaps the most important signal concerning his support for abortion rights, however, was his appointment of the women's rights, pro-choice pioneer Ruth Bader Ginsburg to the Supreme Court.

After *Casey*, even before Ginsburg's nomination, many in the right-to-life movement stepped up their efforts in the states to secure new abortion restrictions. Others began to direct more hostility, harassment, and violence at abortion clinics, providers, and those seeking abortions. One NARAL official speculated, "opponents haven't won in the political system, so they're apparently determined to shoot, stalk, and murder their way to their goal."[78]

Litigating to Stop Violence

Pro-choice groups initially were caught off guard by clinic violence. They realized, however, the tremendous toll that years of right-to-life activism were taking on the right to choose. By the end of the Reagan years, in spite of the fact that the vast majority of all obstetricians-gynecologists believed that "abortion should be legal and available," most did not perform any abortions. The few who did, didn't perform many.[79] At the same time, fewer medical schools were even training medical students to perform abortions. To stop this backslide, and energized by the Reagan administration's refusal to investigate clinic violence, NOW decided to take legal action to stop groups that were attempting to interfere with the daily routine of abortion clinics.

In 1986, long before Clinton's election, in the wake of an upsurge of clinic violence, NOW filed suit on behalf of two clinics' owners trying to stop Joseph Scheidler's Pro-Life Action League (PLAL) from picketing their clinics and disrupting their businesses. NOW argued that PLAL's activities were part of a massive conspiracy to shut down clinics. After a series of legal maneuverings, the Court finally slated *NOW v. Scheidler* for oral argument in 1993.

In *Scheidler*, NOW alleged that the Racketeer Influenced and Corrupt Organizations Act (RICO), which was initially enacted by Congress as a prosecutorial tool against mob activity and organized crime, could be applied to anti-choice violence even though the perpetrators were not trying to interfere with business practices for their own economic gain.[80]

By the time *Scheidler* got to the Court, President Clinton had replaced one of the original dissenters in *Roe* with the pro-choice Ginsburg. Just the year before, however, only days before Clinton took office, the Court had ruled that an old federal law designed to stop KKK activity could not be used to deter abortion protestors because their activities were not designed to discriminate against women as a class. *Bray v. Alexandria Women's Health Center* (1993) called into question the legality of at least twenty injunctions that were in place around the nation.

Congress Acts

The Court's decision appeared to embolden some in the right-to-life movement. *Scheidler*, in fact, called clinic bombers "good citizens," and the month of February saw a rash of clinic fire bombings nationwide at the same time that the homes of physicians who performed abortions were picketed and their children followed to school.[81] In response, the Fund for a Feminist Majority offered a $20,000 reward for the arrest of clinic harassers and urged pro-choice supporters in Congress to enact legislation to outlaw violent protest activity.

Just as pro-choice groups began to press for legislation to guarantee clinic safety, Dr. David Gunn was shot and killed outside a clinic in Florida where he worked. Two weeks later, in her first press conference, Clinton's attorney general, Janet Reno, called for federal legislation to protect women. The Freedom of Access to Clinic Entrances Act (FACE) was also introduced in both houses of Congress in March.

As FACE was debated in Congress, another physician was shot by an associate of Gunn's murderer. Reno then testified before Congress on behalf of the administration, urging congressional passage of FACE, saying that it was "essential legislation." FACE, as proposed, made it a federal crime to block access to reproductive health clinics and to harass or use violence against women seeking reproductive health care and those providing it. The proposed legislation also gave federal courts jurisdiction to order injunctive relief and damages while specifically allowing for First Amendment protections for peaceful demonstrations. While versions of the bill were passed in both houses, the House and Senate were unable to reconcile the differences in their bills prior to the Christmas recess.

Meanwhile, in response to *Bray*, while waiting for the U.S. Congress to act, several states enacted their own antiviolence clinic statutes. A Florida antistalking law, however, did not deter Paul Hill of Defensive Action from shooting and killing a physician and his escort as they were leaving a Pensacola clinic where the physician performed abortions. With national attention focused on this latest incidence of violence, it was the straw that broke the camel's back. FACE was passed by the House on May 5, 1994, on a vote of 241 to 174 and by the Senate on May 15 by a vote of 69 to 30.

NOW v. Scheidler *Decided*.   While Congress was considering FACE, the Court heard oral arguments in *Scheidler*. The Clinton administration filed an amicus curiae brief on the side of pro-choice activists and became the first administration ever to weigh in on the side of abortion rights. In January 1994, the Court ruled unanimously that economic motive was not critical to RICO actions so long as a conspiracy that negatively affected a business was present.[82] This ruling gave the pro-choice movement a "powerful tool" in its arsenal to combat the escalation of violence, said Ellie Smeal of the Feminist Majority Foundation.[83] In 1997, the Supreme Court ruled that a fifteen-foot barrier around abortion clinics was also constitutional.

The Freedom of Choice Act.   FACE was not the only pro-choice legislation debated by Congress, although, ultimately, it was the only pro-choice legislation passed. As early as 1990, sensing the direction the Supreme Court was going in terms of accepting restrictions on abortion rights, the ACLU and other pro-choice groups began to seek cosponsors for the Freedom of Choice Act (FOCA), which would prohibit state restrictions on abortion. It initially was drafted to codify *Roe* by protecting the right of a woman to an abortion before viability and prohibit restrictions such as parental notification and consent, as well as any requirements that all abortions be performed in hospitals, at a time when the Court appeared poised to overrule *Roe*. President George H. W. Bush had promised to veto the act, so House and Senate leaders did not push for a vote.

After Clinton's election and the election of more than twenty new pro-choice women to the Democratic-controlled Congress, pro-choice activists failed to seize upon the opportunity to pass pro-choice legislation without fear of a presidential veto. In August 1993, FOCA became bogged down over major issues such as minors' access to abortion and public funding of abortions for indigent women. The ACLU and NOW withdrew their support, arguing the deletion of those provisions would discriminate against poor women and minors. In contrast, NARAL and Planned Parenthood believed that compromise on minors' access and funding was reasonable.

Congress Votes to Roll Back Reproductive Rights

In 1994, speaking about the new Republican majority in Congress, Kate Michelman of NARAL remarked, "The 104th Congress could well be the most anti-women, anti-choice Congress in our history."[84] The 104th Congress reversed the pro-choice 103rd Congress's liberalization of the Hyde amendment, which for the first time had eased the restrictions on federal funding of abortions to include instances of rape and incest. The 104th Congress also enacted a ban on abortion coverage for federal employees and refused to remove a ban on abortions in overseas military hospitals. (In prior years, the ban was implemented through a 1988 agency memo interpreting a federal law; in January 1993, President Clinton reversed that interpretation.) It also passed an unprecedented law called the Partial Birth Abortion Act that was an attempt to criminalize the performance of certain infrequently used abortion techniques for late-term abortions. President Clinton vetoed this bill when it reached his desk. It was reintroduced in the 105th Congress, where it passed the House with a veto-proof majority. The bill also was reintroduced in the Senate but came up three votes shy of the majority it needed to override a presidential veto. In October 1997, President Clinton vetoed the Partial Birth Abortion Act a second time. The bill also received House and Senate approval in the 106th Congress, and once again, it was vetoed by President Clinton. Pro-life forces argued that repeated veto of the Partial Birth Abortion Act demonstrated the necessity of electing a pro-life president in 2000.

Many in Congress continued to seek ways to restrict abortion rights. Moreover, since *Webster* and *Casey*, nearly all of the states enacted one or more abortion-specific restrictions. Some states have no restrictions; others have a variety, including bans on the performing of abortions in public hospitals or by physicians on the public payroll, parental consent requirements, twenty-four-hour waiting periods that often require women to travel long distances and spend the night before obtaining an abortion, and detailed informed consent procedures designed to deter a woman from exercising what is still a constitutional, albeit limited, right.

A Pro-Life Administration

The controversy surrounding the election of George W. Bush (a son of George H. W. Bush) to the presidency in 2000 was an electoral representation of a divided nation, and no other public policy issue seems to divide Americans as does a woman's right to choose. Pro-life organizations worked hard to put a president in the White House who personally opposed abortion. Candidate George W. Bush argued that *Roe v. Wade* "overstepped the constitutional bounds," as he delivered campaign speeches across the country. Pro-choice organizations emphasized that the next president would have the opportunity to appoint up to three justices to the Supreme Court who could tip the balance on the abortion issue. Soon after his election, Bush nominated former Missouri Senator John Ashcroft for attorney general. Ashcroft, who had made a brief run for the 2000 Republican presidential nomination himself, had claimed on the campaign trail that ending abortion was the "most noble and worthy objective that we could have." Both pro-life and pro-choice forces believed that the Ashcroft nomination signaled a policy shift toward restricting reproductive rights. During his Senate confirmation hearings, Ashcroft stated that as attorney general he would accept *Roe v. Wade* as the law of the land. Bush also appointed former Wisconsin Governor Tommy Thompson to lead the Department of Health and Human Services. Thompson indicated during his Senate confirmation hearings that because of safety concerns, he would review the recent Food and Drug Administration decision to approve the medical use of the abortion drug, RU-486.

Shortly after his inauguration, George W. Bush marked the twenty-eighth anniversary of *Roe v. Wade* on January 22, 2001, by signing an executive order reinstating the "global gag-rule." The global gag-rule restricts international family planning organizations that receive U.S. aide from distributing information about abortion or lobbying their governments for less restrictive laws regarding abortion. The George W. Bush administration also made public its support of efforts to ban partial birth abortions as well as new restrictions on federal employee health plans that cover the cost of some contraceptives. On April 26, 2001, the House passed the Unborn Victims of Violence Act, which imposes federal penalties on a criminal who harms a fetus in an attack on a pregnant woman. While the bill explicitly excludes abortion, it represents an important legislative step in recognizing the legal status of a fetus by according it the same right as a woman. Carolyn Maloney (D-N.Y.) warned, "Make no mistake, this is an attack on a woman's right to choose, and we know clearly and squarely where the Bush administration stands."[85] The country's largest pro-life group, the National Right to Life Organization, applauded passage of the bill within the House of Representatives, but the bill never reached the floor for debate in the Senate. President Bush, however, indicated that he would sign the bill if it won approval in the Senate. Some political observers see such legislative action as an attempt to undermine *Roe v. Wade* without a confrontation in the Supreme Court. According to NARAL, Congress voted 134 times on reproduction rights from 1995 to 2000, and pro-choice supporters won a mere twenty-four of these votes.[86] The author of an op-ed piece in the *New York Times* put it this way: "Congressional opponents of abortion have no appetite for a direct and politically unpopular assault on *Roe v. Wade*. So they are pursuing other legislative strategies that would undermine women's reproductive freedom.[87] Twenty eight states have passed laws similar to the Unborn Victims of Violence Act as of April 2003.

President Bush made good on his promise to ban partial birth abortions. On November 5, 2003, he signed into law legislation banning the procedure. The president told audience members, "For years, a form of violence has been directed against children who are inches from birth, while the law looked the other way. Today, at last, the American people and our government have confronted the violence and come to the defense of the innocent child."[88]

NEW FRONTIERS IN REPRODUCTIVE RIGHTS

RU-486, a drug that induces abortions without surgery, became available following approval by the Food and Drug Administration (FDA) during Bill Clinton's presidency. Initially, RU-486 was available by prescription in only France and Germany. Two additional drugs—methotrexate and misoprostol—can be used to produce a "safe and effective alternative" to surgical abortions when used in combination.[89] Initial tests show that RU-486 is more reliable than currently used morning-after pills to terminate pregnancies. When taken within the first seven weeks of pregnancy, RU-486 causes shedding of the fertilized embryo after implantation in the uterine wall 95 percent of the time. There are also indications that it can be used to treat endometriosis, a leading cause of infertility. Thus, somewhat ironically, the same drug that can be used to terminate a pregnancy can potentially be used to facilitate pregnancies. This possibility, however, did not stop right-to-life activists and the Catholic Church from denouncing the drug and pressuring the Reagan and George H. W. Bush administrations to outlaw its testing or use in the United States, despite the fact that it had been used with such success in France that Sweden and Great Britain also licensed the drug.

In 1989, after pressure from the Catholic Church and pro-life groups, the FDA issued an "Import Alert" barring the import of RU-486 into the United States, even for personal use, because it had not been approved by the agency. The federal government also prohibited trials of the drug here.

Immediately after taking office in 1993, President Clinton ordered his administration to "promote the testing, licensing, and manufacturing" of RU-486. He also lifted the Import Alert, thus allowing importation of RU-486 for personal use.

RU-486 and combination medications move many first-term abortions out of clinics and into physicians' offices, allowing abortion to become a truly private decision, although still not an easy one for millions of women. The widespread availability of RU-486 and the use of methotrexate and misoprostol could truly transform the abortion debate, a possibility that is all too real for those who oppose abortion under any circumstances. "You can't stop a woman from visiting a doctor," said one drug industry analyst. "It becomes a private transaction. And that's the end of the abortion battle."[90] Thus, abortions at least during the first seven weeks of pregnancy would be much more difficult to regulate as they become simpler, safer, much cheaper, and able to be done anywhere at any time.

Right-to-life activists condemned the FDA approval of RU-486 and vowed to deny women access to the drug by targeting doctors who offer their patients medical abortions. Jim Rudd, editor of *The Covenant News*, issued a warning to women and their doctors that private decisions to terminate an unwanted pregnancy will have public consequences. "It has been rumored that RU-486 will change the face of abortion in America because doctors who prescribe the poison can do so in secret anonymity. Well that's simply not true. As the Pro-life community reaches out to find these injured women, they will eventually find their doctors."[91]

THE FOOD AND DRUG ADMINISTRATION APPROVES RU-486

Since 1988, RU-486 has been safely used by 600,000 women in Europe and more than 3 million women in China. More than 2,000 women participated in drug trials in the United States sponsored by the Population Council and conducted by Planned Parenthood and other health centers between 1994 and 1995. The study found that mifepristone (the drug known as RU-486) was effective in terminating 92 percent of pregnancies up to forty-nine days in duration, and the results were published in the *New England Journal of Medicine* and the *Archives of Family Medicine* in 1998.[a] The *Journal of the American Women's Medical Association* published a special issue on medical

(continued)

abortion in June 2000, calling for Food and Drug Administration approval of mifepristone. Noting that the number of surgical abortions has declined in America over the last decade, Dr. Felicia Stewart argued that "unintended pregnancy is very common, and abortion remains one of the most frequently needed of all reproductive health services." From her perspective as a practitioner, mifepristone represents an "opportunity . . . to improve care for many women who undergo early abortion."[b]

In September 2000, the FDA approved the use of mifepristone for terminating early pregnancy. The drug is distributed in the United States under the brand name Mifeprex. Women under a doctor's care can be prescribed Mifeprex to end an early pregnancy without surgical intervention. The drug works by blocking a hormone necessary for pregnancy to progress and is used in conjunction with another drug, misoprostol, which causes the uterus to expel the embryo. NARAL Pro-Choice America calls the approval of Mifeprex "a milestone for women's reproductive health," which gives women "a new choice for abortion—a safe, private method of terminating a very early pregnancy that is non-invasive (no surgery) and does not require anesthesia."[c] Mifeprex has been approved for use within the first seven weeks after the first day of a woman's last menstrual period—usually within the first three weeks after a woman knows she is pregnant.

The use of the drug mifepristone to induce a medical abortion is a safe alternative to surgical abortion. The drug's widespread availability in the United States will greatly increase women's access to early abortion because it is prescribed in a doctor's office. Currently, 86 percent of the counties in the nation do not have an abortion provider. Many doctors who do not offer surgical abortions have expressed a willingness to prescribe Mifeprex to their patients for medical abortions.

The FDA approved a fourteen-day treatment regime that requires a woman to visit her doctor three times within a two-week period. On day one, the doctor confirms that the woman is pregnant. At this visit, she is asked to read a Medication Guide and to sign a Patient Agreement, stating that she understands the information about the drug. She then receives mifepristone from her doctor. On day three, the patient returns to the doctor's office to check on the status of the pregnancy. If a woman is still pregnant, she is given misoprostol tablets. On day fourteen, the woman returns so that the doctor can confirm the pregnancy has been terminated. If the woman is still pregnant, the doctor discusses options, including a surgical abortion. Jane Henney, M.D., Commissioner of Food and Drugs, stated in 2000 that "the approval of mifepristone is the result of the FDA's careful evaluation of the scientific evidence related to the safe and effective use of this drug."[d] However, congressional opponents of abortion have introduced legislation to restrict women's access to Mifeprex by allowing the drug to be prescribed only by doctors who already perform surgical abortions.[e]

---

[a] "Mifepristone: A Brief History," Planned Parenthood Fact Sheet, http://www.planned parenthood.org/library/ABORTION/Mifepristone.html.

[b] Felicia Stewart, "Improving Early Options for Abortion: It's Time to Stop Waiting," editorial, *Journal of the American Medical Women's Association*, Medical Abortion Supplement, 55, no. 3 (June 2000), http://www.jamwa.org/ vol55/ 55_3_ed.htm.

[c] "What You Should Know About Mifeprex," National Abortion Rights Action League Fact Sheet, http://www.naral.org/mediaresources/fact/mifeprex.html.

[d] "FDA Approves Mifepristone for the Termination of Early Pregnancy," U.S. Department of Health and Human Services, Press Release (September 28, 2000).

[e] "Congress and RU-486," editorial, *Washington Post*, April 26, 2001, A26.

CONCLUSION

Women's family status and their reproductive choices have improved remarkably since women met in Seneca Falls in 1848. Women are no longer civilly dead upon marriage, and family law reform continues today.

Birth control has also improved, yet debate continues over issues of access and health. In recent years, much of the debate and controversy in women's rights has focused on abortion.

The abortion issue clearly mobilized members of a flagging movement to act. But unless abortion is in imminent danger of being dramatically limited, marginal changes in abortion law have failed to draw concerted, prolonged mobilization of women. Issues of child care, pay equity, and how to combine both family and career are central concerns to most women, yet unlike threatened abortion rights, they are hard to sum up on a bumper sticker. Many laws are now in place to prevent discrimination against women in marriage. Yet the combined weight of her motherhood role and gender-based assumptions about her abilities that often stem from her childbearing capabilities still leave women as less than full citizens.

NOTES

1. Carl N. Degler, *At Odds: Women and the Family in America from the Revolution to the Present* (New York: Oxford University Press, 1980), chap. 1.
2. Ibid., 8–9.
3. Joanna Powell, "Invisible Mom," in *Working Mother*, July/August 2000, 52.
4. "In order to render their private virtue a public benefit, they must have a civil existence in the state, married or single; else we shall continually see some worthy woman, whose sensibility has been rendered painfully acute by undeserved contempt, droop like 'the lily broken down by a plow-share.'" Mary Wollstonecraft,

A Vindication of the Rights of Woman, ed. Carol Poston (New York: W.W. Norton, 1988, 148–9.

5. Quoted in Ida Husted Harper, *The Life and Work of Susan B. Anthony,* vol. 1 (Indianapolis, Ind., and Kansas City, Mo.: Bowen Merrill, 1899), 67.

6. Quoted in Degler, *At Odds,* 175.

7. Quoted in Elizabeth Cady Stanton, *Eighty Years and More: Reminiscences 1857–1897* (1898; reprint, ed. T. Risher Urwin, New York: Schocken Books, 1971), 215–26.

8. Ibid., 225.

9. Quoted in Sara M. Evans, *Born for Liberty* (New York: Free Press, 1989), 143.

10. "Lucy Stone to Elizabeth Cady Stanton, October 22, 1856," *Elizabeth Cady Stanton as Revealed in Her Letters, Diaries and Reminiscences,* vol. 2, ed. Theodore Stanton and Harriet Stanton Blatch (New York: Harper, 1922), 67–8.

11. Lois Banner, *Women in Modern America* (New York: Harcourt Brace Jovanovich, 1974), 17.

12. James Reed, *From Private Vice to Virtue: The Birth Control Movement in American Society since 1830* (New York: Basic Books, 1978), 37. The inadequacies of birth control and ignorance about fertile periods may have helped make birth control unpopular. For example, one popular pamphlet on birth control counseled women to refrain from sex at all times except in the middle of the menstrual cycle.

13. Kristin Luker, *Abortion and the Politics of Motherhood* (Berkeley: University of California Press, 1984).

14. Linda Gordon, *Woman's Body, Woman's Right: A Social History on Birth Control* (New York: Penguin Books, 1977), 95–8.

15. Degler, *At Odds,* 204.

16. Charlotte Perkins Gilman, *Women and Economics* (New York: Harper Torchbooks, 1966) 270.

17. Diemut Bubeck, *Care, Gender, and Justice* (New York: Oxford University Press, 1995).

18. Sheila M. Rothman, *Woman's Proper Place* (New York: Basic Books, 1978), 221.

19. The National Woman's Party was not against the act itself, but it believed that the orientation of the proposed legislation should be changed so that pregnancy would not be treated as something that made woman unique. Rothman, *Woman's Proper Place,* 157–8.

20. William L. O'Neill, *Everyone Was Brave* (Chicago: Quadrangle, 1969), 303.

21. For more on the impact of functionalism on women as citizens, see Susan Moller Okin, *Women in Western Political Thought* (Princeton, N.J.: Princeton University Press, 1979), and her more recent study of functionalism and public policy, *Justice, Gender, and the Family* (New York: Basic Books, 1991).

22. Stanley J. Lemons, *The Woman Citizen: Social Feminism in the 1920s* (Urbana: University of Illinois Press, 1973).

23. Reed, *From Private Vice to Virtue,* 87.

24. Gordon, *Woman's Body, Woman's Right,* 221.

25. Quoted in ibid., 228.

26. Ibid., 242.

27. Flora Davis, *Moving the Mountain: The Women's Movement in America since 1960* (New York: Simon and Schuster, 1991), chap. 8.

28. Shulamith Firestone, *The Dialectic of Sex: The Case for Feminist Revolution* (New York: Bantam Books, 1970).

29. See Deborah L. Rhode, *Justice and Gender* (Cambridge, Mass.: Harvard University Press, 1989), 10, 24, 25.

30. In 1972 and late 1976, the Court upheld the right of Alabama and Kentucky to mandate a woman's use of her husband's surname when applying for a driver's license. The Kentucky suit was brought by a NOW member with NOW support. A woman's right to retain her maiden name is clearly a right largely determined by state law, and the Supreme Court is unwilling to get involved in the issue of sex discrimination as found in Kentucky/Alabama-type statutes.

31. Quoted in Evans, *Born for Liberty*, 304.

32. Report of the President's Commission on the Status of Women, 1963, 46–48.

33. *What Women Want*, from the Official Report to the President (New York: Simon and Schuster, 1979), 129.

34. Ibid.

35. Susan E. Marshall, "Who Speaks for American Women? The Future of Antifeminism," *Annals* (May 1991): 57.

36. See *Kirchberg v. Feenstra*, 450 U.S. 455 (1981), and *Farrey v. Sanderfoot*, 1991 U.S. LEXIS 2906.

37. For an excellent discussion of divorce reform, see Martha Fineman, *Divorced from Reality, the Illusion of Equality: The Rhetoric and Reality of Divorce Reform* (Chicago: University of Chicago Press, 1991).

38. Georgia Commission on Gender Bias, Task Force Report, 1991.

39. David Bradvica, "Life with a Father . . . and a Father," *Press Enterprise*, February 23, 1997, NEXIS. See also *Bottoms v. Bottoms*, 1997, Va. App. LEXIS 505.

40. See New York Task Force on Women in the Courts, "Report of the New York Task Force on Women in the Courts," *Fordham Law Review* 15 (1986): 211–35.

41. See Jana B. Singer, "The Privatization of Family Law," *Wisconsin Law Review* 5 (1992): 1497–1567 in particular.

42. Ibid.

43. Judith A. Baer, *American Women in Law* (New York: Holmes and Meier, 1991), 179.

44. Laura Woliver, "The Deflective Power of the New Reproductive Technologies: The Impact on Women," *Women & Politics* 9 (1989): 17–49.

45. Michael Lollar, "Alternate Path to Parenthood," *Commercial Appeal*, December 10, 1995, 1E.

46. See Gayle Binion, "Surrogate Parenting, Reproductive Freedom and Public Policy" (paper prepared for delivery at the Western Political Science Association, San Francisco, 1988).

47. Lollar, "Alternate Path."

48. Lori B. Andrews, "Surrogate Motherhood: Should the Adoption Model Apply?" *Children's Legal Rights Journal* 7 (Fall 1986): 13.

49. Janice G. Raymond, "International Traffic in Reproduction," *Ms.*, May/June 1991.

50. See, for example, Woliver, "New Reproductive Technologies."

51. *What Women Want*, 16.

52. Boston Women's Health Book Collective, *The New Our Bodies, Ourselves* (New York: Simon and Schuster, 1992).

53. 381 U.S. 479 (1965).

54. *Eisenstadt v. Baird*, 405 U.S. 438 (1972).

55. Rhode, *Justice and Gender*, 216–7.

56. Quoted in ibid., 216.

57. *Bowen v. Kendrick*, 487 U.S. 589 (1987).
58. Ruth Marcus, "President Clinton Fires Elders," *Washington Post*, December 10, 1994, A1.
59. Loretta Ross, Sherrilyn Ifill, and Sabrae Jenkins, "Emergency Memorandum to Women of Color," in Marlene Gerber Fried, ed., *From Abortion to Reproductive Freedom: Transforming a Movement* (Boston: South End Press, 1990), 148.
60. Lawrence H. Lader, *Margaret Sanger and the Fight for Birth Control* (Boston: Beacon Press, 1955).
61. National Organization for Women, *NOW Bill of Rights*, Washington, D.C., 1967.
62. See Karen O'Connor, *Women's Organizations' Use of the Courts* (Lexington, Mass: Lexington Books, 1980), chap. 5.
63. 410 U.S. 113 (1973).
64. 410 U.S. 179 (1973).
65. Constance Balides et al., "The Abortion Issue: Major Groups, Organizations and Funding Sources," in *The Abortion Experience*, ed. Howard Osofsky and Joy Osofsky (New York: Harper and Row, 1973), 513.
66. Deirdre English, "The War against Choice—Inside the Antiabortion Movement," *Mother Jones*, February/March, 1981, 17.
67. See Eva R. Rubin, *Abortion, Politics, and the Courts* (Westport, Conn.: Greenwood Press, 1982).
68. *Planned Parenthood v. Danforth*, 428 U.S. 52 (1976).
69. *Maher v. Roe*, 432 U.S. 464 (1977); *Beal v. Doe*, 432 U.S. 438 (1977); *Poelker v. Doe*, 432 U.S. 519 (1977).
70. *What Women Want*, 160.
71. 462 U.S. 416 (1983).
72. 492 U.S. 490 (1989).
73. Quoted in Lawrence H. Tribe, *Abortion: The Clash of Absolutes* (New York: Norton, 1992), 176.
74. See American Civil Liberties Union, *Reproductive Rights Update*, July 27, 1990.
75. 111 S.Ct. 1759 (1991).
76. Quoted in R. Berke, "Groups That Back Right to Abortion Ask Court to Act," *New York Times*, November 8, 1991, A1.
77. Quoted in R. Marcus, "Court's Ruling Assures More Abortion Litigation," *Washington Post*, July 1, 1992, A1.
78. Much of this section is derived from Karen O'Connor, *No Neutral Ground: Abortion Politics in an Age of Absolutes* (Boulder, Colo.: Westview Press, 1996), chap. 7.
79. Dallas A. Blanchard, *The Anti-Abortion Movement and the Rise of the Religious Right: From Polite to Fiery Protest* (New York: Twayne, 1994).
80. 506 U.S. 263 (1993).
81. Blanchard, *The Anti-Abortion Movement*, 100.
82. 510 U.S. 249 (1994).
83. Quoted in Steve McGonigle, "Abortion Rights Backers Win High Court Ruling," *Dallas Morning News*, January 1, 1994, 1A.
84. "Election Heightens Pro-Choice Rhetoric," *Charlestown Gazette*, December 10, 1994.
85. Alison Mitchell, "House Approves Bill Criminalizing Violence to Fetus," *New York Times* (April 27, 2001).
86. Quoted in Laurence Pantin, "Anti-Choice Stealth Strategy Focuses on States," Women's enews (May 6, 2001) http://www.womensnews.com/article, NOW Legal Defense Fund.

87. "Reproductive Rights Under Attack," op-ed piece *New York Times* (April 25, 2001).
88. Press release, White House, "President Bush Signs Partial Birth Abortion Ban Act of 2003," November 5, 2003, http://www.whitehouse.gov.
89. Mathew Brelis, "Drug Induced Abortions Cleared for Trial in Boston, Other Cities," *Boston Globe*, September 12, 1996, A3.
90. David Van Bierra, "But Will It End the Abortion Debate?" *Time*, June 14, 1993, 52.
91. Jim Rudd, quoted in News Service Launches RU-486 Campaign, http://www.CovenantNews.com, October 11, 2000.

Women's Place in the Family

The review presented in Chapter 5 of the struggle for women's rights as they relate to marriage, the family, and reproduction sets the stage for an examination of the current status of women in these areas. As we saw in our discussion of political and economic rights, laws alone are rarely sufficient to bring about full equality. The situation is little different with respect to the position of women in the family. Indeed, as we have seen, women's family roles and positions generally serve to undermine efforts to implement women's legal achievements in the political and economic sectors. More specifically, assigned the extra duties of wife, mother, and homemaker, women often find they are hindered in their attempts to achieve an equal footing with men in the wider public world. Hence, an examination of the problems and barriers preventing an improved status for women in this last area is critical to our understanding of why women's progress in other sectors has been delayed.

One of the problems limiting progress of women in the family has been the nature of many of the proposed new rights. Women's rights advocates often encounter staunch opposition in this sphere because the changes they seek are seen by some as undermining the institution of the family. One result, as we saw in Chapter 5, is that the current women's movement has faced strong opposition from organizations opposed to change. Moreover, women who benefit, or believe they benefit, from the current structure of the family, have joined the opposition, often dividing many homemakers from women's rights advocates.

In addition to the organized opposition and conflict among women themselves, efforts to alter women's reproductive and family roles have confronted many of the same barriers that we identified as factors limiting women's equality in the political and economic realms, namely, cultural stereotypes, differential resources of men and women, and discrimination or at least a reluctance to change by men. In the sections that follow, we discuss these barriers, how they have been modified over time, how they have prevented or delayed change, and what the prospects are for their elimination in the near future. We focus first on the most immediate and important

"I'm tired of this full-time job. I want a part-time job."

barrier: cultural stereotypes concerning women's role in the family and a woman's right to control her reproductive capabilities.

ATTITUDINAL CHANGE TOWARD MARRIAGE AND THE FAMILY

As noted earlier, our ability to gauge public attitudes before the 1930s is hampered by the absence of public opinion polls. In the case of the family, we have even fewer data sources before the 1950s than we did for the political and economic realms, perhaps reflecting the perception that the institution of the family was immutable. We can get some idea of societal views during earlier periods, however, by examining actual marital practices or what popular writers and average citizens had to say about marriage.

Pre-Twentieth-Century America

In colonial times, marriage was perceived as a virtual economic necessity. Divorce was infrequent, and most marriages lasted until the death of one of the partners. The nature of the marital relationship and cultural attitudes about the appropriate placement of authority favored a male-dominated union. However, the scarcity of women relative to men, the need for workers to grow food and deliver rudimentary services, and the predominantly Protestant faith of the colonists all created a situation of somewhat greater equality in marriage in the colonies than in Europe.

Homemaking was often a shared task, with both spouses responsible for providing food and basic needs for the family. Housekeeping was of less concern in the barren existence of most colonial homes. The mother's role was also diminished, in part because of high infant mortality that lessened the importance of individual children and made pregnancy an almost constant condition. Abortion, legal until "quickening" (movement in the womb, or "life" in the science of the day), may have been common.[1] Child rearing was a joint endeavor, although the primary parent was the father. This is reflected in parental guides, which stressed the father's responsibilities and rarely mentioned the mother.[2]

The roles of men and women in the family, though more equitable than in the Old World, were far from equal. Only women could be found guilty of adultery.[3] More importantly, by law, men were the ultimate authority in all family decisions, and women were cautioned that the "proper attitude of a wife toward her husband was a reverend subjugation."[4]

On account of slavery, family life for African American men and women was different from that of whites. Robert Staples and Leanor Boulin Johnson note that the institution of marriage "was one of the most important survival mechanisms for African people held in bondage."[5] Although marriage between slaves lacked legal guarantees because slaves could not sign contracts, men and women in bondage still were intensely committed to their families. Masters knew this and often threatened to sell or punish members of a slave's family to keep him or her from rebelling or escaping.[6] On occasion, owners arranged marriages between slaves to encourage the birth of slave children, which added value to the owners' property. This practice increased after the importation of slaves was halted in 1808.

Slave family life was often very difficult. Men and women worked hours in the fields and had few resources with which to create a home. Nevertheless, sex roles existed, with men claiming the position of head of the family and women assuming more responsibility for child rearing. On at least some plantations, domestic tasks were undertaken communally to allow time for women slaves to work in the cotton fields or in the "Big House."[7]

One substantial difference between slaves and other women was the precarious status of slave women's control of their sexuality. Slave owners and other white men could rape African American women with no fear of retribution. Many slave women and their husbands put up a fierce resistance, but there was little either could do in a society that considered them the property of their masters.[8] After emancipation, African Americans made every effort to create family structures that solidified the bonds that were maintained with great difficulty under slavery. Thus, in the 1890 U.S. Census, the first to collect information on family status, marital patterns of African Americans and whites differed little.

In the postcolonial era, the "modern family" emerged, with its emphasis on love or mutual attraction rather than economic necessity as the basis of marriage. Remaining single and even divorce in rare circumstances became alternatives to an unhappy marriage. However, mutual emotional support was probably still more an ideal than a reality, and unlike earlier times, women's sexual needs were increasingly downplayed in a Victorian culture that expected only men to have such urges.[9]

Moreover, the "separate spheres"—women in the home and men in the business world—divided women's and men's roles in the family more clearly than they had been divided in the past. Men became the breadwinners, and women assumed responsibility for housekeeping and the children. Men's authority in important family decisions remained supreme, although their increasingly long absences from the home gave women an opportunity for daily decision making on many child-rearing and housekeeping matters.[10]

After slavery was abolished in 1865, African American women often tried to confine their activities to the home at least in part to limit the prospect of rape by white bosses or other men. The economic needs of their families often made this impossible. Sharecropping by whole families became the preferred solution. Many women, however, were forced to spend hours away from their families working as domestics.

With the division of roles in place, homemaking and motherhood achieved a new importance, and the status of women often depended on how well they performed these roles. Few persons, with Elizabeth Cady Stanton being one notable exception, questioned the primacy of motherhood for a woman. Corresponding to this increased emphasis on motherhood, abortion and the distribution of birth control information were outlawed.

The dawn of the twentieth century reinforced the trends begun in the nineteenth. The romantic ideal, and the increasing importance of sexual satisfaction for women as well as men, became the clear basis of marriage. Role divisions between men and women became more distinct. Housework became a science as home economics courses were developed at the high school and college levels to prepare women for their careers in the home. Motherhood took on a new meaning as well with the development of eugenics and Freudian psychology, which stressed the importance of the mother on the mental and physical development of the child. Even calls to limit the number of children a woman could have were tied to the need for women to devote more time to each child, lest she damage the child's psyche. Accordingly, the desire for birth control information increased. A 1937 poll, for instance, found 79 percent of all women believed in limiting the number of births.[11] As women's ties to the home were strengthened, men continued their retreat from the family. Fatherhood demands were increasingly limited to earning a wage to support the economic needs of wife and children. Automobile magnate Henry Ford's family wage plan sought to advance this notion by setting a man's wage at what was necessary to maintain a family.[12]

Throughout the nineteenth and early twentieth centuries, a period of family transition, many women continued to contribute to the household economy, both through their employment outside the home and their unpaid work in the house or family business. At least one social scientist estimates that women contributed 25 percent of family income, broadly interpreted, in the early part of the twentieth century.[13] Therefore, women's entry into the labor market during World War II was not as dramatic a break with "tradition" as it is so often portrayed.

The movement of women into the marketplace during and after World War II, however, did little initially to alter the public's perception of appropriate role divisions. Indeed, the 1950s saw the development of, in Betty Friedan's terminology, the *feminine mystique*, that is, the notion that a woman's fulfillment in life could only come through her total commitment to the roles of mother, wife, and homemaker.[14] Interviews with wives living in the Chicago area in the late 1950s and 1960s found considerable support for the triple roles of mother, wife, and homemaker. Almost all full-time homemakers identified their most important job as that of mother. The roles of wife and homemaker were close seconds. Even among women working outside the home, the same three roles dominated.[15]

Correspondingly, this era saw men's tasks as limited to breadwinner, with only a handful rating fatherhood as the most important role for a man. Men assumed the breadwinner position even if their wives went to work. Domestic and parental role sharing was rejected.[16] Authority in family decision making remained with husbands. To illustrate this point, only a third of all women in a Detroit area poll disagreed with the following statement: "Most of the important decisions in the life of the family should be made by the man of the house."[17] Thus, it appears that the initial entry of large numbers of women into the workplace did little to alter views about family life that had been in place since the Industrial Revolution.

The Women's Rights Movement and Attitudes Toward Marriage and Family

As recounted in previous chapters, one of the main goals of the current women's rights movement is the abolition of the stereotype that a woman's place is solely in the home. Paralleling this objective, and partially as a result of it, has been the massive flow of married women into the workforce. Moreover, the working wife has increasingly become the working mother and, since the 1980s, the working mother of very young children. The combination of the movement's ideology and the changing demands on women has had a major effect on attitudes toward marriage and family roles.

Attitudes Toward Marriage. In the mid-1950s, nearly every woman believed that to find fulfillment in life she had to marry. This view may be less common today. Many women are overwhelmingly in agreement that a woman can have a complete and happy life if she remains single.[18] Relatedly, there is nearly universal disagreement with the statement that a bad marriage is better than no marriage at all.[19]

The desire to marry, however, continues to be very strong.[20] In 1974, only 2 percent of women opted for an unmarried lifestyle. Twenty years later, this figure was only 8 percent. What had changed is the type of family desired. In 1974, the "ideal" was a traditional marriage with a husband assuming responsibility for providing for the family and the wife running the house and taking care of the children. By 1994, a shared marriage with both spouses

Global Awareness

ABORTION RATES WORLDWIDE

Abortion Rate per 1,000 women, by age group, and total abortion rate according to country and year of statistics.

Country, year of statistic	<20	20-24	25-29	30-34	35-39	>40	Total Abortion Rate*
Australia, 1995-1996	23.9	36.9	29.3	21.9	15.2	6.2	.67
Belgium, 1995	6.2	10.1	8.4	6.7	4.5	1.7	.19
Bulgaria, 1995	32.7	85.4	84.1	60.1	30.8	10.9	1.52
Canada, 1995	21.8	31.5	20.9	12.9	8.0	2.8	.49
Czech Republic, 1996	12.4	26.7	30.8	28.0	18.9	9.5	.63
Denmark, 1995	14.8	22.5	21.4	19.1	12.5	5.4	.48
England/Wales, 1996	19.2	25.5	18.6	12.4	7.9	3.2	.43
Estonia, 1996	33.1	85.3	80.5	62.1	44.2	21.6	1.63
Finland, 1996	9.6	15.6	13.8	11.2	7.5	3.9	.31
Germany, 1995	3.1	7.5	7.6	7.1	5.3	2.6	.17
Hungary, 1996	30.4	46.8	48.7	43.5	30.7	13.0	1.07
Israel, 1996	10.2	16.3	16.8	17.0	15.9	9.9	.43
Kazakhstan, 1995	14.4	72.3	106.8	76.6	50.8	19.9	1.7
New Zealand, 1995	20.3	29.1	21.4	14.6	8.7	3.4	.49
Norway, 1996	15.8	25.7	21.1	15.9	10.1	4.3	.46
Scotland, 1995	16.6	19.5	12.4	8.0	4.8	2.0	.32
Slovenia, 1996	10.9	26.3	27.7	32.1	27.3	14.8	.7
Sweden, 1996	17.7	27.5	24.7	20.9	14.8	6.5	.56
United States, 1995	32.1	50.3	32.6	17.9	9.8	3.2	.73

*The total abortion rate represents that number of abortions that an average woman will have in her lifetime if she experiences the prevailing period age-specific abortion rates.

Source: Akinrinola Bankole, susheela Singh, and Taylor Haas, "Characteristics of Women Who Obtain Induced Abortion: A Worldwide Review," *International Family Planning Perspectives*, Volume 25, Issue 2 (June, 1999), 66-77.

Numerous factors help to explain variances in reproduction preferences and behavior worldwide, including perceived opportunity costs of having a child; legal, moral and religious contexts; and patterns of contraceptive use. A recent study of fifty-six countries reported that the highest proportions of abortions occur among women in their twenties, unmarried women, and women who already have at least one child. In the few countries where more detailed socioeconomic characteristics were provided the results indicated that, "for some women in every context, personal, social, or family circumstances make it unacceptable to carry a

(continued)

pregnancy to term."[1] The authors conclude that "analyses that demonstrate the extent to whichabortion is obtqained by women of all socioeconomic and demographic characteristics document the universality of women's need for abortion when faced with an unplanned pregnancy."[2]

[1]Akinrinola Bankole, susheela Singh, and Taylor Haas, "Characteristics of Women Who Obtain Induced Abortion: A Worldwide Review," *International Family Planning Perspectives*, Volume 25, Issue 2 (June, 1999), 66.

[2]Ibid, 77.

working, raising the children, and doing the housework was the preferred choice of a majority of women and men.[21]

Other evidence that Americans favor shared roles can be found when questions are raised about housework. Research by Arland Thornton and Deborah Freedman found that in one sample of married women taken between 1962 and 1977, the percentage believing a woman should expect help from her husband around the house increased from 46 to 62 percent. The more educated, younger, or working women were even more likely to favor this practice.[22] More recent research suggests women are increasingly willing to share domestic roles with men. For example, the 2000 Virginia Slims Poll found that 71 percent of the women polled believed that men should help out more with household and child-care responsibilities to allow working women to balance their jobs, marriages, and children.[23] In a similar vein, both men and women are more willing to assign the breadwinning and parental roles equally. Thus, whereas in the early 1970s most men and women said they would lose respect for a man who stayed home to take care of the children while the wife worked, two decades later only one-fifth of men and women said they would lose respect for a man who made such a decision.[24]

Men and women are also in agreement on the need for emotional expression in a marriage. As indicated in Table 6.1, majorities of men and women believe the ingredients to a good marriage include "being in love," "keeping romance alive," "being able to talk together about your feelings," and "your spouse having an understanding of what you do every day." Women are somewhat more likely to think these dimensions of a marriage are important.

With marriage increasingly based on mutual emotional satisfaction, divorce has become the answer to an unhappy marriage. The proportion of women who find it an acceptable solution rose from 52 percent in 1970 to 62 percent in 1979, declining to 57 percent in 1985.[25] In 1994, 48 percent agreed and 32 percent disagreed that divorce is usually the best solution when a couple can not work out their disagreements.[26] Divorce is seen as less acceptable if there are children under the age of five.[27] Moreover, older and less educated women are less willing to see divorce as an acceptable solution. Interestingly, a plurality of the population would like to see divorce made more difficult to obtain.[28]

Perhaps because of these changing attitudes and the practices that accompany them, there is growing concern about the future of marriage. In the 2000

TABLE 6.1 Important Qualities in a Good Marriage

	Men (%)	Women (%)
Having respect for each other	83	85
Liking the same kinds of life, activities, and friends	44	45
Being in love	75	78
Keeping romance alive	71	69
Having children	41	44
Having similar ideas about how to raise children	56	62
Sexual fidelity on the part of your spouse	76	77
Having similar ideas about how to handle money	54	60
Having similar backgrounds	34	34
Being able to talk together about your feelings	70	75
Your spouse understanding what you do every day	55	59

Source: Data from the 2000 Virginia Slims Poll, conducted by Roper Starch Worldwide Inc. Data provided by Philip Morris USA.

Virginia Slims Poll, 63 percent of the women polled and 58 percent of the men reported that the institution of marriage is weaker than it was ten years ago. Only 6 percent of the women and 8 percent of the men thought that marriage is weaker because women are working, are more independent, or are neglecting their families. Instead the men and women both blamed a lack of commitment, a lack of communication, and a lack of respect. A small percentage (9 percent of men and 10 percent of women) blamed external factors, including financial problems, stress, or career demands.[29]

Attitudes Toward Motherhood. In the past, motherhood ranked second only to marriage as a woman's objective in life. Today, however, many women no longer identify motherhood as the route to happiness or the primary goal in life. As early as 1979, 82 percent of women in one poll disagreed that children are essential to a full and happy marriage.[30] By 1994, only 13 percent of the public believed the main purpose of marriage is to have children.[31]

Attitudes are also changing on the acceptability of having a child outside of marriage. A 1994 poll found that although a sizable majority of the public agreed, almost one out of five disagreed with the statement that people who want children ought to get married. Other polls have found young people are more accepting of out-of-wedlock births.[32]

Polls, moreover, continue to show that among those desiring a family, the ideal number of children has declined dramatically since the 1950s. In the 2000 Virginia Slims Poll, a plurality of women (48 percent) and a majority of men (52 percent) said the ideal number of children in a family is two. The second most popular response was three children (23 percent women and 20 percent men).[33]

Along with a decreased emphasis on motherhood has come an increased focus on fatherhood. In a recent poll, 82 percent of males age twenty-one to

Women and Politics
MOBILIZING MOTHERS

Economist Arleen Leibowitz predicted in the 1970s that "as the average American woman gained better schooling and spent more of her life in the paid labor force, she would also probably spend more time with her children, not less" as the focus shifted from quantity to quality child rearing.[a] A majority of women with children today are employed. At the same time, Generation X wants to spend more time with family than ever before. As outlined by Ann Crittenden in *The Price of Motherhood*, women pay a price referred to as the "mommy tax" when they become mothers. Crittenden argues that whether a mother chooses to stay at home, work full or part time, or reenter the workforce after a leave of absence, mothers pay a penalty—estimated at $1 million in lost earnings for the typical college-educated woman. Whereas the wage gap is nearly nonexistent among single, childless workers, working mothers earn only 73 percent of others in the workforce.[b] Economists estimate a 7 percent penalty for each additional child a woman bears.[c] The wage gap results in part from leave time, reduced work hours, a loss of experience, and a loss in seniority. Although difficult to measure, employers also may discriminate against the perceived loyalty and commitment of working mothers. The mommy tax also includes a loss in benefits, such as Social Security and unemployment compensation; tax penalties pushing married working mothers into the highest tax brackets; and fewer promotions and raises as women care for their children during the prime years for establishing a career.[d] Ultimately, two out of three working mothers average less than 40 hours of work each week. Their work is "marginalized," as part-time workers are typically paid less, receive no benefits, and are not in line for promotions.[e]

Realizing the difficulties in either choosing between the mommy track or the fast track, or balancing the two, women have begun to mobilize for change. In the workplace, groups such as MOTHERS (Mothers Ought to Have Equal Rights) and 9to5 are fighting for paid family leave, shorter work weeks without jeopardizing advancements in rank and salary, and flexible work schedules.[f] While family-friendly practices benefit working fathers as well as working mothers, childless employees complain that they unfairly pay the price tag. Childless workers argue that since childbearing is a choice, why should they be forced to subsidize families? Elinor Burkett writes in *The Baby Boom* that benefits for mothers would comprise "an affirmative action program for mothers that would shelter them from the difficulties created by their own choices."[g]

(continued)

Other groups, including Mothers and More, are fighting for policies to enable mothers to stay home longer. Kristin Maschka, president of Mothers and More, argues: "If we think care giving is really valuable, mothers shouldn't be paying a penalty for performing it in terms of retirement and other benefits."[h] Ann Crittenden makes the case for adding value to women's unpaid labor, advocating including caretaking in the GDP and in Social Security calculations. She argues that stay-at-home moms should also be entitled to the child-care tax credit that working mothers are eligible to receive. If unpaid work in the home came with a price tag, women would receive more equitable distribution of property in the event of a divorce.[i] Gloria Steinem argues, for example, that "If two homemakers were to cross the street and work for each other's husbands, they would be entitled to an eight-hour day and a forty-hour week, Social Security, disability pay and unemployment compensation—and perhaps paid vacations, transferable health benefits and a retirement plan."[j] Critics oppose placing a monetary value on mothering, however, arguing that it overlooks the emotional rewards mothers experience in their choice to stay at home. Maggie Gallagher, author of *The Case for Marriage*, adds: "To say that someone who has taken 10 years out of the work force should make as much as if they had not taken 10 years off strikes me as living in some sort of utopia."[k]

Mothers are divided in their perspective on changing the workplace versus changing incentives to stay at home. For the movement to succeed, it will have to reconcile these differences and, at the same time, further mobilize young women professionals. When feminist Gloria Steinem questioned why young feminists have not taken the lead on family-friendly issues such as child care, Min Jin Lee responded in an essay, "Do you have any idea what would happen, if, as a junior associate, I created a committee to push for childcare in a Wall Street firm? I'd be ostracized, and I'd never make partner. If I ever met her [Steinem], I'd say 'You don't get it; you're out of touch.'"[l] Ann Crittenden observes that "American mothers are their own worst enemies; and that this explains, more than anything else, why caring labor is so undervalued in this country."[m] She warns that mothers divided are conquered:

> I knew that women (like men) are divided, over the issue of abortion, and matters of class and race. And we know that many mothers of young children are too hard-pressed to have time to support women's causes—in many cases, even to vote. But it is nonetheless disturbing to find mothers actively engaged in sabotaging one another, blind to their common ground. Think about it: women against poor mothers on welfare; women against rich Zoe Baird. Women against their husbands' first wives; mothers embroiled in endless mommy wars. Working mothers aren't "doing their job" at home, while mothers at home don't have a "real" job. The net effect of all this belittling is to obscure the

larger reality that mothers as a group are performing an enormous amount of essential unpaid labor force.[n]

---

[a] Ann Crittenden, *The Price of Motherhood* (New York: Henry Holt, 2001), 20.

[b] Crittenden, *The Price of Motherhood.*

[c] Sarah Glazer, "Mothers Movement," *CQ Researcher*, April 4, 2003, 300.

[d] Crittenden, *The Price of Motherhood.*

[e] Joan Williams, *Unbending Gender: Why Family and Work Conflict and What to Do About It* (London: Oxford University Press, 2000), 2.

[f] See http://www.mothersoughttohaveequalrights.com, and http://www.9to5.org/.

[g] Elinor Burkett, *The Baby Boom* (Free Press, 2000), 173.

[h] http://www.mothersandmore.org.

[i] Crittenden, *The Price of Motherhood.*

[j] Gloria Steinem, *Moving Beyond Words* (New York: Touchstone Books, 1994), 221.

[k] Glazer, "Mothers' Movement," 303.

[l] Min Jin Lee, "Pushing Away the Plate," quoted in Glazer, "Mothers' Movement," 302.

[m] Crittenden, *The Price of Motherhood*, 250.

[n] Ibid.

---

twenty-nine prioritized family at the top of their agenda, and 70 percent were
willing to trade a lower salary for more time with their families. The majority
of these men (70 percent) grew up with a mother who worked outside the
home, in contrast to only 32 percent of males age sixty-five or older.[34] As Ros-
alind Chait Barnett, director of the Community, Families, and Work program
at Brandeis University, commented: "If men start to take advantage of work-
life programs, it will destigmatize what women have been doing."[35]

Sexuality and Birth Control

One of the most controversial issues of the women's rights movement has been
the effort of women to control their reproductive capabilities. The major battles in this area have been over abortion. Closely tied to this effort has been the
notion that women as well as men have sexual drives independent of the
desire to have children.

Attitudes on abortion (see Figure 6.1) have been among the most frequently polled in the past two decades. Over time, the polls show that the proportion of the public favoring legality under all circumstances has grown only
marginally, rising from 21 percent in 1975 to 24 percent in 2002.[36]

When pollsters ask general questions about the legality of abortion, majorities appear to support a woman's right to choose. But when more specific questions are asked about the legality of abortion in a variety of circumstances,
support drops off considerably, as revealed in Table 6.2. When asked if abortion
should be legal if the woman's life is endangered or if her pregnancy is the result
of rape or incest, clear majorities support a woman's right to choose. More than

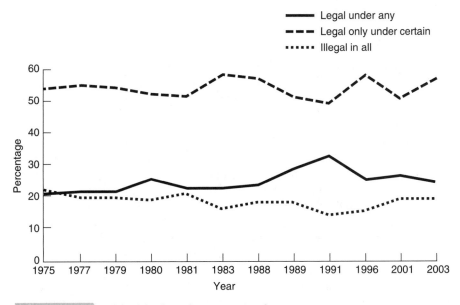

FIGURE 6.1 **Should Abortion Be Legal?**

The question asks: "Do you think abortions should be legal under any circumstances, legal only under certain circumstances, or illegal in all circumstances?"

Source: George Gallup Jr., "Poll Topics and Trends: Abortion," *Gallup Polls* (2003).

TABLE 6.2 **Circumstances When Abortion Should Be Legal, 2003**

Survey question: Now I am going to read some specific situations under which an abortion might be considered. For each one, please say whether you think abortion should be legal in that situation, or illegal.

	Percent Answering Legal
When the woman's life is endangered	85
When the woman's physical health is endangered	77
When the woman's mental health is endangered	63
When there is evidence that the baby may be physically impaired	56
When there is evidence that the baby may be mentally impaired	55
When the pregnancy was caused by rape or incest	76
When the woman or family cannot afford to raise the child	35

Source: George Gallup Jr., "Abortion Issues," *Gallup Polls,* http://www.gallup.com/poll/indicators/indabortion.asp.

half of the public supports abortions in cases where the baby has a physical or mental defect. On the other hand, if the decision is a function of economics, support for abortion declines to 35 percent. Support for abortion also declines as a woman's pregnancy progresses. Whereas 66 percent of Americans support abortion during the first three months of pregnancy, support drops to only 25 percent in the second trimester and 10 percent in the third trimester.[37]

During the past two decades, the proportion opposing abortion under all circumstances has declined slightly, from 22 percent in 1975 to 18 percent in 2003. The majority of Americans surveyed in both 1975 and 2003 favor some restrictions on abortion. In 2003, about a third of Americans said they would like to see abortion laws in this country made more strict. The public is evenly divided in its attachment to the "pro-life" (46 percent) and "pro-choice" positions (47 percent). Women are as likely as men to call themselves either pro-choice or pro-life. Older Americans and those living in the South tend to be the most conservative on abortion. Support for abortion increases with education and is highest among those with postgraduate education[38]

African Americans are less supportive of abortion than are whites.[39] While controls for demographic characteristics reduce the differences, they do not eliminate them. Moreover, attitudinal controls for sexuality and women's rights increase racial disparity. Factors associated with pro-choice views are also different for the races. For whites, being Catholic, living in a rural area, or having a low income or a low education is linked to a pro-life position on abortion. For African Americans, the key correlates of pro-life views are being male and growing up in the South.[40]

It is, of course, the question of what restrictions should be imposed that has engaged the public and courts in heated battles during the past decade. In a 2003 Gallup Poll, a vast majority of the public favored the following laws restricting abortion: doctors required to inform patients of alternatives to abortion (88 percent), a twenty-four hour waiting period (78 percent), parental consent for women under eighteen (73 percent), and spousal notification (72 percent).[41] Additionally, 63 percent of Americans supported a ban on partial birth abortions, although support varied widely depending on the phrasing of the question.[42] Only 30 percent, however, supported a constitutional ban on abortion.[43]

Since the Supreme Court's first major case upholding a wide variety of abortion restrictions in *Webster v. Reproductive Health Services* in 1989, public attitudes on abortion are increasingly finding their way into state and national elections. Research by the Center for the American Woman and Politics during four gubernatorial campaigns held in 1989 and 1990 found that attitudes on abortion influence the voting behavior of many citizens.[44] Women and persons with consistent pro-choice or pro-life positions were the most likely to cite the abortion issue as an important concern for them in the election. Similarly, both pro-choice and pro-life voters who felt strongly about the issue and were aware of the candidates' positions were most prone to cast their ballots for the candidate who closely reflected their views. This was especially true in the campaigns held a few months after *Webster*, and where the abortion issue was politicized by the media and the candidates.[45]

At the presidential level, Alan Abramowitz's research on the 1992 election found abortion was the most important issue for voters, and Mark J. Wattier, Byron W. Daynes, and Raymond Tatalovich report that pro-choice women were particularly mobilized by the election that year.[46] As revealed in Table 6.3, in the last three presidential elections, only a small percentage of voters said they would vote exclusively for a candidate with the same views on abortion. About a third do not consider abortion a major issue affecting their vote choice. With three Supreme Court justices nearing retirement, NARAL attempted to mobilize voters by running ads with the slogan "It's the Supreme Court, Stupid" during the 2000 Democratic National Convention. Although NARAL warned that Republican candidate George W. Bush's model justices are Antonin Scalia and Clarence Thomas, the issue failed to gain salience.[47] Democratic candidate Al Gore had an advantage among voters on reproductive rights, but the difference was less than 10 percent. When asked "Which candidate do you think would appoint Supreme Court justices whose opinions would be closest to your own on issues like abortion," 47 percent said Gore and 38 percent said Bush.[48]

Beliefs about a woman's right to abortion are often linked more generally to attitudes about a woman's right to control her sexuality. Earlier generations clearly thought men had this freedom, but only in the past few decades have public attitudes begun to allow women some of the same privileges. In 1953, for instance, 33 percent of the public agreed that no decent man can have respect for a woman who has had sexual relations before marriage.[49] Today, most young Americans do not believe premarital sex is always or almost always wrong. Moreover, most men and women think a single woman should enjoy the same kind of freedom as a single man, although few people today believe that it is a good idea for a couple to live together before marriage.[50]

There are, however, large differences between women and men in this area. Though, overall, 42 percent of all first-year college students in 2001 agreed with the view that "it is all right for two people who really like each other to have sex even if they've known each other for a very short time," men

---

TABLE 6.3 **Impact of Abortion Issue on Electoral Politics**

Survey question: Thinking about how the abortion issue might affect your vote for major offices, would you: only vote for a candidate who shares your views on abortion or consider a candidate's position on abortion as just one of many important factors? (responses include only registered voters)

	Candidate must share views	One of many important factors	Not a major issue
1992	13	46	36
1996	16	51	30
2000	15	49	33

Source: George Gallup Jr., "Abortion Issues," *Gallup Polls,*
http://www.gallup.com/poll/releases/pr010122.asp.

were much more likely to agree (55 percent) than women (32 percent).[51] Men and women also have very different views about when sexual behavior is appropriate. Among young men, one-fifth disagreed with the view that "just because a man thinks that a woman has 'led him on' does not entitle him to have sex with her." Virtually all young women (93 percent) agreed with this view.[52] Similarly, 88 percent of women but only 77 percent of men consider it rape when a man has sex with a woman who has passed out from drinking too much.[53] In a variety of other circumstances, men are more likely than women to think forced or pressured sex is not rape.[54] Attitude differences such as these help to explain the inability of many men who rape their dates to recognize that they have committed a crime or the failure of (mostly male) district attorneys to believe victims or to prosecute cases of acquaintance rape.[55] Not surprisingly, given these mixed messages about women who are sexually active and men's continuing belief in their "right to sex," women and men in national samples agree that the double moral standard still exists.[56]

In polls, majorities of Americans are still strongly opposed to instances of homosexual relations.[57] This seems to be particularly true of men. For instance, even among men in their first year of college, 33 percent support laws prohibiting homosexual relations, while only 19 percent of first-year college women support such laws.[58] Less than a fifth of Americans say that it is acceptable for same-sex couples to raise children (18 percent of women and 16 percent of men).[59]

Differences Among Women. The dynamic attitudinal changes in the past two decades have been more warmly supported by some women than by others. Feminists have generally been the most willing to endorse new views, while conservative women have been strongly opposed to any change that threatens the traditional division of family roles.[60] Working women are also more likely to take more progressive positions. Homemakers, however, have increasingly diverged from the feminists and working women in their views on changing marital and sexual relationships.

Jennifer Glass's research on attitudinal change of working women and homemakers from 1972 to 1986 found a widening gap among women on a range of issues. Part of the difference was attributable to growing demographic differences. Housewives were older, less well educated, and had more children and lower incomes than working women. Even controlling for these variables, however, women working full time were more accepting of abortion for married women, less willing to think a husband's career should come first, less willing to think men should run the country and women run the homes, and less in agreement with the view that maternal employment was detrimental to young children. Glass argued that the political implications of the class and ideological gap between working wives and housewives was "profound."[61] That the women's rights movement has played a role in this gap is reflected in a poll question that found most people (90 percent) believed the movement had benefited professional women and working-class women (75 percent) but had actually been detrimental (20 percent) or had made little difference (33 percent) to housewives.[62]

Homemakers' more traditional views of women's roles are not the only problem limiting women's attainment of equal status in marital and sexual relationships. In addition to organized opposition, women's own lack of preparation (or their socialization to traditional roles) also hampers them as they bargain for greater equality.

WOMEN'S AND MEN'S RESOURCES IN THE STRUGGLE FOR EQUAL ROLES

In attempting to explain the subordinate position of women in the family, many sociologists have focused on the wives' inferior resources with which to demand or to bargain for more equitable roles in marriage. The lack of resources is partly traceable to the cultural stereotypes discussed previously. With respect to economic worth, for example, one of the direct results of the traditional cultural view that the proper role for women is to marry was that, until recently, few women prepared for a full-time career. As a result, as we have seen in Chapter 4, few women had jobs. If they worked, few had jobs that paid as well as their husbands'. Related resource discrepancies still exist in age and educational attainment, with women generally marrying men who are older and who have more formal years of schooling.

Women also are often at a disadvantage when physical force becomes an issue in marital relationships. Studies of family violence make it clear that men are much more likely than women to use acts of violence in a dating or marital relationship. Among the 2.7 million violent crimes against women in 2001, one in five was attacked by an intimate partner, but intimate partners committed only 3 percent of violent crimes against men. Only 32 percent of the crimes against women but more than half of the crimes against men are committed by strangers. Fortunately, violent crimes against women have decreased, from forty-one per 1,000 women age twelve or older in 1993, to twenty-three per 1,000 in 2001.[63]

Most women have also not been as well prepared as men to bargain or negotiate. Women have especially been less conditioned to engage in conflict or to be assertive, which may be necessary prerequisites for getting a spouse to do housework, for example.[64] The inability to change men's behavior is also conditioned by sex-role socialization that makes talking about certain topics taboo or potentially explosive. Researchers who have studied women partners of men who are intravenous drug users, for instance, find the women are often reluctant to raise the issue of condom use even though they recognize they are at risk to contract AIDS.[65] Among the women there was a general expectation that their partners would respond violently or simply refuse to consider the woman's request. Hispanic women, whose culture tends to frown on women talking about sex, were even more reluctant to ask their partner to practice safe sex. For women who did ask, the predicted reactions were indeed what they encountered.[66] With heterosexually transmitted AIDS among women the major factor in making women the fastest growing number of AIDS cases (accompanied by the very real threat of giving birth to infected babies), we can see that unequal sex roles in relationships can have deadly consequences.

The lack of a strong sense of independence in women also limits women's ability to leave bad relationships. Socialization studies find that while young boys are encouraged to be independent, young girls often are not.[67] This may result in women's unwillingness to leave less-than-satisfying relationships or marriages. The added responsibility of children may also limit a woman's sense of independence.

In the twin areas of child care and housework, however, women may have been overtrained to take charge. Studies measuring differences in play activities encouraged or discouraged, toys purchased, and household chores assigned make it clear that parents, especially fathers, encourage sex-role-type activities in their children.[68] As a result, girls are trained to be homemakers and parents, and boys are not. At adulthood, these roles are hard to change. Moreover, because of their early training, women's expertise in these tasks may make some unwilling to give up the jobs to not-as-well-trained males. Correspondingly, males may feel inadequate to undertake the task, having little experience in cleaning the house or taking care of babies.

Thus, until very recently, as a result of cultural stereotypes that narrowly defined their roles as wife and mother, women have not always had the same resources as men to assume, negotiate, or demand. Our review of cultural stereotypes suggests some of these barriers may be changing, especially among the young, educated, and working women. For some segments of women, however, traditional views persist. Even if all women were to demand an equitable, shared marriage, their success in achieving that goal would be limited unless they can overcome another important barrier—men's attitudes, prejudices, and simple unwillingness to change.

DISCRIMINATION BY MEN IN THE FAMILY

Men's reluctance to share in all facets of marriage is conditioned by a number of factors. Among the most important has been the unwillingness of men to give up the privileged position that they hold even in modern-day marriages. The system benefits men, and most proposed changes would require them to give something up, either time or power or both. The unequal benefits of traditional marriage help to explain the more conservative or traditional views of men on the gender roles. This seems to be especially noticeable among the young, where women's attitudes have changed more rapidly than men's. Even in 2002, first-year male college students were much more likely than women students (28 versus 17 percent) to agree that married women's activities are best confined to the home.[69] Often, men's ideas on gender roles cover hidden qualifications of women.

Even among men who want to share, they may find their own socialization has ill prepared them for certain tasks, such as laundry or mending. Although parents may be more willing today than in the past to assign certain chores to both boys and girls, research suggests that in many homes, boys and girls do not have the same responsibilities.[70]

Another barrier to equality may be the attitudes of employers. Some evidence suggests that employers do not think family-friendly issues are as important to men as they are to women.[71] This may make it hard for men to ask for time off for child-care or household responsibilities. For women, marriage signals other priorities than work. In contrast, married men are viewed as more stable, more reliable, and less likely to leave a position than unmarried men. The male image as breadwinner may contribute to what economists refer to as the male marriage wage premium. Married men earn approximately 11 percent more than men who have never married.[72]

Although men may be beginning to want more equitable marital arrangements, alteration of old practices will not come quickly or easily. Even more so than political and economic changes, new proposals regarding family life require men to relinquish some of the power and leisure that they have enjoyed in the past. As we shall see, for many men, these changes are very difficult to make.

IMPACT OF CULTURAL ATTITUDES, LACK OF RESOURCES, AND DISCRIMINATION ON THE POSITION OF WOMEN IN THE FAMILY

Marriage Rates

During the colonial period, cultural standards and the economic needs of both women and men resulted in virtually all men and women marrying. Unlike their Western European counterparts, women settlers in the New World married at a relatively young age.[73] In the nineteenth century, the new emphasis on marrying "for love" and the initial drive for autonomy on the part of women resulted in a gradual increase in the number of women remaining single. Yet the absence of economic alternatives for most women kept this figure low.[74] In the first half of the twentieth century, this pattern was reversed. With the exception of the Great Depression years, the percentage of women who never married and the age at which women actually married fell steadily until 1960. This corresponds to our discussion of the popularity of marriage, especially in the profamily era of the "feminine mystique."

Starting in the mid-1960s, the age of women marrying and percentage of women and men not marrying rose (see Figure 6.2). For instance, in 2000, the median age of first marriage for women was twenty-five and for men it was twenty-seven (see Figure 6.3). Additionally, among persons age fifteen and over in 2000, 31 percent of men and 25 percent of women had never married. In 1965, 22 percent of men and 14 percent of women in this age category were unmarried.[75] The probability of marrying is very much related to race. Among whites, 22 percent of all persons age fifteen and over have never married; among African Americans the figure is 42 percent.[76]

Explanations for the declining marriage rate are varied. One issue is the availability of "marriageable" mates, men who by traditional standards

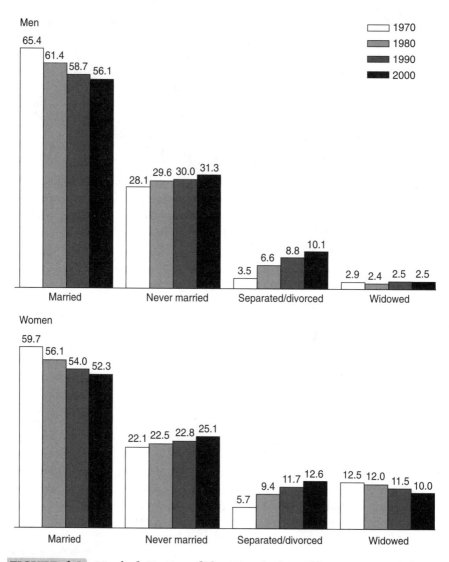

FIGURE 6.2 **Marital Status of the Population Fifteen Years and Over (in percentages)**

Source: U.S. Census Bureau, "America's Families and Living Arrangements: June 2001," *Current Population Reports*, Series P20-537 (Washington, D.C.: U.S. Government Printing Office).

would be good providers. In the past, this meant a man who was older than the woman, better or as well educated as the woman, and gainfully employed. A reason for the lower marriage rates of African American women, then, is the lack of men with jobs or an education equal to or greater than that of the women.[77]

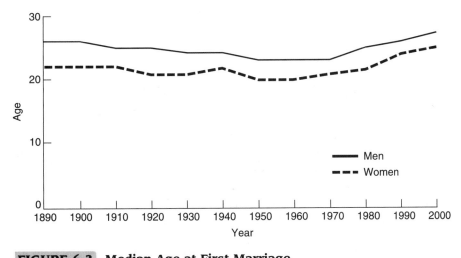

FIGURE 6.3 **Median Age at First Marriage**
Source: U.S. Census Bureau, "America's Families and Living Arrangements: March 2000," *Current Population Reports*, Series P20-537, http://www.census.gov, and earlier reports.

The declining importance of marriage in women's lives, noted in our earlier discussion of attitudes toward marriage, and the increased importance of obtaining an education and pursuing a career are also important factors in the avoidance or delay in marriage among young women. In 2000, 43 percent of women and 56 percent of men age eighteen to twenty-four were living with their parents.[78] As Frances Goldscheidner, an editor of *Demography* magazine, notes, "Unmarried women do well if they have enough money. They can support themselves in reasonable style. They don't define themselves around men." She calls women's growing lack of interest in marriage in the past twenty years "a real revolution."[79] Just as revolutionary is the dramatic jump in marriage age, which has risen five years for women since 1960. By delaying marriage until their mid-twenties, more women have experienced work outside the home before marriage.

Although demographers and sociologists expect most persons will eventually marry, it is estimated that as many as 15 percent of young adult women may not.[80] Some researchers believe that many women with successful careers may avoid marriage if they perceive the conflicts between marriage and career that may await them. One result is that many women "go it alone," living by themselves and often buying their own homes.[81] Other women prefer female partners.

Another indicator of the trend away from marriage is the phenomenal growth in the number of couples who live together without the benefit of marriage. Cohabitation has increased from 1.1 percent of couples in 1960 to 5.1 percent by 2000. A plurality of Americans in the 2000 Virginia Slims Poll (42 percent of women and 46 percent of men) said that it is acceptable for couples to live together before marriage. However, nearly a third of both men and women said that people who live together before marriage are more likely to get divorced.[82]

Companionship Marriage

Our earlier discussion of changing public views toward marriage found that, whereas few reject the institution, most prefer a role-shared union where both spouses work and take care of children. This attitude, however, is relatively recent. In the 1950s and 1960s, most women expected to take care of the home and children while the husband financially supported the family. Given the relatively recent change in public attitudes, we might expect to find that behavior has not "caught up" with opinions. As we saw in Chapter 5, in at least two aspects of role sharing—working outside the home and contributing to the family income—wives are increasingly assuming an equal role with husbands. But what about the reverse of this? Are men sharing housekeeping and child-rearing roles?

Research conducted in the 1950s and 1960s reveals that most men did little role sharing in the first wave of women's move into the workforce. An examination of the way women and men spent their days in 1965 and 1966, for instance, found that husbands with employed wives contributed no more time to housework than those with nonemployed spouses.[83] More recent studies still find little evidence that the desired equality in task sharing has been put into practice. Most men are doing more than their fathers, but the amount of time they contribute is still only a small proportion of that given by women.

Examining the period from 1965 to 1985, one researcher found that the proportion of traditionally female tasks (cooking, meal clean-up, housecleaning, laundry, and ironing) done by women had only decreased from 92 to 80 percent.[84] The number of hours women spend with their children has remained stable. As Daphne Spain and Suzanne Bianchi comment, "We tend to inflate nostalgically the hours mothers in the past had available to spend interacting with their children and forget all the adjustments working mothers today make in order to find time for their children."[85] Women have traded increased hours in paid work for declining hours of housework. In the mid-1960s, women spent approximately half of their time on housework, a quarter on paid work, and the remaining quarter on errands and child care. Today, women spend about half of their time in paid work, a quarter on housework, and the same amount on errands and child care. Smaller, planned families probably enable women today to spend more time with each child than was possible for their own mothers.[86]

Still, the unequal distribution of housework and child-care responsibilities requires women to perform a stressful balancing act. Recent polls indicate that nearly 60 percent of working mothers feel their work is an obstacle to their family life.[87] In the 2000 Virginia Slims Poll, women revealed that they feel guilty leaving their children in the morning for work, that the conflicting demands of family and job puts them under a lot of stress, and that the demands of family life make it hard to devote complete attention to work. Men were less likely to report such conflicts. Women also perceive more negative consequences at work when day-care arrangements fall through. Having men help more with the household and child-care responsibilities is the primary way women foresee being able to balance their lives.[88]

More than 70 percent of women say they do most or all of the housekeeping and child care.[89] As revealed in Figure 6.4, men have a slightly different perspective. Overall, a majority of Americans agree that women end up doing more of the household chores than men and that stereotypes about women are still firmly in place or just beginning to change. Forty-one percent of the public agrees that "whether or not they work outside the home, women primarily are responsible for household chores such as cooking, shopping, and cleaning" is a stereotype that is still in place today, 40 percent say that it is starting to change, and only 17 percent believe that this stereotype has been broken. Similarly, 51 percent agree that "whether or not they work outside the home, women are the primary caregivers for children" is a stereotype that persists, 33 percent say that it is starting to change, while only 12 percent say that it has been broken. How much change is needed before women can achieve equality with men in running the household? Three in ten say a great deal of change and four in ten say a moderate amount of change would be required.[90]

Although men may be contributing more time to housework today, research indicates that most of the similarity in hours spent by men and women in housework is a function of working women doing considerably less housework than their mothers. Because women average more hours of family responsibilities, men gain a substantial "leisure gap." Thus, most of the role-sharing changes today seem to be the result of women annexing men's role as breadwinner, not men taking on traditional women's roles.

Researchers have attempted to explain this failure to share roles by focusing on four sets of variables: ideological acceptance of role sharing, relative resources of men and women, economic dependency, and time availability. These overlap with the three barriers to women's equality that we identified earlier: cultural stereotypes, differential resources, and discrimination or unwillingness on the part of men to change. With respect to ideology, most

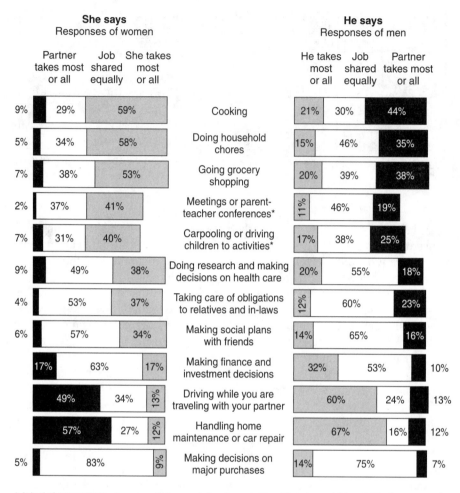

She says Responses of women				**He says** Responses of men		
Partner takes most or all	Job shared equally	She takes most or all		He takes most or all	Job shared equally	Partner takes most or all
9%	29%	59%	Cooking	21%	30%	44%
5%	34%	58%	Doing household chores	15%	46%	35%
7%	38%	53%	Going grocery shopping	20%	39%	38%
2%	37%	41%	Meetings or parent-teacher conferences*	11%	46%	19%
7%	31%	40%	Carpooling or driving children to activities*	17%	38%	25%
9%	49%	38%	Doing research and making decisions on health care	20%	55%	18%
4%	53%	37%	Taking care of obligations to relatives and in-laws	12%	60%	23%
6%	57%	34%	Making social plans with friends	14%	65%	16%
17%	63%	17%	Making finance and investment decisions	32%	53%	10%
49%	34%	13%	Driving while you are traveling with your partner	60%	24%	13%
57%	27%	12%	Handling home maintenance or car repair	67%	16%	12%
5%	83%	9%	Making decisions on major purchases	14%	75%	7%

* Asked of respondents who are part of a couple in a household and they have children. 20% of women and 23% of men said the school question did not apply to them; 21% of women and 18% of men said the carpooling question did not apply.

FIGURE 6.4 **Perspectives of Women and Men on Domestic Responsibilities**
Source: Survey by Peter D. Hart Research Associates for Shell Oil, January 7–13, 2000. "Living Female: A Roper Center Data Review," *Public Perspective*, July/August 2000.

researchers find that in couples with more egalitarian attitudes, men generally do more around the house than when attitudes are more traditional. Only in households where *both* the man and the woman hold egalitarian views do men contribute much to household labor. Egalitarian wives married to men with traditional views can expect little assistance.[91] The more egalitarian views of African American men and women contribute to the greater role sharing found in such families.[92] However, even in families (including African

American families) where men agree that women should be equal or that the man should not be the sole breadwinner, tasks are far from equally shared. Philip Blumstein and Pepper Schwartz report egalitarian men with working wives did 8.4 hours of housework, only a slight increase compared to the 7.33 hours for all men with working wives.[93] Findings that African American men are more likely to share housework and Hispanic men are less likely to do so probably reflect the cultural differences between the two groups in their attitudes toward men's and women's roles.[94] In the same vein, the presence of young children increases family workload considerably and reinforces stereotyped roles. Even though men help out, studies indicate that young children may actually increase role divisions, as women take on even more responsibility under these circumstances.[95]

Feminists argue further that the failure of men and women to share housekeeping may stem from the meaning each assigns to housework. For many if not most people, housework "defines" a person's gender. People who do it are gendered women; people who avoid it are gendered men. To quote Sara Fenstermaker, "The doing of housework provides the occasion for the accomplishment of work and the affirmation of the essential natures of women and men."[96] Thus, both men and women may avoid role sharing because role sharing threatens not only their sense of self-identity as men or women but also the proper fulfillment of roles that identify men and women in the larger society.

Another critical factor is the resources of the spouses. In general, the more money a woman makes, the less housework she does. The same, however, is true of men. Because in most families men earn more (hence women are economically dependent), they are able to "buy their way" out of housework. This phenomenon persists even when both spouses work full time,[97] although the influence of money is lessened when couples reject the view that the man should be the breadwinner.[98] Another resource that has been found to influence division of housework is workplace authority. When women have more power on the job than their husbands and more power than most women, they tend to do less housework.[99] It should be noted, however, that even when women's resources exceed their husbands', women still do more of the household tasks than do their husbands.

Not surprisingly, women feel deeply resentful and stressed by the inequality in the home. Most believe more of the daily tasks should be shared, and two-thirds feel men are not doing their fair share of the household chores. One-half of all women indicated they feel resentful often or from time to time about the amount of work their mate does around the house. Moreover, nearly half of all women feel some level of resentment about not having enough free time.[100] Some social scientists believe that the failure of most husbands to take an equal role not only fuels resentment from their wives but also contributes to a lack of marital contentment and an increase in divorce.

Aside from the sharing of household tasks, is the rest of the marriage relationship becoming more equal? One area of consideration is power over family decisions. As we noted earlier, most reports from the past century find that husbands dominated family decision making. As recently as the 1950s, just before the dawn of the current women's rights movement, wives indicated the balance of power favored the male head of the household, with the husband making most of the important economic decisions and wives' decision making tending to be limited to areas closely connected with their roles as mothers and housewives.[101] The locus of authority in the era of the feminine mystique can perhaps be best seen in the contrast between two areas of family decisions: what job a husband should take and whether the wife should work. With respect to the first, 90 percent of women said it was the husband's decision alone to make. By contrast, in a third of the families, the husband also determined whether the wife should seek paid employment.[102]

Although views about the appropriate division of authority in the family have changed since the 1950s, there is still a tendency to give men the final say. In one poll, 44 percent of men sampled reported that ultimately they were the main decision makers when it came to what the family could or could not afford. Nearly a third of all women in the poll agreed with that assessment.[103] In 1999, however, a majority of men and women claimed that investment decisions and planning family vacations were jointly shared in their home.[104]

Research by scholars on family leadership and decision making still reports that men have an edge. This is because social scientists continue to discover that it is a husband's superior financial resources that give him greater authority.[105] Although in gender-egalitarian families the relationship is weaker, generally, the more a husband makes, the more power he has in family decisions and the more leadership he exercises. Wives' power on both measures is also affected by their income levels, but generally women need to earn many more dollars than their husbands to obtain an equal increment in authority.

Blumstein and Schwartz find that a key intervening variable is the relative income dependency of the wife. More specifically, as the gap in what the two spouses earn increases, so too does the tendency of men to dominate family decision making.[106] Thus, contributing to women's increased power is their movement into the workforce and the narrowing wage gap. However, Blumstein and Schwartz find the most important asset men have in determining family policy is their greater assertiveness.[107] As this may be tied to more immutable role socialization, men's authority in the family may not be easily eliminated by women's movement into well-paying jobs.

The overall test of marital quality, however, may not be how much roles are shared or decision making is equalized. Rather, it may be how happy or satisfied a couple is with their marriage. Social scientists have begun to examine this in great detail, and their research suggests a number of factors contribute to marital success. The results show that some of the indicators we have identified indeed do contribute to a decline in marital quality. More specifically, the presence of children and stepchildren affects marital happiness negatively, in part because they lower satisfaction with role sharing and companionship.[108] This finding is not surprising, given the extra burden young children place on women. A key factor may also be whether each spouse perceives the other as doing a fair share.[109] A wife working does not necessarily lower marital happiness, but differences in views about appropriate roles of husbands and wives or men and women do depress marital quality. This is especially true for couples where the husband holds traditional views about sex roles and the wife has more modern notions.

Research by Norval D. Glenn on marital quality in the 1980s finds that because of the strain brought about by the attempt to share roles in marriages, marital happiness has deteriorated, both for long-term and relatively recent marriages.[110] He attributes the decline to changed expectations about marriage, as well as to a waning of the ideal of marriage permanence. He argues that rising divorce rates are not only a function of growing acceptance of divorce but also of a decline in marital quality.[111] Media depictions of relationships reinforce romantic expectations that many do not find in their own relationships.

Surveys report that the percentage of people who say they are very happy with their marriages declined from 68 percent in the early 1970s to a low of 56 percent in 1985 and then increased again to 63 percent by 2000.[112] Although both marital happiness and marriage rates have declined over time, married people are still happier in general than unmarried people. Forty percent of married people say they are very happy, compared to only 23 percent of the widowed, 19 percent of divorced, 16 percent of separated, and 23 percent of people who have never married.[113]

Divorce.   As Glenn anticipated, even when women and men do marry today, they are less likely to stay married than they were in previous eras. Since the mid-nineteenth century, the divorce rate has risen almost tenfold. The 1970s saw the fastest increase in divorce, with the rate in the 1980s and 1990s remaining at a rather stable high. Today, the chance of a marriage ending in divorce is triple the rate of the 1920s and 1930s, and double the rate of 1950 to 1965. (See Table 6.4 for Census Bureau findings on marital status from 1950 to 2000.)

Seen another way, in the late 1800s, only one in ten marriages ended in divorce; in the 1950s, the rate was one in three; and today, about half of first marriages are not expected to survive. Arguing that the divorce rate ignores those who separate permanently without formally divorcing, at least some scientists think two-thirds of all marriages may fail.[114]

Lynn K. White, in a review of the literature on the reasons for the high marital instability in the United States (higher than in Europe since records have been kept), finds several factors to be important.[115] Among the most significant may be the notion that a marriage should be based on love and on sexual attraction. This has come to mean that when a marriage does not live up to the ideal of a companionship union giving a couple emotional or sexual fulfillment, it is seen as failed. In addition, as we have noted, in the past two decades women's and men's notions of marriage have changed to include the concept of "role-shared" unions. The inability of most marriages to achieve this sharing, especially as it relates to housework and child care, may also result in more people being convinced their marriage has not achieved the goals they have set for it.

TABLE 6.4   **Marital Status, by Race, 1950 to 2000**

	1950[a] (%)	1960[a] (%)	1970 (%)	1980 (%)	1995 (%)	2000 (%)
All Races						
Married	66.6	67.6	64.2	61.0	57.6	56.2
Divorced	2.2	2.3	2.9	5.8	8.7	9.3
Never married	23.1	22.0	25.0	25.9	27.1	28.1
Widowed	8.1	8.3	8.0	7.4	6.6	6.4
White						
Married	67.0	68.4	65.3	62.8	60.0	58.7
Divorced	2.2	2.2	2.8	6.2	8.1	9.3
Never married	23.0	21.5	24.1	24.4	24.7	25.5
Widowed	7.8	8.0	7.8	7.3	6.7	6.5
Black						
Married	63.2	60.3	55.4	46.5	40.0	39.2
Divorced	2.3	3.2	3.8	7.6	9.9	10.7
Never married	24.4	26.7	31.4	37.0	43.0	43.5
Widowed	10.1	9.8	9.5	8.8	7.1	6.6

[a]1950 and 1960 data are for the population 14 years old and over. All other years are for 15 and older.

Source: U.S. Census Bureau,"America's Families and Living Arrangements: June 2001," *Current Population Reports*, Series P20-537, http:// www.census.gov, and earlier reports.

The causes of divorce also reflect generational differences. Pamela Paul, author of *The Starter Marriage and the Future of Matrimony*, explains the high divorce rate among baby boomers.

> The widespread introduction of the Pill and the sexual revolution, the advent of feminism and "Consciousness-raising groups," and the freedoms extolled by the "Me Generation" demonstrated to women in their twenties that they didn't *have* to marry, that marriage was unnecessary. A pop-psychological shift taught men and women in their thirties that if their marriage wasn't serving them well, it was "okay" to divorce—even better for them in the end. The underlying core value, enthusiastically embraced, was *independence*.[116]

The divorce rate leveled off in the 1990s in part because baby boomers entered their forties and fifties, an age less likely to divorce. A new trend among Generation X and Y, however, is the "starter marriage." These marriages average less than five years, ending before children are born and before the couple reaches age thirty. As Paul explains, these younger generations embrace the ideals of matrimony of their parents' parents, but lack an understanding of what commitment to marriage really involves.[117]

Also contributing to the rising divorce rate has been the movement of women into the marketplace. The ability to achieve a measure of economic resources, and thus independence, may have allowed women in unhappy marriages to leave. Data also suggest, however, that work per se may not be as important as women's autonomy from her spouse or her commitment to the workforce. Indeed, there is some evidence that more equitable marriages in which the wife's share of the income is high may actually be more stable unions, perhaps because they more closely approach the kind of "role-sharing" marriage that is seen as desirable.

Some researchers, notably Lenore Weitzman, believe that the advent of no-fault divorce may have expedited the exit of men and women from unhappy marriages.[118] At the least, it has detracted from the notion that a man is obligated to support his wife for life. As with the decline in marriage rates, the oversupply of women of marriageable age and status in comparison to men may also be a factor in the increase of divorce. Men who have many "wife options" may be less interested in maintaining their current marriage. Support for this proposition can be found in the higher divorce rates of African Americans, where the numbers of marriageable women far exceed those of marriageable men.

Fueling these trends, or resulting from them, has been the growing acceptance of divorce as an answer to failed marriage. There is at least some indication, however, that attitudes toward divorce may be changing, with large segments of the public wanting to make divorce more difficult to obtain, especially when there are children in the family. A 2000 survey reported that 52 percent of Americans think it should be more difficult to obtain a divorce (49 percent of men and 54 percent of women).[119] It should also be noted that most divorced persons remarry, although rates for remarriage have also declined. In large part, this seems to be a function of women not wanting to remarry. Barbara Foley Wilson of the National Center for Health Statistics claims, "It's hard for men to remarry when women aren't interested."[120]

The sources of marital instability are not completely understood, but most observers agree that the impact of divorce on the American family has been overwhelming. For example, the cultural stereotype that the responsibility for child care should remain with the mother means that in most divorces where there are children, the mother gets custody. Even in the large number of states that encourage joint custody, the mother remains the primary parent.[121] The result of such practices has been the burgeoning number of single-parent families headed by women. In 2000, in families with children under eighteen, 21.9 percent were headed by the mother only, whereas 6.2 percent were in 1950.[122] The largest proportion of these households were the result of divorce or separation (51 percent); a growing number were the product of never-married women having children (40 percent).[123] The remainder of such families are headed by widows. Because of the complementary trends of divorce and childbirth without marriage, it is estimated that somewhere between one-half and three-quarters of all children will spend part of their youth in a family headed by a woman.[124] Among African Americans, where both trends are more pronounced, more than 80 percent of all children will live in a single-parent household at some time during their youth.[125] However, in any one year, the majority of children live in two-parent families. In 2000, for instance, 69 percent of children under eighteen were living in a household with two parents.[126]

Divorce not only alters the family structure but also often brings dramatic income inequalities between the women and men who experience the dissolution of their marriages. Under traditional divorce laws, husbands were assumed responsible for the support of their wives and their children. Since the adoption of no-fault laws, this has changed. Today, when marriages dissolve, both spouses are assumed to be able to "make it on their own." One result of this change is the virtual elimination of most permanent alimony awards. Today, when alimony is awarded (only in about 15 percent of divorces), it is usually for a short duration, generally two years or less.[127] Moreover, no matter how limited a woman's preparation for employment, judges assume women are able to support themselves. Rarely is there an awareness of the wage discrepancies between working women and men noted in Chapter 4. The difficulty in finding a good job is particularly hard on women who have been full-time homemakers, especially if they are older and have spent most of their adult years raising children. Few can ever make up for the time they were out of the job market, losing experience and work-related skills.

Most people assume that women with children get child support. The reality is that less than two-thirds of custodial mothers are awarded child support, and even fewer receive it (see Table 6.5). A study by the U.S. Census Bureau in 1999 found child support was conferred by the court to only 62 percent of all women with children. The figure is far lower for African American and Hispanic women, only 46 and 48 percent of whom, respectively, are awarded child support.[128] Because more stringent enforcement has been shown to increase compliance, it is likely that stricter prosecution of dead-beat dads should result in more full and partial payment of awards. A key factor in the lack of awards to African American women is out-of-wedlock births. Welfare reform, however, includes more stringent efforts to identify birth fathers and may result in

TABLE 6.5   **Child Support Payments by Race, 1999**

	All (%)	White (%)	African American (%)	Hispanic (%)
Women awarded child support	62	63	46	48
Women receiving full payments	46	48	34	43
Women receiving partial payments	29	28	31	29
Women receiving nothing	25	24	35	28

Source: U.S. Census Bureau, "Custodial Mothers and Fathers and Their Child Support: 1999," *Current Population Reports*, Series P60-217, http://www.census.gov.

more awards to women of color, although negative attitudes toward the legal system and the low income of minority fathers will continue to keep awards and payment of awards to women of color low.[129]

As indicated in Table 6.6, the only significant change in recent years has been the percentage of women receiving full payments. The percentage of women receiving the full amount of child support due increased from 35 percent in 1993 to 46 percent in 1999. Though the lack of compliance is often tied to fathers' inability to pay child support, research suggests fathers could be paying almost twice as much.[130] The average child-support award in 1999 was $3,787.[131]

The standard of living for most divorced women and their children falls dramatically after divorce but increases among divorced men. On average, men increase their disposable income by 15 percent, but there is a 28 percent decrease in income for women.[132] Three factors explain the difference between women's and men's economic status. First, mothers typically get custody of children, which raises their cost of living. Second, men earn more than women, especially if the wife has been a full-time homemaker or has young children. Third, few men pay "fair" child support, and some pay none. As a result, one-fourth of divorced women and their children are living in poverty—a phenomenon referred to as the feminization of poverty.[133]

Motherhood.   More pressing demands on single mothers are not the only sign of changes in the maternal role. Although, in the past, one of the most defining characteristics of women has been the enduring cultural stereotype of the importance of motherhood in women's lives, this is increasingly less true.

One indication of change can be found in birth rates, which have steadily declined. The one exception to this trend occurred in the late 1940s through the early 1960s. Because of the delayed births brought about by World War II and the emphasis on women's maternal role that characterized the era of the feminine mystique, the United States experienced a baby boom from 1946 to roughly 1965. Correspondingly, the number of births per 1,000 for women of childbearing age was 121 in 1921, 89 in 1930, rising again to a peak of 123 in 1957, and declining from that point to a nearly stable rate of 65 to 68 since the early 1970s.[134]

TABLE 6.6   **Child Support for Custodial Mothers, 1993–1999**

	1993	1995	1997	1999
Awarded child support	60	61	59	62
Due child support	86	88	89	86
Received any child support	71	70	68	75
Received full amount of child support	35	40	42	46

Source: U.S. Census Bureau, "Custodial Mothers and Fathers and Their Child Support: 1999," *Current Population Reports,* Series P60-217, http://www.census.gov.

Of course, a critical factor in the probability of a woman having a child has been access to birth control. In the latter part of the nineteenth century, with the decrease in infant mortality and the increased emphasis on the mother in shaping a child's development, women began to limit their pregnancies. However, this was difficult because of changes in the medical profession (male doctors increasingly replaced women doctors and midwives) and Victorian attitudes toward women's sexuality, which resulted in the illegality of both abortion and the dissemination of birth control information. With abstinence as the only acceptable method, it is probable that the real birth rate far exceeded the desired birth rate. The renewed realization of female sexuality in the early twentieth century, as we saw in the last chapter, led to more widespread access to birth control and a corresponding decline in the birth rate, with the baby-boom period as an aberration in the trend.

In the early 1960s, however, the birth control revolution began. New forms and methods of limiting pregnancy, including the pill and abortion, were critical to a renewed downward trend in fertility. Joan Huber and Glenna Spitze even attribute the move toward equality for women to their being able to control the timing and number of children.[135] The most recent Survey of Family Growth found that among women age fifteen to forty-four, 98.4 percent have used some method of birth control, with the fastest-growing method being sterilization. About half of all unintended pregnancies ended in abortion, with unmarried women making up the largest number of those obtaining them. Increased use of birth control contributed to record low pregnancy rates by the mid-1990s, particularly among teens.[136] The number of abortions decreased at the same time. (See Figure 6.5.)

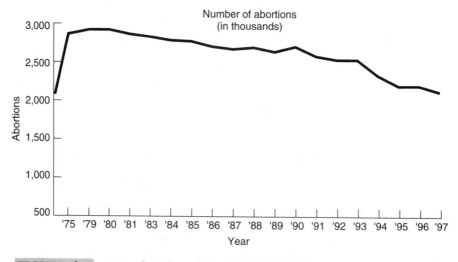

FIGURE 6.5   **U.S. Abortion Rates, 1974–2000**
Source: Lawrence B. Finer and Stanley K. Henshaw, "Abortion Incidence and Services in the United States in 2000," *Perspectives on Sexual and Reproductive Health,* January/February 2003, Alan Guttmacher Institute.

As Table 6.7 shows, the largest percentage of abortions involves non-teenage women, white women, and unmarried women. Stanley K. Henshaw and Katherine Kost, who calculated the rate of abortion for different groups, found abortions were most likely to be obtained by women under thirty, never-married women, women without a religious affiliation, and poor women.[137]

Roe v. Wade (1973) had a dramatic effect on the number of legal abortions obtained. In 1973, there were 745,000 abortions. This number increased to a peak of 1,609,000 abortions in 1990 and then decreased to 1,328,000 by 1997.[138]

TABLE 6.7 **Abortions by Selected Characteristics, 1997**

	Percent Distribution
Age	
19 years old or younger	20
20 to 24 years old	32
25 to 29 years old	24
30 to 34 years old	14
35 to 39 years old	8
40 years old and over	3
Race	
White	58
Black and other	42
Marital Status	
Never married	81
Married	19
Number of Prior Induced Abortions	
None	51
One	28
Two or more	20
Weeks of Gestation	
Less than 9 weeks	55
9 to 10 weeks	22
11 to 12 weeks	11
13 weeks or more	12

Source: U.S. Census Bureau, *Statistical Abstract of the United States: 2002,*
http://www.census.gov/prod/www/statistical-abstract-US.html.

However, birth control information is still not available to all women who want such information, nor is abortion accessible to all women. Few states provide funding for Medicaid recipients, whereas a growing list of other states require parental notification or consent, spousal notification or consent, counseling or informed consent, a waiting period, or tests to determine fetal viability. Were birth control information and abortion more widely available, the birth rate might fall even more.

Another indicator of changes in attitudes toward childbearing that have accompanied the women's rights movement is the practice of delaying the birth of the first child. Unlike the women of the 1950s and 1960s, women today are likely to remain child-free until well into their late twenties or even their thirties and forties (see Table 6.8). Although there are several reasons for the delay in childbearing, perhaps one of the most significant is the practice of many women to postpone childbirth to concentrate on the development of their careers. Research suggests that women who have babies later in life are better educated, have higher-status jobs, are more likely to have planned the birth, will have fewer children, and are more likely to return to work soon after the baby is born.[139] As a result, there has been much talk and often heated debate about the ticking of women's "biological time clocks."

For some women, there may be a growing realization that they have waited too long or that they do not want a family after all. Caroline Bird quotes a reporter as saying:

> When I was growing up, I never questioned that I would one day have a child. But now I'm not so sure. I've found a job that I really like and I now can see what children really mean—a lot of time, a lot of expense, a lot of frustration—and I am sure, too, a lot of satisfaction. But I can't see myself quitting my job and staying home with the kids.[140]

Delayed childbearing may eventually mean no children for some women. For example, in 2000, 44 percent of women age twenty-five to twenty-nine were

TABLE 6.8 **First Births per 1,000 Women, by Age and Race, 2000**

	All Races	White	Black	Asian and Pacific Islander	Hispanic
15 to 19 years	38.7	37.2	48.8	15.6	64.4
20 to 24 years	47.1	47.4	40.9	52.9	79.8
25 to 29 years	43.7	49.4	13.6	45.6	43.0
30 to 34 years	27.5	30.2	13.1	32.6	27.7
35 to 39 years	9.6	8.3	11.1	27.4	10.0
40 to 44 years	2.3	1.7	1.9	3.1	—

Source: U.S. Census Bureau, "Fertility of American Women: June 2000," *Current Population Reports*, Series P20-543RV (Washington, D.C.: U.S. Government Printing Office), 2001.

childless, as were 27 percent of women age thirty to thirty-four, 20 percent of women thirty-five to thirty-nine, and 19 percent of women forty to forty-four. The corresponding figures for 1976 were 31 percent, 16 percent, 11 percent, and 10 percent.[141]

Rather than have no children at all, others, especially working women, are choosing to limit their families to one or two children. The total fertility rate, which measures the number of children a woman can expect to have in her lifetime, has fallen from 3.7 children in 1957, the height of the baby boom, to approximately 2 over the last twenty years with minor fluctuations. The current figure is below the replacement level for the population at about 2.1 births per woman.[142]

An apparent trend contrary to the declining emphasis on motherhood has been the rising percentage of babies being born to women who are not married. In 1960, if a woman became pregnant while not married, she generally married the father. Thus, only 14.5 percent of all women having their first child in 1960 were unmarried. With changing attitudes toward marriage and premarital sex, this figure had risen to 22.3 percent in the late 1970s, decreasing to 20.2 percent in 2000. Part of the explanation for this phenomenon is the rising percentage of young women who engage in premarital sexual intercourse, up nearly 100 percent from 1978.[143] Eighty-three percent of births to teenagers in 2000 were out of wedlock. Forty-four percent of births to women in their early twenties occur out of wedlock, but only 13 percent to women over thirty. Among African American women, 62 percent of first births are to women who are unmarried; among Hispanics, nearly one in three; among white women, one in four. Fifty-four percent of first births to women without a high school degree occurred out of wedlock, 32 percent to women with some college, and only 4 percent to women with a bachelor's degree or higher.[144]

Most observers note that unmarried women who are having babies are not really countering the trends in motherhood that we have discussed. If anything, the number of children born to individual unwed mothers is declining in a parallel trend to the declining number born to married women.[145] What has changed is the desire and the opportunity to marry. Larry Bumpass, a professor at the University of Wisconsin, claims: "This is more a change in marriage behavior than a change in child-bearing behavior."[146] Jane Mattes, the founder of Mothers by Choice, agrees. She notes, "I decided I couldn't go through life without a child, and I put the child first, marriage later."[147] For many women who have children without a husband, however, the resultant economic hardship of not being in a dual-income family can be devastating for the woman and her children. As we noted, a very large proportion of these women and their families have incomes that place them below the poverty level.

One of the results of today's smaller families and decisions to remain childless is that both married and unmarried women are devoting less time to motherhood. Unless there is a complete reversal of these trends, the data suggest that motherhood in the future will loom as even less of an important role for women. If the proportion of one's life devoted to a particular pursuit determines its importance, the worker role may replace the mother role in the value hierarchy of at least some women. The growing practice of returning to work shortly after the birth of a child, especially for professional women, may indicate this reversal has already occurred for some. A more likely scenario for most women is that the two roles will have equal importance. For this to occur, however, either men will have to share family responsibilities more than they do now or the government will have to adopt policies to make the executions of joint mother-worker roles more manageable. We turn now to see whether fathers' role changes have kept pace with mothers'.

Profiles in Leadership

BLANCHE LINCOLN

Blanche Lincoln is the youngest woman ever elected to the United States Senate and the third woman ever to hold a seat on the Senate Finance Committee. She is also the mother of twin boys—joining a mere handful of working mothers of young children in the Senate.

Lincoln graduated with a bachelor's degree from Randolph Macon Women's College in 1982 and went to work on Capitol Hill as a receptionist for Rep. Bill Alexander (D-Ark.). After two years, she left for a series of research positions at lobbying firms that solidified her interest in pursuing a career in politics. As she wrote in *Nine and Counting*, "Daddy always said, 'I don't want to hear you whining

Source: Focused Images Photograpy, Inc.

about things you're not willing to do something about. Either stop griping, or get out there and change it.'"[a] Lincoln won a seat in the U.S. House of Representatives during the historic "Year of the Woman," easily defeating her former boss in the midst of revelations of his involvement in the House check-bouncing scandal.

Lincoln married during her first term, won reelection, but decided not to seek a third term when she became pregnant with twins in 1996. As she explained, "I just didn't see myself riding around on flatbed trucks being eight months pregnant with twins, and seventy-five extra pounds out to there."[b] An open Senate seat tempted her back into the political ring in 1998, drawing criticism from columnist Mona Charen, who wrote: "Running for the U.S. Senate is incompatible with being a good mother to very young children."[c] Lincoln made it clear during her campaign that she would strive to balance work and family, telling constituents, "I'm moving my family with me because I want to watch my family grow up. I want to see their school plays. We'll be back here every holiday and every chance I get, but I'm not going to sacrifice my family for this job."[d] She was elected with 55.1 percent of the vote, entering the Senate as one of nine women.

Lincoln is a champion for issues relating to children, women, and working mothers in particular, including social security, geriatric medicine, health care, and education. As Lincoln explains, "My perspective is a little different, since I'm a working mom and understand what other working mothers are going through." She has worked with Senate colleague Mary Landrieu and a handful of Senate dads to press for family-friendly scheduling in the Senate.[e] Catherine Whitney writes in *Nine and Counting*, "Lincoln's days are a juggling act that all working mothers can identify with. She is up at the crack of dawn to get the family ready, feed her sons, Reece and Bennett, and then bundle them up and take them to preschool. Sticky hugs and kisses and reassurances trail her as she leaves: 'Mommy's going to work. I love you.'"[f] Lincoln is also a member of the "sandwich generation," caring for young children and aging parents simultaneously. As one reporter commented, "She may seem like living proof that women can have it all, but it's clear that life as a Senator and a mother is a constant juggling act bolstered by some serious time management and late-night cram sessions."[g]

Although Lincoln claims that "It's hard to be high-and-mighty when you've got peanut butter on your sleeve," she has impressed her colleagues with her grasp of the issues and her people skills.[h] Lincoln is described as "savvy and polished" and someone who "knows how to make deals."[i] Landing a seat on the coveted Finance Committee acknowledges the respect she has earned. The product of a farming family, Lincoln is a vocal advocate for rural America, serving on the Agriculture, Nutrition and Forestry Committee, and chairing the Forestry, Conservation and Rural Revitalization subcommittee. She is also a member of the Senate Special Committee on Aging, the Select Committee on Ethics Agriculture, the Social Security Task Force, and the Rural Health Caucus. Joining the New Democrat Coalition and the Senate Centrist Coalition, Lincoln takes a moderate approach to policy making, recognizing the value of "governing from the center."[j] Lincoln has also solidified her support among constituents, frequently criss-crossing the state to visit all twenty-five counties. Once telling a

(continued)

reporter that she would like to grace the cover of *Field and Stream Magazine*, Lincoln enjoys fishing and duck hunting with constituents.[k] Undaunted by the challenges of balancing family and a political career, Lincoln advises young women: "Don't limit yourself in what you want to do by what you think you ought to do. Don't limit yourself—if you have an idea, don't be afraid . . . and don't ever think you're limited by the color of your skin or your sex or your age or anything else."[l]

---

[a] The Women of the Senate and Catherine Whitney, *Nine and Counting* (New York: William Morrow, 2000), 90.

[b] *Nine and Counting*, 92.

[c] "Senator Speaks Out on Behalf of Working Mothers," *Washington Times*, June 29, 1998, A16.

[d] Brian Nutting, "Sen. Blanche Lincoln," *CQ Weekly*, December 28, 2002, 30.

[e] Allison Stevens, "For Parents, There's No Vacation Like Home," *The Hill*, June 14, 2000.

[f] *Nine and Counting*, 93.

[g] Susan Crabtree, "With Finance Seat, Lincoln Hits Stride," *Roll Call*, February 19, 2001.

[h] *Nine and Counting*, 88.

[i] Nutting, "Sen. Blanche Lincoln," 29.

[j] "Blanche Lambert Lincoln, United States Senator, Arkansas," http://www.senate.gov/~lincoln/html/biography.html.

[k] Marjorie Margolies-Mezvinsky, *A Woman's Place: The Freshmen Women Who Changed the Face of Congress* (New York: Crown, 1994), 104.

[l] *A Woman's Place*, 211.

Fatherhood.   Often in the public discussions about changing motherhood practices, little is said about the changing role of fathers. Social scientists have attempted to fill this void with research on the "other parent." What they find is often a paradox. On the one hand, there is some still very limited evidence that men are taking their job as parent more seriously. On the other hand, there is disturbing evidence that some men are "abandoning the good provider role."[148]

On the positive side, many married men now take an active part in their wives' pregnancies, go to childbirth classes, and are in delivery rooms. Many men now help their wives with child care, although the bulk of the work and the responsibility to see that the work gets done still generally stay with the mother. Fathers' "help" is often limited to taking care of the children while the wife is engaged in some other household chore or at work. Even fathers in delayed families (where the first child was born to a mother after age twenty-eight), who are better educated, older, and more egalitarian in their views, contribute only marginally more to household tasks than all fathers in two-parent families with children under age eighteen.[149]

If this relatively modest change is the "good dad" side of the equation, the "bad dad" side is even more disturbing.[150] Several authors present convincing evidence that men are, in many ways, abandoning their parental role. One indicator of this is the declining proportion of time that men spend with their children, down 43 percent between 1960 and 1980.[151] If we focus on divorced dads and fathers of children born to unmarried mothers, the evidence of declining notions of fatherhood become even more convincing. Few divorced dads, as we already noted, make a very serious effort to take care of the financial needs of their children, often ignoring court orders to pay child support. In a similar vein, Frank F. Furstenberg Jr.'s research found divorced fathers maintain only minimal contact with their children from a former marriage. Among children whose parents had been divorced two to nine years, more than 20 percent of the children had not seen their father in five years; this percentage rose to nearly 50 percent for children of parents who were divorced for ten years or more. As Furstenberg notes, "Men often sever ties with their children in the course of establishing distance from their former wives."[152] Remarriage appears to hasten the exit, with fathers often apparently too busy with the responsibilities of their new family to maintain contact with the children from a former marriage.[153]

Fathers of children from unions where there was no marriage are even less attached to their children. Few give any child support. Moreover, many seem to "forget" the child completely, not even recalling their existence when asked to list or name their children on social surveys.[154]

The failure of fathers to assume an equal parenting role seems traceable to the same problems we have identified as limiting the movement to an equitable marital or parental relationship. First, society does not encourage, and may discourage, especially in the workplace, role sharing by men. Few fathers can take time off to stay home with sick children, whereas women are more likely to find they can do this, although not without damage to their careers. Research on the implementation of the Family and Medical Leave Act of 1993, for example, finds far higher numbers of women than men take advantage of its provisions to care for a family member. Second, men are inadequately trained to assume the parental role. Fathers of babies and young children seem to be the least prepared to assume an equal role. Third, men are not motivated to change.[155] Fourth, some men may find that economic conditions make it financially difficult or impossible to live up to the culturally defined provider role assigned to men. Young white men and African American men more generally may find they are unable to support their children.

The New Families

The intersection of the trends we have been discussing in marriage, divorce, and parenthood has produced a radical alteration in what we might call the typical family. As Table 6.9 makes clear, the typical family is no longer a married couple with children. Moreover, if we were to divide this latter group into families where only the father works, we would find less than 21 percent of all families meet the historically defined "traditional" family.[156] The implications for women's status in the family are far reaching. For many women living

TABLE 6.9   **Household Composition, 1960 to 2010 (in percentages)**

	1960	1990	1995	2010[a]
Married couples with children	44.2	26.3	25.2	20.1
Married couples without children	30.3	29.8	29.5	31.5
Other families with children	4.4	8.3	8.2	7.9
Other families without children	6.4	6.5	7.1	8.3
Living alone	13.0	24.6	24.9	26.8
Other nonfamily households	1.7	4.6	5.2	5.4

[a]Projected.

Source: Jennifer Classen Day, "Projection of Number of Households and Families in the U.S., 1995–2010," *Current Population Reports*, Series P25-1129 (Washington, D.C.: Department of Commerce, 1996).

alone, their status is solely a function of their own self-determined lifestyle and their earning power. For women who head single-parent families, they are both parent and breadwinner. Their ability to share family responsibilities may depend on the number and ages of their children and the support from their extended family, but for most important decisions they alone are responsible. Women living with a spouse find their status depends on whether they work, what their earning capacity is relative to their spouse's, whether they have children, and the willingness of their spouse to "role-share."

A very important variable in the status of women is the relative economic position of the family in which the woman lives. Figures from the U.S. Census Bureau indicate that families of married couples where both partners work have the highest earnings, followed by families where only the husband works, and then families headed by a woman.[157]

Thus, women's status in the family is variable and can become even more so in the decades to come as the trends we have been describing continue to affect even more women. How the women's movement and the government react to this growing diversity may be critical to all women's futures.

CONCLUSION

Although there has been considerable progress in the direction of creating a more equitable institution of marriage, many of the traditional practices remain. This lack of equality of men and women in marriage is of considerable consequence for the position of women, not only within but outside the family. Women cannot achieve an equal position in politics or the marketplace as long as they have the primary responsibility for housework and child care. For equity in these areas, women need what men have: "a wife." The situation, of course, is even more precarious for the women who head families alone. They lack even the "help" that husbands and fathers provide. Perhaps more importantly, they lack the second, and still generally primary, income that comes from a man's paid employment.

Many feminists argue that the institution of the family may be particularly resistant to change because it signifies and creates our understanding of gender roles. The same could be said of motherhood. A person's sense of self-identity and society's definition of woman and man may be intimately linked to what happens in the family. Relatedly, as we saw in Chapter 4, what transpires at work may also seek to create gender. Thus, women are not merely socialized to become wives and homemakers; rather, the social structures in which they live act to reinforce the notions of what women must or should do if they are "to be a woman." The same argument can be made perhaps even more forcefully for men, who seem particularly concerned about confirming "their manhood." Thus, in making any prognosis about further change in the institution of the family, not only do we need to look at the barriers we have identified, but also we must be sensitive to how altering the family is seen as threatening to many people's very sense of gendered self.

With respect to the first of our three barriers, cultural attitudes about the family, we expect that further change can be predicted. Even during the 1980s, when the political leadership in Washington emphasized traditional family values, an evolution in the desired family structure continued. By the 1990s, more men and women wanted a role-shared relationship. While both political parties now seem generally concerned that the trends we have identified have not always been beneficial, especially for children, there seems to be little public policy can do to alter public opinion or social practices.[158]

It is likely that the conflict between feminists and conservative women will continue, each claiming the other's proposals will not solve the decline of the family. Correspondingly, the divisions between women who stay at home and those who work full time about what impact the women's rights movement has had on women's status in the family will also not go away. Feminists will continue to push for policy changes in an attempt to give women greater independence and to allow them to blend their marital and work roles. Homemakers, however, may increasingly resist what they see as changes undermining their way of life.

With respect to the other two barriers (differential resources of men and women and discrimination or reluctance to change by men), women, especially young women, seem increasingly better equipped to demand equal role sharing. They are more likely to work and to work at well-paying jobs. Men, however, seem only marginally inclined to adopt the practices that would produce equitable unions. The resultant resentment by women may contribute to marital dissolution and to women's increasing reluctance to marry and to have children. Men's "flight from commitment" may symbolize their own reluctance to save the institution.

Betty Friedan's comments about the restructuring of the institution of home and work several years ago still seem applicable. She claims, "We will never bring about these changes unless fathers demand them too."[159] Because the pressure on the traditional institution of marriage is not likely to diminish, we may expect men to soon join the chorus of voices calling for change.

NOTES

1. Linda Gordon, *Woman's Body, Woman's Right: A Social History of Birth Control in America* (New York: Viking Press, 1976), 18, 48–49.
2. Carl N. Degler, *At Odds: Women and the Family in America from the Revolution to the Present* (New York: Oxford University Press, 1980), 73.
3. John Demos, "Husbands and Wives," in *Our American Sisters: Women in American Life and Thought*, ed. Jean E. Friedman and William G. Shade (Boston: Allyn and Bacon, 1973), 36–41.
4. Quoted in Ibid., 31.
5. Robert Staples and Leanor Boulin Johnson, *Black Families at the Crossroads* (San Francisco: Jossey-Bass, 1993), 7.
6. Herbert G. Gutman, "Marital and Sexual Norms among Slave Women," in *A Heritage of Her Own*, ed. Nancy F. Cott and Elizabeth H. Pleck (New York: Simon and Schuster, 1979), 305–6.
7. Susan A. Mann, "Slavery, Sharecropping, and Sexual Inequality," *Signs* 14, no. 4: 779–81, 786–7.
8. Staples and Johnson, *Black Families at the Crossroads*, 7–8; Gutman, "Marital and Sexual Norms," 306–7.
9. Michael Gordon, *The American Family: Past, Present, and Future* (New York: Random House, 1978), 201–9; Carroll Smith-Rosenberg, "Sex as Symbol in Victorian Purity: An Ethnohistorical Analysis of Jacksonian America," in *Turning Points: Historical and Sociological Essays on the Family*, ed. John Demos and Sarane Spence Boocock (Chicago: University of Chicago Press, 1978), 212–47.
10. Mary Frances Berry, *The Politics of Parenthood* (New York: Viking, 1993); Barbara Welter, "The Cult of True Womanhood: 1820–1860," in *Our American Sisters*, ed. Friedman and Shade, 102–3.
11. Gordon, *Woman's Body, Woman's Right*, 320.
12. Myra Marx Ferree, "Beyond Separate Spheres: Feminism and Family Research," *Journal of Marriage and the Family* 52, no. 4 (1990): 872.
13. Ibid.
14. Ibid.
15. Helena Znaniecki Lapata, *Occupation Housewife* (New York: Oxford Press, 1991), 48–53.
16. Arland Thornton and Deborah Freedman, "Changes in the Sex Role Attitudes of Women, 1962–1977," *American Sociological Review* 44, no. 4 (1979): 833.
17. Ibid., 833–5.
18. The 1985 Virginia Slims Poll found 70 percent of women believed they could have a happy and complete life without marriage. Data made available by the Roper Center for Public Opinion Research, Storrs, Conn. A 1989 poll found the proportion of women who believed they could be happy without marriage had risen to 90 percent. Cited in Susan Faludi, *Backlash: The Undeclared War against American Women* (New York: Crown, 1991), 15.

19. James Allan Davis and Tom W. Smith, *General Social Surveys, 1972–1996*, National Opinion Research Center, distributed by Roper Center for Public Opinion Research, Storrs, Conn.

20. A 1987 survey found 81.5 percent of all men age eighteen to twenty-four agreed (strongly agree, agree) that they would like to get married someday. For young women, the desire to be married was equally strong, although women were more likely to strongly agree they would like to marry. Bruce A. Chadwick and Tim B. Heaton, *Statistical Handbook on the American Family* (Phoenix, Ariz.: Oryx Press, 1992), 22.

21. The Virginia Slims Polls: 1970, 1974, 1979, 1985, 1990, 1995. Data made available by the Roper Center, Storrs, Conn.

22. Thornton and Freedman, "Changes in the Sex Role Attitudes of Women," 833, 837–8.

23. The 2000 Virginia Slims Poll.

24. The 1994 *General Social Survey*.

25. Ibid.

26. The 1994 *General Social Survey*.

27. Chadwick and Heaton, *Statistical Handbook*, 94.

28. In the 1996 *General Social Survey*, 52.1 percent of those who had an opinion favored making divorce more difficult, 28.6 percent favored making it easier, and 19.4 percent did not want any change.

29. The 2000 Virginia Slims Poll.

30. The 1980 Virginia Slims Poll.

31. The 1994 *General Social Survey*.

32. Ibid.; Chadwick and Heaton, *Statistical Handbook*, 129.

33. The 2000 Virginia Slims Poll.

34. Charles Pappas. "21st Century Dad," *Working Mother*, September 2000, 20.

35. Sharman Stein, "Make Room for Daddy," *Working Mother*, October 2002, 45.

36. George Gallup Jr., "Poll Topics and Trends: Abortion" *Gallup Polls* (2003), http://www.gallup.com/poll/topics/abortion/asp.

37. Lydia Saad, "Roe v. Wade Has Positive Public Image," *Gallup Polls* (2003), http://www.gallup.com/poll/releases/pr030120.asp.

38. Ibid.

39. Elaine J. Hall and Myra Marx Ferree, "Race Differences in Abortion Attitudes," *Public Opinion Quarterly* 50, no. 1 (1986): 197–9.

40. Ibid., 199–204.

41. Saad, "Roe v. Wade Has Positive Public Image."

42. Lydia Saad, "Public Opinion on Abortion Policies Making News," *Gallup Polls* (2003), http://www.gallup.com/poll/releases/pr020724.asp.

43. George Gallup Jr., "Abortion Issues," *Gallup Polls*, http://www.gallup.com/poll/releases/pr010122.asp.

44. Debra L. Dodson, *Abortion Politics in State Elections: Comparisons Across States* (New Brunswick, N.J.: Center for the American Woman and Politics, 1991).

45. Ibid.

46. Alan I. Abramowitz, "It's Abortion, Stupid: Policy Voting in the 1992 Presidential Election" (paper prepared for delivery at the annual meeting of the American Political Science Association, Washington, D.C., 1992); Mark J. Wattier, Byron W.

Daynes, and Raymond Tatalovich, "Abortion Attitudes, Gender, and Candidate Choice in Presidential Elections: 1972 to 1992," *Women and Politics* 17, no. 1 (1997): 55–72.

47. http://www.naral.org/mediasources/press/goulding.pdf.

48. CBS News/*New York Times* Poll, September 27–29, 2000, http://www.pollingreport.com/court.htm.

49. Chadwick and Heaton, *Statistical Handbook*, 145.

50. The 2000 Virginia Slims Poll.

51. Linda J. Sax, Alexander W. Astin, William S. Korn, and K. M. Mahoney, *The American Freshman: National Norms for Fall 2001* (Los Angeles: Higher Education Research Institute, UCLA, 2001).

52. "Attitudes and Characteristics of Freshmen, Fall 1991," *Chronicle of Higher Education Almanac* (Washington, D.C.: Chronicle of Higher Education, 1992), 13.

53. "What's OK on a Date," *Public Perspective* 3, no. 2 (1992): 102.

54. Ibid. Only 40 percent of men over age fifty think it is rape when a husband has sex with his wife even if she does not want to; among young men, 69 percent think it is rape. In general, young men seem much more sensitive to the fact that sex must be by mutual agreement.

55. Susan Estrich, *Real Rape* (Cambridge, Mass.: Harvard University Press, 1987).

56. The 1990 Virginia Slims Poll.

57. Chadwick and Heaton, *Statistical Handbook*, 146.

58. *The American Freshman: National Norms for Fall 2002.*

59. 2000 Virginia Slims Poll.

60. Susan Cohen and Mary Fainsod Katzenstein, *Feminism, Children, and the New Families* (New York: Guilford Press, 1988), 25–46. See also Jeanne J. Flemming, "Public Opinion on Change in Women's Rights and Roles," in *Feminism, Children, and the New Families*, ed. Stanford M. Dornbush and Myra H. Strober (New York: Guilford Press, 1988), 47–66.

61. Jennifer Glass, "Housewives and Employed Wives: Demographic and Attitudinal Change, 1972–1986," *Journal of Marriage and the Family* 54, no. 3 (1992): 559–69.

62. The 1996 *General Social Survey.*

63. U.S. Department of Justice, "Criminal Victimization: 2001," Bureau of Justice Statistics (September 2002), http://www.ojp.usdoj.gov/bjs/pub/pdf/cv01.pdf.

64. Caroline Bird, *The Two-Paycheck Marriage* (New York: Rawson, Wade, 1979), 43.

65. Laurie Wermuth, Jennifer Ham, and Rebecca L. Robbins, "Women Don't Wear Condoms: AIDS Risk Among Sexual Partners of IV Drug Users," in *The Social Context of AIDS*, ed. Joan Huber and Beth E. Schneider (Newbury Park, Calif.: Sage, 1992), 83.

66. Ibid., 78–9.

67. Constantina Safilios-Rothschild, *Sex Role Socialization and Sex Discrimination: A Synthesis and Critique of the Literature* (Washington, D.C.: National Institute of Education, 1979), 35.

68. Ellen Wood, "The Impact of Parenting Experience on Gender Stereotyped Toy Play of Children," *Sex Roles*, July 2002.

69. *The American Freshman: National Norms for Fall 2002.*

70. The 1974 and 1979 Virginia Slims Polls both questioned women about whether boys should do laundry and mend clothes. In the earlier survey, only three out of five mothers thought a boy should do laundry and four out of ten thought he should sew. By 1979, these figures were four out of five and nearly six out of ten, respectively.

71. *The General Mills American Family Report*, 41. The report found that while 72 percent of all men and 77 percent of all women reported they take their families into consideration in deciding the amount of on-the-job travel they will accept, interviews with executives in large corporations found only 34 percent believed this was a consideration for men. Sixty-four percent said it was important for women.

72. Abbigail J. Chiodo and Michael T. Owyang. "Marriage, Motherhood and Money: How Do Women's Life Decisions Influence Their Wages?" *Regional Economist* (April 2003): 5–9.

73. Degler, *At Odds*, 7–8.

74. Ibid., 152.

75. U.S. Census Bureau, "Marital Status and Living Arrangements," *Current Population Reports*, Series P20-514.

76. U.S. Census Bureau, "America's Families and Living Arrangements," *Current Population Reports*, Series P20-537.

77. Scott J. South and Kim M. Lloyd, "Marriage Opportunities and Family Formation: Further Implications of Imbalanced Sex Ratios," *Journal of Marriage and the Family* 54, no. 2 (1990): 440–51. They find, however, that availability of men is only a partial explanation for the lower marriage rates among African Americans. See also Maxine Baca Zinn, "Family, Race, and Poverty in the Eighties," *Signs* 14, no. 4 (1989): 867–8.

78. U.S. Census Bureau, "America's Families and Living Arrangements."

79. Quoted in Jane Gross, "Divorced, Middle-Aged, and Happy: Women, Especially, Adjusted to the '90s," *New York Times*, December 7, 1992, A14.

80. Andrew Cherlin, "Women and the Family," in *The American Woman: 1987–1988*, ed. Sara E. Rix (New York: Norton, 1987), 75.

81. Jean Seligmann et al., "The Art of Flying Solo," *Newsweek*, March 1, 1993, 70–71, 73.

82. The 2000 Virginia Slims Poll.

83. Joann Vanek, "Housewives as Workers," in *Women Working: Theories and Facts in Perspective*, ed. Ann H. Stromberg and Shirley Harkess (Palo Alto, Calif.: Mayfield, 1978), 402.

84. John P. Robinson, "Who's Doing the Housework?" *American Demographics* (December 1988): 24–8, 63.

85. Daphne Spain and Suzanne M. Bianchi, "Mother's Day and Other Days," *Public Perspective* (July/August 2000): 18.

86. Ibid.

87. Diane Crispell, "Super Woman Gives Way to Sensible Woman," *Public Perspective* (July/August 2000): 15.

88. The 2000 Virginia Slims Poll conducted by Roper Starch Worldwide, Inc. Data provided by Philip Morris USA.

89. Crispell, "Super Woman Gives Way."

90. "Living Female: A Roper Center Data Review," *Public Perspective* (July/August 2000).

91. Scott Coltrane and Masako Ishii-Kuntz, "Men's Housework: A Life Course Perspective," *Journal of Marriage and the Family* 54, no. 1 (1992): 46, 52–3; Blumstein and Schwartz, "Money and Ideology," 268–70; Theodore N. Greenstein, "Husbands' Participation in Domestic Labor: Interactive Effects of Wives and Husbands' Gender Ideologies," *Journal of Marriage and the Family* 55, no. 3 (1993): 585–95.

92. Robert Joseph Taylor, Linda M. Chatters, M. Belinda Tucker, and Edith Lewis, "Developments in Research on Black Families: A Decade Review," *Journal of Marriage and the Family* 52, no. 4 (1990): 995.

93. Blumstein and Schwartz, "Money and Ideology," 272.
94. Chadwick and Heaton, *Statistical Handbook*, 69. See April A. Brayfield, "Employment Resources and Housework in Canada," *Journal of Marriage and the Family* 54, no. 1 (1992): 28, for a discussion of ethnic group differences in Canada.
95. Coltrane and Ishii-Kuntz, "Men's Housework," 44.
96. Sara Fenstermaker, Candace West, and Don H. Zimmerman, "Gender Inequality: New Conceptual Train," in *Gender, Family, and Economy: The Triple Overlap*, ed. Rae Lesser Blumberg (Newbury Park, Calif.: Sage, 1991), 301. See also Ferree, "Beyond Separate Spheres," 866–85.
97. Blumstein and Schwartz, "Money and Ideology," 265–8; Coltrane and Ishii-Kuntz, "Men's Housework," 45–6, 52.
98. Blumstein and Schwartz, "Money and Ideology," 265–8.
99. Brayfield, "Employment Resources," 25.
100. The 1989, 1994, and 2000 Virginia Slims Polls.
101. Robert O. Blood and Donald M. Wolfe, *Husbands and Wives: The Dynamics of Married Living* (Glencoe, Ill.: Free Press, 1960), 2–23.
102. Ibid., 21.
103. *The General Mills American Family Report*, 46.
104. The 2000 Virginia Slims Poll.
105. Blood and Wolfe, *Husbands and Wives*, 40; Stephen J. Bahr, "Effects on Power and Division of Labor in the Family," in *Working Mothers*, ed. Lois Wladis Hoffman and F. Ivan Nye (San Francisco: Jossey-Bass, 1974), 173–7; Cynthia Fuchs Epstein, "Toward a Family Policy: Changes in Mothers' Lives," in *The Changing American Family and Public Policy*, ed. Andrew J. Cherlin (Washington, D.C.: Urban Institute, 1988), 169–70; Blumstein and Schwartz, "Money and Ideology," 273–6.
106. Blumstein and Schwartz, "Money and Ideology," 276–7.
107. Ibid., 277–8.
108. Norval D. Glenn, "Quantitative Research on Marital Quality in the 1980s: A Critical Review," *Journal of Marriage and the Family* 52, no. 4 (1990): 818–32.
109. Ibid., 826–7.
110. Norval D. Glenn, "The Recent Trend in Marital Success in the United States," *Journal of Marriage and the Family* 53, no. 2 (1991): 261–70.
111. Ibid., 269–70.
112. The 1972–2000 *General Social Surveys*.
113. Tom W. Smith, "The Ties That Bind," *Public Perspective* (January/February 2001): 35.
114. Frank F. Furstenberg Jr., "Divorce and the American Family," *Annual Review of Sociology* 16 (1990): 381–2.
115. The following discussion draws heavily on Lynn K. White, "Determinants of Divorce: A Review of Research in the Eighties," *Journal of Marriage and the Family* 52, no. 4 (1990): 904–12. See also Furstenberg, "Divorce and the American Family," 379–81.
116. Pamela Paul, *The Starter Marriage and the Future of Matrimony* (New York: Villard Books, 2002), x–xi
117. Ibid.
118. Lenore J. Weitzman, "Women and Children Last: The Social and Economic Consequences of Divorce Law Reforms," in *Feminism, Children, and the New Families*, ed. Sanford M. Dornbusch and Myra H. Strober (New York: Guilford Press, 1988), 241–3.
119. The 1972–2000 *General Social Surveys*.
120. Quoted in Gross, "Divorced," A14.

121. Furstenberg, "Divorce and the American Family," 384–5; Leslie A. Morgan, "The Multiple Consequences of Divorce: A Decade Review," *Journal of Marriage and the Family* 52, no. 4 (1990): 917.

122. U.S. Census Bureau, "America's Families and Living Arrangements: March 2000," *Current Population Reports*, Series P20-537, and earlier reports.

123. Ibid.

124. Furstenberg, "Divorce and the American Family," 383.

125. Ibid.

126. U.S. Census Bureau, "Custodial Mothers and Fathers and Their Child Support: 1999" *Current Population Reports*, Series P60-217.

127. Weitzman, "Women and Children Last," 224–5; Chadwick and Heaton, *Statistical Handbook*, 104.

128. U.S. Census Bureau, "Custodial Mothers and Fathers and Their Child Support: 1999."

129. Daniel R. Meyers and Judi Bartfeld, "Compliance with Child Support Orders in Divorce Cases," *Journal of Marriage and the Family* 58, no. 1 (1996): 210–2; John W. Graham and Andrea H. Beller, "Child Support in Black and White: Racial Differentials in the Award and Receipt of Child Support in the 1980s," *Social Science Quarterly* 77, no. 3 (1996): 528–42.

130. Morgan, "Multiple Consequences," 914; Meyer and Bartfeld, "Compliance with Child Support Orders," 201–12.

131. U.S. Census Bureau, "Custodial Mothers and Fathers and Their Child Support: 1999."

132. Carol Sarler, "Divorce Your Husband and Watch Him Get Rich," *New Statesmen*, October 30, 2000.

133. Furstenberg, "Divorce and the American Family," 386.

134. Wetzel, "American Families," 8; U.S. Census Bureau, "Fertility of American Women: June 2000," *Current Population Reports* P20-543RV (October 2001), http://www.census.gov.

135. Joan Huber and Glenna Spitze, *Sex Stratification: Children, Housework, and Jobs* (New York: Academic Press, 1983).

136. National Center for Health Statistics, *National Survey of Family Growth*, http://www.cdc.gov/nchs.htm.

137. Stanley K. Henshaw and Kathryn Kost, "Abortion Patients in 1994–5: Characteristics of Contraceptive Use," *Family Planning Perspective* 28 (1996): 140–7. Catholic and Jewish women were more likely to get an abortion than Protestant women, although the abortion rate for all religious groups was one-quarter that for women without a religious affiliation.

138. U.S. Department of Commerce, *Statistical Abstract of the United States: 2002*, 70.

139. Ibid.; Coltrane and Ishii-Kuntz, "Men's Housework," 44.

140. Quoted in Bird, *The Two Pay-Check Marriage*, 158–9.

141. U.S. Census Bureau, "Fertility of American Women: June 2000," *Current Population Reports*, series P20-543RV and earlier reports.

142. Ibid.

143. David Popenoe, "Flight from the Nuclear Family: Trends of the Past Three Decades," *Public Perspective* 2, no. 3 (1991): 19.

144. U.S. Census Bureau, "Fertility of American Women: June 2000."

145. Mary Jo Bane and Paul A. Jargowsky, "The Links Between Government Policy and Family Structure: What Matters and What Doesn't," in Cherlin, ed., *The Changing American Family*, 223.

146. Margaret L. Usdansky, "A Baby Doesn't Mean Marriage Anymore," *USA Today*, December 4, 1991, 8A.

147. Ibid.

148. Jessie Bernard introduced this idea. Jessie Bernard, "The Good Provider Role: Its Rise and Fall," *American Psychologist* 36, no. 1 (1981): 1–12. See also Barbara Ehrenreich, *The Hearts of Men: American Dreams and the Flight from Commitment* (New York: Anchor Press, 1983); Frank F. Furstenberg Jr., "Good Dads–Bad Dads: Two Faces of Fatherhood," in Cherlin, ed., *The Changing American Family*, 193–218.

149. The 1989 Virginia Slims Poll.

150. Furstenberg, "Good Dads–Bad Dads."

151. Ibid., 201.

152. Ibid., 388.

153. Ibid., 203–4.

154. Ibid., 201–2.

155. Ibid., 209–10.

156. Howard V. Hayghe, "Family Members in the Work Force," *Monthly Labor Review* 113, no. 3 (1990): 18.

157. U.S. Department of Labor, "Highlights of Women's Earnings in 2001" *Bureau of Labor Statistics*, Report 960 (May 2002).

158. Bane and Jargowsky, "Government Policy and Family Structure," 227–47.

159. Quoted in "The Superwoman Squeeze," *Newsweek*, May 19, 1980, 78. See also Betty Friedan, *The Second Stage* (New York: Summit Books, 1981), especially chaps. 3, 6, and 8.

The Future of the Movement

In evaluating the impact of the women's rights movement, 80 percent of women polled in 2003 agreed its impact on society was mostly or completely positive. Six in ten women agreed that a strong women's movement is still needed to push for changes that benefit women.[1] Many of the goals of the women's rights movement remain unmet, and the list of concerns continues to grow. As issue priorities have evolved and diversity within the movement has increased, a feminist realignment appears to be on the horizon. Yet the current status of the movement seems to be plagued by a "feminist malaise." As indicated in Table 7.1, only a small percentage of women are engaging in the most active forms of political participation on behalf of women's rights. While four in ten women say they have voted for a candidate because of his or her support for women's rights, only 11 percent have joined an organization concerned with women's rights.[2] Lacking a unifying symbol, crisis, or mobilizing event, women today have failed to join forces behind a general movement for women's rights.

TABLE 7.1 Political Participation of Women on Behalf of Women's Rights

Question: Have you ever . . .	Yes
Voted for a candidate because of his or her support for women's rights?	42%
Given money to an organization concerned with this issue?	26
Phoned, written, or sent e-mail to a public official expressing your views on women's rights?	19
Joined an organization concerned with women's rights?	11
Taken ANY ACTION on behalf of the rights of women in other countries?	9

Source: "Progress and Perils: New Agenda for Women," Center for the Advancement of Women (April 2003), http://www.advancewomen.org.

"When did you become the voice of the disenfranchised?"

Our discussion of the various women's movements' attempts to gain greater political, employment, educational, and personal rights has revealed both periods of progress and periods of stagnation and even retrenchment. To evaluate the advances of women and these respective movements, we use as our standard the goals movements set for themselves. Table 7.2 highlights the demands made by women at Seneca Falls and then again at the next woman's rights meeting, which was held in Rochester, New York, on August 2, 1848, just two weeks after the Seneca Falls Convention. The Declaration of Sentiments and the Resolutions issued in Seneca Falls were a bit vague; the Rochester Resolutions were an effort by Elizabeth Cady Stanton to make lofty goals more concrete. The early goals for the current women's movement are derived from the National Organization for Women's Bill of Rights, which was drafted in 1967. Look closely at the demands made by women in 1848. Although women got the right to vote in 1920, they continue to be underrepresented at all levels of lawmaking. Women have yet to gain an equal standing with men in social, political, or religious life.

The Married Women's Property Acts that were passed in the states in the 1800s were a first step on the long road to equality within marriage. Women and men are far more equal within the institution of marriage today than they were

TABLE 7.2 **Goals of the Women's Movements**

Woman's Movement The Declaration of Sentiments/ Rochester Resolutions[a]	Women's Rights Movement NOW Bill of Rights[b]
The right to vote	Passage of an ERA
Equal representation in the government	
Equal standing in social, political, and religious life —an end to the double standard	
Equal rights for women in marriage, including: —estate law —control of her own wages and services —reform of the marriage contract including coverture (civil death) and obedience	
Equal educational opportunities for women	Equal educational opportunities
Fairer wages for women	Equal job training opportunities for women in poverty
	Enforcement of laws banning discrimination in employment
	Maternity leave rights in employment and in social security benefits
	Tax deductions for home and child-care expenses
	Government creation of child-care centers
	Right of women to control their reproductive lives

[a] For the full text of the Declaration of Sentiments, see
http://www.rochester.edu/SBA/declare.html.

[b] For an explanation and excerpts of the NOW Bill of Rights, see
http://www.feminist.org/research/chronicles/early2.html.

in 1848, yet, as we saw in Chapter 6, many women often now have not one, but two places where they suffer from inequality—in their homes and in the workplace. Divorce laws, however, even after no-fault reforms, still often result in the unequal treatment of women, and child custody laws and child support enforcement lag behind the goals of most women's organizations today.

Employment opportunities for women are also limited and alone are insufficient to bring equity to women in the workplace. And, although women attend college in greater numbers than men, challenges to Title IX continue, hindering full implementation. A chilly climate for girls and women prevails in many schools, colleges, and universities.

Women at the Seneca Falls Convention also demanded greater participation in church affairs. Today, many major religions still prevent women from becoming ministers or priests. In medicine and law, women's opportunities are also far from equal to men's. The double moral standard, while weakened, continues to limit women's progress. Women's "sphere of action" is still more confined than men's to the home and to "women's" jobs, and the public continues to harbor doubts about women's ability to manage in certain fields and to lead independent lives.

NOW's goals, as well as those of the larger women's rights movement, have only been partially achieved. There is no equal rights amendment (ERA). In spite of passage of the Pregnancy Discrimination Act and the Family and Medical Leave Act, maternity leave is limited, and adequate child care is unavailable for most working women. Poverty continues to strike women disproportionately, and welfare reform, in some cases, has made it more difficult for many women to raise their children and be employed outside the home. And while secure for the moment, the right to control one's reproductive life is restricted by the limited availability of abortion and birth control.

In previous chapters, we identified public attitudes, role conflict, women's lack of preparation, and male resistance and discrimination as some of the barriers to full equality and securing women's demands. These hindrances have been considerably weakened since 1848 (and even since 1967). Many of the most dramatic changes that have occurred during the past three decades were a result of pressure from the women's rights movement. (See Table 7.3.) But whether the roadblocks to women's full equality will continue to fall is an open question.

Some commentators argue that women's progress is only partially dependent on the existence of a women's movement. Anne N. Costain, for example, argues that the government often took the lead in passing policy proposals beneficial to women.[3] Our review suggests that without the prodding and pressure of organized women, not only will many advances not occur, but also gains won can quickly become gains lost. The decades of the 1920s and 1930s are particularly instructive. Split into two camps divided over whether working women needed differential (protective) or equal treatment, women witnessed few gains and, more ominously, were unable to prevent their economic opportunities from being undermined during the Depression. Differences in tactics and goals also hindered the progress of the first woman's movement. During the Reagan-Bush years, the continued onslaught of government attacks on women's programs and policies not only hurt women, but women's rights groups seemed unable to counter those actions until abortion rights truly

TABLE 7.3 **Factors Changing Women's Lives During the Twentieth Century**

	"Most Important" Rank Order	
	Women	Men
Women getting the right to vote	1	1
More women earning college and graduate degrees	2	2
Women entering the workforce in large numbers	3	4
The 1964 Civil Rights Act banning employment discrimination based on gender or race	4	3
Increasing attention to the problem of violence against women	5	7
Birth control pills becoming available	6	6
Development of home appliances	7	9
The women's movement	8	5
The Supreme Court ruling that sexual harassment is illegal employment discrimination	9	10
The Family Medical Leave Act protecting maternity and family leave rights	10	11
More women entering politics	11	8
More women postponing marriage and children until later in life	12	13
The legalization of abortion	13	12
More comfortable and less restrictive clothing for women	14	16
More social acceptance of unmarried women having children	15	17
The higher divorce rate	16	15
Sandra Day O'Connor's appointment to the Supreme Court of the U.S.	17	14
Title IX, which bans athletic or academic discrimination in schools	18	18

Source: The 2000 Virginia Slims Opinion Poll, conducted by Roper Starch Worldwide Inc. Data provided by Philip Morris USA.

seemed threatened in the late 1980s. This threat, when coupled with the Senate's treatment of Anita Hill during the Clarence Thomas confirmation hearings, seemed to energize the movement and produced considerable results in the 1992 elections. Women were united on two fronts—the need to keep abortion safe and legal and the clear need for more women in elected positions. This seemed to happen with the election of the first pro-choice president, record numbers of women in the House and Senate, and the appointment of a female, pro-choice justice to the Supreme Court. These 1992–1993 successes, however, appeared to lull some women into thinking that the fight was over. Women stayed home from the polls in droves in 1994, and the most antifemale Congress ever was elected.

Currently, President George W. Bush and the Republican-controlled Congress continue efforts to roll back many gains made by women in the political, employment, educational, familial, and reproductive spheres discussed throughout this volume. The question then remains, what is necessary to reenergize the women's rights movement and get it back on the solid road to equality?

PREREQUISITES FOR A REENERGIZED WOMEN'S RIGHTS MOVEMENT

In our introduction to this volume, we outlined the prerequisites for a women's movement. We argue that unless many of these factors are present, the kind of sustained activity for women's rights displayed in the 1970s will not occur. Instead, sporadic events may energize some women for short periods of time to act for easily identifiable goals, but this activity will be insufficient to bring about the kind of dramatic changes in women's status that occurred in the 1960s and 1970s.

Organizational Base and Organizational Support

The first prerequisite for a revitalized movement is an organizational base. Although the membership of many feminist and traditional women's rights groups wavered or declined in the 1980s, women's organizations continue to proliferate. In the wake of the Clarence Thomas hearings, many groups reported sharp increases in membership.[4] Mary Fainsod Katzenstein, moreover, argues that the unobtrusive mobilization by women in women's caucuses and within existing organizations long dominated by men "drives second-wave feminism ahead into the 1990s."[5] Still, these groups, while undoubtedly changing existing traditionally male-dominated organizations, have yet to form a sufficient base necessary to reenergize the movement.

As Nancy F. Cott's analysis of women's activity in the 1920s found, women's associations proliferated in the decade after suffrage was attained, but their growth drew potential membership from the more clearly defined pro-women's groups such as the national League of Women Voters.[6] Much of the same sort of phenomena may have happened in the 1980s and 1990s, contributing to the recent feminist realignment or malaise. Women's caucuses in the professions and new women's groups that organized around new or reinvigorated issues such as abortion, peace, nuclear disarmament, or domestic violence siphoned off members from NOW, the National Federation of Business and Professional Women's Clubs, the League of Women Voters, and other pro–women's rights groups.

Even earlier, the younger branch of the women's movement witnessed most of its constituent organizations' fading or their transformation into local associations with more narrow focuses. Flora Davis notes that between 1972 and 1975, a "metamorphosis" occurred in the women's movement. As original women's liberation groups died, what she terms *liberal feminism* became the mainstream of the movement.[7] This growing mainstream, however, was soon affected by the proliferation of women's groups in the 1980s, which often meant, as it did in the 1920s, a dispersal of women's energies and a resultant lack of focus on a single agenda at the same time that there was outside pressure from the government and even the media *against* the women's rights movement and its goals.

Countering this trend somewhat has been the development of "permanent flexible alliances" of women's groups that agree to work together on a common agenda.[8] Perhaps the most notable of these are the National Women's Conference Committee and the Council of Presidents. The former has established coalitions of women's groups in almost all the states. These state coalitions have agreed to work together on the twenty-five-point National Plan of Action for Women adopted at the 1977 National Women's Conference held in Houston, Texas. Growing out of and usually working in concert with the remaining state commissions on the status of women, these alliances are based on the premise that groups will work together to reform state laws. Like the Women's Joint Congressional Committee (WJCC), which was national in scope, members do not have to work on all issues, but affiliated organizations must agree not to work in opposition to items on the common agenda. Success in changing state laws involving marital property reform, domestic abuse, pay equity, child support, and gender discrimination in insurance rates can be partially attributed to these coalitional efforts.

Whereas the National Conference Committee works for state law reform, the Council of Presidents works on the national level. It is composed of women representatives from more than one hundred national women's groups. Since it was organized in 1985, it annually adopts a set of legislative priorities, called the Women's Agenda. Like the WJCC, its member organizations agree to jointly lobby the Congress and executive branch on agenda items.

In conjunction with these coalitions, national and state governments, as they have in the past, may also play an important role in providing organizational support for the women's rights movement. The Clinton administration was committed to women's rights, and many more feminists were appointed to positions of authority, including more cabinet-level jobs, than in any previous administration. Secretary of State Madeleine Albright was able to push the goal of more equitable treatment for women in all nations to the forefront of national foreign policy. Clinton's appointment of Ruth Bader Ginsburg, a pioneer in women's rights litigation and an advocate of stricter constitutional protections for women, immediately affected the Supreme Court's decision making on women's rights issues, as witnessed by her majority opinion in *United States v. Virginia Military Institute*, discussed in Chapter 3. The election of a Republican Congress in 1994 and Clinton's own increased conservatism, however, had the effect of slowing or reversing women's progress. Welfare reform, most notably, is having a disastrous impact on poor women. Furthermore, in 2001, President George W. Bush not only reinstated the global gag rule, but he placed new restrictions on access to contraception through federal employee health plans. One lesson is clear. Women cannot rely on others to be as committed to their agenda.

Leaders and Organizers

The second criterion for a successful movement is the availability of leaders and organizers. There is a pressing need for a new generation of feminist spokespersons. Most of the foremothers of the current movement are ready to retire or have moved on to other issues. The younger branch has aged alongside the older branch, symbolizing the shifting demographics of the aging baby-boom generation. Those who will shepherd the movement in the twenty-first century may well be found among the many newly elected and appointed women public officials who have already begun to parlay their positions in Washington and in state capitals into a platform from which to champion women's issues.

Moreover, NOW and several other women's rights groups, including the White House Project, realize how important it is to attract young, energetic women to the cause as organizers and potential leaders. Still, a cadre of nationally known young organizers of the same renown as those women who came to the forefront in the 1960s has yet to emerge.

Communications Networks

Communications networks are a third key to a reenergized women's movement. Although women's networks and coalitions continue to play an important role in getting the message of the movement to supporters, a question remains about the willingness of the media to provide favorable coverage. Although the national media are not the kind of communications network historically discussed by social movement theorists, the impact of the news media as a way of conveying information about the women's rights movement cannot be ignored. In her best seller, *Backlash: The Undeclared War Against American Women*, Susan Faludi argued persuasively that the media in the 1980s were a critical coplayer with the New Right in a tacit alliance to undermine the movement. She cited several examples of the media backlash, including coverage of the "marriage crunch," the problem of getting pregnant when over the age of thirty (the ticking biological clock), and other (often mythical) miseries besetting professional women. Just as most magazine editors after World War II urged women to adopt the feminine mystique, leave their jobs, and return to homes in the suburbs, the hidden message in the media in the 1980s was that the women's rights movement was responsible for the supposed problems besetting women. Faludi was quick to point out that she did not believe the backlash was an overt conspiracy, but the results were the same.

Not all reviewers have seen a media backlash against feminism. Surely, the coverage of the "Year of the Woman" in 1992 or the attention paid to the "Year of the Woman Governor" in 2002 helped to fuel the success of women candidates. Perhaps it is best to note that the media can be both friend and foe of the movement, but they cannot always be relied on to motivate women to support the movement.

One new avenue that has yet to be fully explored in terms of reaching women is the Internet. Hundreds of women's rights and feminist home pages, chat rooms, and lists abound, facilitating communications among women, some of them probably previously unorganized. The women regularly logging on to the Internet may prove to be the critical mass yet to be mobilized. Still, women's movement leaders will have to develop more effective strategies to organize this untapped force.

Critical Mobilizing Events

Communication networks often serve as signals to participants that the time has come to act. In the 1980s, there were few events that roused women to action. Indeed, the defeat of the ERA in 1982 seemed to have the opposite effect, warning movement activists that it was not an auspicious time to seek major change. Other critical demobilizing events were the election and reelection of Ronald Reagan, an avowed foe of many items on the women's agenda, particularly the ERA and freedom of choice. George H. W. Bush's victory in 1988 reinforced the message that the 1980s were not a time to advance the agenda of the women's movement.

In 1989 and into the 1990s, however, a few critical events served notice to women that they must act. The first was the U.S. Supreme Court's decision in *Webster v. Reproductive Health Services* (1989), which sent a strong signal to women that the right to control their bodies might soon be lost. In reaction, women by the thousands took to the streets, contributed money, or joined women's rights organizations. This behavior was quite understandable. Research suggests that threats to public goods (in this case, freedom of choice) are more powerful motivators of action than are attempts to mobilize for new or yet-to-be-won public goods.

Fear about the loss of abortion rights also played a role in the next critical event, the Clarence Thomas hearings. When Anita Hill testified that Thomas (a conservative who was expected to provide the critical vote to overturn *Roe v. Wade*) had subjected her to sexual harassment, the "treatment" she received by the all-male Senate Judiciary Committee served as another critical mobilizing event. Again, many women vowed to work to put more women in the Senate and House, and millions of dollars were raised and votes secured for women candidates.

The election of Bill Clinton to the White House in 1992 activated women elected to the 103rd Congress to push a women's agenda. But the sudden political shift in 1994 cut short some major gains and reversed others. With the election of George W. Bush in 2000, many gains women made were jeopardized.

The battle over late-term abortions and abortion rights after fetal viability is just one signal that the rear-guard action to protect gains won in the 1970s is not yet over.

Political Mobilization

The factors discussed previously are critical to forging a movement, but no movement can succeed unless it can mobilize the potential beneficiaries, in this case, women. The need to do so is particularly critical for women of color, who in the twenty-first century will become the majority of American women. Polls reveal that African American and Hispanic women are very strong proponents of the movement. However, the movement has not always embraced these women. Both the early woman's movement and even more so the suffrage movement were flawed by racism that drove women of color out of mainstream women's organizations. In the modern era, the issue has been less one of overt racism than an inability of white women leaders to recognize the biases built into their structures and the movement's focus on issues that have not always been a high priority to women of color. Abortion, for instance, is less strongly supported by both Hispanics and African Americans than whites. The women's movement, moreover, has not placed racism, an issue of extreme importance to women of color, very high on its agenda. Likewise, even though welfare reform was in many ways a targeted attack on poor African American women, mainstream women's groups lined up uneasily behind Clinton's efforts to change the system. The key to a reenergized women's movement, therefore, depends on a set of goals that will strengthen the resolve of the traditional core of the movement while attracting a much broader and more diverse constituency.

GOALS FOR THE WOMEN'S RIGHTS MOVEMENT

Widespread support continues among women for changes in all of the three spheres that have been the focus of women's movements: politics, economics, and the family. The unmet goals of 1848 or 1967 can and still do serve, with some minor modification, to set a possible platform for the movement. A 1996 U.S. Department of Labor Women's Bureau survey of 250,000 working women supports this. It found that women were very concerned with improving their pay and career advancement opportunities. Finding affordable child care and securing paid sick and family leave also topped the list of needs for working women.[9] Considerable consensus exists among women about the need to focus on three problems of particular concern to working women: (1) combining work and family, (2) discrimination in hiring, and (3) low pay. Women of color were particularly likely to identify these issues as important.[10] Interviews with women in focus groups found "real anger about equal pay and not getting a decent wage for working all day long."[11]." Women in the study complained not only about the lack of money but also the lack of time, with middle-class women more concerned about the latter, and poor and working-class women the former. Pay equity, family leave, and flextime were seen as solutions to the dual demands on women to provide for, and take care of, their families. Also high on women's list of concerns was national health care. Further down in the rankings of priorities, however, were crime, child support, and abortion rights.

In the 2000 Virginia Slims Poll, both men and women reported high levels of stress. In order to balance their lives, both genders seek family-friendly work policies. In addition, women are looking for greater support within the home. Seventy-one percent of women want men to increase their household and child care responsibilities. Nearly half of women think that women should put less pressure on themselves to be "superwomen," and four in ten want less pressure put on them by men.[12]

The message to the movement is clear. Women are suffering under their dual roles as worker and homemaker-mother, and they need help. The problem for women's organizations is framing a solution that will mobilize women—who are already stressed from combining roles with little actual time to spare—to act in concert for change. Woman's suffrage served in that capacity during the early years of this century, and the ERA filled the role during the 1970s. Throughout most of the 1980s, however, the movement remained adrift with no central or core issue around which to mobilize women. In the late 1980s and early 1990s—at least until the Clinton victory—abortion rights appeared immediately threatened, and women did mobilize to march on Washington, D.C., *and* to go to the voting booth. Similarly, the Clarence Thomas hearings encouraged a national debate about sexual harassment. Sexual harassment, however, is not perceived by most women as one of the major problems facing them. Although the abortion issue did not mobilize voters against George W. Bush in 2000 to the extent that many predicted, the first pro-life Supreme Court appointment of the Bush administration may be the next critical event.

The issue of political underrepresentation of women might provide a unifying issue. In the 2000 Virginia Slims Poll, a majority of both men and women agreed that for women to be treated fairly, equal numbers of men and women are needed in Congress and in leadership positions in the federal government. Additionally, 59 percent of women and 48 percent of men agreed on the need for gender equality in representation on the Supreme Court.[13] If women in the United States can be made to believe that political representation is the key to policy success, in the same manner that they were convinced that the right to vote itself was key to obtaining a wide range of goals, the movement may have its mobilizing issue. What do women have to gain? Table 7.4 reveals the optimism women have about their status in the year 2020.

TABLE 7.4 **Ways Women Twenty Years From Now Will Have a Better Life**

Survey question: "In which of these ways, if any, will women twenty years from now have a better life?"

	Total Women (%)	Executive/ Professional (%)	White Collar (%)	Blue Collar (%)
More equal opportunities for women in the workplace	53	55	56	51
Women will have more choices about what types of lives they choose to lead	47	50	47	44
Women will have more control over the way things go in their lives	46	46	50	47
More opportunities for women in leadership positions in business	43	49	48	38
Men will look at women more as equals	40	39	39	38
More opportunities for women in leadership positions in politics	39	44	41	38
More help from men with household chores and child rearing	38	44	39	33
Employers will be more accommodating of the needs of working mothers	37	38	37	35
It will be less of a man's world	26	28	28	25
Men will be more sensitive to women's needs	25	27	25	23
Other (vol.)	*	—	1	—
Don't Know	2	2	3	2

Source: 2000 Virginia Slims Opinion Poll, conducted by Roper Starch Worldwide Inc. Data provided by Philip Morris USA.

CONCLUSION

The nation's priorities shifted to national defense and homeland security after the terrorist attacks of September 11, 2001. Yet increased spending on the nation's defense, the rising federal budget deficit, and a weak economy threaten to undermine many of the gains women have made as a result of the women's rights movement. Still, there is hope that the feminist realignment or malaise that seemed to mark the 1990s may be followed by renewed commitment to women's rights. In the 2000 presidential election and the 2002 midterm elections, women continued to vote in larger numbers than men, and to cast their votes more frequently for women, Democrats, or pro-choice female Republicans. This political clout may help elect more women legislators who will be more likely to advance and secure the wide array of issues that make up the women's agenda. The "Year of the Woman" saw unprecedented numbers of women elected to Congress in 1992. A decade later, in 2002, a record number of women were elected governors, and women are fast gaining strength in numbers in state legislatures across the country. The United States faces many challenges as we enter a new millennium. Women's active engagement in the nation's politics as citizens and leaders is essential to meeting these challenges. The future of the movement depends on attracting a diverse constituency who will elect women committed to work for issues that will ease the burden of the average working woman.

NOTES

1. *Source:* "Progress and Perils: New Agenda for Women," Center for the Advancement of Women (April 2003), http://www.advancewomen.org.
2. Ibid.
3. Anne N. Costain, *Inviting Women's Rebellion: A Political Process Interpretation of the Women's Movement* (Baltimore: Johns Hopkins University Press, 1992), chap. 6. See also Georgia Duerst-Lahti, "The Government's Role in Building the Women's Movement," *Political Science Quarterly* 104 (1989): 249–68.
4. See Sarah Slavin, *Women's Issues Interest Groups* (Westport, Conn.: Greenwood Press, 1995).
5. Mary Fainsod Katzenstein, "Feminism within American Institutions: Unobtrusive Mobilization in the 1980s," *Signs* 16 (1990): 28.
6. Nancy F. Cott, *The Grounding of Modern Feminism* (New Haven, Conn.: Yale University Press, 1987), chap. 3.
7. Flora Davis, *Moving the Mountain: The Women's Movement in America since 1960* (New York: Simon and Schuster, 1991).
8. Sarah Harder, "Flourishing in the Mainstream: The U.S. Women's Movement Today," in *The American Woman, 1990–1991*, ed. Sara E. Rix (New York: Norton, 1990), 278.
9. U.S. Department of Labor, Women's Bureau, *The Working Women Count Honor Roll Report* (Washington, D.C.: Author, 1996), 1–2. See also Women's Voices Project, commissioned by the Ms. Foundation and the Center for Policy Alternatives.
10. Linda Tarr-Whelan, quoted in Marcia Eldredge, "Women's Voices: An Agenda for Change," *National Business Woman*, Winter 1992, 14.
11. Ibid., 14–15.
12. The 2000 Virginia Slims Opinion Poll conducted by Roper Starch Worldwide Inc. Data provided by Philip Morris USA.
13. Ibid.

Index

Note: Pages followed by *f* and *t* indicate figures and tables, respectively.